BUSHWHACKER!

Cole Younger & the Kansas-Missouri Border War

John Koblas

NORTH STAR PRESS OF ST. CLOUD, INC.

ISBN: 0-87839-207-6

First Edition: July 2004

Printed in the United States of America by Versa Press, Inc., East
Peoria, Illinois.

Published by:
North Star Press of St. Cloud, Inc.
P.O. Box 451
St. Cloud, Minnesota 55320
nspress@cloudnet.com

1 2 3 4 5 6 7 8 9

For my favorite bushwhacker—Emmett C. Hoctor

Table of Contents

Introduction

by Chuck Parsons

O F THE THOUSANDS OF MEN AND A FEW WOMEN who fought in the terrible War Between the States, few—save for some generals—became household names. All Americans know something of Grant, Robert E. Lee, or Stonewall Jackson. Fewer still know of the hundreds who fought as guerrillas, today rarely known outside their immediate area of action. Jesse and Frank James, William Clarke Quantrill, and "Bloody Bill" Anderson are a few of a handful who are the exception, whose names are familiar to all who have even a smidgen of familiarity with the War Between the States.

To a lesser degree, Americans are somewhat familiar with Thomas Coleman Younger. His renown, however, rests more on his post-Civil War activities—finally meeting his Waterloo along with his brothers James Hardin and Robert Ewing Younger in a slough in southern Minnesota two weeks following the foiled bank robbery attempt at Northfield.

These men—the Youngers—were brutalized by the Civil War. Born on January 15, 1844, the second son of fourteen children born to W.H. and Bursheba Younger, Cole matured early in the violent years before war was declared. In those years prior to the start of the Civil War, the border war between free territory Kansas and pro-slave state Missouri raged. Although the political concept had been to allow the resident people decide whether the new territory of Kansas would become free or slave holding, unscrupulous bands of brigands became the reality, their political ideologies often cast aside in order to plunder and kill. Bands from Missouri were known as Bushwhackers or Border Ruffians; bands from Kansas were called Jayhawkers or Redlegs. John Brown's raid and the subsequent events of the late 1850s guaranteed that the nation would agonize through a Civil War, making the casualties of the earlier "border wars" seem inconsequential.

For the Youngers, tragedies came early. On the night of December 15, 1861, Cole, in defending his sister's honor at a dance near Harrisonville, knocked out a Union officer, Captain Irvin Walley. To avoid military punishment, Cole was compelled to take to the brush. During the ensuing months, the Younger brothers' father was murdered. Their mother was forced to set fire to their home, losing all the family's possessions. Not surprisingly, the children, Cole and Jim, vowed vengeance (younger brothers Bob and John were too young for any type of service during the war). The two brothers, along with other friends and neighbors and relatives, became guerrillas—or bushwhackers as they were also called. They joined Quantrill. Cole Younger was nineteen when Quantrill led the successful punishing raid on Lawrence, Kansas, and he no doubt killed his share.

The Youngers became notorious in the decade following the end of the War Between the States. Bank robbery became a new phenomenon—and the Youngers were accused of participating in several. Cole, Bob, Jim, and John became embroiled in difficulties not only in Missouri but in Texas as well, where John killed a man. Back in Missouri, they were accused of being bank and train robbers. In a battle with Pinkerton agents, brother John was killed. The three remaining brothers continued their lawless life until they—along with the James brothers and three lesser known outlaws—failed in their raid on the bank at Northfield, Minnesota, on September 7, 1876. A citizen and a bank employee were killed during the raid and ensuing street battle. Leaving two of their own men dead in the streets of Northfield, the remainder of the gang fled south. Two weeks following the Northfield fiasco, the Youngers were captured after a gun battle with Watonwan County Sheriff James Glispin and a posse near Madelia. At their trial they surrendered their liberty after pleading guilty to bank robbery and murder charges. Cole, Jim, and Bob were sentenced to life in Minnesota's prison at Stillwater. Bob died there in 1889; Jim committed suicide in 1902. Cole alone was eventually pardoned and returned home to Missouri. He died on March 21, 1916, at his home.

The outlaw career of the Youngers, as well as their better-known companions, the James brothers, has been told and retold in various degrees of historical accuracy. Author John J. "Jack" Koblas has established his preeminence among James-Younger scholars and western history buffs in general with his previous books focusing on the Northfield Raid and Jesse James. Now he brings bushwhacker Cole Younger into prominence for the first time with this full-length study of the man prior to his notoriety as a bank and train robber.

For those who want to follow Cole Younger's career after his bushwhacking days were behind him, one can do not better than to refer to Koblas' *Faithful Unto Death: The James-Younger Raid on the First National Bank*; *When the Heavens Fell: The Youngers in Stillwater Prison* and *The Great Cole Younger & Frank James Historical Wild West Show*.

With this biography of Cole Younger before his outlaw career, the Missouri guerrilla/bank and train robber/lifer in Stillwater/Wild West show promoter and in his final years a "new born" Christian, we have the story of his life complete. No doubt there may be snippets of information about Cole Younger discovered by some other fortunate researcher, but for all intents and purposes we have with this work and Koblas' other works, the complete biography of Thomas Coleman Younger—bushwhacker.

Luling, Texas
January 5, 2004

BUSHWHACKER JUSTICE

Missouri darkened from her rising Osceola smoke
    And Jim Lane's raiding Kansas Redleg dust.
They'd looted, burned and murdered underneath the guise of war
    To label their barbaric crimes as "just"
For purposes of beating us into submission while
    Their Union motto says, "In God we trust."

With Osceola disappearing from Missouri's map,
    As our beloved Confederacy bleeds,
To rally "blood for blood" is not enough to compensate
    For laws that such atrocity exceeds,
Thus in the name of Justice shall our vengeance wreak its hell.
    We'll leave the Union wounded on her knees!

Guerrilla bands arose with William Quantrill in command
    Who rode through Union camps with blood to shed.
One night a social dance in honor of a southern belle
    Was crashed by Captain Walley, Union-bred,
Demanding Coleman Younger tell him Quantrill's whereabouts.
    Their fighting left a price on Younger's head.

Then back and forth across the borders Quantrill's raiders rode,
    Self-righteous in their callous butchery.
"We need no courts to sentence any Jayhawker to death:
    Our saddles hold the jurors verily.
On this side of the border there's no questions asked--you die!
    Each man among us lost his family!"

At Independence, Lawrence, and Lone Jack, guerrilla crimes
    Of carnage escalated till the line
Between a war-torn soldier and an outlaw had been crossed.
    Where murdering and robbery combine
As skills of daily life, there is no room for amnesty:
    The James and Younger Gang emerged refined.
                     —Roger Brezina

Cole Younger. (Courtesy Northfield Historical Society)

Chapter One

Victims of Geography

"Political Hatreds are always bitter, but none were ever more bitter than those which existed along the border line of Missouri and Kansas during my boyhood in Jackson County in the former state from 1856 to '60. These hatreds were soon to make trouble for me of which I had never dreamed."
                                                                    —Cole Younger[1]

C OLE YOUNGER PASSED AWAY AT 8:45 in the evening of March 21, 1916, at the age of seventy-two, following a long illness. He was unconscious for several hours before his death. His last words were: "I have tried to make amends for the crimes of my younger days and hope, under God's mercy, for forgiveness."[2]

Cole had remained a life-long bachelor. On the afternoon of March 24, 1916, a large crowd assembled at a cemetery in Lee's Summit, Missouri. The silent gatherers, many of them weeping, watched as the casket was lowered into the grave. The graveside services were brief, as the longer service had been held earlier in church. Cole Younger, often called the last of the great outlaws of the West, was laid to his eternal rest beside his mother.[3]

A simple headstone bore the inscription: "Cole Younger, 1844-1916, Rest in Peace Our Dear Beloved." The Daughters of the Confederacy later placed a marble plaque next to the headstone, which reads, "Cole Younger, Quantrill's Co., C.S.A."

Cole, loved by some, hated by others, died a much different man than the young outlaw who had wreaked havoc from the Kansas-Missouri Border War of the 1860s to the bungled robbery attempt in Minnesota two decades later. Those in the South—enemies of the Yankee carpetbaggers—had never forgotten his exploits, and to them, he would be remembered as a hero and friend of the common man. But to the former Jayhawkers and Redlegs who fought against him on the border, the name Younger was synonymous with the dreaded black flag of the bushwhacker.

The institution of slavery had been a divisive issue in the United States for decades before the territory of Missouri petitioned Congress for admission to the Union as a state in 1818. Since the Revolution, the country had grown from thirteen states to twenty-two and had managed to maintain a balance of power between slave and free-states. There were eleven free-states and eleven slave states, a situation that gave each faction equal representation in the Senate and the power to prevent the passage of legislation not to its liking. The free-states, with their much larger populations, controlled the House of Representatives, 105 votes to eighty-one.

In February 1819, New York Representative James Tallmadge proposed an amendment to ban slavery in Missouri even though there were more than 2,000 slaves living there. The country was again confronted with the volatile issue of the spread of slavery into new territories and states. The cry against the South's peculiar institution had grown louder through the years. "How long will the desire for wealth render us blind to the sin of holding both the bodies and souls of our fellow men in chains?" asked Representative Livermore from New Hampshire.

The South's economy was dependent upon black slavery, and 200 years of living with the institution had made it an integral part of Southern life and culture. The South demanded that the North recognize its right to have slaves as secured in the Constitution. Through the efforts of Henry Clay, "the great pacificator," a compromise was finally reached on March 3, 1820, after Maine petitioned Congress for statehood. Both states were admitted, a free Maine and a slave Missouri, and the balance of power in Congress was maintained as before, postponing the inevitable showdown for another generation. In an attempt to address the issue of the further spread of slavery, however, the Missouri Compromise stipulated that all the Louisiana Purchase territory north of the southern boundary of Missouri, except Missouri, would be free, and the territory below that line would be slave. The state of Missouri was up for grabs, and its residents were trapped in the crossfire of political hatreds.

Cole Younger, named after an uncle, was born near Lee's Summit, Jackson County, Missouri, on January 15, 1844, one of fourteen children born to Henry Washington Younger and Bursheba Leighton Fristoe. Three of these children, however, died in infancy. The fourteen children were Laura, Isabelle, Anne, Richard, Mary Josephine, Caroline, Thomas Coleman (Cole), Sally, James Hardin, Alphae, John Harrison, Emma, Robert Ewing, and Henrietta (Retta).[4]

The somewhat prominent couple had been married in 1830. Henry was originally from Crab Orchard, Kentucky, and he settled near Kansas City in 1825 where he was heavily engaged in a political career. The title "Colonel," was purely honorary, for he was never in the military, nor had he fought in any war. "Colonels," according to one biographer, "were as thick as blackbirds on a barbed wire fence; anybody so far down the line to be called 'Major' was sensitive about it."[5]

The Colonel, a tall, handsome man with a flowing moustache and goatee, acquired some degree of wealth upon being elected to the Missouri State Legislature three terms. He went on to become County Judge of Jackson County as what was called a "court judge," whose responsibility was to lay out roads, supervise the building of bridges and oversee the voting of road bonds. His brother, Coleman Younger, represented Clay County in the legislature. Cole's great-grandmother on his father's side was a daughter of "Lighthorse Harry" Lee.[6]

The Youngers had come to America from Strasburg, Germany, which was settled a few decades before Jesus Christ, in the Rhenish Valley, between the Vosges Mountains and the Black Forest. Strasburg was established as a military camp by the Eighth Roman Legion, instructed to protect the annexed territories on the west side of the Rhine River against the Germanic tribes. Surrounding the military camp was a sprawling civilian town of Celtic craftsmen and merchants, who acted as legion's commissary. The borough received the Roman name of "Argentoratum" (colloquially "Argentina"), because of the silver color of the Rhine's water.[7]

Many centuries later, the Free City of Strasburg began to lose its glamour with the appearance of the national states. After the Thirty-Years War, during which the Strasburgers had much to suffer, the town was annexed to the Crown of France (1681). It lost all autonomy in 1789 with the French Revolution. Following the Napoleonic wars, Strasburg experienced a peaceful life. In 1862, Otto von Bismarck became President of Prussia, and over the next few years he helped to reorganize Germany under Prussia's leadership. In 1870 Bismarck ordered the Prussian Army into France. As a result of the Franco-Prussian War, France lost Alsace and Lorraine, Strasburg, and the great fortress of Metz to Germany. During the terrible siege, the west section of Strasburg was burned down. In the decades 1880 and 1890, Strasburg was enlarged and became a modern shipping port, after the canalization of the Rhine River. This was the Germany of Younger ancestry.

Todd M. George, a friend of Cole Younger, later stated in a letter: "Cole's father, Henry Washington Younger, made his way from Virginia in a very early day to become a resident of Jackson County, Missouri. He brought with him quite a cash estate besides a number of his slaves. His first and only marriage was to Bursheba Fristoe, the oldest daughter of Richard Fristoe, the first presiding judge of our county court here in Jackson County, Missouri."[8]

Bursheba was, in fact, the daughter of Richard Fristoe, a highly respected judge, who fought under General Andrew Jackson at the Battle of New Orleans and had been responsible for the christening of Jackson County. Bursheba was descended from the Sullivans, Ladens, and Percivals of South Carolina, the Taylors of Virginia, and the Fristoes of Tennessee. Cole's Grandfather Fristoe was a grand nephew of Chief Justice John Marshall of Virginia.

Cole later discussed some of his ancestors hailing from Knoxville, Tennessee: "My grandfather, Richard Fristoe, was born here about 1790.[9] His father was a Baptist preacher. My grandfather married in McMinnville and he and his brother, Tom, were in the Indian wars with General Jackson, and were with him at the Battle of New Orleans. Richard Fristoe and brother went from Nashville to Missouri. They went to the "6 mile" country, and were about the [seventeen]th family to settle in Jackson [County] where my father and I were born. I was the seventh son of fourteen children. My grandfather was a judge in that country, and was a nephew of Chief Justice Marshall. My grandfather must have had relatives [in Knoxville] who never moved away as he did."[10]

Cole's father, Colonel Younger, quickly accumulated 3,500 acres of land and bought two slaves to work it. He procured a contract with the United States government as mail agent, in which he delivered the mail in an area encompassing 500 miles, which necessitated a considerable investment in horses, wagons, and stables. He was occasionally summoned to Washington to devise methods of transporting the mail.

According to Todd M. George: "The first land purchase made by Mr. Younger was about 1800 [sic] acres six miles due north of the little village of Lee's Summit at that time. For quite some years Mr. Younger prospered with raising livestock on a large portion of his farm and at one time served on the Missouri State Legislature. For several years he had a contract with the federal government to drive a stagecoach where he delivered mail and carried passengers all the way over the hills and valleys that led from a prosperous active village then known as Westport to a prosperous town over 150 miles to the southeast of Westport known as Neosho."[11]

The year of Cole's birth—1844—was one of turmoil for both the United States and the state of Missouri, as violence loomed on the horizon, and men prepared for a fight of one kind or another. Nationally, James K. Polk was elected president of the United States that same year on an expansionist platform that focused upon the re-annexation of Texas, which in 1836 had claimed its *de facto* independence from Mexico. Congress, however, passed a joint resolution annexing Texas just prior to Polk's inauguration, even though Mexico had threatened war if the United States claimed Texas. Mexico, however, merely severed diplomatic relations.

Relations were further strained when Polk supported Texas' claim to the land between the Nueces River and the Rio Grande. In June 1845, Polk directed Zachary Taylor to lead a detachment of troops to the Nueces as a protective measure should Mexico decide to launch an attack. He also ordered the commander of the Pacific naval squadron to seize San Francisco if Mexico did attack.

Cole Younger stated in a November 1880 interview with author J.W. Buel that, "Independence was, for a long time previous to the war with Mexico, headquarters for Mexican freighters. The freight passing between Mexico and Missouri was carried on pack-mules, many Jackson countymen being engaged in that business. It was in Jackson County chiefly, also, that Colonel [Alexander William] Doniphan recruited his famous regiment for

5

the Mexican war and made that wonderful march known in history as *De rando del murato*, (the journey of death). After subduing New Mexico, Doniphan marched to Chihuahua, which then had 40,000 inhabitants, and raised the United States flag over the citadel; and from this latter place he continued his march to the Gulf of Mexico."[12]

Missouri was affected not only by the fight with Mexico the year of Cole's birth but with an eruption of violence with Mormons who had settled within the state's borders in 1831. Joseph Smith and his followers were convinced that God had selected Jackson County as the place where the Saints should gather to await the holy summons. Independence was chosen as the Saints' Zion, which angered many Missourians, who feared the Mormons would drive all other settlers away.[13]

By 1833, a third of Jackson County's population was Mormon. The area's first settlers, mostly Southerners who had come to Missouri with slaves, kept a spiteful eye on both the Mormons and the Indians, who had settled just across the border. The Southerners were uncomfortable and angry over the religious sect, composed mostly of wealthy Yankees, because they not only welcomed the Indians into their fold, but the free blacks as well.

Church members were also heavily persecuted, largely because the non-Mormons believed that the church was promoting the establishment of a religious dictatorship (a theocracy). They were also distressed at the Mormon's belief that the *Book of Mormon* was the revealed work of God, with the same status as the Hebrew Scriptures (Old Testament) and Christian Scriptures (New Testament). In spite of the opposition, much of it state sponsored or condoned, the church increased greatly in numbers.

The persecution of the Mormons commenced in November 1833 with a frightening meteor shower. Citizens of Jackson, Clay, Ray, Caldwell, and Daviess counties concluded that the meteors were a sign that the end predicted by the Mormons was near, and they gathered a force to drive the Saints from their area. For six years, from 1833 to 1839, the Mormons endured brutality. Their homes were destroyed; many Mormons died while trying to survive winter without adequate shelter. The church was expelled from Jackson County and settled in Far West, Missouri, in Caldwell County, which had been reserved for them.

A public *Danite* organization was formed in the Mormon community to organize defense, construct homes and obtain provisions. The original settlers were concerned that the Latter Day Saints might become a political majority in their locality and planned an attack as a method of preventing Mormons from voting. The state militia became involved. Sampson Avard, believed to have been both a captain within the Danites and an officer in the militia, persuaded his men to become a "covert renegade band" and to avenge outrages against the Mormons. When Joseph Smith heard of this group's illegal activity, he removed Avard from command and disbanded his criminal group.

On October 27, 1838, Governor Boggs of Missouri had issued an "Extermination Order" to treat all Mormons as enemies and exterminate them or force them out of Missouri. Ignorance, fear, and rumors fueled the fire of hatred against the Mormons which finally led to the extermination order by Governor Boggs.

Governor Boggs Extermination Order read "The Mormons must be treated as enemies and must be exterminated or driven from the state if necessary for the public peace."

With this Order the Missouri Militia dispatched a party of men on October 30, 1838, to a small Mormon settlement at Jacob Haun's Mill in Caldwell County, Missouri, where they massacred seventeen persons. The Militia consisted of 200 men while only thirty families resided at Haun's Mill. The residents were unaware of the extermination order and believed they were living under a truce that had been reached several days earlier between the Missouri Government and the Mormons. They were totally shocked and unprepared for the brutal attack.

When the militia invaded the settlement on horses and began firing rifles, the women and children ran across a stream and into the woods to hide. The men ran indoors to find a defense but were massacred by bullets from the militia fired through the wood slats of the cabin. Any Mormons that were found alive were summarily shot.

When the massacre ended, seventeen Mormons had been killed, including a ten-year-old boy. The boy had been huddling behind a stove, unable to escape with his mother into the forest. When the militia found him they blew his head off. Another victim was a seventy-eight-year-old, feeble grandfather. He was shot by one of the militia and then was mutilated with a knife. Thirteen Mormons had been injured, including women and children. Three Militia men were injured, which indicates there had been some fighting back.

After the militia left, the frightened settlers stayed in hiding until after dark, afraid the militia would return to finish them off. When it was clear they were safe, they hid the bodies of their dead in a well, and ran into neighboring settlements for help. The Mormons surrendered after being faced with diminishing supplies, the approach of winter, an aggressive militia, and an anti-Latter Day Saints extermination order from the federal governor.

"The people of western Missouri are, in some respects, very peculiar," stated Cole Younger years later. "We will take Jackson County (where I was born) for instance. In that section the people seemed to be born fighters, the instinct being inherited from a long line of ancestors.

"Joe Smith and Brigham Young laid out Independence, but very soon thereafter enough citizens of the county collected to drive them off, after several stubborn fights. The Mormons withdrew from the state and settled their community at Nauvoo, Illinois, but in a few years afterward about fifty of them again came into Missouri and settled in Platte County. They had scarcely established themselves, however, before another company of Jackson County citizens, chiefly from around Independence, organized to drive them off. Among these determined citizens were Richard Fristoe, my grandfather, Wood Nolen, Smallwood Nolen, and Sam Owens. While crossing the river in a hand-ferry-boat, the ferryman, who had been bribed by the Mormons, succeeded in turning the boat over midway in the Missouri River. A large number were drowned, but the four I have mentioned succeeded in swimming ashore."[14]

A St. Louis newspaper reported the following in February 1844, one month following Cole's birth: " MORMON DIFFICULTIES IN ILLINOIS. —The *Quincy Herald* of the 9th instant states that four wagons passed through that place on Tuesday previous, on their way to the State arsenal at Alton, for the purpose of procuring arms to be used against the Mormons. The difficulties and the prospect of an immediate breach between the citizens and the Mormons has been brought to the knowledge of Governor Ford, and he has been earnestly appealed to, to maintain the peace and to protect the innocent. The state of exasperation between the Mormons and citizens is such that we will not be surprised to hear of actual hostilities at any time quite as violent as formerly existed between them and a portion of our own citizens."[15]

That same newspaper announced in June of the same year:

TROUBLES IN ILLINOIS: A new aspect is given to the proceedings of Joe Smith and his adherents at Nauvoo, in the destruction of the printing press of the *Nauvoo Expositor* of which we give an account to-day. If the corporate authorities of Nauvoo, of which Joe Smith is the head, can compass their lawless ends by such means as were adopted on this occasion, then similar measures may serve to rid them of all persons who may become obnoxious to them. Neither person nor property can be safe where such a control is exercised by reckless men, and in the present state of affairs there, it is not improbable that violence will be resorted to, to put down all opposition. If the authorities of Illinois had any respect for themselves-any regard for the law-any desire to protect the person and property of citizens from outrage and destruction, they would at once adopt measures to put an end to these arbitrary acts; but we have little hope of seeing this done so long as Joe Smith controls so many thousands of votes, and purchases an immunity from punishment by casting them for the Locofocos.

LATEST FROM THE MORMONS—By the last accounts from Nauvoo we learn that Joe Smith had issued a proclamation declaring martial law. The greatest excitement prevailed in the neighborhood, and the whole upper country was under arms. The streets of Warsaw were patrolled by armed men, and sanguinary results were anticipated.[16]

On September 28th, it was reported:

. . . We learn from the officers and passengers of the steamer *Osprey* that Governor Ford and his troops have reached Carthage. The purpose of the Governor in ordering out the troops seems to be a determination to bring the murderers of Joe and Hiram Smith to trial. The troops are under the command of General J.J. Hardin, subject, of course, to the direction of the Governor. The reason assigned by the Governor's friends for ordering out the troops in the first instance was a "wolf hunt," advertised by a portion of the people of Hancock County to come off on the 26th and 27th instant. This hunt, it was believed by the Governor, was a pretext to get the people assembled, aroused, and then to make an attack on the Mormons at Nauvoo, or some other Mormon settlement. From all we can learn, we suppose that the wolf hunt was abandoned after the orders of the Governor were issued.

The Governor was at Carthage. Writs were issued and placed in the hands of the Sheriff, for the arrest of Thomas C. Sharp, editor of the *Warsaw Signal*, and for Col. Williams, of the same place, both charged with participating in the murder of the Smiths. The Sheriff came to Warsaw and attempted to arrest Sharp, but he refused to surrender himself, and in this resolution was sustained by the people of Warsaw. The Sheriff returned and reported his inability to arrest him, when three hundred of the troops were ordered to march to Warsaw. The troops had not arrived at Warsaw before the Osprey left, but Sharp and Williams had escaped to the Missouri side of the river, and, we presume, will not be taken.[17]

Between 1807 and 1847, every able-bodied white male in Missouri, aged eighteen to forty-five, was required to serve in the regular militia. These men were ordered to arm and equip themselves to attend musters and serve when called to active duty. Between 1835 and 1847, four musters were required by state law. Men who opted to not serve in the regular militia could enroll in the volunteer militia. This organization elected its own officers, equipped themselves at its own expense, and answered directly to the governor. Although the state pledged to furnish arms, it had only public arms that had come into its possession via the federal government. The policy of forcing men during peace time to perform military functions never proved satisfactory. The policy was scrapped in 1847 in favor of uniform militia companies which compromised the State Militia.[18]

In 1850, Henry Younger purchased over a hundred acres of prime farmland and erected a two-story farmhouse in the community of Strother, which later became incorporated into the town of Lee's Summit. James Younger had been born January 15, 1848, exactly four years after his brother Cole. John was born in 1851, one year after construction of the Strother house, and Robert in 1853.

Cole would entertain a long-standing love affair with Lee's Summit. The community was founded in 1865, the final year of the Civil War by a successful farmer and stockman, William B. Howard. Originally the town consisted of only seventy acres of land, in which Howard named Strother, after his wife's maiden name. During the Civil War, the village was continually subject to border raids and repeated violence. In 1867, the community had to be renamed, at the request of the United States Post Office, because there was already another existing town named Strother.

Lee's Summit, it is claimed, took its name from General Robert E. Lee with "Summit" referring to the city's location on the highest point on the railroad line between Kansas City and St. Louis. But the origin of the name is not conclusive. Many Missourians believe the name was incorrectly spelled on the side of a Missouri Pacific boxcar, which was supposed to read "Lea's Summit," in honor of respected citizen Dr. Pleasant Lea, who lost his life in the Civil War.

Although the Younger family prospered during this period of military buildup, the question of slavery hovered over the people of both Missouri and Kansas. Nearly a decade before the first shots were fired in the Civil War, a border war waged between Missouri and Kansas. Missouri was the only state north of the Mason-Dixon Line which was pro-slavery. Fewer than two percent of the population owned slaves, and Missouri never joined the Confederacy. However, many viewed the radical abolitionist movement as a threat to their safety, property, and sovereignty.

In 1853, Harriet Beecher Stowe had published *Uncle Tom's Cabin*, the novel whose bold and passionate attack upon slavery thrilled millions of readers in the North and throughout the world. Abolitionist John Brown, having read the book from cover to cover, took the book with him on his travels and wrote to his wife that, "The star of hope is slowly and steadily rising above the horizon. As one sign of these times I would like to mention the publication of *Uncle Tom's Cabin* . . . which has come down upon the abodes of bondage like the morning sunlight unfolding . . . in a manner which has awakened a sympathy for the slaves in hearts unused to feel. . . ."[19]

All eyes focused upon Kansas, which was approaching statehood. There was much dissention over its status of entering the Union as either a pro-slavery or free-

Harriet Beecher Stowe, author of Uncle Tom's Cabin. (National Archives

11

state. Most of the residents were peaceful farmers, but radical groups, rabble-rousers, and ruffians conducted raids on farms and towns to the extent that it was difficult, if not imprudent, to maintain neutrality. Missouri was already a state, admitted in 1821 as a slave state under the Missouri Compromise. Kansas was not yet a state but was to resolve its status through a referendum in accordance with the 1854 Kansas-Nebraska Act. Virtually no one in the sparsely settled Kansas frontier owned slaves, and the territory was being rapidly settled by abolitionist "Free-Soilers" from Eastern states and Germany. On the Missouri side, most of the slave-owners lived in the eastern half of the state along the Mississippi River, but some lived near Kansas City and adjacent counties along the Kansas frontier.

This was an explosive mixture. First, radical abolitionists from Kansas raided Missouri farms to liberate slaves they found there. Finding few slaves to liberate, they looted as necessary so as not to return home empty-handed. In response, Missourians raided Kansas to recapture their property. Sparsely populated, the Kansas territory was up for grabs. Forces on both sides of the slavery issue sent settlers into Kansas to take up claims and tip the scales in their favor . . . Kansas was settled in strife.

Many people in Missouri were pro-slavery and did what they could to make Kansas a slave state. Abolitionists, however, insisted that Kansas enter the union as a free state. The Kansas-Nebraska Act of 1854, which called for the opening of the two territories, permitted the voters in each state to decide whether slavery would be legal or prohibited. Though most Kansans settlers favored slavery at this time, many were more concerned with settling the territory then arguing over slavery issues.

The majority of Missourians were made up of individuals loyal to the federal government. They approved of slavery but wanted some compromise to be found that would keep the Southern states in the Union. If Kansas entered the Union as a free state, Missouri would be bordered on the east, west and north by states that prohibited slavery, providing abolitionists with an opportunity to liberate slaves and also make it easier for slaves to escape from Missouri. Even though the number of slave owners in Missouri was small, Southerners largely populated the state, making up about seventy-five percent of the total population. These slave owners owned just a few slaves, and the types of crops they raised did not require a large number of slaves to plant and cultivate. Most of the residents worked their own small farms.

The Kansas-Nebraska Act became law on May 30, 1854, by which the U.S. Congress established the territories of Kansas and Nebraska. By 1854 the organization of the vast Platte and Kansas rivers country west of Iowa and Missouri was overdue. As an isolated issue, territorial organization of this area was no problem. It was, however, irrevocably bound to the bitter sectional controversy over the extension of slavery into the territories and was further complicated by conflict over the location of the projected transcontinental railroad. Under no circumstances did proslavery Congressmen want a free territory (Kansas) west of Missouri. Because the West was expanding rapidly, territorial organization, despite these difficulties, could no longer be postponed.

Four attempts to organize a single territory for this area had already been defeated in Congress, largely because of Southern opposition to the Missouri Compromise. Although the last of these attempts to organize the area had nearly been successful, Stephen A. Douglas, chairman of the Senate Committee on Territories, decided to offer territorial legislation making concessions to the South. Douglas's motives have remained largely a matter of speculation. Douglas's desire for the Presidency focused upon his wish to cement the bonds of the Democratic Party, his interest in expansion and railroad building, or his desire to activate the unimpressive Franklin Pierce administration.

The bill he reported in January 1854 contained the provision that the question of slavery should be left to the decision of the territorial settlers themselves. This was the famous principle that Douglas called popular sovereignty though actually it had been enunciated four years earlier in the Compromise of 1850. Douglas's bill, in its final form, provided for the creation of two new territories—Kansas and Nebraska—instead of one. The obvious inference—at least to Missourians—was that the first would be slave, the second free. The Kansas-Nebraska Act flatly contradicted the provisions of the Missouri Compromise (under which slavery would have been barred from both territories); indeed, an amendment was added specifically repealing that compromise. This aspect of the bill in particular enraged the antislavery forces, but after three months of bitter debate in Congress, Douglas, backed by President Pierce and the Southerners, saw it adopted. Its effects were anything but reassuring to those who had hoped for a peaceful solution. The popular sovereignty provision caused both proslavery and antislavery forces to marshal strength and exert full pressure to determine the

13

"popular" decision in Kansas in their own favor, using groups such as the Emigrant Aid Company. The result was the tragedy of "bleeding" Kansas. Northerners and Southerners were aroused to such passions that sectional division reached a point that precluded reconciliation. A new political organization, the Republican Party was founded by opponents of the bill, and the United States was propelled toward the Civil War.[20]

When the Kansas-Nebraska Act was passed, most Southern state senators counted on Nebraska joining as a free-state and Kansas joining as a slave state; however Eastern abolitionists had different ideas. They raised money to assist abolitionists who wished to settle in Kansas territory, and over 700 settlers arrived in Kansas during the summer of 1854 with the specific intentions of abolishing slavery in that state.

With the passage of the act, there was a feeling of despondency all over the North. The discussion of the bill had been long and exciting, and the whole country had joined in it. It was discussed in every newspaper, in every gathering of citizens, in every school lyceum. It was everywhere felt that its passage opened Kansas to slavery, and that was thought to be equivalent to making Kansas a slave state. Kansas lay beyond Missouri, and Missouri was a slave state. The border counties of Missouri had a large slave population, and an intense pro-slavery sentiment. The South pressed the passage of the bill for the sole purpose of securing Kansas to slavery, and when the bill had passed the South felt assured that her end was gained. In the natural order of things this conclusion would have been justified by the sequel. In the natural order of things the people of Missouri would have passed over into Kansas and shaped her institutions to suit themselves. Therefore, the South was jubilant and the North despondent when the bill passed.[21]

But after the first shock was over, people began to ask what could be done. The question so long discussed had taken too strong a hold on the public mind to be dropped. Congress had thrown the territory open to slavery. Was there any other way of keeping it out? Mr. Eli Thayer, of Worcester, Massachusetts, proposed to meet the question on the terms of the bill itself. The bill provided that the people of the territory should themselves determine whether it should be slave or free. "Let us settle Kansas with people who will make it free by their own voice and vote." William H. Seward had foreshadowed this policy in a speech in the United States Senate. "Come on, then, gentlemen of the slave states. Since there is no escaping your challenge, we accept it in the name of freedom. We will engage in competition for the virgin soil of Kansas, and God give the victory to the side which is stronger in numbers, as it is in right."

The contest, therefore, was transferred to the plains of Kansas. The north had been defeated in Congress; she would try again in Kansas. In accordance with this purpose, "The Emigrant Aid Company" was formed in Massachusetts. Its purpose was to encourage and aid immigration to Kansas. Many leading men joined in the movement. Amos A. Lawrence, of Boston, a man of wealth and honor and large influence, was prominent among those who gave the movement not only their sanction, but their active cooperation. These men never faltered in the long struggle but were always ready with voice and purse to help the cause along.

"But many of those who came to Kansas under the auspices of this society were undesirable neighbors, looked at from my standpoint," recalled Cole Younger years later. "Their ideas on property rights were very hazy, in many cases. Some of them were let out of Eastern prisons to live down a 'past' in a new country. They looked upon a slave owner as legitimate prey, and later when lines became more closely drawn a secessionist was fit game, whether he had owned slaves or not."[22]

Many New Englanders settled around Lawrence, Kansas, and it became known as "The Boston Colony" and "Yankee Town." Lawrence became the headquarters for a group of citizens known as Jayhawkers. They were guerillas who raided nearby pro-slavery settlements, pillaging and murdering along the way.

The interest was not confined to New England but was general and widespread. The rising tide of anti-slavery sentiment was rapidly centering upon one practical point: "Slavery must not secure another foot of the public domain." Men anxious to check slavery felt that here was the opportunity to do something effective. They could not vote in Congress, but they could go to Kansas and vote, and that would accomplish the same thing. Even before the bill passed, this thought began to mature, and people here and there were preparing for what they saw was coming.

"These new neighbors ran off with the horses and Negroes of Missouri people without compunctions of conscience," penned Cole Younger, "and some Missourians grew to have similarly lax notions about the property rights of Kansans. These raiders on both sides, if interfered with, would kill, and ultimately they developed into what was known during the war as 'Freebooters,' who, when they found a stable of horses or anything easily transportable, would take it whether the owner be abolitionist or secessionist in sympathy."[23]

Early in May 1854, the Barber brothers, Thomas W. and Oliver P., with Samuel Walker and Thomas M. Pearson, made a tour in the territory with a view to settlement. They had all been "boys, together" in Franklin County, Pennsylvania, but the Barbers now lived in Indiana. They came to Westport, Missouri, by public conveyance. Here they hired a half-breed Indian to take them over the territory with his team. They spent a night at "Blue Jacket Crossing" on the Wakarusa River, and passed over what was to be the site of Lawrence, traveling up the spur of the hill. They went up as far as Topeka where there was an old-fashioned rope ferry; they then went across the prairies to Fort Leavenworth and then back to their home. The Kansas-Nebraska Bill passed while they were in the territory. All four afterwards removed to Kansas, and were largely instrumental in inducing others to come.

The most systematic and extensive movement, however, was made in New England. "The New England Emigrant Aid Company," which had been chartered by the legislature of Massachusetts in April, was then called "The Massachusetts Emigrant Aid Society." But afterwards a new charter was obtained for "The New England Emigrant Aid Company." The men engaged in it, Eli Thayer, Amos A. Lawrence, and others, commenced their work at once, arousing public interest and making arrangements to facilitate immigration to Kansas.

As early as June 1854, they sent Dr. Charles Robinson, of Fitchburg, and Mr. Charles H. Branscomb, of Holyoke, to explore the territory and select a site for a colony. Dr. Robinson was just the man for such a mission. Besides being in full sympathy with the ideas of Mr. Thayer, he knew the methods of the frontier. In 1849 he had gone to California with the gold seekers, and was prominent in the stirring events which characterized the early history of that state. In those turbulent times, he had been severely wounded, and had been placed under arrest and locked in prison for several months. But he and his friends finally won the day, and California was saved from the rule of the thieves.

He was just the man needed in the new emergency. He was calm and brave, and knew the conditions which he had to meet. In going to California, he had passed through Kansas by what was afterwards known as the "California Road." This road began at Westport, crossed the Wakarusa beyond Franklin, and wound up the spur of the hill. It then passed along the high prairie, which divided the valley of the Kansas River from that of the Wakarusa.

Dr. Robinson and his party climbed the hill along this spur and looked off over what became the site of Lawrence. They marked the beauty of the spot and the magnificence of the view. Whether they thought then of what might afterwards occur is not known, but when the time came to select a location for the first colony, Dr. Robinson remembered this view from the hilltop, and this doubtless had much to do in the final decision.

When he was asked, therefore, to go and explore the country with a view to locating colonies, it was not altogether an unknown terrain to him. Neither was pioneering altogether a new experience to him, as he knew something of the men and methods of pioneer life. On arriving in Kansas, Mr. Branscomb and some others passed again over the Lawrence town site, while Dr. Robinson went up the Missouri River to Leavenworth and other points.

While the pair was exploring the territory, their friends were getting ready to send out the initial party of immigrants. There were only twenty-nine in this first party, but they went out to prepare the way for others, and to show that the thing could be done. They were accompanied as far as Buffalo by Eli Thayer himself, the founder of The New England Emigrant Aid Company. The pioneer colony left Boston July 17, 1854. Immense crowds had gathered at the station to give them a parting God-speed. They moved out of the station amid the cheering of the crowds who lined the track for several blocks.

"The emigrants remained in Worcester the first night, and received a suitable ovation," wrote one of the men. "Several of the leading citizens called upon them, and applauded their patriotic devotion, and pledging remembrance in any emergency. The next day we were met in the evening at Albany by a good number of citizens who welcomed us with great cordiality. The next day we were cheered at all the principal stations as we passed on our westward journey. The president of the Monroe County Bible Society made an address, and presented the colony with a large and elegant Bible."

They crossed Lake Erie in the steamer *Plymouth Rock*, and went by way of Chicago to St. Louis. Here they were met by Dr. Robinson, who gave them the benefit of his experience. He procured transportation for them on board the steamer *Polar Star*, and they left St. Louis July 24th, arriving at Kansas City the Friday evening following, July 27th. The journey from there was well described in a letter by Mr. B.R. Knapp, published in the *Boston News*, and dated August 9, 1854:

> We prepared ourselves at once for starting. An ox team was purchased to transport the baggage and at ten o'clock Saturday evening we started on foot for our destination across the prairie. We traveled as much as possible during the night as the weather was very hot during the middle of the day. We saw occasionally a log house as we passed along, inhabited by farmers, of whom we obtained milk, etc. On the evening of Sunday we encamped on the lands of the Shawnee Indians. On Monday morning we started early, and in the evening arrived at the Wakarusa River, within ten miles of our destination. Here we camped, and the next day reached our new home. Here we established our camp, and pitched our twenty-five tents, which made a fine appearance though somewhat soiled. On Wednesday the second day of August, we went to work setting up our claim to the lands, and preparing for permanent settlement.[24]

This party arrived August 1st, ate their first meal on a hill, and conducted a meeting for organization. Ferdinand Fuller was selected as chairman. They were in good position to "view the landscape o'er," which they proceeded to do. They also delivered some speeches, and discussed the merits of the location and the best methods of procedure. The situation seemed to please them, and they voted to remain there. They named the hill on which they met "Mount Oread."

They remained on the hill a day or two, and then moved down, and camped near the Kansas River. The members of the party spent several days hunting for claims and selected them all around the proposed town site. Half the party returned East with the intention of bringing their families in the spring once the claims were agreed upon.[25]

The second party of emigrants left Boston in late August. It was a much larger party than the first, boasting sixty-seven members when leaving the city. They received accessions on the way, swelling their numbers to 114. There were eight or ten women in the company and several children, as well as several musicians, among them Joseph and Forest Savage from Hartford, Vermont.

These musicians carried their instruments with them and enlivened the journey with music whenever opportunity offered. Before departing, they assembled in the Boston and Worcester Station in Boston and sang and played Whittier's "Hymn of the Kansas Emigrant," which became a sort of national hymn to the colonists. These musicians became afterwards the nucleus of the "Lawrence Band" and were its main reliance for many years. They did noble service in stimulating an interest in music in the early times.

When the second party arrived, they met the members of the first party and soon agreed upon terms of union with them in laying out the town. The newcomers were soon scattered, seeking claims for themselves. On September 18th, a meeting of the settlers was conducted to effect a town organization. The necessity for this arose from the fact that there were no laws regulating such matters. The only thing they could do was to set up a sort of voluntary municipal government, and they lost no time in adopting a constitution and agreeing upon rules for the choice of claims.

The next day officers were chosen and a full city government set up. Dr. Charles Robinson was chosen president; Ferdinand Fuller, vice-president; Caleb S. Pratt, secretary; Levi Gates, treasurer; E.D. Ladd, register of deeds; A.D. Sean, surveyor; Joel Grover, marshal. The councilmen were Messrs. J.S. Emery, J.F. Morgan, Franklin Haskell. S.C. Harrington, A.H. Mallory, Samuel F. Tappan, S.P. Lincoln, S.J. Willis, N.T. Johnson, Joseph H. Cracklin. At an early meeting of the council, the principles of the Maine law were proposed and adopted almost unanimously. Thus Lawrence commenced its being as a prohibition town.

On September 20th, another public meeting was held by members of the first and second parties. Terms of agreement were arranged and unanimously adopted, by which they were to lay out the town together. It was agreed that the choice of shares should be sold to members of the town association. Time was allowed for payment, and the proceeds were to constitute a fund for public improvements. The choices were sold at prices varying from fifty cents to over three hundred dollars. The fifty-six claims sold aggregated the sum of $5,040. At the end of the year, the association gave up the notes, and the obligation was cancelled and the money never called for. In the distribution of shares, lots were reserved for a college, for schools, for state buildings, and for other public purposes.

At midnight of this same day, September 20th, the surveyor, A.D. Sean, with Charles W. Smith and three others, went out upon the high ground on Massachusetts Street, near the river, and took the observations necessary to establish the meridian line. September 25th the surveyor commenced the survey of the town, and marked off the lots and streets.

The name of the town had not been determined. It had been called Wakarusa, Yankee-town, and New Boston. After a full discussion, it was decided to give it the name of Lawrence, after Amos A. Lawrence, of Boston. Mr. Lawrence was one of the first men of means to endorse the movement for the settlement of Kansas in the interest of freedom. He was a man of large wealth and belonged to one of the most distinguished New England families. He was also a man of wide personal influence. He was treasurer of The New England Emigrant Aid Company and a very liberal contributor to its funds. A little later he gave some twelve thousand dollars to help found a college at Lawrence, which ultimately became a part of the endowment of the state university. His interest in Kansas, and especially in Lawrence, never faltered. His father and uncle were Abbott and Amos Lawrence, who were long distinguished in business and political circles in eastern Massachusetts. Abbott Lawrence had been a member of congress several times, and was minister to England for a number of years. Amos A. Lawrence inherited the wealth and reputation and business capacity of the family. He also inherited their public spirit and large liberality. The naming of the first free-state town in Kansas after him was a very fitting recognition.

Sara T.L. Robinson described Lawrence two years later:

> The town reaches to the river, whose further shore is skirted with a line of beautiful timber, while beyond all rises the Delaware lands, which in the distance have all the appearance of cultivated fields and orchards, and form a back-ground to the picture of singular loveliness. To the eastward the prairie stretches away eight or ten miles, and we can scarcely help believing that the ocean lies beyond the low range of hills meeting the horizon. The line of travel from the east, or from Kansas City, passes into the territory by this way. Blue Mound rises in the south-east, and, with the shadows resting over it, looks green and velvety. A line of timber between us and Blue Mound marks the course of the Wakarusa, while beyond the eye rests upon a country diversified in surface, sloping hills, finely rolling prairies, and timbered creeks. A half mile to the south of us, Mount Oread, upon which our house stands, becomes yet more elevated, and over the top of it passes the great California road. West of us also is a high hill, a half mile in the distance, with a beautiful valley lying between, while to the north-west there is the most delightful mingling together of hill, valley, prairie, woodland, and river. As far as the eye rests, we see the humble dwellings of the pioneer, with other improvements.[26]

On October 16, 1854, President Abraham Lincoln delivered the following speech on the Kansas-Nebraska Act:

> It is argued that slavery will not go to Kansas and Nebraska, in any event. This is a palliation—a lullaby. I have some hope that it will not; but let us not be too confident. As to climate, a glance at the map shows that there are five slave States—Delaware, Maryland, Virginia, Kentucky, and Missouri —and also the District of Columbia, all north of the Missouri compromise line. The census returns of 1850 show that, within these, there are 867,276 slaves—being more than one-fourth of all the slaves in the nation.
>
> It is not a climate, then, that will keep slavery out of these territories. Is there anything in the peculiar nature of the country? Missouri adjoins these territories, by her entire western boundary, and slavery is already within every one of her western counties. I have even heard it said that there are more slaves, in proportion to whites, in the north western county of Missouri, than within any county of the State. Slavery pressed entirely up to the old western boundary of the State, and when, rather recently, a part of that boundary, at the north-west was moved out a little farther west, slavery followed on quite up to the new line. Now, when the restriction is removed, what is to prevent it from going still further? Climate will

President Abraham Lincoln, ca. 1863. (Photo by Mathew B. Brady. Courtesy of the National Archives)

not. No peculiarity of the country will—nothing in nature will. Will the disposition of the people prevent it? Those nearest the scene are all in faver of the extension. The Yankees, who are opposed to it may be more numerous; but in military phrase, the battle-field is too far from their base of operations.

But it is said, there now is no law in Nebraska on the subject of slav-ery; and that, in such case, taking a slave there operates his freedom. That is good book-law; but is not the rule of actual practice. Wherever slavery is, it has been first introduced without law. The oldest laws we find concerning it are not laws introducing it; but regulating it, as an already existing thing. A white man takes his slave to Nebraska now; who will inform the negro that he is free? Who will take him before court to test the question of his freedom? In ignorance of his legal eman-cipation, he is kept chopping, splitting and plowing. Others are brought, and move on in the same track. At last, if ever the time for voting comes, on the question of slavery the institution already in fact exists in the country, and cannot well be removed. The facts of its presence and the difficulty of its removal will carry the vote in its favor. Keep it out until a vote is taken, and a vote in favor of it cannot be got in any pop-ulation of forty thousand, on earth, who have been drawn together by the ordinary motives of emigration and settlement. To get slaves into the country simultaneously with the whites, in the incipient stages of settlement, is the precise stake played for, and won in this Nebraska measure.

The question is asked us, "If slaves will go in, notwithstanding the general principle of law liberates them, why would they not equally go in against positive statute law?—go in, even if the Missouri restriction were maintained?' I answer, because it takes a much bolder man to venture in, with his property, in the latter case, than in the former—because the positive congressional enactment is known to, and respected by all, or nearly all; whereas the negative principle that no law is free law is not much known except among lawyers. We have some experience of this practical difference. In spite of the Ordinance of '87, a few negroes were brought into Illinois, and held in a state of quasi slavery; not enough, however, to carry a vote of the people in favor of the institution when they came to form a constitution. But in the adjoining Missouri country, where there was no ordinance of '87—was no restriction—they were carried ten times, nay a hundred times, as fast, and actually made a slave state. This is fact—naked fact.

Another LULLABY argument is that taking slaves to new countries does not increase their number-alms nor make any one slave who other-wise would be free. There is some truth in this, and I am glad of it, but it

[is] not WHOLLY true. The African slave trade is not yet effectually suppressed; and if we make a reasonable deduction for the white people amongst us, who are foreigners, and the descendants of foreigners, arriving here since 1808, we shall find the increase of the black population out-running that of the white, to an extent unaccountable, except by supposing that some of them too, have been coming from Africa. If this be so, the opening of new countries to the institution increases the demand for, and augments the price of slaves, and so does, in fact, make slaves of freemen by causing them to be brought from Africa, and sold into bondage.

But, however this may be, we know the opening of new countries to slavery, tends to the perpetuation of the institution, and so does KEEP men in slavery who otherwise would be free. This result we do not FEEL like favoring, and we are under no legal obligation to suppress our feelings in this respect.

Equal justice to the South, it is said, requires us to consent to the extending of slavery to new countries. That is to say, inasmuch as you do not object to my taking my hog to Nebraska, therefore I must not object to you taking your slave. Now, I admit this is perfectly logical, if there is no difference between hogs and negroes. But while you thus require me to deny the humanity of the negro, I wish to ask whether you of the south yourselves, have ever been willing to do as much? It is kindly provided that of all those who come into the world, only a small percentage are natural tyrants. That percentage is no larger in the slave States than in the free. The great majority, south as well as north, have human sympathies, of which they can no more divest themselves than they can of their sensibility to physical pain. These sympathies in the bosoms of the southern people, manifest in many ways, their sense of the wrong of slavery, and their consciousness that, after all, there is humanity in the negro. If they deny this, let me address them a few plain questions. In 1820 you joined the north, almost unanimously, in declaring the African slave trade piracy, and in annexing to it the punishment of death. Why did you do this? If you did not feel that it was wrong, why did you join in providing that men should be hung for it? The practice was no more than bringing wild negroes from Africa, to sell to such as would buy them. But you never thought of hanging men for catching and selling wild horses, wild buffaloes, or wild bears.

Again, you have amongst you, a sneaking individual, of the class of native tyrants, known as the "SLAVE-DEALER." He watches your necessities, and crawls up to buy your slave, at a speculating price. If you cannot help it, you sell to him; but if you can help it, you drive him from your door. You despise him utterly. You do not recognize him as a friend, or even as an honest man. Your children must not play with his; they may rollick freely with the little negroes, but not with the "slave-dealers" children. If you are obliged to deal with him, you try to get through the job without so much as touching him. It is common with you to join hands with the men you meet; but with the slave dealer you avoid the ceremony—instinctively shrinking from the snaky contact. If he grows rich and retires from business, you still remember him, and still keep up the ban of non-intercourse upon him and his family. Now why is this? You do not so treat the man who deals in corn, cattle, or tobacco.

And yet again, there are in the United States and territories, including the District of Columbia, 433,643 free blacks. At $500 per head they are worth over two hundred millions of dollars. How comes this vast amount of property to be running about without owners? We do not see free horses or free cattle running at large. How is this? All these free blacks are the descendants of slaves, or have been slaves themselves, and they would be slaves now, but for SOMETHING which has operated on their white owners, inducing them, at vast pecuniary sacrifices, to liberate them. What is that SOMETHING? Is there any mistaking it? In all these cases it is your sense of justice, and human sympathy, continually telling you, that the poor negro has some natural right to himself—that those who deny it, and make mere merchandise of him, deserve kickings, contempt, and death.

And now, why will you ask us to deny the humanity of the slave? And estimate him only as the equal of the hog? Why ask us to do what you will not do yourselves? Why ask us to do for nothing, what two hundred million of dollars could not induce you to do?

But one great argument in the support of the repeal of the Missouri Compromise, is still to come. That argument is "the sacred right of self-government." It seems our distinguished Senator has found great difficulty in getting his antagonists, even in the Senate to meet him fairly on this argument—some poet has said "Fools rush in where angels fear to tread." At the hazard of being thought one of the fools of this quotation, I meet that argument—I rush in, I take that bull by the horns.

I trust I understand, and truly estimate the right of self-government. My faith in the proposition that each man should do precisely as he pleases with all which is exclusively his own lies at the foundation of the sense of justice there is in me. I extend the principles to communities of men, as well as to individuals. I so extend it because it is politically wise, as well as naturally just: politically wise, in saving us from broils about matters which do not concern us. Here, or at Washington, I would not trouble myself with the oyster laws of Virginia, or the cranberry laws of Indiana.

The doctrine of self-government is right—absolutely and eternally right—but it has no just application, as here attempted. Or perhaps I should rather say that whether it has such just application depends upon whether a negro is not or is a man. If he is not a man, why in that case, he who is a man may, as a matter of self-government, do just as he pleases with him. But if the negro is a man, is it not to that extent, a total destruction of self-government, to say that he too shall not govern himself? When the white man governs himself, and also governs another man, that is more than self-government—that is despotism. If the negro is a man, why then my ancient faith teaches me that "all men are created equal," and that there can be no moral right in connection with one man's making a slave of another. Judge Douglas, frequently with bitter irony and sarcasm, paraphrases our argument by saying "The white people of Nebraska are good enough to govern themselves, but they are not good enough to govern a few miserable negroes!"

Well I doubt not that the people of Nebraska are, and will continue to be, as good as the average of people elsewhere. I do not say the contrary. What I do say is that no man is good enough to govern another man, without the other's consent. I say this is the leading principle—the sheet anchor of American republicanism. Our Declaration of Independence says: "We hold these truths to be self evident: that all men are created equal; that they are endowed by their Creator with certain inalienable rights; that among these are life, liberty, and the pursuit of happiness. That to secure these rights governments are instituted among men, DERIVING THEIR JUST POWERS FROM THE CONSENT OF THE GOVERNED."

I have quoted so much at this time merely to show that according to our ancient faith, the just powers of governments are derived from the consent of the governed. Now the relation of masters and slaves is, PRO TANTO, a total violation of this principle. The master not only governs the slave without his consent; but he governs him by a set of rules altogether different from those which he prescribes for himself. Allow ALL the governed an equal voice in the government, and that, and that only is self-government.

Let it not be said I am contending for the establishment of political and social equality between the whites and blacks. I have already said the contrary. I am not now combating the argument of NECESSITY, arising from the fact that the blacks are already amongst us; but I am combating what is set up as MORAL argument for allowing them to be taken where they have never yet been—arguing against the EXTENSION of a bad thing, which where it already exists, we must of necessity, manage as we best can.

In support of his application of the doctrine of self-government, Senator Douglas has sought to bring to his aid the opinions and examples of our revolutionary fathers. I am glad he has done this. I love the sentiments of those old-time men, and shall be most happy to abide by their opinions. He shows us that when it was in contemplation for the colonies to break off from Great Britain, and set up a new government for themselves, several of the states instructed their delegates to go for the measure PROVIDED EACH STATE SHOULD BE ALLOWED TO REGULATE ITS DOMESTIC CONCERNS IN ITS OWN WAY. I do not quote; but this in substance. This was right. I see nothing objectionable in it. I also think it probable that it had some reference to the existence of slavery amongst them. I will not deny that it had. But had it, in any reference to the carrying of slavery into NEW COUNTRIES? That is the question; and we will let the fathers themselves answer it.

This same generation of men, and mostly the same individuals of the generation, who declared this principle—who declared independence—who fought the war of the revolution through—who afterwards made the constitution under which we still live—these same men passed the ordinance of '87, declaring that slavery should never go to the northwest territory. I have no doubt Judge Douglas thinks they were very inconsistent in this. It is a question of discrimination between them and him. But there is not an inch of ground left for his claiming that their opinions—their example—their authority—are on his side in this controversy.

Again, is not Nebraska, while a territory, a part of us? Do we not own the country? And if we surrender the control of it, do we not surrender the right of self-government? It is part of ourselves. If you say we shall not control it because it is ONLY part, the same is true of every other part; and when all the parts are gone, what has become of the whole? What is then left of us? What use for the general government, when there is nothing left for it [to] govern?

But you say this question should be left to the people of Nebraska because they are more particularly interested. If this be the rule, you must leave it to each individual to say for himself whether he will have slaves. What better moral right have thirty-one citizens of Nebraska to say, that the thirty-second shall not hold slaves, than the people of the thirty-one States have to say that slavery shall not go into the thirty-second State at all?

But if it is a sacred right for the people of Nebraska to take and hold slaves there, it is equally their sacred right to buy them where they can buy them cheapest; and that undoubtedly will be on the coast of Africa; provided you will consent to not hang them for going there to buy them.

26

You must remove this restriction too, from the sacred right of self-government. I am aware you say that taking slaves from the States to Nebraska does not make slaves of freemen, but the African slave-trader can say just as much. He does not catch free negroes and bring them here. He finds them already slaves in the hands of their black captors, and he honestly buys them at the rate of about a red cotton handkerchief a head. This is very cheap, and it is a great abridgement of the sacred right of self-government to hang men for engaging in this profitable trade!

Another important objection to this application of the right of self-government, is that it enables the first FEW, to deprive the succeeding MANY, of a free exercise of the right of self-government. The first few may get slavery IN, and the subsequent many cannot easily get it OUT. How common is the remark now in the slave States—"If we were only clear of our slaves, how much better it would be for us." They are actually deprived of the privilege of governing themselves as they would, by the action of a very few, in the beginning. The same thing was true of the whole nation at the time our constitution was formed.

Whether slavery shall go into Nebraska, or other new territories, is not a matter of exclusive concern to the people who may go there. The whole nation is interested that the best use shall be made of these territories. We want them for the homes of free white people. This they cannot be, to any considerable extent, if slavery shall be planted within them. Slave States are places for poor white people to remove FROM; not to remove TO. New free States are the places for poor people to go to and better their condition. For this use, the nation needs these territories.

Still further; there are constitutional relations between the slave and free States, which are degrading to the latter. We are under legal obligations to catch and return their runaway slaves to them—a sort of dirty, disagreeable job, which I believe, as a general rule the slave-holders will not perform for one another. Then again, in the control of the government the management of the partnership affairs—they have greatly the advantage of us. By the constitution, each State has two Senators—each has a number of Representatives in proportion to the number of its people—and each has a number of presidential electors, equal to the whole number of its Senators and Representatives together. But in ascertaining the number of the people, for this purpose, five slaves are counted as being equal to three whites. The slaves do not vote; they are only counted and so used, as to swell the influence of the white people's votes. The practical effect of this is more aptly shown by a comparison of the States of South Carolina and Maine. South Carolina has six representatives, and so has Maine; South Carolina has eight presidential electors, and so has Maine. This is precise equality so far; and, of course they are equal in Senators, each having two. Thus in the control of the government, the two States are equals precisely. But how are they in the number of their white people? Maine has 581,813—while South Carolina has 274,567. Maine has twice as many as South Carolina, and 32,679 over. Thus each white man in South Carolina is more than the double of any man in Maine. This is all because South Carolina, besides her free people, has 384,984 slaves. The South Carolinian has precisely the same advantage over the white man in every other free state, as well as in Maine. He is more than the double of any one of us in this crowd. The same advantage, but not to the same extent, is held by all the citizens of the slave States, over those of the free; and it is an absolute truth, without an exception, that there is no voter in any slave State but who has more legal power in the government than any voter in any free State. There is no instance of exact equality; and the disadvantage is against us the whole chapter through. This principle, in the aggregate, gives the slave States, in the present Congress, twenty additional representatives-being seven more than the whole majority by which they passed the Nebraska bill.

Now all this is manifestly unfair; yet I do not mention it to complain of it, in so far as it is already settled. It is in the constitution; and I do not, for that cause, or any other cause, propose to destroy, or alter, or disregard the constitution. I stand to it, fairly, fully, and firmly. But when I am told I must leave it altogether to OTHER PEOPLE to say whether new partners are to be bred up and brought into the firm, on the same degrading terms against me, I respectfully demur. I insist, that whether I shall be a whole man, or only the half of one in comparison with others, is a question in which I am somewhat concerned; and one which no other man can have a sacred right of deciding for me. If I am wrong in this—if it really be a sacred right of self-government, in the man who shall go to Nebraska, to decide whether he will be the EQUAL of me or the DOUBLE of me—then after he shall have exercised that right, and thereby shall have reduced me to a still smaller fraction of a man than I already am, I should like for some gentleman deeply skilled in the mysteries of sacred rights, to provide himself with a microscope, and peep about, and find out, if he can, what has become of my sacred rights! They will surely be too small for detection with the naked eye.

Finally, I insist, that if there is ANY THING which it is the duty of the WHOLE PEOPLE to never entrust to any hands but their own, that thing is the preservation and perpetuity of their own liberties and institutions. And if they shall think, as I do, that the extension of slavery

28

endangers them, more than any, or all other causes, how recreant to themselves, if they submit the question, and with it, the fate of their country, to a mere hand-full of men, bent only on temporary self-interest. If this question of slavery extension were an insignificant one having no power to do harm-it might be shuffled aside in this way. But being, as it is, the great Behemoth of danger, shall the strong gripe of the nation be loosened upon him, to entrust him to the hands of such feeble keepers?[27]

Stephen A. Douglas' hopes for national political peace were dashed, as the repeal of the Missouri Compromise excited widespread indignation and opposition in the North. Douglas was burned in effigy across the North and shouted down when he attempted to speak before a crowd in Chicago. The act also roused Abraham Lincoln by paving the way for the extension of slavery, a prospect he had long opposed.[28]

Lincoln laid out his objections to the Act and resurrected his political career in a brilliant speech at Peoria on October 16, 1854. In it he vigorously attacked the repeal of the Missouri Compromise line, noting that restricting slavery above that geographical boundary had been a Southern concession to match northerners' accession to allowing Missouri to enter the Union as a slave state. Now that concession had been inexplicably withdrawn,

Stephen A. Douglas, Senator from Illinois. (Courtesy of the National Archives)

and with it, the sixty-year-old policy of restricting the expansion of slavery. Lincoln invoked the founding fathers, specifically Thomas Jefferson, as he contended that the Sage of Monticello had originated the restriction of slavery with his Northwest Ordinance's prohibition of slavery in the Northwest Territories.

Lincoln criticized popular sovereignty, questioning how it was that this doctrine could supersede the famed Northwest Ordinance and the sacred Missouri Compromise. Congress had purchased the territory, yet under Douglas' reasoning, it had no control over the disposition of slavery there. The entire nation was interested in the slavery issue, and properly so. Lincoln dismissed arguments that climate and geography rendered slavery impossible in Kansas and Nebraska. Only an explicit statutory prohibition was a true guarantee.

Most important, Lincoln attacked the morality of slavery's extension and of slavery itself, while tempering this assault on the "peculiar institution" with moderate rhetoric toward the South. Douglas' contentions were perfectly acceptable if the black man were no different than a hog. But Lincoln argued for the humanity of the slaves. They were people, not animals, and consequently possessed certain natural rights. "If the negro is a man, why then my ancient faith teaches me that 'all men are created equal,' and that there can be no moral right in connection with one man's making a slave of another."

Still, Lincoln attached no blame to the South for slavery, and confessed that he was not ready to accept black social and political equality. Though he strongly condemned any extension of slavery, he was still willing to tolerate even that to preserve the Union. Despite the radical nature of some of his statements, Lincoln was still a Whig, not an abolitionist.

Lincoln's speech was a success. By linking moral condemnation of slavery with appeals to the founding fathers, Lincoln legitimated the oft-criticized antislavery movement. Because Lincoln had spoken immediately after Stephen A. Douglas, who was touring Illinois to explain and defend the Kansas-Nebraska Act, he began to be thought of as Douglas' political foe.

Lincoln was drafted to run for the state legislature in 1854, which he reluctantly agreed to do in the hope of assisting the congressional candidate for his district. He won handily but immediately resigned to contest for a U.S. Senate seat, then decided by the Illinois General Assembly. The anti-Nebraska forces had won the General Assembly in 1854, but they were a queer political mix of Whigs, Democrats who had broken with Douglas over

Kansas-Nebraska, and "Know Nothings." The latter party had formed in response to perceptions that the country was being overrun with immigrants, many of whom were Catholic in faith. Thus it was an essentially bigoted, anti-immigrant party seeking to protect old-line Protestants' prerogatives and power. The old Whig party had broken down after the 1852 election, driven by insoluble sectional tensions. These disparate political groups were united in a common distaste for the Kansas-Nebraska Act. They squabbled over the Senate appointment, and Lincoln was forced to throw his support behind the anti-Nebraska Democrat Lyman Trumbull.

Notes

[1]Cole Younger (edited by Marley Brant), *The Story of Cole Younger by Himself*, St. Paul, Minnesota Historical Society Press, 2000, p. 5.

[2]Newspaper clipping, Northfield Public Library, Newspaper unknown, dated March 22, 1916.

[3]A. Huntley, "Cole Younger," *Famous Outlaws of the West*, Fall 1964, p. 27.

[4]Homer Croy, *Cole Younger Last of the Great Outlaws*, Lincoln, University of Nebraska Press, 1999 (reprint edition), pp. 3-4; Augustus C. Appler, *The Guerrillas of the West, or the Life, Character and Daring Exploits of the Younger Brothers*, St. Louis, Eureka Publishing Company, 1876, p. 5.

[5]Harry Sinclair Drago, *Outlaws on Horseback*, Lincoln & London, University of Nebraska Press, 1998, p. 24.

[6]Cole Younger, *The Story of Cole Younger by Himself*, p. 5.

[7]Philippe Charles Edel, *History of Strassburg, Alsace, France*, North Dakota State University, The Libraries, Germans from Russia Heritage Collection, September 1975.

[8]Todd M. George letter to Owen Dickie dated February 27, 1968, Le Sueur County Historical Society, Elysian, Minnesota.

[9]Richard Marshall Fristoe was born on March 22, 1789 in Knoxville, Tennessee, to Elizabeth Lovell and Reverend Robert Fristoe.

[10]*Knoxville Journal*, June 15, 1903.

[11]Todd M. George letter to Owen Dickie dated February 27, 1968, Le Sueur County Historical Society, Elysian, Minnesota.

[12]November 7,1880, author J.W. Buel visited Cole Younger and his brothers Jim and Bob in the Stillwater, Minnesota, Prison where they were serving life sentences for the Northfield robbery and murders. They had exchanged letters before this with Cole willing to talk about his war history but insisting he would divulge

nothing else. His interview with Cole Younger was published in his book *The Border Outlaws: An Authentic and Thrilling History of the Most Noted Bandits of Ancient or Modern Times, The Younger Brothers, Jesse and Frank James, and Their Comrades in Crime.*

[13]Paul C. Nagel, *Missouri: A History*, Lawrence, University of Kansas Press, 1977, pp. 120-121.

[14]J.W. Buel, *The Border Outlaws: An Authentic and Thrilling History of the Most Noted Bandits of Ancient or Modern Times, The Younger Brothers, Jesse and Frank James, and Their Comrades in Crime.*

[15]*Missouri Daily Republican* (St. Louis), February 1844.

[16]*Missouri Daily Republican* (St. Louis), June 1844.

[17]*Missouri Daily Republican* (St. Louis), September 28, 1844.

[18]Missouri State Archives.

[19]John Anthony Scott & Robert Alan Scott, *John Brown of Harper's Ferry*, New York, Facts on File, 1988, p. 88.

[20]P.O. Ray, *The Repeal of the Missouri Compromise* (1909, reprinted 1965).

[21]Richard Cordley, D.D., *A History of Lawrence, Kansas, from the Earliest Settlement to the Close of the Rebellion.* Lawrence, Kansas, E.F. Caldwell, Lawrence Journal Press, 1895.

[22]Cole Younger, *The Story of Cole Younger by Himself.* p.11.

[23]Ibid., p. 12.

[24]*Boston News*, August 9, 1854.

[25]Richard Cordley, D.D., *A History of Lawrence, Kansas from the Earliest Settlement to the Close of the Rebellion.*

[26]Sara T.L. Robinson, *Kansas: Its Exterior and Interior Life*, 1856.

[27]Founder's Library, The 19th Century Letters, Writings and Speeches of Abraham Lincoln.

[28]R.D. Monroe, Ph D, "The Kansas-Nebraska Act and the Rise of the Republican party, 1854-1856," Internet; David Donald, *Lincoln.* New York: Simon and Schuster, 1995; Eric Foner, *Free Soil, Free Labor, Free Men: The Ideology of the Republican Party before the Civil War.* New York: Oxford University Press, 1970; William E. Gienapp, *The Origins of the Republican Party, 1852-1856.* New York: 1987; Abraham Lincoln, *Abraham Lincoln: Speeches and Writings, 1832-1858.* Edited by Don E. Fehrenbacher. New York: Literary Classics of the United States, inc., 1989; Leon Litwack, *North of Slavery: The Negro in the Free States.* Chicago; 1961; Robert W. Johannsen, *Stephen A. Douglas.* New York; Oxford University Press, 1973; Mark E., Neely, *The Abraham Lincoln Encyclopedia.* New York, McGraw-Hill, 1982.

Chapter Two

Trouble along the Border

"Outrage follows outrage with frightful rapidity. The list is swelling. Every day some new crime is brought to light which equals in enormity its predecessors. The reign of terror has commenced. The bowie-knife and revolver, the hatchet, and hempen rope are the instruments brought into requisition to awe, intimidate, and crush out the liberty-loving portion of our fellow-citizens. As affairs are working now, no earthly power can prevent a bloody collision. If it must come, the sooner we have whipped out our enemies, the sooner will quiet be restored to the country. Human patience cannot long endure this system of terrorism and persecution." —THE HERALD OF FREEDOM[1]

IN OCTOBER 1854, KANSAS' FIRST territorial governor, Andrew H. Reeder, arrived in the territory for a tour of inspection to aid him in becoming familiar with conditions. Although Reeder was an advocate of slavery, he was heartily welcomed by the people of the territory. A number of settlements were being formed in eastern Kansas while tents and cabins were scattered over the prairies. The pro-slavery settlers had already brought slaves with them, and Reeder found many Indians, for only part of the tribes had as yet been removed.[2]

33

Following his return from such remote settlements as Council Grove and Fort Riley, Governor Reeder issued a proclamation for the first election to be held in Kansas. This action prepared the way for a delegate to Congress to be selected. Many Kansans paid little attention to the election, but Missourians under the leadership of Senator David Rice Atchison, were determined to control Kansas. Atchison's Blue Lodge voters began crossing the border into Kansas the day prior to the election. In the morning, they proceeded to the polling place, well armed and organized into companies.

The local press in Missouri encouraged Missourians to relocate in Kansas so they could influence the pending election and push the northeasterners north or west. Many Missourians did move to Kansas, but the majority if border-county residents stayed in Missouri to protect their interests. Although Colonel Henry Younger remained in Missouri with a large number of slaves, he was elected to the Kansas legislature with A.M. Coffee and David Lykins as a resident of the Kansas-Missouri Border District of Shawnee Mission, Kansas, on March 30, 1855. Younger, a conservative unionist, extolled the virtues of order and liberty.[3]

In the Kansas election of November 29, 1854, thousands of Missourians crossed the border to vote for a delegate to Congress; so many appeared that they were able to outnumber the legal voters in many of the precincts. They felt they had as much right to vote in the election as the newly arrived New Englanders. It was also their impression that the New Englanders were hired to sway the vote in favor of anti-slavery delegates. Election judges, who refused to accept the Blue Lodge votes were removed and pro-slavery judges installed in their place.

The pro-slavery candidate won the election easily, but he would most likely have won nonetheless had the Missourians stayed home since most of the area, except for Lawrence, was pro-slavery. The Territorial Census taken in the spring revealed that 8,601 people lived within the territory, only about 3,000 of whom that could vote. Soon a date was set for the election of a territorial legislature.

Abolitionist societies from the free-states encouraged abolitionists like John Brown to move to Kansas and settle so that they could vote for Kansas to be a free state. Frederick Douglass later said of Brown, "His zeal in the cause of my race was far greater than mine. I could live for the slave, but he could die for him."[4]

Frederick Douglass. (Courtesy of the National Archives)

During the first fifty years of his life, Brown had worked as a tanner, a sheep farmer, a land speculator, and a wool broker. He was extremely diligent and hardworking, but he was also stubborn, and refused to take advice from those who could have helped him become successful. John Brown was married twice. His first wife, Dianthe, died after bearing him seven children. Shortly after her death, he married Mary, who bore him an additional thirteen children. He believed in corporal punishment and would often use a switch to enforce his rules. He also showed affection, and on more than one occasion, stayed up all night comforting a sick child.

In 1854 five of Brown's sons—Owen, Frederick, Salmon, Jason, and John, Jr.—had moved to Kansas to settle and support the free-state cause. At the time, John Brown was living in North Elba, New York, where he had established a farm with the hopes of training escaped slaves in citizenship and farming methods. However, when he heard of the troubles in Kansas, the enactment of the "bogus laws" and his sons' ill health, he collected arms with his son Oliver and son-in-law Henry Thompson and moved to Kansas. When he arrived there, his sons were all sick, and he began immediately clearing land for them and helping them build houses.

In the spring of 1855, the election of the first territorial legislature was conducted. As the Organic Act allowed the people to determine their own domestic institutions, the first legislature might establish or exclude slavery by law, and so might settle the whole question. Governor Andrew H. Reeder ordered the election to be held on the thirtieth day of March. Both sides understood the importance of this election and put forth their strongest efforts to carry it. Whoever secured the first legislature would make the first laws. A pro-slavery legislature could establish slavery and pass laws protecting slave property. Then the people of the South could come with their slaves, and slavery would actually exist in Kansas. If once a considerable number of slaves were settled in Kansas, it would be very difficult to dislodge them.[5]

On the other hand if the free-state men secured the legislature, they would establish freedom by law. Pro-slavery men could come to Kansas still, but they would not dare bring their slaves. This would practically settle the question for freedom. The canvas, therefore, was a lively one, and all felt that the contest was vital. The pro-slavery people, however, carried on their canvas in Missouri. They were not disposed to trust to the doctrines of popular sovereignty, of which they had boasted. They proposed to go over and help settle the question. For weeks before the election, the border counties of Missouri were all astir. Meetings were held and flaming speeches made, and the excitement knew no bounds. There were secret societies, called Blue Lodges, in which the main purpose was to control Kansas for slavery. The members were bound together by pledges, and armed for the battle. The plan advocated in all these meetings was to have the members of these lodges march into Kansas on the day of election, take possession of the polls, and vote, and so get control of the legislature. They proposed to go in sufficient numbers to secure their end beyond all doubt, and they proposed to go thoroughly armed so as to overcome all resistance. They would depend on numbers and bluster and threats to carry the scheme through. The plan of the campaign was perfectly laid. It was arranged that bands of Missourians should enter every election district in Kansas, and enter in sufficient number to out-vote the settlers.

General B.F. Stringfellow declared in a speech at St. Joseph: "I tell you to mark every scoundrel among you that is the least tainted with free-soilism or abolitionism, and exterminate him. I advise you, one and all, to enter every election district in Kansas, in defiance of Reeder and his vile myrmidons, and vote at the point of the bowie knife and revolver. Never give or take quarter from the rascals."[6]

The Missourians came to Lawrence one thousand strong, March 29th, the day before the election, and camped in the ravine near the town. In all, five thousand men armed with guns and knives marched into Kansas and more than 6,000 ballots were cast. Disorderly, vulgar, and dangerous, they boasted they were from Missouri and drove many of the legal voters from the polls. The company that came to Lawrence was led by Colonel Samuel Young, a leading lawyer of Boone County, and Claiborne F. Jackson. It was not a burst of ignorant passion but the deliberate purpose of the leading men of Missouri and of the South. Kansas had to be secured for slavery by fair means or foul. The report of the congressional committee, which investigated the affair, gave a very vivid description of the scene at Lawrence:

> The evening before, and the morning of the day of the election, about one thousand men arrived at Lawrence, and camped in a ravine a short distance from the town, and near the place of voting. They came, in wagons (of which there were over one hundred) or on horseback, under the command of Colonel Samuel Young, of Boone County, Missouri, and Claiborne F. Jackson, of Missouri. They were armed with guns, rifles, pistols, and bowie knives; and had tents, music, and flags with them. They brought with them two pieces of artillery, loaded with musket balls.
>
> The evening before the election, the Missourians were called together at the tent of Captain Claiborne F. Jackson, and speeches were made to them by Colonel Young and others, calling on volunteers to go to other districts where there were not Missourians enough to control the election, as there were more at Lawrence than were needed. On the morning of the election, the Missourians came over to the place of voting from their camp, in companies, or bodies, of one hundred at a time. Mr. Blanton, one of the judges, not appearing, Colonel Young claimed that as the people of the territory had two judges, it was nothing more than right that the Missourians should have the other one to look after their interests. Robert A. Cummins was elected in Blanton's stead because he considered that every man had a right to vote if he had not been in the territory but an hour. The Missourians brought their tickets with them. Not having enough they had three hundred more printed in Lawrence the evening before and on the day of election. They had white ribbons in their buttonholes to distinguish them from the settlers.
>
> When the voting commenced, the question of the legality of the vote of a Mr. Page was raised. Before it was decided, Colonel Samuel Young stepped to the window where the votes were received and said he would

settle the matter. The vote of Mr. Page was withdrawn, and Colonel Young offered to vote. He refused to take the oath prescribed by the governor, but said he was a resident of the territory. He told Mr. Abbott, one of the judges, when asked if he intended to make Kansas his future home, that it was none of his business; if he were a resident then he should ask no more. After his vote was received, Colonel Young got upon the window sill and announced to the crowd that he had been permitted to vote, and they could all come up and vote. He told the judges that there was no use swearing the others, as they would all swear as he had. After the other judges had concluded to receive Colonel Young's vote, Mr. Abbott resigned as judge of election, and Mr. Benjamin was elected in his place.

The polls were so much crowded till late in the evening that for a time they were obliged to get out by being hoisted up on the roof of the building, where the election was being held, and passing out over the house. Afterwards a passageway was made through the crowd by two lines of men being formed, through which voters could get to the polls. Colonel Young asked that the old men be allowed to go up first and vote, as they were tired with the traveling and wanted to get back to camp. During the day, the Missourians drove off the ground some of the citizens, Mr. Stearns, Mr. Bond and Mr. Willis. They threatened to shoot Mr. Bond, and made a rush after him, threatening him. As he ran from them, shots were fired at him as he jumped off the bank of the river and escaped.[7]

The Missourians mostly started for home as soon as they had voted. A few remained until the next day. According to the census taken in February, the district contained 369 legal voters. The whole number of votes cast was 1,034. A careful examination of the poll lists showed that 232 of these were legal votes, while 802 votes were cast by non-residents.

What was done in Lawrence was done everywhere, and while the census showed only 2,905 legal voters in the territory, there were 6,307 votes cast. It was a clean sweep, Missourians electing the entire legislature with one exception. There was no denial of the invasion, but the pro-slavery press boasted of it as a great victory. Abolition had been rebuked in its own stronghold.

Many free-staters gathered and appealed the fraudulent election to Governor Reeder and demanded another voting. Angry Missourians, however, threatened Reeder's life should he take such action. While angry mobs from both sides gathered outside the governor's office, Reeder recognized the validity of the election except where proof of fraud was shown. In these cases, he called for new elections to which the pro-slavery element took no part. Several free-state candidates were elected to the legislature.

When the legislature met, however, the pro-slavery majority ousted the free-state members and recognized the men originally elected. The all-proslavery or "Bogus Legislature," leaders were B.F. Stringfellow and David Rice Atchison. Adopting the entire body of Missouri laws, Atchison declared, "We wish to make Kansas in all respects like Missouri."[8]

Meanwhile, the "bogus legislature," assembled and began their work. They met at Pawnee July 2nd, but adjourned to Shawnee Mission, where they reassembled July 12th. They excluded all those elected at Reeder's special election and admitted all those chosen March 30th. There was only one free-state member left in the whole lot, and he soon became disgusted and left. To save time and toil, they adopted the Missouri code of laws, simply directing the clerk to make the necessary verbal changes to adapt it to Kansas. In the matter of slavery, however, they favored Kansas with special legislation. As slavery in Kansas was in peculiar danger, it must be protected by laws peculiarly searching and strong. In this matter they acted like men whose reason had left them. They enacted an absurdly severe slave code, which stated:

> Section 1. If any person shall entice, or decoy, or carry out of this territory, any slave belonging to another, he shall be adjudge guilty of grand larceny, and on conviction thereof shall suffer death. Section 2. If any person shall aid or assist in enticing, carrying away, or sending out of the territory, any slave belonging to another, he shall be adjudge guilty of grand larceny, and on conviction hereof suffer death. Section 3. If any person shall entice, decoy, or carry away out of any state or other territory of the United States, any slave belonging to another, and shall bring such slave into this territory with the intent to procure the freedom of such slave, the person thus offending shall suffer death.
> Section 11. If any person shall print, write, publish, or circulate within the territory any book, magazine, hand-bill or circular containing any statements, arguments, opinions, sentiments, doctrine, advice or innuendo calculated to promote a disorderly, dangerous or rebellious disaffection among the slaves in this territory, or to induce such slaves to escape from their masters, or to resist their authority, he shall be guilty of a felony, and be punished by imprisonment and hard labor for a term of not less than five years.

Section 12. If any free person, by speaking or by writing, assert or maintain that persons have not the right to hold slaves in this territory, or shall introduce into this territory, print, publish, write or circulate, or shall cause to be introduced in this territory, any book, paper, magazine, pamphlet or circular containing any denial of the right of persons to hold slaves in this territory, such person shall be deemed guilty of felony, and punished by imprisonment at hard labor for a term of not less than two years.[9]

If anything were needed to confirm the free-state men in their attitude towards the "bogus legislature," the conduct of the legislature itself furnished it. The outrageous invasion of March might have been forgotten if the legislature itself had been moderate and fair. But first of all they broke with Governor Reeder because he would not accede to all of their demands. Then they purged themselves of free-state members wherever any pretext could be found for doing so. Then they enacted a slave code more severe than was found in the slave states themselves. By the twelfth section of that bill it was made a penitentiary offense to express an opinion adverse to slavery. Self-respecting free-state men must either leave the territory or repudiate such laws. As the legislature itself was elected by non-resident votes, they pronounced the whole concern a fraud, and repudiated the legislature and its laws. As the work of the legislature went on, the idea of repudiation was being matured. The numerous conventions in Lawrence grew more and more distinct in their tone as the spirit and work of the legislature became more and more manifest.

Because Governor Reeder had refused to accede to all the demands of the pro-slavers, they successfully petitioned the president for his removal. By the summer of 1855, the territory was divided into two bitter factions evidenced by the election of two territorial governors. Wilson Shannon operated the pro-slavery government out of Topeka. Free-soiler Charles Robinson chose Lawrence as his headquarters.

Again, in the summer of 1855, many more emigrants arrived from the East Coast but instead of bringing their families and farm implements, they brought with them rifles. Many rumors abounded, and Missourians became worried about the new inhabitants and their intentions. Crates of rifles and some cannons were shipped to Kansas under disguised labels, and it appeared that Kansas was preparing for war. John Brown and Jim Lane also arrived in

Kansas in the summer of 1855. John Brown was well known for his antics against slave owners and his desire to wage war against them. Jim Lane was a politician and was looking for political opportunities but at the time had no qualms over slavery. Seeing political opportunity, he switched sides and became a free-soil advocate. In 1856, he led pillage-and-burn raids in eastern Kansas and western Missouri, freeing numerous slaves, but he also passed a "Black Law" in Kansas, which prohibited residency to all Negroes. Men like Lane, Brown, and other abolitionists justified their raids into Missouri as doing the Lord's work. Kansas was politically and residentially being set up to be a free-soil state and its new residents (Jayhawkers) were conducting raids against pro-slavery residents and establishments on both sides of the border.[10]

Charles Robinson, first governor of Kansas. (Author's collection)

The free-staters were led by Charles Robinson of Lawrence, ex-Governor Reeder, and James H. Lane. James Henry Lane was one of the most bizarre and compelling characters ever to ride the prairies of Kansas. His career was one of obsessive ambition and, until the end, surprising success. His military victories in the Mexican War acted as a springboard for a political career, and there was no better climate for a man of these two talents than the Kansas Territory.[11]

Atrocities took place on both sides as the free-staters ignored the proslavery government, organized one of their own, and drew up their own constitution. The free-state leaders held a meeting to gain the support of the people and of Congress. Each claimed its own breed of logic and extremism. But the tension appeared greatest where the Missouri Border Ruffians and Jayhawkers crossed paths. In this region, zealotry to the cause resulted in heinous retaliatory actions. With forts and meeting spots scattered throughout Miami, Linn, and Bourbon counties, direct confrontations were a daily occurrence. As strong personalities congregated in the area, tensions rose.

A convention was held in Topeka during the fall of 1855, and a state constitution proclaimed: "There shall be no slavery in the state." The state constitution was submitted to a vote of the people and was approved by an immense majority. Only free-staters voted in the election since the proslavery element did not recognize the rival government. Dr. Charles Robinson was made governor and James Lane, senator. In the spring of 1856, the constitution was dispatched to Washington requesting that Kansas be admitted to the Union, but the bill failed to pass.

Reverend Pardee Butler, a preacher of the Christian Church, denounced the outrage in the streets of Atchison, and was seized by a mob, his face was painted black, and he was bound upon a raft and sent floating down the Missouri River. He escaped after a few miles. Some time afterwards, he was seized again. The mobs were disposed to hang him but finally were content to give him a coat of tar and feathers, and let him go. As these outrages and many more were approved by a large portion of the "law and order" party, no attempt was made to punish the perpetrators of them, although they were well known and did not bother to conceal themselves or their crimes.

The violence finally culminated in the first killing on November 21, 1855, when a proslavery man named Coleman shot a young free-state man named Dow ten miles south of Lawrence. It all grew out of a claim dispute. Charles W. Dow and Franklin M. Coleman occupied adjoining claims at Hickory Point, about ten miles south of Lawrence. Dow was a free-state man and Coleman was a pro-slavery man, and they frequently quarreled about their claims.

On November 21st, Dow was at Coleman's cabin, talking over the inevitable subject in the inevitable temper. As he started home, Coleman shot him down in the road. Coleman fled to Westport, Missouri, and sought protection from a border ruffian with legal power, Sheriff Jones. Jacob Branson, a friend of Dow, threatened the life of a friend of Coleman's, whereupon Sheriff Jones arrested Branson. The man was rescued by an indignant party of free-staters, who took him to Lawrence, the settlement most despised by the proslavery faction.[12]

Jones appealed to Sheriff Shannon for 3,000 men. Fifteen hundred men assembled, however, and camped on the banks of the Wakarusa River, about three miles south of Lawrence. Although Sheriff Jones carried a warrant, Branson and his followers had already left Lawrence. Two free-staters crept through enemy lines and convinced Governor Shannon that he was being deceived by the Missourians. Governor Shannon hastened to Lawrence, arranged a treaty between the two factions, and Jones and his men dispersed without a single shot fired.

But pitched battles erupted between the two factions, and small parties of federal troops patrolled Clay County, Missouri. Two hundred men from Clay County responded by collecting $1,000 from area citizens, purchased weapons and equipment, and ferried across the Missouri River to fight the Jayhawkers.[13]

On December 4th, a hundred Missouri men stormed the Federal Arsenal in Liberty, arrested the major in command and appropriated arms and ammunition, which were dispatched to border ruffian camps in Kansas. A meeting at the courthouse in Liberty in March 1856 raised a great deal of money for the Missouri cause, and on May 21st, 800 border ruffians looted the town of Lawrence, Kansas. Pro-slavery leader David Rice Atchison ordered the Missouri River closed to free-state migrants and goods, while armed squads of men stood guard along the waterfront in Platte, Clay, Lafayette, and Jackson counties.

Among those participating in the sacking of Lawrence was Joseph Orville "Jo" Shelby. Although born into an aristocratic Kentucky family in 1830, Shelby had moved to Waverly, Missouri, in 1852 where he built an agrarian empire that included several plantations, warehouses, and a steamboat. Waverly's economic interests were tied to the South, and as a proponent of slavery, he became a leader of the border ruffians although he had never had any formal military training.[14]

Many Northerners hated the newspaper coverage of hostilities because it implied that they could not stop the spread of slavery into new territories before statehood. If slavery could establish itself, then slave owners could, by means fair or foul, create a slave state when the state was admitted to the Union—as the Jayhawkers in Kansas had attempted to do, with their fraudulent Lecompton Convention establishing a Kansas Constitution, a blatant act of force having little support among the majority of Kansans.

The Missourians continued to cross the Kansas border and vote in the elections in an attempt to sway a pro-slavery vote and to elect the politicians that supported slavery. This caused much turmoil between the two states, and the federal government sent troops to occupy the area. These troops were from Kansas, Iowa, Illinois, Michigan, and Wisconsin.[15]

43

This action, however, exacerbated the situation. First, the Missourians viewed the federals as an occupying army, but most important, the soldiers in the militia were Kansas volunteers, many of which were ruffians, but now wore blue uniforms. Two of the most famous ruffian bands were the Jayhawkers (named for a mythical Irish bird) and the Redlegs (named for their maroon leggings). The founder of the Jayhawkers, Charles R. "Doc" Jennison, once declared an outlaw by the federal government, was commissioned to command the Seventh Kansas Volunteer Cavalry Regiment. The Redlegs, under command of General James C. Blunt and Kansas Senator Jim Lane, became the Ninth Kansas Volunteer Cavalry Regiment.

When President Lincoln sent in the federal occupational troops, they took full advantage of their position and soon began traumatizing much of Western and West Central Missouri by committing unspeakable crimes. Innocent families became their victims, including women, children, and the elderly.

An unscrupulous opportunist in both his personal relations and political associations, Jim Lane nevertheless became the Hero of Free Kansas by leading the Free State volunteers in a coordinated defense of Lawrence in the Wakarusa War of 1856. He had previously led the convention of Free-State representatives which produced the anti-slavery Topeka Constitution, and would go on to represent the fledgling state as a senator.[16]

In addition to the Jayhawkers and Missouri bushwhackers, border ruffians, who had no interest in Missouri and Kansas politics inhabited the border. Their sole intention of inhabiting the area was to initiate terror tactics of pillaging and murder. This added to the conflict as often times, either side was blamed for their crimes.

On the morning of May 21st, Marshal Donaldson with a posse of several hundred men and some pieces of artillery, appeared on Mount Oread, the hill overlooking Lawrence. As these came under United States authority, it was decided to make no resistance. Deputy Marshal Fain rode into town about eleven o'clock. The streets were very quiet. Some of the citizens were in prison, some who did not like the decision not to resist, stayed out of the way.

The deputy marshal rode up to the Free-State Hotel where the committee of safety was in session, and summoned a number of citizens to act as his posse in serving writs. He then arrested G.W. Smith, Gaius Jenkins, and G.W. Deitzler, who had been indicted for treason. The marshal and his men were invited to dine at the Free-State Hotel.

After dinner the marshal returned to the camp and told the men he had made all the arrests he desired at this time and that they were dismissed. As soon as they were dismissed as the marshal's posse, Sheriff Jones summoned them to act as a posse for him, as he had some writs to serve. This then was their shrewd game. This mob was brought to Lawrence as the posse of the United States marshal.

The people of Lawrence had determined in no case to resist United States authority. The town came easily into their possession. But an officer of the United States was limited by law and was compelled to pay some regard to decency and justice. All he could do was to make a few arrests to which the people made no objections. But as soon as the town had submitted and was helpless, he turned his posse over to Sheriff Jones, who was hampered by no restrictions. The sheriff rode into town with a company of men and drew up in front of the hotel. He demanded first that all the arms in the place be given up to him. He gave the committee five minutes to decide. If the arms were not surrendered, he would bombard the town. A hurried consultation was held, and it was decided to give up the cannon and the arms in possession of the committee of safety. They told him the other arms were private property and not at the disposal of the committee.

The one cannon they possessed was hidden under a building and never could have been found by the invaders. But so anxiously nervous were they to appease the fussy sheriff and save the town, that General Samuel C. Pomeroy crawled under the building where the cannon was hidden, dragged it out, and turned it over to Jones. But neither their promises nor their humiliation availed anything.

As soon as Jones had possession of the cannon and other arms, he proceeded to carry out his purpose to destroy the Free-State Hotel. He gave the inmates till five o'clock to get out their personal effects. When all was ready he turned his cannon upon the hotel and fired. The first ball went completely over the roof, at which all the people cheered, much to the disgust of Jones. The next shot hit the walls but did little damage. After bombarding away with little or no effect till it was becoming monotonous, they attempted to blow up the building with a keg of powder. But this only made a big noise and a big smoke, and did not do much towards demolishing the house. With every failure, the citizen spectators along the street commenced shouting. At last Jones became desperate, and applied the vulgar torch, and burned the building to the ground. Meanwhile the two newspaper offices had been ransacked, the presses broken and the type thrown into the river, or scattered along the street. The mob by this time had become thoroughly reckless and was ransacking the town. Nearly every house was entered, and many of them robbed. Trunks were broken open, clothing stolen, and everything taken off to which they took a fancy. In the evening Governor Robinson's house was set on fire and burned to the ground.

Jones was exultant as his revenge was complete. "This is the happiest moment of my life," he shouted, as the walls of the hotel collapsed. He then dismissed his posse and left. The losses sustained by the people of Lawrence and surrounding country were quite heavy. It was estimated that the value of the property destroyed and stolen amounted to nearly $200,000. The Missourians had demolished the hotel. Two printing presses were thrown into the river, and the Missourians ransacked stores and homes and burned down the home of Governor Robinson.[17]

Between November 1, 1855, and December 1, 1856, an estimated 200 people lost their lives, and the amount of property destroyed was valued at two million dollars. After the town of Lawrence was sacked, Jayhawkers hunted down the raiding party and killed three men. While on their hunt, they raided a Missourian's store, taking over $4,000 worth of merchandise and set fire to several pro-slavery cabins.

On May 21, 1856, the Pottawatomie Rifles were called together, when it was heard that an attack was to be made on Lawrence, for the purpose of going to the defense of the town. On the way, they learned that Lawrence had been destroyed, when James Towsley, one of the eye-witnesses, brought news that an attack was expected on the Pottawatomie. Owen Brown, and later John Brown, asked Towsley to take a party down to watch what was going on. The party consisted of John Brown, his four sons—Frederick, Oliver, Owen, and Watson—his son-in-law, Henry Thompson, Theodore Weiner, and James Towsley. They left Shore's about two o'clock of May 23. They went into camp about a mile west of Dutch Henry's Crossing, and after supper John Brown revealed his plan, which was to "sweep the Pottawatomie of all pro-slavery men living on it."[18]

Among the pro-slavery men were Allen Wilkinson, who operated the post office; James P. Doyle, who took up a claim north of the Pottawatomie in the fall of 1854; Henry and William Sherman, who settled on an abandoned Indian farm at the ford of the creek, which became known as Dutch Henry's crossing. Some of the free-state men regarded Wilkinson, Doyle, and the Shermans as harmless pro-slavery men, but as the first had been elected by fraud and violence to a legislature where he voted for a black code; the second had his sons, William and Drury, keep free-state men from the polls by force, and the Shermans entertained lawless invaders, this view was not held by all.

John Brown, ca. 1856. (Engraving from daguerreotype. Courtesy of the National Archives)

On May 24th, John Brown, his sons and several of his followers used double-edged artillery cutlasses to hack to death five men near Dutch Henry's Crossing on Pottawatomie Creek in Franklin County. The victims were accused of being pro-slavery ruffians and were dragged from their cabins despite the pleas of their wives and children. Three of these men were a father and his two sons. Their bodies were found the next morning by their kin in various stages of mutilation that included cut throats, multiple stab wounds and fingers, arms, and legs chopped off. This became known as the "Pottawatomie Massacre."

"Many and various were the instructions he gave us," one of his young followers remembered. "He expressed himself to us that we should never allow ourselves to be tempted by any consideration to acknowledge laws and institutions to exist as of right if our conscience and our reason condemned them. He admonished us not to care whether a majority, no matter how large, opposed our principles and opinions, the largest majorities being sometime only organized mobs whose howlings never changed black to white or night into day. . . . While it was true that the pro-slavery people had the upper hand at present, and the Free State organization had dwindled to a handful in the bush, nevertheless we ought to be of good cheer and start the ball rolling at the first opportunity, no matter whether its starting motion would even crush us to death."[19]

Brown's party had crossed the Pottawatomie and Mosquito creeks and continued north until Doyle's house was reached. Frederick Brown, Theodore Weiner, and James Towsley stood guard in the road, while the rest went to the house. They brought out Doyle and his sons—William and Drury—and went back south across the Mosquito Creek. Doyle attempted to escape, and John Brown shot him. When the boys attempted to get away, Brown's sons killed them with swords.

Salmon Brown later described the killings: "We went to Doyle's first and encountered a number of savage dogs. Old man Tousley [Townsley] went after the dogs with a broadsword, and he and my brother Fred soon had them all laid out. Tousley then went in without being asked. . . . The three Doyles were taken out of the house to a point a half mile or so away and were slain with broadswords. Owen Brown cut down one of them, and another of the Browns cut down the old man and the other. Old man Doyle's wife gave the Doyles a terrible scoring as they were being taken from the house. She said, 'I told you would get into trouble for all your devilment, and now you see it has come.'"[20]

The party then proceeded to Wilkinson's house and ordered him out. He had gone but a short distance with them when one of the Brown boys killed him with a sword. They then crossed the creek at Dutch Henry's and took William Sherman to the river, where he was killed with short swords and his body thrown into the stream.

"Henry Sherman was killed by Henry Thompson, and also Wilkinson, at about the same time the Doyles were," related Salmon Brown. "Our party divided, Thompson and Winer [Weiner] in one party and Owen Brown, Fred Brown, Salmon Brown, Oliver Brown, and old man Tousley in the other, father running back and forth between the two parties. Father never raised a hand in slaying the men. He shot a bullet into the head of old man Doyle about a half hour after he was dead, but what for I do not know."[21]

When Brown started out that night, he had intended to capture these men and hold a trial, but after Doyle's effort to escape, the plan was changed. This massacre greatly terrified the pro-slavery settlers of Pottawatomie Creek, who concluded that the whole rifle company had returned to commit the deed.

Missourians crossed the border looking for Brown and found one of his sons. They turned him over to federal authorities who chained him to a tent pole and beat him with rifle butts and fists. Brown launched a pre-dawn attack to rescue his son, killing four and wounding several others. When approached by a U.S. deputy marshall under a flag of truce, Brown held a pistol to the deputy's head and demanded the company's unconditional surrender.

Stories of John Brown and his sons hacking people to death with their swords spread across Missouri almost overnight. Cole Younger, Frank and Jesse James, among other children of proslavery families, played a game called Old John Brown. One of the children would take the role of John Brown, and another his victim. The other children would come to rescue the victim, and together they would drive the hated Brown back to Kansas, swearing to get revenge on him someday.[22]

During the first week of August, proslavers received word that Jim Lane was coming with his "Army of the North." The Missourians began rallying their men along the border and Governor Shannon hastily resigned. Secretary of the Treasury Daniel Woodson became acting governor until a new governor arrived. Woodson, in full sympathy with the Missourians, opened the border, and the proslavery army moved into Kansas. Upon reaching Osawatomie, the headquarters of John Brown, they attacked the town leaving only four cabins standing.

During this action, new Territorial Governor John W. Geary arrived in Kansas and described the scene before him: "I reached Kansas and entered upon the discharge of my official duties in the most gloomy hour of her history. Desolation and ruin reigned on every hand; homes and firesides were deserted; the smoke of burning dwellings darkened the atmosphere; women and children, driven from their habitations, wandered over the prairies and among the woodlands, or sought refuge even among the Indian tribes. The highways were infested with numerous predatory bands, and the towns were fortified and garrisoned by armies of conflicting partisans, each excited almost to frenzy, and determined upon mutual extermination. Such was without exaggeration, the condition of the Territory at the period of my arrival."[23]

49

The Missourians continued their march towards Lawrence but were met there by Governor Geary and United States soldiers. The town was poorly fortified, and the defenders had little ammunition and provisions. On the morning of September 15th, Governor Geary marched out to the Missouri army encampment and held a conference with its leaders. When it concluded, the Missourians consented to disperse, and 2,700 well-equipped men went home.

"In the war of 1856 Jackson County and the settlement about Independence especially, was more largely represented, perhaps, than any other section," recalled Cole Younger years later. "This diabolical war, distinguished by the most atrocious cruelties the conqueror can inflict upon his captive, prepared the way, and created the guerrilla in 1862. Natural fighters, conducting a war of spoliation and reprisal—through the brush—trained to quick sorties and deadly ambuscades, how easily they drifted as their instincts inclined, and became guerrillas by an irresistible combination of circumstances, such as I have explained."[24]

The organization of such armed mobs resulted in pleas to the territorial governor of Kansas for military intervention. On December 21, 1857, two companies of the First Cavalry arrived at Fort Scott from Fort Leavenworth with Captain Samuel D. Sturgis in command. Strife in the immediate area quieted, and the troops marched back to Fort Leavenworth on January 10, 1858. But tension was high inside the fort's compound. The former officers' quarters at the north end of officers' row were located in the Fort Scott Hotel, nicknamed the Free-State Hotel. Directly across the old parade ground, the former barracks, the Western Hotel, was dubbed the Proslavery Hotel.[25]

The following month, the two companies of First Cavalry returned to Fort Scott under Captain George T. Anderson. Fighting, however, continued outside the fort and more troops were dispatched to the scene. Most, however, withdrew on May 17th, leaving a battery of artillery at the fort.

During this period, Henry Younger prospered by leasing much of his land as well as the house to tenant farmers, and he quickly purchased an additional several hundred acres northwest of his original farm in Jackson County. He, Bursheba, and the children decided to live upon this new acreage, while by then he owned several thousand acres of land in Jackson County. Life was good to Henry and his family except for the death of eighteen-month-old Alphae during this period.[26]

In 1856, Henry acquired several hundred acres of farmland in adjacent Cass County and built a home on the property. Cass County had been organized March 3, 1835, from Jackson County and named for Lewis Cass, Michigan senator and presidential candidate. Originally organized as Van Buren County in honor of Martin Van Buren, the Democratic legislature changed the name to Cass on February 19, 1849, to honor Van Buren's Democratic opponent Lewis Cass. Van Buren ran as the Free-Soil candidate for president in 1848.

Although Henry deeded some of his property to his daughters—Laura Kelley, Belle Hall, and Anne Jones, who were already married—most of his holdings were divided for lease or sale to tenants.

When Cole was asked about his early advantages in a 1907 interview, he replied, "They were much better than I took advantage of."[27] He added that Jackson County was one of the oldest counties in Missouri and there had been good schools long before he had been born. Cole attended school in a one-room building on Big Creek. One of his teachers had been Stephen B. Elkins, a United States Senator from West Virginia at the time of the interview. While many of the other children displayed rough and rowdy behavioral traits, Cole did not. He was well liked by his schoolmates and teachers.

During an interview years later, Cole related: "As a young man I had three goals in my life: to become a Mason, to marry a good woman and to become a Christian."[28]

The railroads had not yet come to Jackson County, and game was plentiful on the Younger farm. The boys fished on the nearby streams, and Cole hunted geese before he was old enough to carry his quarry home.

Cole later discussed his boyhood with a friend and former next door neighbor, Harry C. Hoffman. According to Hoffman, Cole claimed that the feeling was so deep in the county that the schoolboys did not play ordinary running games but instead engaged themselves in only war games. After drawing lots, the boys formed squads of soldiers, brandished sticks which they pretended were guns and charged and counter charged each other. The boys representing the Missourians dubbed their numbers "South Side," and, of course, they always won the contests, while those less fortunate were the "Redlegs," of Kansas, and they were frequently beaten up on their way home from school.[29]

The Younger boys, while attending country school, were considered bright students, and unlike many of their frontier schoolmates, were seldom rowdy. When Cole later attended the Academy in Harrisonville, the head-master, Stephen Carter Reagan, who later became a captain in the Con-federate Army, called him one of the finest students in the school.[30]

Through school, Cole and his brothers met and became close friends of the four Brown brothers—William G. (Will), born April 11, 1838; John (Jack), March 29, 1840; Thomas (Tom), March 24, 1842; and Robert A. (Bob), December 3, 1844. Two younger brothers, Samuel and Walter, were born in 1850 and 1853. Cole was particularly close to Tom, and the two became good friends. Cole, however, was especially interested in their sister, Elizabeth "Lizzie" Brown, who was born on October 25, 1847, and was three years his junior.[31]

The Brown family had moved into a new Classic Revival home three miles northwest of Harrisonville in 1851. Lizzie's parents, Robert and Mary Brown, opened their house to friends, relatives, and even strangers, and these visitors gave the house its name—Wayside Rest. Cole Younger was among the guests who spent a great deal of time in the Brown home. With six brothers, a caring mother and father, and faithful servants, Lizzie Brown enjoyed all the advan-tages she was blessed with. Although Lizzie was shielded from the growing hor-ror choking western Missouri, the presence of Home Guards made her well aware of the impending conflict. The oppressive gloom forced her teacher, Reverend W.H. Lewis, a longtime friend of the family, to close the school.

Upon their arrival in Harrisonville in 1858, Henry Younger opened a dry goods store before taking over a livery business with his son Dick and his half brother C. Frank Younger. Henry and his family purchased a home in the center of town from Dr. Henry D. Palmer in 1859, and he made several busi-ness trips to Independence and Kansas City. That same year, Henry became Harrisonville's second mayor and the first to be elected; S.G. (Squire) Allen had been appointed the first mayor of the town in 1857

The City of Harrisonville had had its beginnings as early as 1830 as set-tlers from Kentucky, Tennessee, and Virginia moved west, drawn by the rich farmland and numerous streams and rivers. In 1835, the Missouri General Assembly had enacted a measure to appoint three state commissioners to establish a seat of justice within five miles of the center of this county, and a year later 160 acres of land was selected for the site of the county seat. The town of Harrisonville was established in 1837 and was named in honor of Albert G. Harrison, one of the first two U.S. Congressional representatives elected from the state of Missouri.

The town began to take shape as the land was surveyed and platted into lots and blocks. Four streets were established to outline the town square: Wall and Pearl streets running east and west, and Lexington and Independence streets running north and south. Lots were sold on the square for twenty dollars apiece for those facing the square and ten dollars for those that did not. The first house was built by Jason L. Dickey in that first year, and the city's first business was started by Henry F. Baker, who moved from New York to open a mercantile store in a log cabin on the southwest corner of the square. The town's first courthouse and jail were built in 1838, and the town's first church—the New Hope Church, a Baptist mission—was built two miles southwest of town. A public school was established in 1839.

Harrisonville finally became incorporated in 1851 after an unsuccessful attempt to do so in 1845. The town's first newspaper, the *Cass County Gazette*, was established by Nathan Millington in 1854 and renamed the *Western Democrat* in 1856. The town continued to grow as churches, schools, and businesses sprouted up throughout the 1850s, so that, by the onset of the Civil War, the population of Harrisonville had grown to 675, making it the thirty-seventh largest town in the state.

During the 1850s, Colonel Younger was one of the richest men in the state.[32] His affluence was the envy of less fortunate persons and the reason for his forced payment of heavy tribute to the Kansas Jayhawkers under the leadership of Jim Lane, James Montgomery, and Doc Jennison, who kept the Missouri citizens along the border with Kansas in constant fear of their lives. Several men, women, and children were murdered by the Jayhawkers for no other reason than that they were Missourians.[33]

Because of the hostilities launched by Missourians and Kansans against each other, Cole's father insisted the boy learn the art of firearms, and he quickly became proficient with both pistol and shotgun. Cole frequently accompanied his father on his mail routes, and by the time the boy was seventeen, he carried the mail alone between Harrisonville and Butler. On one of these trips he witnessed the hanging of a Kansas man by William Clarke Quantrill.[34]

Todd M. George later recalled: "During the time that he operated this stagecoach delivery he was much troubled by the Kansas Redlegs coming across the Missouri line where they robbed the mail and passengers as far south as the village of Butler, Missouri, in Bates County. Mr. Younger made a special trip all the way back to Washington, D.C., in an effort to get more protection while serving his contract for the mail and passengers delivery. He failed to get any support whatsoever and was forced to give up this contract with the government. At the same time, he had purchased 800 acres of land in Cass County where he built a garage and some large barns for the breeding of horses and mules that he used in this mail delivery service."[35]

When asked his opinion of the border situation and the men who led the raiders, Henry Younger always talked freely of his convictions. One of these men was James Montgomery. After moving to Kansas in 1854, Montgomery, a preacher from Ohio, immediately became embroiled in the territorial struggles of "Bleeding Kansas." An avid free-stater, Montgomery organized the "Self-Protective Company" to protect local free-state residents and harass area pro-slavers. A leader of the notorious Jayhawkers, Montgomery and his men countered the equally brutal actions of the Border Ruffians.[36]

In the spring of 1858, Montgomery and his band of Jayhawkers drove a group of pro-slavery partisans out of Fort Scott, Kansas, and across the Missouri border. This group of proslavery partisans joined with a man named Charles A Hamilton who led them back across the Kansas line. Hamilton had been a native of Cass County, Georgia, where his father, Dr. Thomas A. Hamilton, was a wealthy and influential citizen. When the Territory of Kansas was organized, Milton McGee went to Georgia to recruit men to aid in making Kansas a slave state. At Cassville he made a fiery speech, and Charles Hamilton and his brother were among the first to rally to McGee's standard. Dr. Hamilton contributed $1,000 to the cause.[37]

Hamilton had rounded up a party of neighbors and acquaintances for a fight. On May 19, 1858, this band of Border Ruffians, led by Hamilton, traveled to the area surrounding Trading Post, Kansas—on the North-South military trail just on the west side of the Kansas-Missouri border—and seized eleven men.

The band of pro-slavers rode on horseback, marching their hostages to a ravine one mile from the Missouri line, along the Marais des Cygnes River. On Hamilton's order, the prisoners were lined up, and the pro-slavers, still on horseback, took aim at their neighbors and opened fire. Two men died in the initial attack. Hamilton and his men went down into the gulch and repeatedly kicked their victims to be sure that they were dead. The survivors tried to play 'possum but three of the wounded were discovered. One was shot in the mouth, one through the head, and the other was shot twice. Of the other six men, five were wounded and another miraculously escaped injury and detection because he was covered with the blood of his comrades. This incident became know as the Marias des Cygnes Massacre. Only one Border Ruffian, William Griffith, was ever held accountable for his actions. Found guilty, he was hanged in Mound City on October 23, 1863.[38]

As the fiery situation exploded out of control, Kansas Territorial Governor James W. Denver arrived at Fort Scott with additional troops, commanded by Captain Nathaniel Lyon. The command consisted of 117 officers and men. Governor Denver arranged a compromise and truce which lasted only until November.[39] With no federal troops in the area, violence erupted again, and Territorial Governor Samuel Medary organized citizen militia groups to restore order.[40]

While many Democrats during this time period, especially those living in the South, believed that slavery should be legal everywhere, Medary and many of his fellow Democrats in the North believed that slavery should only expand if people residing in an area wanted the institution. Despite his strong convictions, it is unclear whether or not Medary believed that slavery was a moral institution, but he did strongly oppose the Civil War. He firmly believed that the North could not defeat the South militarily and utilized his newspaper, *The Crisis*, to criticize President Abraham Lincoln and the war effort.

Lincoln raised the issue of slavery again in 1858 when he made a speech at Quincy, Illinois. Lincoln commented: "We have in this nation the element of domestic slavery. The Republican Party thinks it wrong—we think it is a moral, a social, and a political wrong. We think it is wrong not confining itself merely to the persons of the States where it exists, but that it is a wrong which in its tendency, to say the least, affects the existence of the whole nation. Because we think it wrong, we propose a course of policy that shall deal with it as a wrong. We deal with it as with any other wrong, insofar as we can prevent it growing any larger, and so deal with it that in the run of time there may be some promise of an end to it."

At his inaugural address three years later, however, Abraham Lincoln attempted to avoid conflict by announcing that he had no intention "to interfere with the institution of slavery in the states where it exists. I believe I have no lawful right to do so, and I have no inclination to do so." He added: "The government will not assail you. You can have no conflict without yourselves being the aggressors."

In December of 1858, John Brown and his Jayhawkers raided a Missourian named David Cruise. When Cruise tried to resist, he was murdered. In November 1859, James Montgomery vowed that he would drive every man in favor of slavery out of the territory, invade Missouri to free the slaves, kill their masters and destroy their masters' property.

Missourian, Russell Hinds made the mistake of crossing the Kansas line to visit his mother. Hinds was accused of having caught a fugitive slave and hauling him back to Missouri. Charles Jennison, (a militiaman sent to restore peace to the border) held a vigilante trial. Hinds was found guilty and hanged. A week later, Jennison held another vigilante trial for Samuel Scott of Linn County, Kansas, who was accused of participating in the lynching of two free-state men. He was found guilty and hanged. Another man named Lester D Moore was also accused of the lynching and, knowing the fate of Hinds and Scott, refused to surrender and was killed.

The feared executioner, Charles Ransford Jennison, physician and soldier, had been born in Jefferson County, New York, on June 6, 1834. He was of English descent, some of his father's ancestors having settled in Vermont in the colonial days and fought in the Revolution. He was educated in the common schools until he was twelve years old, when his parents went to Wisconsin. At the age of nineteen years he began to study medicine. After completing his medical courses, he practiced for a short time in Wisconsin and then came to Kansas, settling at Osawatomie in 1857. Within a short time he removed to Mound City, where he remained for three years, and then went to Leavenworth. Dr. Jennison was one of John Brown's staunch supporters.[41]

Cole and Jim, as well as their sisters, attended classes taught by their cousin, Stephen Carter Ragan in Harrisonville. Caroline, perhaps the most attractive of the Younger girls, married George Clayton and bore him two children. Henry's oldest son, Charles Richard Younger, or "Dick" as he was called, attended prestigious Chapel Hill College in Lexington, Missouri, possessing his father's intense interest in civic affairs. He became interested in the Masons and joined the Grand Lodge of Missouri, Prairie Lodge Number 90. Isabella Frances, the second oldest daughter, married shopkeeper/blacksmith Richard S. Hall in Jackson County in 1856, and they settled in Lee's

Summit. Richard owned the first breech-loading shotgun in town, and Belle had a modern folding-leaf Singer sewing machine.[42]

Through the urgings of Richard Hall, Dick Younger and his brother-in-law Will Kelley bought and operated their own small livery business. Kelley, a freighter on the Santa Fe Trail, had married Laura Helen, the oldest daughter of Henry and Bursheba Younger, prior to the border war, and the couple raised three children.

Dick was six years older than the high-spirited Cole, whom their father hoped would follow in his older brother's footsteps. Dick, however, was found dead of unknown causes on August 17, 1860, and buried with full Masonic honors. Upon his brother's passing, Cole considered attending Chapel Hill College but decided he did not want to spend his time in any higher learning institution. Hoping to gain the attention and backing of his father as the favorite son, Cole immersed himself in local politics.[43]

People in the area had often watched Cole's sister, Mary Josephine, born in 1840, race her horse recklessly over the fields at breakneck speed. When "Josie" married an equally daring suitor, John Jarrette, in 1860, her parents and sisters found little to like about the young man. Josie's brothers, especially Cole, however, found him exciting, and it was Jarrette who suggested to Cole that he get involved with Quantrill. Cole and Jarrette became fast friends. Josie and Jarrette eventually had two children, Jeptha and Margaret.[44]

Martha Anne Younger, who had been born January 9, 1835, married a farmer named Lycurgus "Curg" A. Jones and commenced raising a family of six children. In 1861, Curg began making a home for his family near Pleasant Hill, Missouri, upon choice farm land given to Anne by her father's estate. Although Curg was a staunch supporter of the Confederacy, he did not enter military service when the war broke out. But for Henry, Bursheba, Cole, Jim, and the rest of the family, there would be little time to discuss loyalties; the war would come to them.

Notes

[1]*The Herald of Freedom*, May 16, 1856.

[2]Anna E. Arnold, *A History of Kansas*, Topeka, The State of Kansas, 1915, pp. 73-77.

[3]Marley Brant, *Outlaws: The Illustrated History of the James-Younger Gang*, Montgomery, Alabama, Elliott & Clark Publishing, 1997, pp. 19-20.

[4]Marvin Stottelmire, "John Brown: Madman or Martyr?" *Brown Quarterly*, Volume 3, No. 3, Winter 2000, Black History Month Issue.

[5]Richard Cordley, D.D., *A History of Lawrence, Kansas, from the Earliest Settlement to the Close of the Rebellion.* Lawrence, Kansas, E.F. Caldwell, Lawrence Journal Press, 1895.

[6]Ibid.

[7]Ibid.

[8]Anna E. Arnold, *A History of Kansas*, Topeka, The State of Kansas, 1915, pp. 73-77.

[9]Richard Cordley, D.D., *A History of Lawrence, Kansas, from the Earliest Settlement to the Close of the Rebellion.*

[10]Ibid; Phillip W. Steele with George Warfel, *The Many Faces of Jesse James*, Gretna, Louisiana, Pelican Publishing Company, 1995, p. 20.

[11]Albert Castel, *A Frontier State at War: Kansas, 1861-1865*, Cornell UP, 1958.

[12]Anna E. Arnold, *A History of Kansas*, pp. 80-81.

[13]T.J. Stiles, *Jesse James: Last Rebel of the Civil War*, New York, Alfred A. Knopf, 2002. p. 51.

[14]Scott Hosier, "'Jo' Shelby Goes Home to Missouri," *America's Civil War*, January 2003, pp. 35-37.

[15]Kansas State Historical Society.

[16]Albert Castel, *A Frontier State at War: Kansas, 1861-1865.* pp. 81-83.

[17]Albert Castel, *A Frontier State at War: Kansas, 1861-1865*, pp. 86-87.

[18]Frank W. Blackmar, editor, *Kansas: A Cyclopedia of State History, embracing events, institutions, industries, counties, cities, towns, prominent persons, etc.* . . . with a supplementary volume devoted to selected personal history and reminiscence, Volume II, Chicago, Standard Publishing Company, 1912, pp. 492-493.

[19]Richard O. Boyer, *The Legend of John Brown*, New York, Alfred A. Knopf, 1973, p. 65.

[20]Albert Fried, *John Brown's Journey Notes & Reflections of His America & Mine*, Garden City, Anchor Press/Doubleday, 1978, pp. 47-48.

[21]Ibid.

[22]Robert L. Dyer, *Jesse James and the Civil War in Missouri*, Columbia & London, University of Missouri Press, 1994, p. 12.

[23]Anna E. Arnold, *A History of Kansas*, pp. 91-92.

[24]J.W. Buel, *The Border Outlaws: An Authentic and Thrilling History of the Most Noted Bandits of Ancient or Modern Times, The Younger Brothers, Jesse and Frank James, and Their Comrades in Crime. 25 Leo E. Oliva, Fort Scott Courage and Conflict on the Border*, Topeka, Kansas State Historical Society, 1996, p. 66.

[26]Marley Brant, *The Outlaw Youngers: A Confederate Brotherhood*, Lanham, New York, London, Madison Books, 1995, pp. 10-11.

[27]Albert S. Gilles, "Jesse, Frank and Cole," *Frontier Times*, September 1969, p. 47.

[28]Marley Brant, *Outlaws: The Illustrated History of the James-Younger Gang*, p. 207.

[29]Homer Croy, *Cole Younger: Last of the Great Outlaws*, pp. 5-6.

[30]A. Huntley, "Cole Younger," *Famous Outlaws of the West*, Fall 1964, p. 27.

[31]Dr. William A. Settle, *Cole Younger Writes to Lizzie Daniel*, Liberty, James-Younger Gang, 1994, pp. 1-6.

[32]Carl W. Breihan, *Younger Brothers, Cole, James, Bob, John*, San Antonio, The Naylor Company, 1972, p.5.

[33]William Ward, *The Younger Brothers: The Border Outlaws: The Only Authentic History of the Exploits of These Desperadoes of the West*, Cleveland, Arthur Westbrook Company, 1908, pp. 5-6.

[34]Carl W. Breihan, *Younger Brothers, Cole, James, Bob, John*, pp. 4-6.

[35]Todd M. George letter to Owen Dickie dated February 27, 1968, Le Sueur County Historical Society, Elysian, Minnesota.

[36]During the Civil War, he served as colonel of the Second South Carolina Negro Regiment and fought in the East and South.

[37]Frank W. Blackmar, editor, *Kansas: a Cyclopedia of State History, Embracing Events, Institutions, Industries ,Counties, Cities, Towns, Prominent Persons, etc. . . . With a Supplementary Volume Devoted to Selected Personal History and Reminiscence*, Volume I, Chicago, Standard Publishing Company, 1912, p. 803.

[38]John Greenleaf Whittier immortalized the fallen in a poem, "Le Marais du Cygne."

[39]Leo E. Oliva, *Fort Scott Courage and Conflict on the Border*, Topeka, Kansas, State Historical Society, 1996, p. 66.

[40]Samuel Medary was indicted by a federal grand jury in 1864 for conspiracy against the government and was arrested. He was released on bonds but died before he could be tried. He died in Columbus, Ohio, November 7th, 1864.

[41]Frank W. Blackmar, editor, *Kansas: a Cyclopedia of State History, Embracing Events, Institutions, Industries ,Counties, Cities, Towns, Prominent Persons, etc. . . . With a Supplementary Volume Devoted to Selected Personal History and Reminiscence*, Volume II, Chicago, Standard Publishing Company, 1912, p. 27.

[42]Marley Brant, *The Outlaw Youngers: A Confederate Brotherhood*, pp. 13-15.

[43]A.C. Appler, *The Younger Brothers: The Life, Character and Daring Exploits of the Youngers, the Notorious Bandits Who Rode with Jesse James and William Clarke Quantrill*, New York, Frederick Fell, Inc., Publishers, 1955, p. 33.

[44]Marley Brant, *The Outlaw Youngers: A Confederate Brotherhood*, pp. 24-25.

Chapter Three

Under the Black Flag

"Permit me respectfully to call your attention to the condition of the border of Southern Kansas. The frontier on this line is fearfully exposed to guerrilla raids, and needs and should have the amplest military protection. Unless an effective force is detailed along the line it must become depopulated. No house is secure there now. The few heads of families left there feel unsafe, and where these heads are on the battlefield, afar off, their wives and children and their property are hourly exposed to the ruffian invasion of robber and rebel bands."
—Thomas Carney, governor-elect of Kansas, November 1862.

THE CIVIL WAR IN MISSOURI evolved through three distinct phases. The first began with an attack on a Union home guard regiment by pro-Southerners in St. Louis, May 1861. Federal troops quickly occupied the state capital in Jefferson City, driving out the governor and legislature, and installing a pro-Union provisional government. The second phase was due to excesses in martial law and abuses by the federal occupation forces, who considered the citizens disloyal secessionists. Guerrilla bands led by men such as William Clarke Quantrill and "Bloody Bill" Anderson adopted terror tactics and their atrocities were aimed at keeping federal forces off balance. The third phase began when Confederate Major General Sterling Price attempted to recapture control of the state.[1]

Lexington, Missouri, farmer, Isaac Hockaday described the battles in Missouri in 1861: ". . . all is destroyed even the rails & trees fencing of every kind bushes & shrubs nothing left that would hide a chicken. I never expect to witness another just such a sight—and when reflect that it is upon American soil & by American Citizens it is melancholy to think upon . . ."[2]

War was nothing new to the peoples of Kansas and Missouri, who had been involved in armed conflict since 1854 when Kansas was opened to settlement. Atrocities were committed by both sides. But when the Civil War officially commenced, Missouri came under martial law. People were arrested without charges, imprisoned without trials, and executed on flimsy evidence that wouldn't have held up in court in other times. Vengeance and revenge were the order of the day, both from official and unofficial sources. "People weren't particular to a corpse or two," wrote William McWaters, who lived through the horrors of war along the border.[3]

Kansas, meanwhile, possessed only 30,000 men between the ages of eighteen and forty-five when the Civil War erupted in April 1861. Nevertheless, the state ultimately provided nineteen regiments and four artillery batteries in response to President Abraham Lincoln's calls for troops. These units would ultimately suffer nearly 8,500 casualties and sustain the highest mortality rate of any state in the Union—over sixty-one percent.[4] Many Kansas troops saw considerable action along the Missouri border and on the Indian frontier. But they also served in Arkansas, Tennessee, Mississippi, and Alabama. The First and Second Kansas Regiments saw action immediately, participating in the Battle of Wilson's Creek in August of 1861.

Missouri was comprised of numerous Northern and Southern natives and the divided loyalties of the state were evidenced by the fact that 100,000 men enlisted in the federal army and 50,000 joined the rebel forces. This pitted neighbor against neighbor, and no one knew whom they could trust. Even those Missourians who favored the North and organized pro-Union Home Guard units regarded as invaders the Illinois and Iowa regiments sent to their state to keep the peace.[5]

Most Missourians were hard-working and honest people who did not own slaves or condone slavery. They were simple people trying to make a simple living as farmers, carpenters, and cattlemen. They did not wish to get

61

involved in the conflict of the Northern and Southern states and chose to remain neutral. This non-committal stance added to the distrust throughout the state.

Three days after Fort Sumter was fired upon April 12, 1861, President Abraham Lincoln issued a proclamation calling for 75,000 men, from the militia of the several states, to suppress combinations in the Southern states therein named. Simultaneously therewith, the Secretary of War sent a telegram to all the governors of the states, excepting those mentioned in the proclamation, requesting them to detail a certain number of militia to serve for three months, Missouri's quota being four regiments.[6]

In response to this telegram, Missouri Governor Claiborne Fox Jackson sent the following reply: "Executive Department of Missouri, Jefferson City, April 17, 1861. To the Hon. Simon Cameron, Secretary of War, Washington, D.C: Sir: Your dispatch of the 15th inst., making a call on Missouri for four regiments of men for immediate service, has been received. There can be, I apprehend, no doubt but these men are intended to form a part of the President's army to make war upon the people of the seceded states. Your requisition, in my judgment, is illegal, unconstitutional, and can not be complied with. Not one man will the State of Missouri furnish to carry on such an unholy war. —C.F. Jackson, Governor of Missouri."

Four days later the U.S. arsenal at Liberty was seized by order of Governor Jackson, and on the following day, April 22nd, Governor Jackson issued a proclamation convening the Legislature of Missouri, on May following, in extra session, to take into consideration the momentous issues which were presented, and the attitude to be assumed by the state in the impending struggle. That same day the Adjutant-General of Missouri issued the following military order: "Headquarters Adjutant-General's Office Jefferson City, Mo., April 22, 1861 (General Orders No. 7).

> I. To attain a greater degree of efficiency and perfection in organization and discipline, the Commanding Officers of the several Military districts in this State, having four or more legally organized companies therein, whose armories are within fifteen miles of each other, will assemble their respective commands at some place to be by them eventually designated, on the 3rd day of May, and to go into an encampment for a period of six days, as provided by law. Captains of companies not organized into battalions will report the strength of their companies immediately to these headquarters, and await further orders.

II. The Quartermaster-General will procure and issue to Quartermasters of Districts, for these commands not now provided for, all necessary tents and camp equipage, to enable the commanding officers thereof to carry the foregoing orders into effect.

III. The Light Battery now attached to the Southwest Battalion, and one company of mounted riflemen, including all officers and soldiers belonging to the First District, will proceed forthwith to St. Louis, and report to Gen. D.M. Frost for duty. The remaining companies of said battalion will be disbanded for the purpose of assisting in the organization of companies upon that frontier. The details in the execution of the foregoing are entrusted to Lieutenant-Colonel John S. Bowen, commanding the Battalion.

IV. The strength, organization, and equipment of the several companies in the District will be reported at once to these Headquarters, and District Inspectors will furnish all information which may be serviceable in ascertaining the condition of the State forces. By order of the Governor. Warwick Hough, Adjutant-General of Missouri.

Missouri political leaders moved quickly, and on May 2nd, the Legislature convened in extra session. Many acts were passed, among which was one to authorize the governor to purchase or lease David Ballentine's foundry at Boonville for the manufacture of arms and munitions of war; to authorize the governor to appoint one major-general; to authorize the governor, when, in his opinion, the security and welfare of the state required it, to take possession of the railroad and telegraph lines of the state; to provide for the organization, government, and support of the military forces; to borrow one million of dollars to arm and equip the militia of the state to repel invasion, and protect the lives and property of the people. An act was also passed creating a "Military Fund," to consist of al the money then in the treasury or that might thereafter be received from the one-tenth of one percent on the hundred dollars, levied by act of November, 1857, to complete certain railroads; also the proceeds of a tax of fifteen cents on the hundred dollars of the assessed value of the taxable property of the several counties in the state, and the proceeds of the two-mill tax, which had been theretofore appropriated for educational purposes.

On May 3rd, Camp Jackson was organized, and a week later, Sterling Price was appointed major-general of State Guard. That same day, General Daniel Marsh Frost, commanding Camp Jackson, addressed General Nathaniel Lyon, as follows: "Headquarters Camp Jackson, Missouri Militia, May 20, 1861. Capt.

N. Lyon, Commanding U.S. Troops in and about St. Louis Arsenal:
J

I am constantly in receipt of information that you contemplate an attack
upon my camp, whilst I understand that
you are impressed with the idea that an
attack upon the Arsenal and United
States troops is intended on the part of
the Militia of Missouri. I am greatly at a
loss to know what could justify you in
attacking citizens of the United States,
who are in lawful performance of their
duties, devolving upon them under the
Constitution in organizing and instruct-
ing the militia of the State in obedience
to her laws, and therefore, have been
disposed to doubt the correctness of the information I have received.

General Daniel Marsh Frost, C.S.A. (Author's collection)

I would be glad to know from you personally whether there is any
truth in the statements that are constantly pouring into my ears. So far
as regards any hostility being intended toward the United States, or its
property or representative by any portion of my command, or, as far as I
can learn (and I think I am fully informed), of any other part of the State
forces, I can positively say that the idea has never been entertained. On
the contrary, prior to your taking command of the Arsenal, I proffered
to Major Bell, then in command of the very few troops constituting its
guard, the services of myself and all my command, and, if necessary, the
whole power of the State, to protect the United States in the full possession of all her property. Upon General [William S.] Harney taking
command of this department, I made the same proffer of services to him,
and authorized his Adjutant-General, Captain Williams, to communicate the fact that such had been done to the War Department. I have
had no occasion since to chance any of the views I entertained at the
time, neither of my own volition nor through orders of my constitutional commander.

I trust that after this explicit statement that we may be able, by fully
understanding each other, to keep far from our borders the misfortunes
which so unhappily affect our common country. This communication
will be handed you by Colonel Bowen, my Chief of Staff, who will be
able to explain anything not fully set forth in the foregoing. I am, Sir,
very respectfully your obedient servant.

—Brigadier-General D.M. Frost, Commanding Camp Jackson, M.V.M.

Captain Lyon dispatched the following letter back to General Frost the same day:

> Headquarters United States Troops, St. Louis, Mo., May 10, 1861.
> Sir: Your command is recorded as evidently hostile toward the Government of the United States. It is, for the most part, made up of those Secessionists who have openly avowed their hostility to the General Government, and have been plotting at the seizure of its property and the overthrow of its authority. You are openly in communication with the so-called Southern Confederacy, which is now at war with the United States, and you are receiving at your camp, from the said Confederacy and under its flag, large supplies of the material of war, most of which is known to be the property of the United States. These extraordinary preparations plainly indicate none other than the well-known purpose of the Governor of this State, under whose orders you are acting, and whose communication to the Legislature has just been responded to by that body in the most unparalleled legislation, having in direct view hostilities to the General Government and co-operation with its enemies.
>
> In view of these considerations, and of your failure to disperse in obedience to the proclamation of the President, and of the imminent necessities of State policy and warfare, and the obligations imposed upon me by instructions from Washington, it is my duty to demand, and I do hereby demand of you an immediate surrender of your command, with no other conditions than that all persons surrendering under this command shall be humanely and kindly treated. Believing myself prepared to enforce this demand, one-half hour's time before doing so will be allowed for your compliance therewith.
>
> Very respectfully, your obedient servant, N. Lyon.

Lyon, determined to protect the federal arsenal, resolved to eliminate the threat posed to government property by the pro-Southern citizen soldiers. State Guard troops moved into Camp Jackson to capture federal weapons stored in the city. General Francis P. Blair got wind of the plan and decided to take action. On May 10th, Lyon and Blair surrounded and captured the 700 militiamen at Camp Jackson, their training ground, and commenced marching his captives through the streets. Rioting broke out along the way and at least twenty-eight civilians were killed.[7]

General Daniel Frost surrendered Camp Jackson, and all prisoners were released excepting Captain Emmett McDonald, who refused to subscribe to the parole. On May 12th, Brigadier-General William S. Harney issued a proclamation to the people of Missouri, promising "he would carefully abstain from the exercise of any unnecessary powers, and only use the military force stationed in this district in the last resort to preserve peace."

Lyon was promoted to brigadier general and met with Jackson and Price in St. Louis on June 11th to discuss methods that would prevent the state from sliding any farther toward all-out civil war. Lyon stated he would rather see every man, woman, and child in the state dead and buried than relinquish his right to act in protecting the interests of the federal government. Price and Jackson walked and ordered out the State Guard.

With the official declaration of the war, the Redlegs and Jayhawkers increased their presence in Missouri and their crimes became more rampart. One of the most notorious individual units operating in the state was the Seventh Kansas Volunteer Cavalry Regiment. Proclaimed as the "Independent Kansas Jay-Hawkers"; on Doc Jennison's original recruiting poster of August 1861, it was better known as "Jennison's Jayhawkers."

Mustered into United States' service on October 28, 1861, with Jennison as colonel and David Read Anthony as lieutenant colonel, the regiment, comprised of volunteers from Kansas and nearby states, became part of James Lane's Kansas brigade. (Lane also formed a "Frontier Guard" to protect the White House immediately after the attack on Fort Sumter.) Jennison referred to the regiment as "self-sustaining," which meant simply that every foray into Missouri liberated more supplies than were carried into the state. Horses, livestock, and wagonloads of agricultural products were seized from Southern sympathizers, but only a minuscule fraction of those goods found their way to the federal commissary. Slaves, too, gleefully trooped westward to freedom in Kansas. If other items found their way into the Jayhawkers' possession—furniture, silverware, and money—such was the bitter price paid for secession. Jennison's Seventh Kansas Volunteer Cavalry Regiment was often called "The Forty Thieves."

In November 1861, Doc Jennison was ordered to march his regiment from Leavenworth to Jackson County following a bushwhacker attack on a government wagon train. Near Independence, they burned a mill and half a dozen houses, and in Independence, they forced all males into the square at saber and bayonet point. One resident was selected to separate secessionist from Union loyalists while Jennison's raiders looted the private homes of valuables.[8]

A new low in Jennison's depredations occurred at Harrisonburg, Missouri, where another outfit had looted the depository of the American Bible Society before Doc's men arrived, leaving only a stock of Bibles. The Seventh appropriated the Bibles. Although such behavior continued for less than five months, it left an indelible mark on Missouri and the historical reputation of the Seventh. Missouri was technically in the Union, and many of the citizens despoiled by the Jayhawkers were loyal Unionists.

The Seventh remained in Jackson County throughout December. They stole wagonloads of dry goods, groceries, drugs, and every horse and mule and conveyance they could find. Farmers were robbed, men were beaten, and when any persons stood up for their rights, their homes were burned. Jennison's Jayhawkers killed at least two men in Independence, one for refusing to give them liquor, the other for attempting to save his mules. They arrested and shot another man on their return to Kansas.

Concerned that the Jayhawkers would create more rebels than they conquered, federal authorities determined to put them where they could do no further harm and decided upon New Mexico. But instead, in May 1862, they were dispatched to Kentucky, then to Tennessee, and were seen no more in Kansas until their mustering out in September 1865. Jennison, who was seldom with the regiment in the field, departed in April 1862, and Anthony resigned his commission four months later. In a letter penned to the Leavenworth Conservative, Jennison wrote:

> I am informed officially that General R.B. Mitchell uses my regiment principally in the capacity as kidnappers . . . I do not enlist to return slaves or protect rebels but to crush slavery and to kill rebels, and while in the service, I gave a good deal of attention to these two points. When the Government adopts that policy, I shall be again a soldier; until that time, I shall be a citizen.

The murdering of innocent people, pillaging of property and raping of women and children continued on a broader scale, all in the name of the federal government. Attempts by Missourians to get the government to control their troops went unheeded, although Kansas border ruffian Jim Lane had left the area.

Lane had killed Gaius Jenkins, a prominent Free-Soiler, in a dispute over land in 1858. However, his exceptional power as an orator combined with his unique charisma got him elected to the Senate when Kansas became a state in 1861; shortly after his arrival in Washington he added the new president of the United States to his list of admirers. The lack of federal military in Washington immediately after the Confederate attack of Fort Sumter ignited a hysterical fear for Lincoln's safety, so General Lane's "Frontier Guard" took up security positions in the White House and around the city until reinforcements arrived. It goes without saying that Lane basked in the warm glow of political patronage for the next few years.[9]

Nonetheless, Missourians were forced to take matters into their own hands to protect their homes and families. Frank James of Clay County, Missouri, joined the pro-Southern Missouri State Guard, a company which had formed on May 4, 1861, probably at the home of George Claybrook, who lived across the road from the James-Samuel farm.[10]

Frank James. (Courtesy of the National Archives)

At the outbreak of the Civil War, the James and Samuels families lived near Kearney, in Clay County, Missouri. Frank's mother, Zerelda Samuel, being a native of Kentucky, was naturally a Southern sympathizer, as was her husband, Dr. Reuben Samuel. Living in the immediate area were a great many sympathizers with the Northern cause. Many of these had formed orga-

nizations known as "Home Militia" or "Home Guards," and these often operated in conjunction with the raiders from Kansas, who came into Missouri to
pillage and kill. Many members of these militia groups loathed Zerelda James
because she was a Southern sympathizer and outspoken in her loyalty to the
cause of the Confederacy.[11]

Other pro-South Missourians joined groups known as Partisans and
secretly pledged their loyalty to the Confederacy but retained their civilian
status. They aided the Confederacy in supplying them with food, shelter,
clothing and revealing troop movements, when they could. This was not
done with the intent to support the Southern cause but in retaliation against
the crimes that had been committed against them by the federals.

Many of these partisans were farmers by day and raiders by night. Most had
never owned a slave but were fighting against a cruel occupation of federal
forces. Operating behind enemy lines, they raided outposts, burned Yankee
wagon trains, shot pickets, and settled scores with hated Union sympathizers.
The federals considered the guerrilla bands of Quantrill, Anderson, and Todd
little better than highwaymen, and when captured, they were usually hanged.
The irregulars, in retaliation, asked no quarter and gave none.[12]

The Missouri Partisan Rangers was a group of men who formed their
own army to fight the Union troops. These men supported the Confederacy
because they shared the same enemy but not necessarily the same cause.
Most of the Missouri Partisan Rangers were men who had suffered the loss
of family members, property or had some kind of injustice inflicted upon on
them by the federal troops and they vowed revenge against them. Often
times, they would assist in a raid and return to their homes that same
evening to tend to their chores and families.

They were distinguished as "guerillas" or "bushwhackers" because of
their style of warfare. These men were masters of war and introduced new
tactics of warfare, such as disguising themselves as federals or women to
sneak into enemy territory to gain information or to launch a surprise attack.
They continually overcame great odds by defeating Union troops that outnumbered them more than two to one. The capture of these guerilla bands
became a focal point for the Union army.

One element that made the bushwhacker successful was his choice of
weaponry. Although he might wield anything from a shotgun to a Bowie knife,
it was the light, durable, and extremely accurate .36 caliber Colt Navy revolver

that they preferred. Many of the bushwhackers often carried as many as half a dozen Colts in their belts. The federal cavalryman, armed with a carbine, a saber, and a single pistol, was no match for the bushwhacker in firepower.[13]

Another advantage of the bushwhacker over his enemy was in the quality of their mounts. The region was known for its fine horses, and the guerrillas had their choice of Missouri's best. Most bushwhackers had been in the saddle since early childhood and, by the time the war started, were already masters on horseback. Under fire through much of the war, man and beast worked as one and depended on each other for survival. Recalled an appreciative bushwhacker:

> There was some sort of affinity between a guerrilla and his horse. I have slept in my saddle and trusted my faithful horse to keep out of danger. I have sometimes, when alone and tired, dismounted, lay down in the grass or thicket, and left my horse on guard. I always found him there when I awoke. . . .
>
> Once my horse called me. I had been in the saddle nearly thirty hours. In that time the rain was incessant. I went to sleep under some branches on the ground. Under such conditions a man will sleep the sleep of the just. I was awakened by the shaking and breaking of the brush. My horse was pulling it from me. I was barely to the saddle when a lot of Jayhawkers were upon me. But for my knowledge of the country I would not have escaped. I think I owe my life to my horse.
>
> I remember I spoke of this once to Quantrill, and he said it

"Bloody Bill" Anderson. (Author's collection)

showed a horse appreciated a low voice, for the guerrilla was never known to speak otherwise; at least, not after he had been a guerrilla very long.[14]

One of the most feared of all Missouri guerillas was William "Bloody Bill" Anderson, who actually considered himself a Kansan. Bloody Bill was born in Randolph County, Missouri, in 1840. His parents were William and Martha (Thomason) Anderson. Bill was one of six children, who included Ellis, James, Mary C, Josephine, and Martha. Also living with them were his grandparents, William and Martha Thomason. His father was a hatter, and the family moved from Palmyra, Missouri, to Huntsville, Missouri, between 1847 and1848.

In 1850, his father went to California to join the gold rush, leaving the family in Huntsville. During this time, Bill and his brothers were the heads of the family, and their relationship with their sisters were both brotherly and fatherly. The father returned in 1854, and the family relocated to Breckinridge County, Kansas, in 1857.

In March of 1862, Bill's father was murdered while he and his brother Jim were on a trip to Fort Leavenworth. The murder was committed by either Pro-Northern neighbors or by a squad of Union soldiers. One account alleged that Union soldiers hanged him because his name appeared on a list of Southern sympathizers while another claimed that a neighbor, who accused him of horse theft, murdered him. Bloody Bill later killed this same neighbor.

When Bill and his brother returned home that evening and found their father murdered, a campaign of revenge began that very night when he crept up behind a Union picket and broke his neck. The next night he killed another Union soldier and was almost caught by a federal cavalryman and had to shoot him in order to escape. He left that same night for the Missouri border and joined up with Quantrill.

It was said that he carried a silk cord on which knots were tied for every Yankee killed and that he sometimes frothed at the mouth during battle. He was also known to scalp his federal victims, which is probably one reason why he received the name of "Bloody Bill." Bill was described as being tall, sinewy and lithe with long black hair that curled and fell to his shoulders. He had prominent cheekbones and small angry eyes, and he usually wore a drab slouch hat, woolen shirts, and high heeled boots.

Bill quickly became the leader of the Missouri Partisan Rangers. He became notorious for his leadership skills, his excellent horsemanship and his

William Clarke Quantrill. (Author's collection)

warfare tactics. He was looked upon as a monster by Unionists and as a hero by Southern sympathizers and Confederates.

William Clarke Quantrill was born July 3, 1837, in Dover, Ohio, to Thomas Henry and Caroline Cornelia (Clarke) Quantrill. He was the oldest of eight children. Four of his siblings died in infancy. William's father, a tin smith, was involved in several scandals that included theft and fraud. His father often beat him, but his mother doted on him. After Thomas Henry Quantrill died of tuberculosis on December 7, 1854, William tried to supplement the income of his family by becoming a schoolteacher. He taught in Dover, Illinois, and Indiana. He was never satisfied with the amount of money he made teaching and even tried his hand at gambling for a while in Utah. Finding no success, he returned home to Dover. His mother made arrangements for two neighboring men to buy a claim for him in Kansas and hold it until he reached the age of twenty-one. He was to pay off his debt by working on their farms.

On February 26, 1857, William left for Kansas with Harmon Beeson and Henry Torrey. They settled in Franklin County. After living with these men for about a year, William became restless and wanted to sell his claim. A dispute arose over the claim and had to be settled in court. He was paid only half of what the court awarded him and then moved into a communal cabin called Tuscarora Lake.

During Quantrill's early years in Kansas, he believed in Northern views and often talked against slavery. His viewpoint began to change once he was hired as a teamster in Fort Leavenworth where he enlisted under the name of Charley Hart. There he met and befriended some Southern sympathizers.

By 1860, William was ready to settle down and start farming. He lived with an Indian family near Lawrence but began to associate with some border ruffians. He quickly learned that capturing runaway slaves for the reward money turned a nice profit. He devised a scheme to help free black men by assisting the Jayhawkers in rescuing them and then helped the border ruffians capture them and collect the reward money. He was soon caught in this charade when he took four free-state men to liberate the slaves at the Morgan Walker farm in Missouri. Quantrill warned the farmer before the raid occurred and three of the Kansas men were killed.

After the war officially started, Quantrill went to Texas and then to the Cherokee Nation where he made friends with a half-breed Confederate sympathizer named Joel Mayes. He rode with Joel and his men for a while, learning many tactics of war. Quantrill joined Sterling Price's Confederate Army shortly after the Confederate victory in Springfield on August 12, 1861. By the end of September, he left Price's army and returned to Jackson County. Here he decided to form his own army and gathered about fifteen men willing to follow him. He would not accept any man into his band unless he were seeking revenge for himself or his family for injuries inflicted by the Union Army or the Jayhawkers. This was in contrast to his own personal history and, therefore, he made up a story to gain the confidence of his men. He told his men that he and an older brother had left for California on the Santa Fe Trail and were ambushed by Jayhawkers while camped beside the Little Cottonwood River deep in Kansas territory. The Jayhawkers opened fire on Quantrill and his brother, and his brother was killed instantly. William claimed to have been shot in the right breast and left leg. After the attack, the murderers rifled their pockets and left them for dead. Quantrill said that for two days he guarded his brother's body from buzzards and prairie wolves, and then on the third day he was found by an old Shawnee Indian who nursed him back to health and buried his brother. His story also included the tale that he vowed vengeance and enlisted as a private in the Union army, quickly rising to the rank of lieutenant. Using his position, he killed all but two of the murderers with a single shot to the forehead between the eyes while on patrol. This story was not true, as Quantrill did not have an older brother, and this lie was told for the sole purpose of gaining the loyalty of his men.

Quantrill and his band assisted the Confederate Army by distracting the Union troops from Confederate movements. They did this by constantly raiding Unionist homes and businesses and ambushing Union troops. In 1862, Quantrill was commissioned as a captain as a Missouri Partisan Ranger by Colonel Thompson, and he also was declared an outlaw by the Union Army. This occurred after Quantrill and his men assisted the Confederate Army in their capture of Independence. A federal order was passed stating that all guerillas and partisans were to be treated as criminals and shot on sight. Quantrill had been in the habit of releasing his Union prisoners. After the order was issued, he felt that if he and his men were not going to be granted the same courtesy as Confederate prisoners of war, that he would apply the shot-on-sight order to Unionists as well. By this time, Quantrill's army band contained well over 300 men. They often rode as separate bands, but would come together for the larger raids when Quantrill summoned them. It was clearly understood among the guerrillas and partisans that Quantrill was in charge, and divided Missouri, bordering on hysteria, was up for grabs.

"I will never forget the first time I saw Quantrill," recalled Frank James. "He was nearly six feet in height, rather thin, his hair and moustache was sandy, and he was full of life and a jolly fellow. He had none of the air of the bravado or of the desperado about him. We all loved him at first sight. . . ."[15]

After refusing President Lincoln's call for troops, Governor Claiborne F. Jackson left St. Louis for Jefferson City on June 11th, burning railroad bridges behind him, and cutting telegraph wires. The following day, Jackson issued a proclamation calling into active service 50,000 militia "to repel invasion, protect life, and property." Jackson conveyed the following message to the state of Missouri in his June 12, 1861, proclamation:

> All our efforts toward conciliation have failed. We can hope nothing from the justice or moderation of the agents of the federal government in this State. They are energetically hastening the execution of their bloody and revolutionary schemes for the inauguration of civil war in your midst; for the military occupation of your State by armed bands of lawless invaders; for the overthrow of your State government; and for the subversion of those liberties which that Government has always sought to protect; and they intend to exert their whole power to subjugate you, if possible, to the military despotism which has usurped the powers of the federal government. . . . You are under no obligation whatever to obey the unconstitutional edicts of the military despotism which has enthroned itself in Washington, not to submit to the infamous and

degrading sway of its wicked minions in this State. . . . Rise, then, and drive out ignominiously the invaders who have dared to desecrate the soil which your labors have made fruitful, and which is consecrated by your homes. Jackson's state government was deposed and his dream for Missouri of Confederate membership sputtered out into an ineffective rump legislature at Neosho.

Three days later, Colonel Frank P. Blair, who had the crucial support to thwart Jackson's plan to take Missouri out of the Union, and Union Brigadier-General Nathaniel Lyon took possession of the State Capital; Governor Jackson, General Price, and other officers had left on the 13th for Boonville. Fortunately for partisans of Confederate Missouri, Jackson had anticipated the federal takeover, and at two o'clock on the morning of June 12th, the governor issued a call for 50,000 Confederate Army volunteers and ordered the evacuation of the capital. Government clerks hastily packed the state's archives and Great Seal into freight wagons, and legislators rushed to their carriages carrying bundles of documents and clothing. By mid-morning, soldiers and refugees were streaming south for the protection of Brigadier-General Ben McCulloch's Confederate Army in northwest Arkansas.[16]

Reaching Jefferson City, the state capital, General Nathaniel Lyon learned of Jackson's and Price's retreat towards Boonville. Lyon re-embarked on steamboats, transported his men to below Boonville, where he then marched to the town and, on June 17th, engaged the enemy. In a short fight, Lyon dispersed the Confederates, commanded on the field by Colonel John S. Marmaduke, and occupied Boonville. This early victory established Union control of the Missouri River and helped douse attempts to place Missouri in the Confederacy.

J.C. Walden of the Missouri State Guard later reported:

> Monday, June 17, 1861, the report came to the state's quota of "rebels" gathered at Boonville under the orders of General Price that General Lyon was landing his men on the Cooper countyside of the Missouri River. General Price had been placed in command of the Southern troops in Missouri after Governor Jackson, incensed at the breaking of the truce made with General Lyon, had ordered them mobilized. Orders were sent for 50,000 men to gather at Boonville, and on Sunday, June 16, they began to arrive, with their leaders, Governor Jackson and General Price, stationed at the old City Hotel.

Sunday afternoon General Price, receiving word that General Lyon was approaching from Jefferson City with a strong force of federal troops, gave orders for the retreat to Lexington. Captain William Brown of Saline County, a firebrand, got up before the men and told them he was going to fight if he had but a handful to face the federals. Some decided to cast their lot with Brown, and the others retreated with Price to Lexington.

Monday morning our scout brought word Union troops were landing three miles east of Boonville on the south side of the river. We immediately were ordered to advance and meet them. Our equipment was poor; most of us had poor rifles, if any, but all went forward with the idea that the enemy soon would be vanquished.

We formed in a wheat field and waited quietly. When we heard the clank of the cannon on the road below us we were told to be ready. "When I raise my hand—fire! The captain said. As the enemy went by us on the road below us, we saw the signal and fired. The federal column paid little attention and didn't even break ranks. We fired a second volley, when someone yelled retreat. I don't know whether it was the captain—but we retreated. I started for the camp at the old fairgrounds where we had left our knapsacks. I found our things taken by the enemy and I ran and hid under the river bank. Finally two other Howard County men and I found our way into Boonville and went to Mrs. Beck's shop on Main Street to get some ginger cake and cider. While we were there, I heard the clanking of the federal cavalry up the street and we hiked without food for the river.

A boat was just leaving for Howard County, and the gangplank was thrown down for us. The federals fired and the captain would have stopped if it had not been for the insistence of Captain Cooper, who was ready to "blow out somebody's brains."[17]

Confederate soldier, H.T. Barnes, M.D., later reminisced:

Marmaduke's Company, which was raised in Saline County, was organized during the latter part of April 1861, and elected John S. Marmaduke captain, Lucian Gaines [fir]st. lieutenant, James H. Akin, [seco]nd. lieut[enant], James Craddock, [thi]rd. lieut[enant]. Our company consisted of from fifty to sixty men. We met about two or three miles south of Marshall and having been ordered to Boonville, we started to that place, arriving there in the evening of June 12 and went into camp on the bluff of the river about two miles east of Boonville.

We were almost without military training. There were many camp rumors concerning the impending battle, and it was generally understood that Colonel Marmaduke was opposed to making the fight because the troops were not sufficiently organized. He favored retreating and

76

joining the reinforcements from the South. On Sunday evening Rev. Frank Mitchell made a speech urging the men to do their duty, telling them they were engaged in a just cause. A captain also made a speech saying, "If every one else leaves I will stay and fight it out by myself." More belligerent than discreet!

The fatal day of June 17, 1861, came on, and we were ordered to fall in by our captain who at that time was Gaines. We moved about two miles down the river to the W.D. Adams place, when our march was changed down a fence on the east side of the Adams farm, with heavy timber east of us. We had no breastworks of any kind. We were halted when we came to the Rocheport road and heard a shot east of us and soon the beat of horses' feet coming up the road. The rider was a handsomely dressed young man mounted on a black horse. He said, "Boys, they are coming. They shot at me down there."

In a short time we were ordered to fall back into a wheat field north of the Adams house. Captain Brown's company formed our extreme right, extending from the Adams house across the road. That company had some protection of trees, fences and outbuildings. Before taking our position we were fired on by the federal troops. In an incredulously short space of time, Captain Totten's federal artillery came down. Our forces, having no protection in that wheat field, were ordered to fall back over the brow of the hill to escape the missiles, the attacking forces being out of reach of our shot guns and rifles.

Colonel Marmaduke, riding along our line, gave the command to advance to the former position. The troops failed to obey the order, only three men responding, William M. Price, of Arrow Rock, a first cousin of Colonel Marmaduke, A.T. Swisher, of Marshall, and the writer. As soon as we were exposed, I saw the flash of a cannon. I dropped down as I heard a shot coming through the wheat. It entered the ground within an arm's reach of my foot. Then we heard in the timber near us the command to advance. Colonel Marmaduke having returned to the Adams house and seeing the troops failing to respond to his orders rode down a second time and finding the men in a little ravine said, "If the Yankees catch you in here, they'll kill half of you. Orders to retreat and every man take care of himself."

The battery kept firing as we retreated through the woods on the west, more for its demoralizing effect than for its execution. Several of us came through our deserted camp and reaching the east part of Boonville we found General M.M. Parsons with his brigade; Governor Claiborne I.[sic] Jackson, Col. Marmaduke, and other officers.

When ordered to fall in to go down to the battlefield a handsome young man, a stranger to me, fell in on my left. In moving our line, we would sometimes get scattered and would have to "double quick" to catch up. The stranger on my left, not used to such violent exercise, would fall behind but when we came to a walk he would overtake us, almost out of breath. In the skirmishing he was struck in the knee by a bullet and died from the wound. I afterwards learned that he was Jeff McCutcheon, a son of Dr. McCutcheon, of Boonville.

I often thought of the young soldier on the black horse who first announced the coming of the federals. In about 1886 and 1887 a gentleman came to Pilot Grove and while he was talking to a friend of mine I felt I had seen him before. Upon inquiring of him whether he was in the battle of Boonville or not I learned he was the rider of the black horse and was Tom Stephens of Bunceton.[18]

Throughout July, the Confederate army, under Generals Price, Jackson, and McCulloch, overran all southern Missouri and constantly threatened the southeast portion of Kansas. Bordering on Missouri, and the hostile Indian Territory easily reached by raiding parties from Arkansas—especially obnoxious to the surrounding slave-holding States with its frontier almost entirely unprotected—it seemed only a measure of ordinary prudence that part of the troops raised in the State should be organized for home defense. Accordingly, at the request of W.C. Ranson, and other citizens of Fort Scott, permission was granted by General Lyon for the organization of three companies of infantry to be stationed at that place, and designated "Home Guards." These companies were soon raised, but being insufficient for the pressing needs of the time, five additional companies, four being cavalry, were organized by authority of Major Prince, commanding at Fort Leavenworth. A regimental organization was effected on the 9th of September, there being at that time eight companies—four cavalry and four infantry.[19]

But federal attacks also continued to escalate during the first year of the war. Doc Jennison and his company of Redlegs attacked Morristown in July of 1861, plundering the village. They took seven men as prisoners. They were court-martialed and sentenced to death. Their graves were dug, and they were forced to kneel down beside them. They were blindfolded and shot. The graves were covered, and Jennison and his men rode off to wreak more havoc.

Meanwhile, the Battle of Carthage took place on July 5th. Brigadier General Nathaniel Lyon had chased Governor Claiborne Jackson and approximately 4,000 State Militia from the State Capital at Jefferson City and from Boonville, and pursued them. Colonel Franz Sigel led another force of about 1,000 into southwest Missouri in search of the governor and his loyal troops. Upon learning that Sigel had encamped at Carthage, on the night of July 4th, Jackson took command of the troops with him and formulated a plan to attack the much smaller Union force.

The next morning, Jackson closed up to Sigel, established a battle line on a ridge ten miles north of Carthage, and induced Sigel to attack him. Opening with artillery fire, Sigel closed to the attack. Seeing a large Confederate force—actually unarmed recruits—moving into the woods on his left, he feared that they would turn his flank. He withdrew.

Twenty-five miles away at Neosho, Union Captain Joseph Conrad of Rifle Company B, Third Missouri, had been left behind to garrison the small town. Having heard the gunnery duel, he dispatched a courier to Sigel to bring back instructions. At one o'clock in the afternoon, Conrad received the ominous dispatch from Sigel's quartermaster, J.M. Richardson "to retreat with my command, if necessary."[20]

The Confederates pursued, but Sigel conducted a successful rear-guard action. By evening, Sigel was inside Carthage and under cover of darkness; he retreated to Sarcoxie. The battle had little meaning, but the pro-Southern elements in Missouri, anxious for any good news, championed their first victory.

Several citizens attended to the gory task of treating the scores of wounded soldiers left behind. Among those who volunteered for nursing duty was a young teenage girl named Myra Maebelle Shirley, whose family owned and operated the Shirley House, a hotel and tavern in Carthage. Later in the war, her brother Bud Shirley was killed by federal troops in a guerrilla skirmish near Sarcoxie, and Myra fled to Seyenne, Texas, with the rest of her family. Myra Maebelle later became the notorious Belle Starr.[21]

Otto C. Lademann, Captain of the Third Missouri Infantry, U.S. Volunteers, later stated in a lecture:

> After the capture of Camp Jackson, May 10, 1861, my regiment, the Third Missouri Volunteer Infantry, Colonel Franz Sigel, remained in the St. Louis Arsenal for some days, and then was moved to a western suburb of St. Louis called Rock Springs, remaining there about two weeks. Returning to the Arsenal, it commenced its reorganization for three years, or during the war. Before that reorganization was completed, the regiment was ordered to take the field leaving the Arsenal about the

middle of June 1861. Our equipment for field service was a very poor one. We had no blankets, no knapsacks, no great coats, and barely any camp and garrison equipage. Our whole outfit consisted of an uncovered tin canteen and a white sheeting haversack, rotten white belts, condemned since the Mexican War, and cartridge boxes made by contract, flat-shaped like cigar boxes, without tin racks to hold the cartridges in place, consequently in a week's marching, you had your cartridge box full of loose powder, and bullets tied to the paper cases. Each company possessed one-half dozen Sibley tents and the same number of camp kettles and mess pans. The baggage and provisions are carried by two four-horse contract teams, for each company. We went by rail to Rolla, Missouri, the then terminus of the Missouri Pacific R.R., Southwest branch, about 120 miles southwest of St. Louis. Here Colonel Franz Sigel established Camp "Lyon" and in a few days our regiment was joined by the Fifth Missouri Volunteers, Colonel Edmund Salomon, a brother of Governor Salomon of Wisconsin: Captain Essig's battery of four [twelve]-pound howitzers, and Captain Wilkin's battery of two [twelve]-pound howitzers and two [six]-pound field guns, forming a battalion of Artillery under Major Backhoff, also a company of pioneers, commanded by Captain Foerster, the whole forming the Second Brigade of General Nathaniel Lyons' army, commanded by Colonel Franz Sigel—say about 2,000 muskets and [eight] guns. From Rolla this brigade marched to Springfield, about 100 miles southwest, arriving there on Friday, June 27, 1861. Continuing our march in a southwestern direction, we arrived in Neosho, Newton County, Missouri, situated in the utmost southwest corner of the state, some [eighty-five] miles southwest of Springfield, on Tuesday, July 2, 1861. Neosho possessed a beautiful spring of clear water gushing forth the size of a brook, where a large fish hatchery is established at the present time. It is also noted because the rebel governor of Missouri Clayborn Fox Jackson assembled his "Rump" Legislature there to pass a futile ordinance of secession for Missouri. Here we remained until Thursday, July 4th, in a rather perilous position. On our right, some [thirty] miles northwest, stood a force of about 4,000 Missouri State Guards, commanded by Major General Sterling Price; a state militia organization, under a recent law of the Missouri legislature, passed at the urgent solicitation of the rebel governor, Clayborn [sic] Fox Jackson. The law contemplated the raising of a Missouri State Guard of 50,000 men ostensibly for the preservation of the neutrality of the sovereign State of Missouri, but virtually as a part and parcel of the Confederate Army.

This infantile organization had been roughly tumbled out of the central part of the state near Booneville, on the Missouri River, on Friday,

June the 17th, 1861, by a quick sharp and victorious attack of Brig. General Lyon, ascending the Missouri River by boat and sending the Missouri State Guard packing to the southwest corner of the State on Cowskin Prairie, in Jasper County, Camp Starvation, Price's men very properly called it.

In sending Colonel Franz Sigel and his brigade to the southwest, General Lyon had intended to capture or destroy the nascent Missouri State Guard, or at least to prevent their proper organization. But General Price had been adding recruits to his numbers on his whole march, and General Lyon had been unable to push Price vigorously, being detained at Jefferson City to organize a loyal state government, and awaiting the arrival of the First Iowa Volunteer Infantry, the First and Second Kansas, and the following regular troops from Fort Leavenworth, Kansas-first battalion of infantry, four troops of cavalry, and Captain Du Bois's battery.

On our left about [thirty] miles southwest of Neosho was a camp of regular Confederate troops, called "Camp Walker," about 5,000 effective men with good artillery, composed of Texas, Louisiana, and Arkansas troops commanded by Brigadier General Ben. McCulloch, a celebrated Texas Ranger, whose adjutant, General McIntosh, was a graduate of West Point and a fine and able officer of the old regular army. Having left garrisons at Springfield, Mt. Vernon, and various other places, Colonel Sigel, marched on Thursday, July 4th, 1861, from Neosho to Carthage, Jasper County, leaving as a garrison at Neosho, Captain Joseph Conrad, and Company "B" Third Missouri Infantry. This was a march of [twenty] miles due north, and we camped southeast of Carthage on Spring River.

Next morning, Friday, July 5th, we marched northwest from Carthage, toward Cowskin Prairie, when about noon, nine miles from town, we came upon the Missouri State Guard, drawn tip in line of battle on a slight rise or swell of the prairie, at the foot of which about 1,000 yards from the enemy, near Dry Fork Creek, we took position. Our train in charge of quartermaster, First Lieutenant Sebastian Engert, was parked in the prairie about three miles in our rear, guarded by Captain Foerster's Company of pioneers.

Colonel Franz Sigel made the following disposition of his command from right to left: Right wing, first battalion, Third Missouri Infantry, Lieutenant Col. Hassendenbel, commanding, and Captain Essig's battery (four guns): center, two battalions, and the Fifth Missouri Infantry, Colonel Edmund Salomon: left wing, Captain Wilkin's battery (four guns), second battalion Third Missouri Infantry, Major Bischoff, commanding 1,000 infantry and [eight] guns according to

Colonel Sigel's official report. Having no cavalry to cover our wings, the whole infantry was formed in column of companies to guard against cavalry attacks.

At about [one] o'clock P.M., after some moving about, using the intervals to gain room for deployments, the battle commenced, consisting mainly of a mutual cannonade which caused few casualties on either side. The Missourians, temporarily commanded by General [James S.] Rains, (General Price being sick) had seven pieces of artillery, but their ammunition consisted of solid shot only, no shells nor shrapnel, while our eight guns fired both of these, and every time one of our shells exploded, we could see a large gap in the enemy's black line against the horizon, and at first we young soldiers, ignorant of war, cheered and rejoiced at seeing so many enemies fall at each explosion of a shell, but they never stayed down, they always got up again, and we soon found that we were doing but little execution.

The enemy had about 4,000 men in line, a part of them without any arms, and nearly one third of them mounted, but in field equipments and armament even worse off than we were. We were armed with the old [sixty-nine]-caliber rifle muskets, each ball weighing an ounce of lead, while the enemy's armament consisted mainly of old Kentucky rifles and shotguns. Our uniform consisted of a grey flannel blouse, grey jeans trousers, and a grey woolen hat. The enemy had no uniforms, being entirely clad in the homespun butternut jeans worn by every Missouri farmer in those days.

The artillery duel had lasted about an hour when the enemy moved out mounted columns from both wings, circling wide round our wings, and taking position in Buck's Branch of Dry Fork Creek, half way between ourselves and our train. This induced Colonel Sigel's retrograde movement. He ordered the battalion of Lieutenant Colonel Hassendenbel, and two guns under Lieutenant Schuetzenbach to dislodge this cavalry, the infantry marching through the prairie in columns of companies to within about 1,000 yards of the enemy, when Schuetzenbach on our left opened fire on the cavalry, whose heads were just visible over the banks of Buck's Branch, while Lieut. Colonel Hassendenbel was deploying his battalion to advance in line. Colonel Franz Sigel galloped up and the following conversation took place. Colonel Sigel: "Colonel Hassendenbel, what are you doing there?" Lieutenant Colonel Hassendenbel: "I am deploying my battalion to advance in line and open fire on them." Colonel Sigel: "For God's sake remain in column, they are cavalry and they will cut you to pieces." Lieutenant Colonel Hassendenbel: "Ah! Nonsense; those fellows haven't got any sabers," and turning to the battalion he commanded "Forward! Double quick! March!" Whereupon with a loud "Hurrah my battalion," (I was first sergeant of Co. 'E' and acting as second lieutenant that day) rushed through the high prairie grass at the enemy's cavalry, posted about 900 yards southeast of us in Buck's Branch, which action was quite a novel spectacle, and contrary to all the orthodox rules of war as known at that time. But Lieutenant Colonel Hassendenbel knew what he was doing. He had served as a lieutenant of artillery under Brigadier General Sterling Price, U.S. Volunteers in the Mexican war, had served as city engineer of the city of St. Louis later, and later still commanded a brigade in 1862, when I was on his staff as an aide de camp. He died in front of Vicksburg in 1863, a piece of shell mortally wounding him.

We ran about 500 yards when the want of breath stopped some one, and he fired his gun; this, of course, brought on a volley and in an instant the whole prairie in front of us was covered with fugitive, mounted men, running away from us at the top of their horses' speed, circling back the way they had come and rejoining their line; only one unfortunate captain, whose horse had been killed, was captured by us. The retrograde movements of our battalion continued until we had joined our train. It was followed by the rest of Colonel Sigel's troops and the whole command preceded by the train, marched back to Carthage followed by the enemy at a respectful distance, and with the exception of the dispute at the crossing of Buck's Branch, which resulted in some sputtering of musketry, our whole retreat was unmolested.

While Colonel Sigel's command was thus engaged at Dry Fork Creek, nine miles northwest of Carthage, Brigadier General Ben McCulloch, of the Confederate Army, with from five to six thousand men, advanced on Neosho, Missouri, in Colonel Sigel's rear, capturing Captain Joseph Conrad and his Company "B" Third Missouri. This gave General McCulloch so much pleasure that he stopped his movement at Neosho. Had he made use of his large number of mounted men and advanced to Sarcoxie, he would have cut off Colonel Sigel's retreat to Springfield, and could easily have captured Colonel Sigel and his whole command. Colonel Sigel's column and train passed through Carthage at about 6:00 P.M. and took the road to Sarcoxie, fifteen miles northeast of Carthage. About an hour later Major General Price and his troops occupied Carthage, and from the public square opened fire with a battery of artillery on our troops, which was returned in a languid manner by two of our guns. Here Colonel Sigel personally ordered my Company "E," Captain John E. Strodtman to remain and hold the enemy in check until further orders.

Captain Strodtman formed the company in column of platoons, across the Sarcoxie road. The sun went down; all troops to the right and left of us marched off, our company being left solitary and alone on the prairie, about 300 yards from the timber fringing Spring River, the place where we had camped the night before. It was nearly dark, when we noticed the edge of that timber filling up with men, and a mounted officer riding toward us was met by our First Lieutenant Poten. They each asked "What regiment do you belong to?" and the enemy answering Second Missouri Infantry. Poten fired his pistol at him, but missed. As soon as the officer had regained his line, we were greeted by a volley that knocked our Captain and three men down and owing to our foolish platoon formation only our 1st platoon could return the fire, and when about three or four hundred of the enemy burst out of the woods rapidly advancing on us, cheering and firing, we picked up our own wounded Captain and "skedaddled."

After running about a mile, and occasionally returning the fire of the enemy, I met, a solitary horseman, our Lieutenant Colonel Hassendenbel, who was greatly astonished when I told him we were Co. "E" of his battalion, remaining behind by special order of Colonel Sigel, and apparently forgotten by him. Here we halted long enough to rally the Company, and a mile further on we joined the rest of Colonel Sigel's command. It was about 9:00 P.M. when the brigade was formed in line of battle, on the edge of the timber, where the Sarcoxie road leaves the prairie.

By word of command of Colonel Sigel, viz., "Ready! Aim! Fire! Load!" three volleys of musketry and three salutes of artillery were fired in this position. Only God and Colonel Franz Sigel know the military reason of this beautiful pyrotechnic display in the dark and silent prairie; no enemy being in sight.

After biding this loud "Adieu" to General Price and his army, two and one-half miles northwest of us at Carthage, we silently ducked into the woods and resumed our march to Sarcoxie, which place we reached about daybreak, Saturday, July 6th, fortunately not occupied by General McCulloch. Having been without food for twenty-four hours, we unpacked our cooking utensils to prepare some breakfast. Our subsistence during the whole campaign consisted mainly of flour and fresh beef, having neither hard bread nor canned meats. When marching we had no meat at all, but where-ever we halted long enough, cattle were killed and we were supplied with fresh beef. Colonel Sigel had established a bakery at Springfield, and we once received a train load of fresh bread in Neosho, but usually we had no means of converting our flour into bread, and substituted a dough made of flour, salt and water, baked in a frying pan in the form of flapjacks, and these being prepared without any yeast or baking powder, possessed the consistency of sole leather. At first we had no cavalry with us, except six mounted orderlies, attending Colonel Sigel, but on arriving at Springfield, we had a couple of squads of mounted Home Guards, loyal men of southwestern Missouri, where loyal men predominated at that time.

These men were dressed and armed like General Price's men: homespun butternut suits, Kentucky rifles, and shotguns, and when Colonel Sigel sent them to reconnoiter, they would frequently sight patrols, mistaking each other for the enemy, and then rush back to camp and report the enemy advancing from two directions. Before our breakfast was ready, a false alarm of this kind reached our camp. "They are coming! They are coming!" Instantly pouring our prospective meal on the ground, and repacking our cooking utensils, we started toward Mt. Vernon, county seat of Lawrence County, twenty-five miles northeast of Sarcoxie on our road to Springfield. It was a very hot and weary march, with frequently halting to rest the troops and no enemy pursuing.

One of our greatest inconveniences in this summer campaign, was the fact that we possessed no clothes whatever, except those on our backs. Marching in a hot July sun produces an abundance of perspiration, and it became imperative to wash our clothes some times. This we accomplished by divesting ourselves of every stitch of clothing, and getting into some convenient creek, washed the same to the best of our ability, remaining in the water until our clothes were sufficiently dried to be worn again.

We arrived at Mt. Vernon about 9:00 P.M., utterly fagged out. We had marched twenty miles from Neosho to Carthage on July 4th, eighteen miles from Carthage to Dry Fork Creek, and return, besides the maneuvering on the battlefield, and fifteen miles to Sarcoxie on July 5th, with twenty-five miles to Mt. Vernon on July 6th, making [eighty-five] miles of marching, with a battle thrown in. This three days' hard work, with barely two meals, was a very creditable military performance for such young and raw troops. In Mt. Vernon we dropped to the ground and went to sleep, where we had stacked our arms, too tired even to cook and eat. On Sunday morning at [three] o'clock, one of those false alarms of our Home Guard friends got us under arms again, the enemy advancing according to their report, from the west and the south. We stood under arms from 3:00 to 10:00 A.M., when Colonel Sigel ordered us back to town and we had a cup of coffee and an abundance of those sole-leather flapjacks. About noon Brigadier General Sweeney, a one-armed Captain of the regular army and veteran of the Mexican war, with about 1,000 St. Louis Home Guards arrived as a reinforcement.

Next morning, Monday, July 8th, we started back to Springfield, thirty-five miles northeast of Mt. Vernon, and we arrived there without any molestation from the enemy, the following day about 10:00 A.M., establishing a regular camp south Lyon and his troops. From a military point

General Sterling Price. (Author's collection)

of view, of the city, on the Forsythe road, awaiting the arrival of General Lyon and his troops. From a military point of view, the battle of Carthage was a very insignificant one, but it will always retain a great deal of historical interest, as being one of the very first very first passages of arms between federal and Confederate troops in our great Civil War.[22]

On July 22, the state convention met and declared the offices of governor, lieutenant-governor and secretary of state vacated. Ex-Governor Jackson, his family, and twenty slaves had fled to Arkansas where he said in an interview published on the 25th, "You see before you a fugitive from my own state, pursued by federal bayonets. With two hundred men we fought the Hessians as long as we could."[23]

Meanwhile, seventy-five miles southwest of Springfield, Major General Sterling Price, commanding the Missouri State Guard, had been busy drilling the 5,200 soldiers in his charge. Frank James saw his first action with the guard at Wilson's Creek when it temporarily joined forces with General McCulloch's Confederate troops.

By the end of July, when troops under Generals Ben McCulloch and N. Bart Pearce rendezvoused with Price, the total Confederate force exceeded 12,000 men. On July 31, after formulating plans to capture Lyon's army and regain control of the state, Price, McCulloch, and Pearce marched northeast to attack the federals. Lyon, hoping to surprise the Confederates, marched from Springfield on August 1st.

The next day the Union troops mauled the Southern vanguard at Dug Springs and followed the enemy as far as McCulloch's ranch. At this point it became evident that the enemy was falling back. To concentrate their columns in one and then attack on his own, getting further from the base of supply, a council of officers was called, to determine the propriety of a retrograde movement on Springfield, General Lyon stating at the same time that this would probably also involve the necessity of falling back all the way to Rolla. Lyon, discovering he was outnumbered and low on supplies, ordered a withdrawal to Springfield.

That same summer General Lyon, then commanding Jefferson Barracks at St. Louis, had given permission to David Moore of Canton to raise troops for the defense of northeastern Missouri. A meeting was held at Kahoka, in Clark County, at which it was determined to raise a regiment and equip it as well as possible for service. By the early part of June a force of seven hundred men had been enrolled and sworn into the United States service for three years, or for the duration of the war. As soon as possible after the organization was completed, the command marched upon Aetna, Scotland County, Missouri, where a Confederate force was stationed under Major Schacklett. This force retreated before Moore, with little resistance, and hoisting the stars and stripes, Colonel Moore and his command proceeded to Athens, where they went into camp to await supplies. While in this camp the men were subjected to military discipline and drill until August 4th when Moore's scouts reported the enemy advancing in strong force from the direction of Edina under command of Colonel Martin E. Green, and another force under Colonel Franklin, from Lancaster County, Missouri.[24]

Colonel Moore's brief account of the fight was as follows: "The two rebel forces, variously estimated at from nine to fifteen hundred men, formed a junction at or near Aetna, Missouri, and camped in the Fox River timber about four miles from Athens. A dispatch was sent to Keokuk notifying the citizens that the enemy was advancing in strong force from Athens, and in two hours two companies of the City Rifles arrived under the command of the gallant William W. Belknap. With this command came Hugh W.E. Sample, John W. Noble, and others, numbering upwards of eighty men. Many who here fired their first shots at an enemy, afterwards joined Iowa regiments and won immortal honors on many great battlefields for the Union and freedom.

> During the night of the 4th, the line of sentinels was often visited by grand-rounds and instructed in their duty. At sunrise on the morning of August the 5th, the advance mounted pickets were driven in, the long roll was beat to arms and in one minute a line of battle was formed and told off in groups of forty men. Each of my commands numbered three hundred and thirty-three in line. Green opened two pieces of artillery

upon the center. The right of his line was touching the river upon my right. Major Schacklet with his battalion was on Green's right with their flank opposite the Iowa boys on the other side of the river. When the artillery opened, my mounted horsemen filed across the river, and Captain Spellman, with his company, also crossed with his colors flying; but Captain Small and his company stood just where they were posted. Nearly all the enemy's cannon shot flew over our heads. The women and children of the village were sent to a big mill under a steep bluff, where they were sheltered from the fire of the enemy; and the prisoners were sent under a strong guard to Croton, opposite Athens. The firing soon became general on the whole line. They were armed with shot-guns and squirrel rifles, which were no match for our improved muskets. The fight had lasted nearly two hours, when those posted on the right and left were ordered by me to stand fast and the center to fix bayonets and move forward in common time. The men, however, soon broke into a charge, and the enemy fled in every direction from the field.

Colonel Moore stated that the number killed and wounded of the enemy was estimated at 31 and over, and that the killed and wounded in his command numbered 23. He also stated, "As the fruits of the victory, we captured many prisoners, four hundred and fifty horses, saddles and bridles complete, hundreds of arms, and a wagon load of long knives with which they expected to fight the infantry."

Immediately after the battle, Colonel Moore, with his command, started in pursuit of the Confederate forces. Later he was joined by other troops under the command of Generals Pope and Hurlbut. Green's command was pursued by these troops for many days, but could not be brought to an engagement. His forces sometimes numbered as high as three or four thousand men, but they would disperse when about to be attacked and reassemble later at another place.

Notes

1War on the Border, Missouri Department of Natural Resources brochure.
2Ibid.
3Elmer D. Mcinnes, "The Terrible McWaters," True West, p. 46.
4Kansas State Historical Society.
5Dave Page, "A Fight for Missouri," Civil War Times Illustrated, August 1995, p. 35.

[6]1884 History of Missouri. Internet.

[7]Jeffrey L. Patrick, "The Travels of a Fallen General Brig. Gen. Nathaniel Lyon, USA," *Blue and Gray*, Volume XVII, Issue 2, January 2000, p. 22; Martin Edward McGrane, *The Home of Jesse and Frank James . . . The James Farm, Kearney, Missouri*, Madison, South Dakota, The Caleb Perkins Press, 1982, p. 18.

[8]Donald R. Hale, *We Rode with Quantrill*, Independence, Blue & Grey Book Shoppe, 1998, p. 28.

[9]Albert Castel, *A Frontier State at War: Kansas, 1861-1865*, Cornell UP, 1958.

[10]Ted P. Yeatman, *Frank and Jesse James: The Story Behind the Legend*, Nashville, Cumberland House, 2000, p. 30.

[11]Jesse James, Jr., *Jesse James, My Father*, Cleveland, Arthur Westbrook Company, 1899.

[12]C.E. Avery and Darryl Stolper, "Confederate Images," *Confederate Veteran*, Volume 1,1999, p. 13.

[13]Thomas Goodrich, *Black Flag Guerrilla Warfare on the Western Border, 1861-1865*, Bloomington and Indianapolis, University of Indiana Press, 1995, p.37.

[14]Ibid.

[15]Thomas Goodrich, *Black Flag Guerrilla Warfare on the Western Border, 1861-1865*, Bloomington and Indianapolis, University of Indiana Press, 1995, p. 35.

[16]Phillip Rutherford, "The Carthaginian Wars," *Civil War Times Illustrated*, February 1987, pp. 40-42.

[17]*Kansas City Times*, June 21, 1929.

[18]*Weekly Advertiser*, Boonville, Missouri, June 13, 1924.

[19]William G. Cutler, *History of the State of Kansas*, Chicago, 1883 by A.T. Andreas, 1883.

[20]David Hinze and Karen Farnham, "Dry Fork Creek," *Confederate Veteran*, Volume I, 1999, pp. 32-34.

[21]Phillip W. Steele and Steve Cottrell, *Civil War in the Ozarks*, Gretna, Louisiana, Pelican Publishing Company, 2000, p. 22.

[22]The Battle of Carthage, Missouri, Friday, July 5, 1861 by Otto C. Ladermann, Captain 3rd Missouri Infantry, U.S. Vols. Companion of the 1st Class, WI Commandery of MOLL US Read March 7, 1907. "War Papers Read Before the Commandery of the State of Wisconsin, Military Order of the Loyal Legion of the United States," Published by the Commandery. Vol.4, Milwaukee: Burdick and Allen ca. 1914, pp.131-139

[23]*The True Democrat*, Little Rock, Arkansas, July 25, 1861.

[24]"The Battle of Athens" by Hon. George W. McCrary, late Secretary of War, Companion of the 3rd Class, MO Commandery of MOLLUS. "War Papers and Personal Reminiscences, 1861-1865, Read Before the Commandery of the State of Missouri, Military Order of the Loyal Legion of the United States," published by the Commandery, Becktold & Co., St. Louis, MO c1892, reprinted by Broadfoot Publishing Co., Wilmington, NC c1992. p.169-176.

Chapter Four

Bushwhackers and Jayhawkers

"... *Camped near the town of California, Missouri-utterly denuded and deserted by its inhabitants. Windows and doors of the dwellings are either fast nailed, or smashed wholly out, and a more melancholy exhibition in its way I have not seen.*"
—Albert Tracy, Union Captain, 1861[1]

O N AUGUST 4TH, GENERAL BEN MCCULLOCH issued General Orders, Number 24 to his Confederate troops at their camp on Crane Creek in the Springfield area:

The army will move at 12:00 P.M. to-night. Colonel Hébert's regiment of Louisiana volunteers, by platoons, with Woodruff's battery, will form the advance guard. The battery will march immediately behind the regiment, and the column will keep 200 yards in advance of the main army and attack the enemy as soon as seen. The main army will march in the following order: First, Colonel Gratiot's regiment; second, Colonel McRae's battalion; third, Colonel Weightman's command of infantry and artillery; fourth, General Pearce's infantry and Reid's battery; sixth, General Price's command of infantry.

In this column no cavalry or mounted men besides the officers will be allowed. These respective commands will form and march in column of platoons. Immediately after the infantry General Price will place his artillery. The cavalry will follow General Price's artillery in the following order, by fours, and whenever possible by platoons: First, Colonel Churchill's regiment of Arkansas Mounted Riflemen; second, Colonel Carroll's regiment of cavalry; third, Colonel McIntosh's regiment of Mounted Riflemen; fourth, Colonel Greer's regiment of Texas volunteers; fifth, General Price's command of cavalry. General Price will order the officer in command of his cavalry, as soon as he learns that the enemy is in force, to make a flank movement to our left, and the general will, as soon as the line of battle is formed, take command of the left in person. The four other regiments of cavalry above enumerated will at the same time make a flank movement to our right, and endeavor to take the enemy in flank. All general officers will lead their respective commands wherever the larger portion of them are. The regiments and batteries of these respective commands which are detached will be led by the immediate commanders. This movement will take place in quietness. Neither shouting nor beating of drums will be allowed, and, especially on the march, strictest silence must be observed.

The canteens will all be filled before starting, and one day's rations (cooked) will be carried by each soldier. Each commander of regiment and company will see that a sufficient amount of ammunition is carried by each man. No unarmed man will be permitted to march with or follow the army. No wagons will move with the command. Each regimental commander will leave a detachment of men to guard their respective wagon trains. The ambulances will move in rear of the army. The general and his aides will be distinguished by a white badge on each arm.

The general takes this occasion to say to his soldiers to look steadily to the front. Remember that the eyes of our gallant brothers in arms, who have so nobly acquitted themselves in the East, are upon you. They are looking for a second victory here. Let us move forward, then, with a common resolve, to a glorious victory.

McCulloch added the following postscript: "Each captain of company will continually caution his men to take aim. As soon as the enemy are driven from their first position; colonels of regiments and captains of companies will at once rally their companies, and hold them in hand for further orders."[2]

The Confederates followed and by August 6th were encamped near Wilson's Creek. Lyon wrote his department commander, Major General John C. Fremont from Springfield on the 9th: "GENERAL: I have just received your note of the 6th instant by special messenger. I retired to this place, as I have before informed you, reaching here on the 5th. The enemy followed to within [ten] miles of here. He has taken a strong position, and is recruiting his supplies of horses, mules, and provisions by foraging into the surrounding country, his large force of mounted men enabling him to do this without much annoyance from me. I find my position extremely embarrassing, and am at present unable to determine whether I shall be able to maintain my ground or be forced to retire. I can resist any attack from the front, but if the enemy moves to surround me, I must retire. I shall hold my ground as long as possible, though I may, without knowing how far, endanger the safety of my entire force, with its valuable material, being induced by the important considerations involved to take this step. The enemy yesterday made a show of force about five miles distant and has doubtless a full purpose of making an attack upon me."[3]

Since Fremont showed no concern for the safety of his force and would give him no support, Lyon determined to take the offensive against the advancing enemy. Despite inferior numbers, Lyon planned a concentric advance against the combined Confederate forces under McCulloch that were camped at Wilson's Creek, southwest of Springfield. Leaving about 1,000 men behind to guard his supplies, the federal commander led 5,400 soldiers out of Springfield. Both forces bivouacked a short distance from the unsuspecting Confederates the night of August 9th. Lyon's plan called for 1,200 men under Colonel Franz Sigel to swing wide to the south, flanking the Confederate right, while the main body of troops struck from the north. Success hinged on the element of surprise. Ironically, the Confederate leaders also planned a surprise attack on the federals, but rain on the night of the 9th caused McCulloch (who was now in overall command) to cancel the operation.

On the morning of the 10th, Lyon's attack caught the Southerners off guard, driving them back. The northern column had moved out at 4:00 A.M. and driven back the outposts of Brigadier General James S. Rains. Lyon's main body then advanced west of the creek, while a flank guard, tinder Captain J.B. Plummer, moved on the opposite side against a Confederate force that had been seen advancing toward the "Corn Field" from the Ray house. Plummer's battalion of Missouri Home Guards was reinforced by the First U.S. Infantry (300 men). In an hour's fight the federals drove the enemy back to the Ray house, but they were then counterattacked and routed with a loss of eighty killed and wounded. Hebert's Third Louisiana ("Pelican Rifles") and McIntosh's Mounted Arkansas were the Confederate troops involved.

About 6:30, following an hour's fight, Price was driven down the hill to Wilson's Creek where he re-formed to counterattack. Greer's cavalry attempted to aid the latter movement by an envelopment of the federal left by way of Skegg's Branch. However, Totten spotted this threat and repulsed it with his guns.

Sigel, meanwhile, had advanced according to plan toward the battlefield from the south. At 5:30 A.M. he was in position near Tyrel's Creek and had placed a battery on high ground east of Wilson's Creek to fire into the cavalry camps of Greer, Churchill, and Major. When he heard Lyon's opening guns, Sigel routed the Confederate cavalry and then advanced toward Sharp's House, taking up an intermediate position on the way. At Sharp's House, he was attacked and routed by McCulloch with Hebert's Third Louisiana and Churchill's cavalry. When Hebert's Pelican Rifles advanced in their natty gray uniforms, Sigel mistook them for the First Iowa and assumed that Lyon had already carried his portion of the field. Reid's battery enfiladed the federals from positions on high ground east of Wilson's Creek, while McCulloch's attack routed them. By eleven o'clock Sigel was out of the fight, and the Confederates could mass their entire strength of two to one against Lyon.

On Oak Hill the federals had repulsed two attacks. It was about this time that the third Confederate charge was under way. The First Iowa was brought up from reserve but when ordered by Schofield to charge initially refused to go forward. Lyon, accompanied by an aide and his six or eight orderlies, advanced towards the right of the Iowa regiment. After proceeding a short distance, his attention was called by the aide to a line of men drawn up on the prolongation of the left of our main line and nearly perpendicular to the 1st Iowa as it moved to the eastward. A party of horsemen came out in front of this line of the enemy and proceeded to reconnoiter. General Price and Major Emmett McDonald (who had sworn that he would not cut his hair until the Confederacy was acknowledged) were easily recognized. General Lyon started as if to confront them, ordering his party to "draw pistols and follow" him, when the aide protested against his exposing himself to the fire of the line, which was partly concealed by the mass of dense underbrush, and asked if he should not bring up some other troops. To this Lyon assented, and directed the aide to order up the Second Kansas. The general advanced a short distance, joining two companies of the First Iowa, left to protect an exposed position.

Colonel Mitchell of the Second Kansas dispatched Colonel Blair to Lyon to ask to be put into action, and the two messengers passed each other without meeting. Lyon repeated his order for the regiment to come forward. The regiment moved promptly by the flank, and as it approached Lyon, he directed the two companies of Iowa troops to go forward with it, himself leading the column, swinging his hat. A murderous fire was opened from the thick brush, the Second Kansas deployed rapidly to the front and with the two companies of the First Iowa swept over the hill, dislodging the enemy and driving them back into the next ravine; but while he was at the head of the column, and pretty nearly in the first fire, a ball penetrated Lyon's left breast, inflicting a mortal wound. He slowly dismounted, and as he fell into the arms of his faithful orderly, Lehmann, he exclaimed, "Lehmann, I am killed," and almost immediately expired. Colonel Mitchell was also severely wounded about the same time and removed to the rear.

Lieutenant Gustavus Schreyer and two of his men of the Second Kansas bore the body of Lyon through the ranks, Lehmann bearing the hat and loudly bemoaning the death of his chief. In the line of file-closers the returning aide was met, who, apprehensive of the effect upon the troops, stopped the clamor of the orderly, covered the general's features with his coat, and had the body carried to a sheltered spot near DuBois' battery. Surgeon Florence M. Cornyn was found and called upon to examine the lifeless body of the dead general, and having pronounced him dead, the aide went to seek Schofield and inform him of the calamity. He was met returning from the successful charge he had led, and at once announced that Major Sturgis should assume command but visited the remains of Lyon on his way to find Sturgis. These were taken charge of by aide, and conveyed to the field-hospital, where the body was placed in a wagon and carefully covered. Strict orders were given that under no circumstances was the body to be removed until the army returned to Springfield, after which the aide returned to the front to report to Major Sturgis for duty.

At 11:30 the Confederates broke off the action and retired down the hill for the fourth time. Major Sturgis, who had succeeded Lyon, then ordered a withdrawal. This controversial decision was apparently prompted by Sturgis' lack of confidence in the ability of his tired troops, who were almost out of ammunition, to withstand another attack.

Sigel filed his report on August 12th:

SIR: I respectfully report to you that after a battle fought [ten] miles south of Springfield, on Saturday, the 10th, between our forces and the rebel army, and in which General Lyon was killed, I have taken temporarily the command of the Union troops. Arrived after the battle at Springfield, on the evening of the 10th, it was found necessary to retreat towards Rolla. We are now here with 3,000 men of infantry, 300 cavalry, and thirteen pieces of artillery. The Irish Brigade, about 900 strong, will meet us at Lebanon. The Home Guards amount to about 200 infantry and 500 mounted men, who are more or less valuable. The enemy's forces cannot be less than 20,000 men, of which about one-fourth are infantry, the others cavalry, besides fifteen pieces of artillery.

Once in possession of Springfield, the enemy will be able to raise the southwest of the State against us, add a great number of men to his army, make Springfield a great depot, and continue his operations towards Rolla, and probably also towards the Missouri (Jefferson City). I do not see the probability of making an effective resistance without reinforcement of not less than 5,000 men, infantry, one or two regiments of cavalry, and at least two batteries. To meet the momentous danger we want re-enforcements, and to be prepared against the last reverses which may befall us in this State, I would respectfully propose to you to make, in the shortest time possible, the necessary preparations for two intrenched [sic] camps, one at Saint Louis, the key to the Southwest, and another at Jefferson City, or, perhaps better, between the Osage River and Moreau Creek, on the heights of Taos Post Office. At the same time it would be necessary to be master of the river between Jefferson City and Saint Louis, and to arm the two intrenched positions by heavy ordnance.

The Missouri will now become our natural line of defense, with the Osage River in advance, and the two places, Tuscumbia and Linn Creek, as the most important points where têtes-de-pont could be constructed. I make these remarks because I am aware of our strength and weakness. Our 4,000 men will be crippled by the discharge of the three-months' men, who cannot be kept longer in our midst because they are anxious to go home, and would be of more damage than use if forced to serve longer.[4]

Sigel penned a second report on the 18th:

GENERAL: I respectfully submit to you the report of the battle at Wilson's Creek, as far as the troops under my command are concerned: On Friday, the 9th of August, General Lyon informed me that it was his intention to attack the enemy in his camp at Wilson's Creek on the morning of the 10th; that the attack should be made from two sides, and that I should take the command of the left. The troops assigned to me consisted of the Second Brigade Missouri Volunteers (900 men, infantry, of the Third and Fifth Regiments, under the command of Lieutenant-Colonel Albert and Colonel Salomon, and six pieces of artillery, under Lieutenants Schaefer and Schuetzenbach), besides two companies of regular cavalry, belonging to the command of Major Sturgis.

I left Camp Frémont, on the south side of Springfield, at 6.30 o'clock in the evening of the 9th, and arrived at daybreak within a mile of the enemy's camp. I advanced slowly towards the camp, and after taking forward the two cavalry companies from the right and left, I cut off about forty men of the enemy's troops, who were coming from the camp in little squads to get water and provisions. This was done in such a manner that no news of our advance could be brought into the camp. In sight of the enemy's tents, which spread out in our front and right, I planted four pieces 'of artillery on a little hill, whilst the infantry advanced towards the point where the Fayetteville road crosses Wilson's Creek, and the two cavalry companies extended to the right and left to guard our flanks. It was 5.30 o'clock A.M. when some musket firing was heard from the northwest. I, therefore, ordered the artillery to begin their- fire against the camp of the enemy (Missourians), which was of so much effect, that the enemy's troops were seen leaving their tents and retiring in haste towards the northeast of the valley. Meanwhile the Third and Fifth Regiments had quickly advanced, passed the creek, and, traversing the camp, formed almost in the center of it.

As the enemy made his rally in large numbers before us, about 3,000 strong, consisting of infantry and cavalry, I ordered the artillery to be brought forward from the hill, and formed them in battery across the valley, with the Third and Fifth Regiments to the left and the cavalry to the right. After an effective fire of half an hour the enemy retired in some confusion into the woods and up the adjoining hills. The firing towards the northwest was now more distinct, and increased till it was evident that the main corps of General Lyon had engaged the enemy along the whole line. To give the greatest possible assistance to him, I left the position in the camp and advanced towards the northwest, to at attack the enemy's line of battle in the rear. Marching forward, we struck the Fayetteville road, making our way through a large number of cattle and horses until we arrived at an eminence used as a slaughtering place, and known as Sharp's farm. On our route we had taken about 100 prisoners, who were scattered over the camp.

At Sharp's place we met numbers of the enemy's soldiers, who were evidently retiring in this direction, and, as I suspected that the enemy on his retreat would follow in the same direction, I formed the troops across this road, by planting the artillery on the plateau and the two infantry regiments on the right and left across the road, whilst the cavalry companies extended on our flanks. At this time, and after some skirmishing in front of our line, the firing in the direction of northwest, which was during an hour's time roaring in succession, had almost ceased entirely. I therefore thought that the attack of General Lyon had been successful, and that his troops were in pursuit of the enemy, who moved in large masses towards the south, along the ridge of a hill, about 700 yards opposite our right.

This was the state of affairs at 8.30 o'clock in the morning, when it was reported to me by Dr. Melchior and some of our skirmishers that Lyon's men were coming up the road. Lieutenant-Colonel Albert, of the Third, and Colonel Salomon, of the Fifth, notified their regiments not to fire on troops coming in this direction, whilst I cautioned the artillery in the same manner. Our troops in this moment expected with anxiety the approach of our friends, and were waving the flag, raised as a signal to their comrades, when at once two batteries opened their fire against us, one in front, placed on the Fayetteville road, and the other upon the hill on which we had supposed Lyon's forces were in pursuit of the enemy, whilst a strong column of infantry, supposed to be the Iowa regiment, advanced from the Fayetteville road and at tacked our right.

It is impossible for me to describe the consternation and frightful confusion which was occasioned by this unfortunate event. The cry 'They (Lyon's troops) are firing against us,' spread like wildfire through our ranks; the artillerymen, ordered to here and directed by myself, could hardly be brought forward to serve their pieces; the infantry would not level their arms till it was too late. The enemy arrived within ten paces from the mouth of our cannon, killed the horses, turned the flanks of the infantry, and forced them to retire. The troops were throwing themselves into the bushes and by-roads, retreating as well as they could, followed and attacked incessantly by large bodies of Arkansas and Texas cavalry. In this retreat we lost five cannon, of which three were spiked, and the color of the Third Regiment, the color-bearer having been wounded and his substitute killed. The total loss of the two regiments, the artillery and the pioneers, in killed, wounded, and missing, amounts to 292 men, as will be seen from the respective lists.

In order to understand clearly our actions and our fate, you will allow me to state the following facts: 1st. According to orders, it was the duty of this brigade to attack the enemy in the rear and to cut off his retreat, which order I tried execute, whatever the consequences might be. 2d. The time of service of the Fifth Regiment Missouri Volunteers had expired before the battle, I had induced them, company by company, not to leave us in the most critical and dangerous moment, and had engaged them for the time of eight days, this term ending on Friday, the 9th, the day before the battle. 3d. The Third Regiment, of which 400 three-months' men had been dismissed, was composed for the greatest part of recruits, who had not seen the enemy before and were only insufficiently drilled. 4th. The men serving the pieces and the drivers consisted of infantry taken from the Third Regiment, and were mostly recruits, who had had only a few days' instruction. 5th. About two-thirds of our officers had left us. Some companies had no officers at all; a great pity, but the consequence of the system of the three-months service.

After the arrival of the army at Springfield, the command was intrusted [sic] to me by Major Sturgis and the majority of the commanders of regiments. Considering all the circumstances, and in accordance with the commanding officers, I ordered the retreat of the army from Springfield. The preparations were begun in the night of the 10th, and at daybreak the troops were on their march to the Gasconade. Before crossing this river I received information that the ford could not be passed well, and that a strong force of the enemy was moving from the south (West plains) towards Waynesville, to cut off our retreat. I also was aware that it would take a considerable time to cross the Roubidoux and the Little and Big Piney on the old road.

To avoid all these difficulties, and to give the army an opportunity to rest, I directed the troops from Lebanon to the northern road, passing Right Point and Humboldt, and terminating opposite the mouth of Little Piney, where, in case of the ford not being passable, the train could be sent by Vienna and Linn to the mouth of the Gasconade, whilst the troops could ford the river at the mouth of Little Piney to re-enforce Rolla. To bring over the artillery, I ordered the ferry-boat from Big Piney Crossing to be hauled down on the Gasconade to the mouth of Little Piney, where it arrived immediately after we had passed the ford. Before we had reached the ford Major Sturgis assumed the command of the army. I, therefore, respectfully refer to his report in regard to the main body of the troops engaged in the battle.[5]

Although a minor engagement, this was one of the most fiercely-contested of the war. The federals were outnumbered 11,600 to 5,400. They lost 1,235 (223 killed, 721 wounded, 291 missing) while inflicting on the Confederates a loss of 1,184 (257 killed, 900 wounded, twenty-seven missing). They killed or wounded 214 Confederates for every 1,000 of their own troops engaged, whereas the Confederates inflicted only eighty-one casualties on the same basis. Considering Sigel's poor performance, this over-all record is particularly remarkable. McCulloch did not pursue the federals, as they retreated to Rolla while Price occupied Springfield. Wilson's Creek, the most significant 1861 battle in Missouri, gave the Confederates control of southwestern Missouri.

Brigadier General Ben McCulloch dispatched reports beginning August 10th from Niangua Crossing, twenty-eight miles east of Springfield to L.P. Walker, Confederate Secretary of War in Richmond, Virginia:

> SIR: I have the honor to report that the enemy, 12,000 strong, attacked us at daylight this morning. Although they were superior in discipline and arms and had gained a strong position, we have repulsed them and gained a decided victory. The enemy fled before us at [one] o'clock, after eight hours' hard fighting, leaving many dead and wounded and prisoners. Six pieces of cannon were taken and many small-arms. Among the dead we found General Lyon, and sent his body to his successor this evening. The loss was also severe on our side. Our men were at great disadvantage, on account of the inferior weapons, but they fought generally with great bravery. I will as soon as possible send a more detailed account. The Missouri and Arkansas State forces were in the battle under my command. Want of arms and discipline made my number comparatively small.[6]

On August 12th, he wrote Brigadier General S. Cooper, Adjutant-General of the Confederate Army from Camp Weightman, near Springfield:

> SIR: I have the honor to make the following official report of the battle of the Oak Hills on the 10th instant: Having taken position about [ten] miles from Springfield, I endeavored to gain the necessary information of the strength and position of the enemy stationed in and about the town. The information was very conflicting and unsatisfactory. I, however, made up my mind to attack the enemy in their position, and issued orders on the 9th instant to my force to start at [nine] o'clock at night to attack at four different points at daylight. A few days before General Price, in command of the Missouri force, turned over his command to me, and I assumed command of the entire force, comprising my own brigade, the brigade of Arkansas State forces under General Pearce, and General Price's command of Missourians.
>
> My effective force was 5,300 infantry, [fifteen] pieces of artillery, and 6,000 horsemen, armed with flint-lock muskets, rifles, and shotguns. There were other horsemen with the army who were entirely unarmed, and instead of being a help, were continually in the way. When the time arrived for the night march, it commenced to rain slightly, and fearing, from the want of cartridge boxes, that my ammunition would be ruined, I

ordered the movement to be stopped, hoping to move the next morning. Many of my men had but twenty rounds of ammunition, and there was no more to be had. While still hesitating in the morning the enemy were reported advancing, and I made arrangements to meet him. The attack was made simultaneously at 5.30 A.M. on our right and left flanks, and the enemy had gained the positions they desired. General Lyon attacked us on our left, and General Sigel on our right and rear. From these points batteries opened upon us. My command was soon ready. The Missourians, under Generals Slack, Clark, McBride, Parsons, and Rains, were nearest the position taken by General Lyon with his main force. They were instantly turned to the left, and opened the battle with an incessant fire of small-arms. Woodruff opposed his battery to that of the enemy under Captain Totten, and a constant cannonading was kept up between these batteries during the battle. Hébert's regiment of Louisiana volunteers and McIntosh's regiment of Arkansas Mounted Riflemen were ordered to the front, and after passing the battery turned to the left, and soon engaged the enemy with regiments deployed. Colonel McIntosh dismounted his regiment, and the two marched up abreast to a fence around a large corn field, when they met the left of the enemy already posted.

A terrible conflict of small-arms took place here. The opposing force was a body of regular United States infantry, commanded by Captains Plummer and Gilbert. Notwithstanding the galling fire poured upon these two regiments, they leaped over the fence and, gallantly led by their colonels, drove the enemy before them back upon the main body. During this time the Missourians, under General Price, were nobly attempting to sustain themselves in the center, and were hotly engaged on the sides of the height upon which the enemy were posted. Far on the right Sigel had opened his battery upon Churchill's and Greer's regiments, and had gradually made his way to the Springfield road, upon each side of which the army was encamped, and in a prominent position had established his battery. I at once took two companies of the Louisiana regiment which were nearest me, and marched them rapidly from the front and right to the rear, with orders to Colonel Mcintosh to bring up the rest.

When we arrived near the enemy's battery we found that Reid's battery had opened upon it, and it was already in confusion. Advantage was taken of it, and soon the Louisianians were gallantly charging among the guns, and swept the cannoneers away. Five guns were here taken, and Sigel's command, completely routed, were in rapid retreat with a single gun, followed by some companies of the Texas regiment and a portion of Colonel Major's Missouri regiment of cavalry. In the pursuit many of the enemy were killed and taken prisoners, and their last gun captured.

Having cleared our right and rear, it was necessary to turn all our attention to the center, under General Lyon, who was pressing upon the Missourians, having driven them back. To this point McIntosh's regiment, under Lieutenant-Colonel Embry, and Churchill's regiment on foot, Gratiot's regiment, and McRae's battalion were sent to their aid. A terrible fire of musketry was now kept up along the whole side and top of the hill upon which the enemy were posted. Masses of infantry fell back and again rushed forward. The summit of the hill was covered with the dead and wounded. Both sides were fighting with desperation for the day. Carroll's and Greer's regiments, led gallantly by Captain Bradfute, charged the battery (Totten's), but the whole strength of the enemy were immediately in rear, and a deadly fire was opened upon them.

At this critical moment, when the fortunes of the day seemed to be at the turning point, two regiments of General Pearce's brigade were ordered to march from their position (as reserves) to support the center. The order was obeyed with alacrity, and General Pearce gallantly marched with his brigade to the rescue. Reid's battery was also ordered to move forward and the Louisiana regiment was again called into action on the left of it. The battle then became general, and probably no two opposing forces ever fought with greater desperation. Inch by inch the enemy gave way, and were driven from their position. Totten's battery fell back. Missourians, Arkansans, Louisianans, and Texans pushed forward. The incessant roll of musketry was deafening, and the balls fell thick as hailstones, but still our gallant Southerners pushed onward, and with one wild yell broke upon the enemy, pushing them back and strewing the ground with their dead. Nothing could withstand the impetuosity of our final charge. The enemy fled, and could not again be rallied, and they were seen at [twelve mile] fast retreating among the hills in the distance. Thus ended the battle. It lasted six hours and a half. The force of the enemy, between nine and ten thousand, was composed of well-disciplined troops, well armed, and a large part of them belonging to the old Army of the United States. With every advantage on their side they have met with a signal repulse. The loss of the enemy is 800 killed, 1,000 wounded, and 300 prisoners. We captured six pieces of artillery, several hundred stand of small arms, and several of their standards.

Major General Lyon, chief in command, was killed, and many of their officers high in rank wounded. Our loss was also severe, and we mourn the death of many a gallant officer and soldier. Our killed amounts to 265, 800 wounded, and [thirty] missing. Colonel Weightman fell at the head of his brigade of Missourians while gallantly charging upon the enemy. His place will not easily be filled. Generals Slack and Clark, of Missouri, were severely wounded; General Price slightly. Captain Hinson, of the Louisiana regiment; Captain McAlexander, of Churchill's regiment; Captains Bell and Brown, of Pearce's brigade; Lieutenants Walton and Weaver, all fell while nobly and gallantly doing their duty. Colonel Mcintosh was slightly wounded by a grape shot while charging with the Louisiana regiment. Lieutenant-Colonel Neal, Maj. H. Ward, Captains King, Pearson, Gibbs, Ramsaur, Porter, Lieutenants Dawson, Chambers, Johnson, King, Adams, Hardesty, McIvor, and Saddler were wounded while at the head of their companies.

Where all were doing their duty so gallantly, it is almost unfair to discriminate. I must, however, bring to your notice the gallant conduct of the Missouri generals—McBride, Parsons, Clark, and Slack, and their officers. To General Price I am under many obligations for assistance on the battlefield. He was at the head of his force, leading them on, and sustaining them by his gallant bearing. General Pearce, with his Arkansas brigade (Gratiot's, Walker's, and Dockery's regiments of infantry), came gallantly to the rescue when sent for, leading his men into the thickest of the fight. He contributed much to the success of the day. The commanders of regiments of my own brigade--Colonels Churchill, Greer, Embry, Mcintosh, Hébert, and McRae--led their different regiments into action with the greatest coolness and bravery, always in front of their men, cheering them on. Woodruff, Bledsoe, and Reid managed their batteries with great ability, and did much execution. For those other officers and men who were particularly conspicuous I will refer the Department to the reports of the different commanders. To my personal staff I am much indebted for the coolness and rapidity with which they carried orders about the field, and would call your attention to my volunteer aides, Captain Bradfute, Messrs. Armstrong, Ben. Johnson (who had his horse killed under him), Hamilton Pike, and Major King. To Major Montgomery, quartermaster, I am also indebted for much service. He cheerfully volunteered his services as an aide during the battle, and was of much use to me. To Colonel Mcintosh, at one time at the head of his regiment and at other times in his capacity of adjutant-general, I cannot bestow too much praise. Wherever the balls flew thickest he was gallantly leading different regiments into action, and his presence gave confidence everywhere.[7]

McCulloch issued General Orders, Number 27, that same day:

The general commanding takes great pleasure in announcing to the army under his command the signal victory it has just gained. Soldiers of Louisiana, of Arkansas, of Missouri, and of Texas, nobly have you sustained yourselves! Shoulder to shoulder you have met the enemy and driven him before you. Your first battle has been glorious, and your general is proud of you. The opposing force, composed mostly of the old

Regular Army of the North, have thrown themselves upon you, confident of victory, but by great gallantry and determined courage you have entirely routed it with great slaughter. Several pieces of artillery and many prisoners are now in your hands. The commander-in-chief of the enemy is slain and many of the general officers wounded.

The flag of the Confederacy now floats over Springfield, the stronghold of the enemy. The friends of our cause who have been imprisoned there are released. Whilst announcing to the army this great victory, the general hopes that the laurels you have gained will not be tarnished by a single outrage. The private property of citizens of either party must be respected. Soldiers who fought as you did day before yesterday cannot rob or plunder.[8]

He wrote Walker again on the 13th:

The battle of the Oak Hills has been fought, and we have gained a great victory over the enemy, commanded by General N. Lyon and the battle was fought [ten] miles from Springfield. The enemy were nine or ten thousand strong; our forces about the same. The battle lasted six and a half hours. Enemy were repulsed and driven from the field, with loss of six pieces of artillery, 700 stands of small-arms, 800 killed, 1,000 wounded, and 300 prisoners. General Lyon was killed and many of their prominent officers. Our loss was 265 killed, 800 wounded, and [thirty] missing. We have possession of Springfield. The enemy are in full retreat towards Rolla.[9]

On August 15th, McCulloch issued the following proclamation from Springfield:

To the People of Missouri: Having been called by the governor of your State to assist in driving the federal forces out of the State and in restoring the people to their just rights, I have come among you simply with the view of making war upon our Northern foes, to drive them back, and give the oppressed of your State an opportunity of again standing up as free-men and uttering their true sentiments. You have been overrun and trampled upon by the mercenary hordes of the North. Your beautiful State has been nearly subjugated, but those true sons of Missouri who have continued in arms, together with my force, came back upon the enemy, and we have gained over them a great and signal victory. Their general-in-chief is slain and many of their other general officers wounded; their army is in full flight, and now, if the true men of Missouri will rise up and rally around their standard, the State will be redeemed.

I do not come among you to make war upon any of your people, whether Union or otherwise. The Union people will be protected in their fights and property. It is earnestly recommended to them to return to their homes. Prisoners of the Union party who have been arrested by the army will be released and allowed to return to their friends, Missouri must be allowed to choose her own destiny; no oaths binding your consciences will be administered. I have driven the enemy from among you. The time has now arrived for the people of the State to act; you cannot longer procrastinate. Missouri must now take her position, be it North or South.[10]

General Price wrote Claiborne Fox Jackson on the 12th:

SIR: I have the honor to submit to your excellency the following report of the operations of the army under my command at and immediately preceding the battle of Springfield: I began to move my command from its encampment on Cowskin Prairie, in McDonald County, on July 25 towards Cassville, in Barry County, at which place it had been agreed upon between Generals McCulloch, Pearce, and myself that our respective forces, together with those of Brigadier-General McBride, should be concentrated, preparatory to a forward movement.

We reached Cassville on Sunday, July 28, and on the next day affected a junction with the armies of Generals McCulloch and Pearce. The combined armies were then put under marching orders, and the First Division, General McCulloch commanding, left Cassville on August 1 upon the road to this city. The Second Division, under General Pearce, of Arkansas, left on August 1; and the Third Division, Brigadier-General Steele, of this State, commanding, left on August 2. I went forward with the Second Division, which embraced the greater portion of my infantry, and encamped with it some 12 miles northwest of Cassville.

The next morning a messenger from General McCulloch informed me that he had reason to believe that the enemy were [sic] in force on the road to Springfield, and that he should remain at his then encampment, on Crane Creek, until the Second and Third Divisions of the army had come up. The Second Division consequently moved forward to Crane Creek, and I ordered the Third Division to a position within three miles of the same place. An advance guard of the army, consisting of six companies of mounted Missourians, under command of Brigadier-General Rains, was at this time (Friday, August 2) encamped on the Springfield road, about five miles beyond Crane Creek.

About 9:00 A.M. of that day General Rains' pickets reported to him that they had been driven in by the enemy's advance guard, and that officer immediately led forward his whole force, amounting to nearly 400 men, until he found the enemy in position some three miles on the road. He sent back at once to General McCulloch for re-enforcements, and Colonel Mcintosh, C.S. Army, was sent forward with 150 men, but a reconnaissance of the ground having satisfied the latter that the enemy did not have more than 150 men on the ground, he withdrew his men and returned to Crane Creek. General Rains soon discovered, however, that he was in presence of the main body of the enemy, numbering, according to his estimate, more than 5.000 men, with eight pieces of artillery, and supported by a considerable body of cavalry. A severe skirmish ensued, which lasted several hours, until the enemy opened their batteries and compelled our troops to retire. In this engagement the greater portion of General Rains' command, and especially that part which acted as infantry, behaved with great gallantry, as the result demonstrates, for our loss was only I killed Lieutenant Northcut) and five wounded, while five of the enemy's dead were buried on the field, and a large number are known to have been wounded.

Our whole forces were concentrated the next day near Crane Creek, and during the same night the Texas regiment, under Colonel Greer, came up within a few miles of the same place. Reasons which will be hereafter assigned induced me on Sunday, the 4th instant, to put the Missouri forces under the direction, for the time being, of General McCulloch, who accordingly assumed the command in chief of the combined armies. A little after midnight we took up the line of march, leaving our baggage trams, and expected to find the enemy near the scene of the late skirmish, but we found as we advanced that they were retreating rapidly towards Springfield. We followed them hastily about [seventeen] miles to a place known as Moody's Spring, where we were compelled to halt our forces, who were already nearly exhausted by the intense heat of the weather and the dustiness of the roads.

Early the next morning we moved forward to Wilson's Creek, [ten] miles southwest of Springfield, where we encamped. Our forces were here put in readiness to meet the enemy, who were posted at Springfield to the number of about 10,000. It was finally decided to march against them in four separate columns at 9:00 o'clock that night, so as to surround the city and begin a simultaneous attack at daybreak. The darkness of the night and a threatened storm caused General McCulloch, just as the army was about to march, to countermand this order, and to direct that the troops should hold themselves in readiness to move whenever ordered. Our men were consequently kept under arms till towards daybreak, expecting momentarily an order to march.

The morning of Saturday, August 10, found them still encamped at Wilson's Creek, fatigued by a night's watching and loss of rest. About 6:00 o'clock I received a messenger [message] from General Rains that the enemy were advancing in great force from the direction of Springfield, and were already within 200 or 300 yards of the position, where he was encamped with the Second Brigade of his division consisting of about 1,200 mounted men, under Colonel Cawthorn. A second messenger came immediately afterwards from General Rains to announce that the main body of the enemy was upon him, but that he would endeavor to hold him in check until he could receive re-enforcements. General McCulloch was with me when these messengers came, and left at once for his own headquarters to make the necessary disposition of our forces. I rode forward instantly towards General Rains' position, at the same time ordering Generals Slack, McBride, Clark, and Parsons to move their infantry and artillery rapidly forward. I had ridden but a few hundred yards when I came suddenly upon the main body of the enemy, commanded by General Lyon in person. The infantry and artillery, which I had ordered to follow me, came up immediately, to the number of 2,036 men, and engaged the enemy.

A severe and bloody conflict ensued, my officers and men behaving with the greatest bravery, and with the assistance of a portion of the Confederate forces successfully holding the enemy in check. Meanwhile, and almost simultaneously with the opening of the enemy's batteries in this quarter, a heavy cannonading was opened upon the rear of our position, where a large body of the enemy, under Colonel Sigel, had taken position in close proximity to Colonel Churchill's regiment, Colonel Greer's Texan Rangers, and 679 mounted Missourians, under command of Colonel Brown and Lieutenant-Colonel Major. The action now became general, and was conducted with the greatest gallantry and vigor on both sides for more than five hours, when the enemy retreated in great confusion, leaving their commander-in-chief, General Lyon, dead upon the battlefield, over 500 killed, and a great number wounded.

"The forces under my command have possession of three [twelve]-pounder howitzers, two brass [six]-pounders, and a great quantity of small-arms and ammunition taken from the enemy; also the standard of Sigel's regiment, captured by Captain Staples. They have also a large number of prisoners. The brilliant victory thus achieved upon this hard-fought field was won only by the most determined bravery and distinguished gallantry of the combined armies, which fought nobly side by side in defense of their common fights and liberties with as much courage and constancy as were ever exhibited upon any battlefield. Where all behaved so well it is invidious to make any distinction, but I cannot refrain from expressing my sense of the splendid services rendered under my own eyes by the Arkansas infantry, under General Pearce; the Louisiana regiment of Colonel Hébert, and Colonel Churchill's regiment of mounted riflemen. These gallant officers and their brave soldiers won upon that day the lasting gratitude of every true

Missourian. This great victory was dearly bought by the blood of many a skillful officer and brave man.

Others will report the losses sustained by the Confederate forces. I shall willingly confine myself to the losses within my own army. Among those who fell mortally wounded upon the battle-field none deserve a dearer place in the memory of Missourians than Richard Hanson Weightman, colonel, commanding the First Brigade of the Second Division of the army. Taking up arms at the very beginning of this unhappy contest, he had already done distinguished services at the bat-tle of Rock Creek, of the lamented Holloway [sic], and at Carthage, where he won unfading laurels by the display of extraordinary coolness, courage, and skill. He fell at the head of his brigade, wounded in three places, and died just as the victorious shout of our army began to rise upon the air. Here, too, died in the discharge of his duty Colonel Ben. Brown of Ray County, president of the senate, a good man and true.

Brigadier-General Slack's division suffered severely. He himself fell dangerously wounded at the head of his column. Of his regiment of infantry, under Colonel John T. Hughes, consisting of about 650 men, [thirty-six] were killed, [seventy-six] wounded; many of them mortally, and [thirty] are missing. Among the killed were C.H. Bennett, adjutant of the regiment; Captain Blackburn, and Lieutenant Hughes. Colonel Rives' squadron of cavalry, dismounted, some 234 men, lost [four] killed and [eight] wounded. Among the former were Lieutenant-Colonel Austin and Captain Engart. Brigadier-General Clark was also wounded. His infantry, 200 men, lost in killed [seventeen], and wounded [seventy-one]. Colonel Burbridge was severely wounded; Captains Farris and Halleck and Lieutenant Haskins were killed. General Clark's cavalry, together with the Windsor Guards, were under the command of Lieutenant-Colonel Major, who did good service. They lost six killed and five wounded. Brigadier-General McBride's division, 605 men, lost [twenty-two] killed, [sixty-seven] severely wounded, and [fifty-seven] slightly wounded. Colonel Foster and Captains Nichols, Dougherty, Armstrong, and Mings were wounded while gallantly leading their respective commands. General Parsons' brigade, 256 infantry and artillery, under command, respectively, of Colonel Kelly and Captain Guibor, and 406 cavalry, under Colonel Brown, lost, the artillery, three killed and seven wounded; the infantry, nine killed and [thirty-eight] wounded; and the cavalry, three killed and two wounded. Colonel Kelly was wounded in the hand. Captain Coleman was mortally wounded, and has since died.

General Rains' division was composed of two brigades. The first, under Colonel Weightman, embracing infantry and artillery, 1,306 strong, lost not only their commander, but [thirty-four] others killed and

111 wounded. The Second Brigade, mounted men, Colonel Cawthorn commanding, about 1,200 strong, lost [twenty-one] killed and [seventy-five] wounded. Colonel Cawthorn was himself wounded, and Major Charles Rogers, of Saint Louis, adjutant of the brigade, was mortally wounded, and died the day after the battle. He was a gallant officer, and at all times vigilant and attentive to his duties, and fearless upon the field of battle. Your excellency will perceive that our State forces consisted of only 5,221 officers and men; that of those no less than 156 died upon the field, while 517 were wounded. These facts attest more powerfully than words can the severity of the conflict and the dauntless courage of our brave soldiers.

It is also my painful duty to announce the death of one of my aides, Lieutenant Colonel George W. Allen, of Saline County. He was shot down while communicating an order, and we left him buried on the field. I have appointed to the position thus sadly vacated Capt. James T. Cearnel, in recognition of his gallant conduct and valuable services throughout the battle as a volunteer aide. Another of my staff, Col. Horace Brand, was made prisoner by the enemy, but has since been released.

My thanks are due to three of your staff-Colonel William M. Cook, Richard Gaines, and Thomas L. Snead—for the services which they rendered me as volunteer aides, and also to my aide-de-camp, Colonel A. W. Jones. In conclusion, I beg leave to say to your excellency that the army under my command, both officers and men, did their duty nobly, as became men fighting in defense of their homes and their honor, and that they deserve well of their State.[11]

After fighting in the conflict alongside Quantrill, Frank James developed a case of the measles and stayed behind at a hotel in Springfield. He was captured by Union troops but released upon his word of honor that he would return home and not fight again for the remainder of the war. Frank did go home to Clay County but did not keep his word to remain a noncombatant. Instead, he joined Price's army in time to fight in the Battle of Lexington.[12]

Union Brigadier-General Benjamin Loan complained to his superiors regarding the resentment of Missouri's pro-Southern citizens: "The inhabitants are generally disloyal, and a large majority of them are actively so. They are fierce, overbearing, defiant and insulting; whilst the Union spirit is cowed and disposed to be submissive . . . [forcing me] to have these disloyal persons arrested . . . to break up the social relations here. Good society here, as it is termed, is exclusively rebel . . . the traders, merchants and bankers who transact the business of the country are all traitors."[13]

On August 24th, Governor Hamilton R. Gamble issued a proclamation calling for 82,000 men for six months to protect the property and lives of the citizens of the State. Colonel H.P. Johnson assumed command of the Fifth Kansas at Fort Scott that same month. James Montgomery had gathered a regiment together, and five companies of the Third Kansas under him arrived at Fort Scott on the 20th of August. Other Kansas troops arrived until the aggregate force was about 2,000 men.[14]

Fort Scott was served as headquarters for General Lane's brigade. The Confederate Generals, Price and Raines, were operating in Western Missouri with several thousand men, and contemplated an attack on Southeastern Kansas. On the first of September, General Raines with his division approached within twelve miles of Fort Scott, on the southeast, and a scouting party came within two miles of town and captured a corral full of mules, and drove in Lane's pickets.

Colonel James H. Lane's cavalry, comprising about 600 men, set out from Fort Scott to learn the whereabouts of a rumored Confederate force. They encountered a Confederate force, about 6,000 strong under General Price, near Big Dry Wood Creek. The Union cavalry surprised the Confederates, but their numerical superiority soon determined the encounter's outcome. They forced the Union cavalry to retreat to Fort Scott and captured their mules, and the Confederates continued on towards Lexington. The Confederates were forcing the federals to abandon southwestern Missouri and to concentrate on holding the Missouri Valley.[15]

The federal infantry, however, occupied the heights east and southeast of town. These troops were reinforced by an impromptu company organized that morning. This company was sworn into service, drew arms and ammunition, and marched to the front in two rows like regulars. The entire force waited on the crest of the hill until night for the expected attack of General Raines. About dark, a raging thunderstorm commenced and the raw recruits returned to town and sought shelter in camp.[16]

That night General Lane ordered the entire force to fall back on Fort Lincoln, twelve miles north, on the Osage, leaving Fort Scott to the mercy of the enemy. General Raines, however, was at that moment conducting a forced march on Lexington by an order received that day from General Price, and Fort Scott thus escaped utter annihilation.[17]

Price decided to follow up his victory at Wilson's Creek by marching north and attempting to win back the towns along the Missouri River. He hoped his march would lead to his recapturing Jefferson City so he could place Jackson back in control of the state government.

While General Price was advancing northeast to Lexington, a body of 2,700 federals under the command of Colonel James A. Mulligan had fortified themselves inside the grounds of the white-pillared, three-storied brick building of the Masonic College on the northern end of town. Around it federal troops had constructed a rampart of sod and earth twelve feet high and twelve feet thick. Beyond was an irregular line of earthworks and rifle pits protected by wire, stakes, and ditches. Patiently waiting behind these obstacles were 3,500 men and seven cannons.

By the first day of the battle, September 18th, Price's army had swelled to 10,000 to 12,000 men and more recruits were pouring in daily from the surrounding countryside. With the strains of "Dixie" in the air, Price's men marched through Lexington and completely encircled the college. For the next nine hours, the huddled Unionists received a galling and continuous bombardment of shot and shell. Meanwhile, the Southerners seized Oliver Anderson's house, which was then serving as a Union hospital. Outraged by what he considered a breach of the etiquette of war, Colonel Mulligan ordered the house to be retaken; in a bloody countercharge, his men stormed the house and took heavy casualties. Soon after, the house changed hands for a third time as the guardsmen drove the Yankees back to their trenches.

On the second day of the battle, the bombardment was continued and the lines around the college were drawn in and tightened. The entrapped blue coats had run out of water by then and were suffering greatly from thirst and heat. The siege ended on the third day in a dramatic and unusual way. The Southerners had discovered a quantity of hemp bales in a nearby warehouse and arranged these bales in a line on the west side of the Union entrenchments. They then began rolling the bales ever closer to the line of trenches. The panicked federals unleashed their artillery into the moving breastwork, but their cannon balls had little effect on the dense bales. By early afternoon, the snakelike line of bales had advanced close enough to the Union trenches for a charge, and the defenders of that sector engaged in a brief but bloody hand-to-hand fight before being driven back into their entrenchments. Mulligan and most of his officers were wounded, and he realized that the time for surrender had come.

The casualty count from the Battle of Lexington was twenty-five killed and seventy-five wounded on Price's side, while the federals had thirty-nine killed and 120 wounded. Price did experience some immediate gains from the battle. He captured five artillery pieces, 3,000 rifles, and 750 horses, all of which were highly beneficial to his under-equipped army. Beyond that, he returned some $900,000 that the federals had looted from the local bank, and he became a hero throughout the South. But his long-term gains were less significant.

In response to the defeat at Lexington, the Union commander in Missouri, General John C. Fremont, mounted a massive force to drive Price from Missouri. In the face of this threat, Price had little choice but to retreat back to southwest Missouri. Lexington and the Missouri River Valley once again returned to Union control.

The Fifth Kansas followed to Morristown, where, on the 17th of September, an attack was made on a rebel force. Colonel Johnson was shot while leading the charge, at the head of his regiment. He was a brave and accomplished officer, beloved by his soldiers, and it was long before the regiment recovered from the effects of the loss of its leader, while yet comparatively undisciplined, and unaccustomed to the reality of war. In the engagement at Morristown, James M. Copeland, of Fort Scott, was killed, and several of the regiment were wounded. The Confederates retreated, and the Union force, after taking possession of their horses, camp equipage, and other effects, moved to West Point, Missouri, thence, with the Third and Fourth Kansas, to Osceola, at which point the rear of the rebel force, then occupying Lexington, was attacked, and large quantities of stores destroyed. General Price, making a feint of advancing on Kansas City, before evacuating Lexington for his retreat to the southwest of Missouri, the Fifth was ordered to that city.

Notes

[1]"War on the Border," Missouri Department of Natural Resources.

[2]Reports of Brig. Gen. Ben. McCulloch, C.S. Army, with orders and proclamation. August 4, 1861. Battle of Oak Hills, Springfield, or Wilson's Creek, Missouri, Official Records of the Rebellion, Series I, Volume 3 [S #3].

[3]Report of Brig. Gen. Nathaniel Lyon, U.S. Army, commanding Army of the West, of operations August 5-9, August 10, 1861. Battle of Oak Hills, Springfield, or Wilson'sCreek, Mo. Official Records of the Rebellion. Series 1, Volume 3.

[4]Reports of Col. Franz Sigel, Third Missouri Infantry, commanding Army of the West. Auguest 10, 1861. Battle of Oak Hills, Springfield, or Wilson's Creek, Missouri, Official Records of the Rebellion, Series I, Volume 3 [S# 3].

[5]Ibid., August 18, 1861.

[6]Report of Brig. Gen. Ben. McCulloch, C.S. Army to L.P. Walker, Auguest 10, 1861. Battle of Oak Hills, Springfield, or Wilson's Creek, Missouri, Official Records of the Rebellion, Series 1, Volume 3 [S #3].

[7]Report of Brig. Gen. Ben. McCulloch, C.S. Army to Adjutant General S. Cooper, Auguest 12, 1861. Battle of Oak Hills, Springfield, Official Records of the Rebellion, Series I, Volume 3 [S #3].

[8]Brig. Gen. Ben McCulloch, General Order, Number 27, August 12, 1861, Official Records of the Rebellion, Series 1, Volume 3 [S #3].

[9]Report of Brig. Gen. Ben. McCulloch, C.S. Army to L.P. Walker, Auguest 13, 1861. Battle of Oak Hills, Springfield, Official Records of the Rebellion, Series 1, Volume 3 [S #3].

[10]Brig. Gen. Ben McCulloch "Proclamation to the People of Missouri," August 15, 1861. Official Records of the Rebellion, Series I, Volume 3 [S #3].

[11]Report of Maj. Gen. Sterling Price, Commanding Missouri State Guard, of Operations from July 25 to August 11, Auguest 10, 1861. Battle of Oak Hills, Springfield, or Wilson's Creek, Missouri, Official Records of the Rebellion, Series 1, Volume 3 [S #3].

[12]Robert L. Dyer, *Jesse James and the Civil War in Missouri*, Columbia, University of Missouri Press, 1994, p. 26; Phillip W. Steele, *Jesse and Frank James: The Family History*, Gretna, Louisiana, Pelican Publishing Company, 1987, p. 46.

[13]Scott E. Sallee, "Porter's Campaign in Northeast Missouri, 1862, Including the Palmyra Massacre," *Blue & Gray*, Winter 2000, p. 7.

[14]T.F. Robley, *Robley's History of Bourbon County*, 1894.

[15]Albert Castel, *General Sterling Price and the Civil War in the West*, Baton Rouge & London, Lousiana State University Press, 1968, pp. 48-50.

[16]T.F. Robley, *Robley's History of Bourbon County*.

[17]Albert Castel, *General Sterling Price and the Civil War in the West*, pp. 48-50.

Chapter Five

On the Run

"Come with your guns of any description that can be made to bring down a foe. If you have no arms, come without them. . . . Bring blankets and heavy shoes and extra bed clothing if you have them. . . . We must have 50,000 men."

—General Sterling Price[1]

J IM LANE, LONG BEFORE 1861, had threatened to make a raid on Osceola, for the purpose of robbing the bank. Osceola, at that time, was the great metropolis of southwest Missouri, and in fact, it was the greatest commercial city west of Jefferson City or southwest of Boonville. The people of St. Clair County had nothing to do with casting illegal votes in the Kansas election, nor had they taken any part in the border war.[2]

About the first of December 1860, Jim Lane collected together about 150 of his followers and started for Osceola. After moving his band as far east as Papinville, he retraced his steps back across the border line, and his band disbanded, subject to the call of their leader. The cause of his sudden change of mind was that the citizens of St. Clair County had been informed of his planned attack, and had collected in force for the defense of the city. Fully 500 well-armed men were ready to meet him, and they remained on guard until all danger was over. Lane refused to abandon his scheme of a raid on Osceola.

When the war broke out, Illinois joined with Kansas and sent untold numbers of plunderers into the richest districts of Missouri. Banks were robbed, the wealthiest citizens plundered, stock driven off, and wagons and teams stolen and loaded with the goods taken from the people, and wearing apparel and jewelry of every description taken from the ladies. There never was a richer field for plunder than Missouri in 1861.

The citizens of Osceola wasted little time in procuring arms. Old men and boys alike, regardless of age, formed themselves into home guards for protection against the numerous bands of outlaws that overran the state. Guerilla bands were organized all along the bloody border, and a Jayhawker and guerilla war began in earnest. Old men and boys were murdered by the Jayhawker bands for opinions' sake, and "blood for blood" became the rallying cry.

As men were rushing off to join the regular army, the Missouri border was left pretty much unprotected, and the Jayhawkers widened their field of operations. In September 1861, while General Price's army was at Lexington, and no Confederate soldiers were in St. Clair County, except a few stragglers and recruiting officers, Lane considered his chance for carrying out his long neglected threat of burning and sacking Osceola.

The town of 2,000 stood on the right or south bank of the Osage River, being situated upon a beautiful elevation of 200 feet above the riverbed and surrounded by beautiful, rolling ridges, at the foot of which gushed forth springs of sparkling water. St. Clair County had been settled up by a thrifty and enterprising people, who turned their attention largely to stock raising, and a majority of them had grown wealthy before hostilities began. Men of wealth and enterprise bought property in Osceola and went into business. The town was considered at the head of navigation, although the boats had ascended as far up the stream as Taberville, at or near the western boundary of the county. Boats ascended the river as far as Osceola regularly before the breaking out of the war, and the town became the great shipping point for eleven counties in the Southwest, and goods were also hauled from this point to Benton County, Arkansas. The town had grown to large proportions, with twelve or fifteen businesses, and several did wholesale as well as retail business.

On September 22, 1861, Lane assembled 200 of his band, and from a point near Fort Scott, made a bee line for the town. The bank deposits, amounting to about $150,000, had been removed to other cities for better security, as the directors knew the exposed condition of the place, and Lane's desire to raid the town. The Jayhawkers proceeded down the south side of the Osage River from Fort Scott to Osceola, a distance of about sixty miles. They crossed Sac River, a small stream that emptied into the Osage two miles above Osceola at the Waldo Ford.

On the 23rd of September, at about eight o'clock P.M., Lane and his band entered the town with torches in hand and two pieces of artillery. No Confederate soldiers were occupying the town at the time of their entrance, but Captain John M. Weidemeyer and forty men chanced to be in the vicinity, and as Lane entered the town, they fired upon him from the brush, and then slowly retreated in the direction of Warsaw.

Instead of pursuing Weidemeyer, the Jayhawkers burst open the doors of the bank and removed the safe that had contained the money, and blew it open, but only a few private papers of no value to anyone except the owners rewarded them for their trouble. Frustrated, Lane flew into a towering rage and swore that the whole town should suffer the consequences and be burned and pillaged. His men were ordered to search the town for anything of value. No citizens from the country were allowed to pass the pickets under any circumstances during the pillaging.

When Lane's troops found a cache of Confederate military supplies in the town, Lane decided to wipe Osceola from the map. First, Osceola was stripped of all of its valuable goods, which were loaded into wagons taken from the townspeople. Nine Osceola citizens were given a speedy trial and were shot by the Jayhawkers. Lane's men went on a wild drinking spree and brought their frenzy of pillaging, murder, and drunkenness to a close by burning the entire town.

The morning of the 24th, Dr. John Trollinger and three companions wished to cross the river into town, not knowing that it was infested by Lane and his band. They arrived on the opposite side of the river and hallooed for a skiff to bring them over. This was done, but no sooner were they safely landed than they were fired upon by fifty to sixty Jayhawkers. The doctor received eleven buckshot wounds, though none serious, but a friend named Summers was shot in the mouth with a minnie ball, which carried away a part of his jawbone and injured him for life. The other two managed to escape, leaving their horses in the hands of the enemy.

As Zachariah Lilley, one of the old pioneers of the county, was fording the river on horseback, aiming to come to town, he was fired upon by the guard, and had to wheel his horse and dash into the timber with bullets whistling around him. The Jayhawkers fired on everyone who dared approach the town. By night the pillage was over, and a large wagon train had been loaded with the spoils. Negroes swarmed around Lane and were permitted to load themselves down with goods of every description. What was considered of little value or too bulky for easy removal was thrown into the streets. Hundreds of barrels of whiskey had their heads knocked out, and the contents formed little rivulets and ran into the river. The courthouse was broken open and the county records destroyed. Lane ordered his men to scatter and apply the torch to every house in town. The band went to work, and soon the business portion of the town was a seething mass of flames.

The fire leaped from house to house. The flames and smoke seemed to have reached their element, but still the storm raged on. The county buildings were soon enveloped by the devouring fiend, but still the flames soared. It was not long before the entire city was a smoking mass of ruins. Not even the women and children were allowed to move anything from their burning houses, and much suffering was the result.

Soon the work of destruction was finished. Lane and his men started with their plunder for Kansas. In Lane's official report to the government he said he had taken $1,000,000 worth of goods away with him.

In late October, a rump convention, convened by Governor Claiborne Fox Jackson, met in Neosho and passed an ordinance of secession. Ransacking and looting continued between the Kansas Jayhawkers and Redlegs throughout the border counties along the Kansas/Missouri state line. Doc Jennison, in one of his raids into Missouri, passed through Jasper, Jackson, and Cass Counties and sacked and burned the town of Harrisonville.[3]

Henry Younger's livery was not exempt from these raids, and in 1861, his business netted a loss of over $4,000 in merchandise during one of these assaults. Several vehicles from his extensive livery were stolen and forty head of horses were confiscated. Over the next year, he would be hit again on several occasions. This angered his son, Cole, who encouraged his father to take a stand against the Kansans, but Henry resisted.

Despite the attacks on his businesses and properties by the Redlegs, Colonel Younger managed to maintain control over the family's wealth.

Willing to put aside the atrocities committed against him, he hoped to see reconciliation between the Union and the fractious South. He regularly invited federal officers to social activities in the Younger home.[4]

On the night of December 15, 1861, Cole, Jim, Sally, and Caroline attended a dance at the home of Colonel Cuthbert and Sarah Mockbee near Harrisonville in honor of their daughter Martha. Mockbee and all in attendance were Southerners, but when a Union militiaman, Captain Irvin Walley, who was stationed at Harrisonville, stopped in, trouble was inevitable. Although he was a married man, Captain Walley insisted that the girls dance with him. When the belles refused, he grabbed Cole's sister and tried to force her to dance with him. Cole, only seventeen, stepped in, and words were exchanged in which Walley asked Cole where Quantrill was hiding. When Cole said he did not know, Walley called him a liar, and Cole responded by knocking him to the floor with a devastating punch to the chin. When Walley pulled a pistol, Cole's friends intervened.[5]

With the Union officer stunned, Cole fled to the brush. Taking to the thicket was not a difficult measure for a Southern sympathizer, since ninety-five percent of the farmers were also Confederate supporters. Plus, wild game was aplenty, and friends were quick to supply him with milk, cheese, and ham.[6]

E.F. Rogers later related his experiences as an officer in the federal army fighting Cole younger, when "not a blot stained his character." Early in the war, Rogers was stationed at Harrisonville, Missouri, where he attended the dance with Captain Walley. According to Rogers, Walley, after dancing with a lady, asked for another, but she informed him she was "engaged" to Cole Younger for that particular dance. Captain Walley was enraged, told Cole he would make no disturbance that evening but would kill him the first opportunity. The captain, according to Rogers, was a vicious man. Cole remained a gentleman through the affair.[7]

After learning of the incident, Henry felt that Cole's safety was at stake, and the Union troops would seek revenge. Henry suggested that Cole leave town and go to the farm in Jackson County as Walley was determined to get him. Henry's instincts proved right when that same evening, Walley did show up at the Younger home accusing Cole of being a spy for Quantrill and demanding that Cole be turned over to him. Henry Younger denounced the charge as a lie.

When Captain Walley learned that Cole had slipped into Jackson County, he reported him as having joined Quantrill's Raiders. Soon, Walley, leading a company of Missouri State Militia, entered the county intending upon arresting Cole, but the party was unable to find him. Cole got word to his father that he "was tired of running like a wild beast, and would not do it much longer without hurting someone."[8]

Colonel A.G. Nugent, in charge of the militia in Harrisonville, also demanded Cole's surrender. Henry and Bursheba wanted Cole to go away to school, and even though he personally wanted to stay and fight the charges, he consented to leave. He quickly found, however, that the railroad stations were being watched, and he had little choice but to remain in the area.[9]

After wandering aimlessly through the bushes, Cole came upon the house of a woman who had earlier refused to give information regarding him to Captain Walley. He was warmly received by the woman and her family and was given food and lodging. In the morning Cole was told that Quantrill was encamped on the Little Blue River in Jackson County.[10]

Cole spent several nights at the home until one morning the woman's brother, having just returned from Harrisonville, awakened him and related that Captain Walley had stolen Cole's father's blooded bays. Captain Walley had gone to Henry's farm and asked to hire the bays and a buggy. Not wishing to widen the breach between the officer and Cole, Henry allowed him to take them.

When, after several days, Henry confronted Walley and demanded his property, the officer snapped his fingers in his face and declared he had decided to keep the horses. Henry reported the incident to the governor, but no action was taken. Infuriated, Cole told the family he was leaving to find Quantrill and strike back at the enemy. The woman urged him to take arms and supplies with him.

Cole rushed into the woods in search of Quantrill's camp on the Little Blue. Armed with both a shotgun and revolver, he was deeply aware of General John C. Fremont's August 30th ruling that any Missourian carrying a gun would be killed. Fremont also passed an edict that all slaves in Missouri were declared free, although President Lincoln promptly overruled this.[11]

When Cole reached Quantrill's encampment, he was greeted by cheers from the guerrillas. According to one source, there were only eight men with Quantrill. Of the eight, Cole knew William Haller, George Todd, Oliver and

118

Al Shepherd, and Kit Childs. Cole's presence in the force pleased Quantill because of Cole's knowledge of the topography.[12]

Cole later wrote that he joined the Missouri guerillas that winter of 1861 with his brother-in-law John Jarrette. Jarrette temporarily became an orderly sergeant before being promoted to an officer, probably because, according to Cole, his brother-in-law never knew fear.[13] William Gregg, on the other hand, insisted that he and Cole were sworn into service together at Widow Ingraham's farm, Jackson County, Missouri, about the 14th day of August 1862, by Colonel Gideon W. Thompson for three years or the duration of the war.[14]

Colonel Thompson, a Missouri recruiting agent, later stated in 1898 that he had sworn Cole into the regular Confederate Army on August 8, 1862. A copy of Colonel Thompson's notarized affidavit was found in the Pinkerton Historical Archives.[15]

Confederate records indicate that he enlisted in Captain John Jarrette's company, Colonel Upton B. Hays' regiment, which was part of General Jo Shelby's Brigade, and he was admitted as a first lieutenant. Shelby's Brigade was recognized by Southerners as part of the Confederacy with official status. However, many of the men in Shelby's unit rode with him one month and Quantrill the next.[16]

Cole later told an interviewer he had always been a strong admirer of William Clarke Quantrill, whom he was closely associated with during the war. Enrolling was a simple procedure. All a recruit had to do was answer "Yes" to the question: "Will you follow orders, be true to your fellows, and kill all those who serve and support the Union?"[17]

Cole, however, later penned a letter to author J.A. Dacus in which he called the rumors of "The Black Oath" absolutely ridiculous. According to several persons, the oath was taken by new recruits into Quantrill's army, which Cole termed, "a myth originating in the brain of some irresponsible, badly informed and reckless chronicler." Cole also blasted the myth that Missouri guerrillas were not recognized by the Confederacy as Confederate soldiers. These men took the same oath as all Confederate soldiers and were recognized as soldiers of the South by all the generals in the Trans-Mississippi Department. Cole maintained that the mix-up may have occurred because the Confederate War Department had refused to give Quantrill a commission as Colonel of partisan rangers; but they did recognize him as captain with all authority to recruit as many companies for the Confederate service as he could.[18]

During January and February of the new year, the federals issued a series of orders designed to discourage Southern sympathizers. On January 8, 1862, Provost Marshal Bernard G. Farrar, of St. Louis, issued General Order Number 10 in reference to newspapers: "It is hereby ordered that from and after this date the publishers of newspapers in the State of Missouri (St. Louis City papers excepted), furnish to this office, immediately upon publication, one copy of each issue, for inspection. A failure to comply with this order will render the newspaper liable to suppression. Local Provost Marshals will furnish the proprietors with copies of this order, and attend to its immediate enforcement."

General Henry Halleck issued General Order 18 on the 26th which forbade, among other things, the display of Secession flags in the hands of women or on carriages, in the vicinity of the military prison in McDowell's College, the carriages to be confiscated and the offending women to be arrested. The bushwhackers were furious. General Halleck issued another order similar to Order No. 18 on February 4th to railroad companies and to the professors and directors of the State University at Columbia, forbidding the funds of the institution to be used "to teach treason or to instruct traitors."

Major General Henry W. Halleck ("Old Brains"). (Courtesy of the National Archives)

120

On February 20th, Special Order No. 120 convened a military commission, which sat in Columbia, and tried Edmund J. Ellis, of Columbia, editor and proprietor of *The Boone County Standard* for the publication of information for the benefit of the enemy, and encouraging resistance to the United States Government. Ellis was found guilty, was banished during the war from Missouri, and his printing materials confiscated and sold.

The forty men in Cole's company were eager for action. "My Grandmother Fristoe used to ask me if I ever prayed before I went to battle," explained Cole after the war. "I told her I always did, which was true. I never rode where the bullets were whistling around me without murmuring a prayer. But I did not tell dear old Grandma that ten minutes after I got into a fight I was cussin' loud enough to be heard a mile. She intended me to be a preacher, but I missed it."[19]

Cole and his men decided one of their first strikes should be against Jennison's Jayhawkers in Kansas, who had raided Henry Younger's farm the year before and driven off his horses and cattle. Although they scoured the border, they found no trace of Jennison or Colonel Younger's stock. Disappointed, they rode back to Missouri, not knowing that Captain Albert P. Peabody, commanding Company D, First Missouri Cavalry, had gathered a force of a hundred federal soldiers and Jayhawkers and were on their trail.[20]

Quantrill, Cole, and company reached the home of a friend named John Flannery in Jackson County in January 1862, where they planned to rest their horses and refresh themselves. While the Union soldiers surrounded the house, Captain Peabody pounded on the front door. Quantrill thrust his head from an upstairs window and asked what he wanted. Peabody demanded his immediate surrender and told him the house was surrounded. Quantrill asked for ten minutes, saying he had to consult with his men.

But Quantrill had no intention of surrendering. Quantrill established his men at the windows of the house, stationing Cole at the attic window of the loft. When everyone was in place, the chieftain opened the front door, allegedly shouted, "Quantrill's guerrillas never surrender," and firing his double barreled shotgun, brought down Peabody's first lieutenant. The other bushwhackers unleashed a deadly fire killing or wounding several of the soldiers.

The Jayhawkers returned the fire and for two hours the battle raged. During the fray, Cole shouted out to Quantrill that there were flames in the attic. He was immediately called downstairs, and while some of the guerrillas continued shooting at the enemy, the others held a council.

Their only chance lay in a sortie, but unless the attention of the soldiers could be distracted by a ruse, there was little hope of escape. The roof of the main portion of the house was blazing as the fire continued to spread, and part of it had collapsed as they discussed their precarious situation. Finding two of his men missing and one wounded, Quantrill told Cole to find them and had the rest of the men gather all the pillows and hats they could find. Cole found the two missing men hiding under a bed, and despite his efforts to get them out, they refused and were burned to death.

Cole reported to his leader, who was ordering the men to place the pillows with hats on them in every window. While the federals reloaded, Quantrill led his men out in a desperate charge for freedom, the bushwhackers discharging their weapons as they ran through the lines. Pursued by the enemy, Quantrill's party crashed into a picket fence. While they tumbled over it, bullets sailed over their heads, but all the men except Cole escaped into the woods.

Cole allegedly took over and fired round after round at the enemy while his comrades scrambled to safety. When he finally halted and dashed into the thicket, his friends were nowhere to be seen. Rushing across an open area, Peabody's men fired at him, mounted their horses, and followed in close pursuit. Cole returned the fire, which initially slowed his adversaries but Peabody's men had no intention of abandoning the chase. After a running battle, Cole again made the woods and lost his enemies.

The bushwhackers were continually on the run when not on the offensive. In the spring of 1862, George Shepherd, Oliver Shepherd, and Cole Younger were trapped in the home of George's brother in Jackson County. Although heavily outnumbered, Cole proposed to lead a charge out from the house when several other Quantrill men attacked the federals from the rear creating a diversion and enabling the boys to escape into the woods.

George Shepherd, one of the more well-known bushwhackers, often rode with Cole during this period of the war. Born on a farm near Independence in Jackson County on January 17, 1842, he joined the troops of Albert Sidney Johnston, who were fighting the Mormons in Utah, when he was only fifteen. He returned to Missouri in 1859 to resume operating the family farm with his brothers, John, James, and William.

Because his family had come from Virginia, he joined the Confederate volunteers when the Civil War broke out and first saw action at the Battle of Wilson's Creek where he met Frank James. He then saw action at the Battle of Pea Ridge in Arkansas where Confederate General Ben McCulloch was killed by a Union sharpshooter. When General Price and his men were ordered east of the Mississippi River, Shepherd went home to Jackson County and joined Quantrill's band.

The guerrillas learned that a Union military force under Lieutenant Colonel John T. Burris was conducting raids on the Independence area and Shepherd, like the other bushwhackers, was furious. Cole later pointed out via an interview the importance of controlling the city:

> Independence was, for a long time previous to the war with Mexico, headquarters for Mexican freighters. The freight passing between Mexico and Missouri was carried on pack-mules, many Jackson County-men being engaged in that business. It was in Jackson County chiefly, also, that Colonel Doniphan recruited his famous regiment for the Mexican war and made that wonderful march known in history as De rando del murato, (the journey of death). After subduing New Mexico, Doniphan marched to Chihuahua, which then had 40,000 inhabitants, and raised the United States flag over the citadel; and from this latter place he continued his march to the Gulf of Mexico.
>
> Independence became also the headquarters and fitting-out post of the Forty-Niners when the great pilgrimage to California began. Majors, Russell & Waddell, the greatest overland freighters the world has ever produced, lived in Independence. In the war of 1856 Jackson County and the settlement about Independence especially, was more largely represented, perhaps, than any other section. This diabolical war, distinguished by the most atrocious cruelties the conqueror can inflict upon his captive, prepared the way, and created the guerrilla in 1862. Natural fighters, conducting a war of spoliation and reprisal—through the brush—trained to quick sorties and deadly ambuscades, how easily they drifted as their instincts inclined, and became guerrillas by an irresistible combination of circumstances, such as I have explained.[21]

On November 10, 1861, the guerrillas struck the federal camp at sunset, and although outnumbered eighty-four to thirty-two, a Confederate volley broke the Union ranks in confusion. Five federals died in the first fire and seven more in the chase. The remaining blue coats rushed into Independence and were saved by their regiment. Cole was proud to have killed a federal with a pistol shot from seventy-one yards away.

Bloody warfare in Independence and the surrounding area continued all through that winter. Captain William S. Oliver, Seventh Missouri Infantry, wrote from Independence on February 3rd:

> I have just returned from an expedition which I was compelled to undertake in search of the notorious Quantrill and his gang of robbers in the vicinity of Blue Springs. Without mounted men at my disposal, despite numerous applications to various points, I have seen this infamous scoundrel rob mails, steal the coaches and horses, and commit other similar outrages upon society even within sight of this city. Mounted on the best horses in the country, he has defied pursuit, making his camp in the bottoms of the _____ and Blue, and roving over a circle of [thirty] miles. I mounted a company of my command and went to Blue Springs. The first night there myself, with three men, were ambushed by him and fired upon. We killed two of his men (of which he had [eighteen] or [twenty]) and wounded a third. The next day we killed four more of the worst of the gang, and before we left succeeded in dispersing them. I obtained six or seven wagon loads and a quantity of tobacco, hidden and preserved for the use of the Southern Army, and recovered also the valuable stagecoach with two of their horses. I was absent a week, and can say that no men were ever more earnest or subject to greater privations and hardships than both the mounted men and the infantry I employed on this expedition.
>
> Quantrill will not leave this section unless he is chastised and driven from it. I hear of him tonight [fifteen] miles from here, with new recruits, committing outrages on Union men, a large body of whom have come in tonight, driven out by him. Families of Union men are coming into the city tonight asking of me escorts to bring in their goods and chattels, which I duly furnished.[22]

Also in February, Captain Quantrill, David Poole, Bill Gregg, George Shepherd, George Todd, and Cole Younger charged in pairs down three streets to the courthouse, while the rest of the men in the company joined them from other streets. Although the guerrillas escaped with badly needed ammunition and supplies, eleven of their men were wounded in the fray. Seven federal militiamen died in the attack.

Another charge into Independence was conducted at daybreak on February 21st. Expecting to be confronted by one militia company, there were four, and although seventeen Unionists were killed, a young man in Quantrill's company was also killed. The band disbanded once they had reached safety, for Quantrill felt it was more difficult to track one man than a whole company. Quantrill's battle policy of strike and disband worked effectively as they could easily rally again at a moment's notice.

During late February, with the weather extremely cold, Quantrill, Cole, and the guerrillas went into camp on Indian Creek in Jackson County, only ten miles from Independence. Learning of the bushwhacker position, Colonel James T. Buel set out from Independence with 200 men for Indian Creek. The federals quickly surrounded Quantrill's camp, although their cavalry could not penetrate the defensive position of the bushwhacker breastworks.

On the morning of the 26th, a shell exploded in Quantrill's camp when the federals opened up with two pieces of artillery. The Confederate pickets were driven in and a surprised Quantrill found that every avenue of escape had been shut off. A guerrilla named William Haller suggested to Quantrill that they look to Cole Younger for an answer because of his thorough knowledge of the countryside and acts of daring already performed.

Cole conveyed to Quantrill that inside the federal lines stood an old farmhouse and several head of cattle in the yards. He suggested they hold the enemy in check until nightfall, make every indication of a stubborn resistance, and then stampede the stock. According to Cole, the stampede would confuse the enemy, draw their fire, and make escape possible.

The fighting continued all day with the loss of several federals. As night came on, the bushwhackers felled several more trees and strengthened their defensive position. The noise deceived the federals in the unusually dark night, and with heavy clouds and the absence of a moon, Cole Younger, William Haller, Dave Pool, and George Todd slipped unseen through the gloom.

Within minutes, a terrible commotion emanated from the barnyard as howling dogs and cackling chickens made way for a dozen charging cattle. Believing they were being attacked by Quantrill's army, the federals unleashed a series of pistol shots at the flying figures. During the chaos, Quantrill and his band escaped in the shadows.

In the morning, the guerrillas positioned themselves in the rear of the federals preparing for an attack engineered by Cole Younger. Quantrill knew the position of the battery and that the federal line would not be able to withstand a determined assault. Cole led the charge on the surprised artillerymen and the battery was quickly captured. As a large federal cavalry force under Doc Jennison approached, Colonel Buel mistook them for Colonel Upton Hays' Confederate force, and opened fire. Taking advantage of the situation, Quantrill rushed among the stunned infantrymen and turned the battery loose on the foe.

Seeing Buel's force cut to pieces, Jennison believed the bushwhackers had mounted a great force, and he withdrew his men. The guerrillas, however, turned from their annihilation of Buel's army and opened up on Jennison's retreating cavalry. The federals fled into a cornfield leaving behind the loss of a hundred men, a large number of horses, and 1,200 rounds of ammunition. The guerrillas lost but eight men. The cannons were spiked and tossed into the Big Blue River.[23]

Following the engagement, Cole paid a visit to his grandmother, Mrs. Fristoe. The house was kept dark as the pair talked late into the night so that no federals would become suspicious at the late hours being kept. When Cole quietly slipped out the door sometime after midnight, he was confronted by a federal officer. In the pale light, Cole was astonished to see that his would-be captor was his cousin, Captain Charles Younger. Upon recognizing his relative, Cole extended his hand in friendship but Charles Younger insisted his cousin was his prisoner. Cole probably believed his cousin was playing a joke on him, but as the conversation continued, he learned otherwise. At an opportune moment, Cole allegedly drew his pistol and shot his cousin in the face, killing him.[24]

The shot attracted several other federal soldiers who quickly surrounded the house. Cole fled into the woods but accidentally fell and injured his knee. The fall, however, perhaps saved his life, for as he went down, musket balls whizzed over his head.

Cole, by this time, had developed a penchant for luring federal patrols into traps. After several such incidents, the ruse no longer worked. Many federal soldiers refused to give chase when they saw him riding or strolling innocently about their lines. But, he would soon have more than Cole Younger to worry about.

Assuming command on March 3rd, Confederate Major General Earl Van Dorn, organizing his forces in northeastern Arkansas, had assembled about 12,000 troops from Arkansas, Louisiana, Missouri, and Texas. Van Dorn developed a simple plan: He would advance northward through Missouri, defeat the federal forces and capture St. Louis, giving the Confederacy full control of the gateway to the West. Van Dorn knew that by taking St. Louis, a major industrial and commercial pro-Union center, the victory would signify Confederate control of the entire state. He wrote to his wife: "I must have St. Louis . . . then Huzza."[25]

Ephraim M. Anderson, a young Missourian, later recalled that Van Dorn possessed "a gay, dashing manner about him. . . . Eyes dark and fiery; lips thin and compressed. . . . He wore a blue uniform coat, a cap of the same color, embroidered with gold lace, dark pants, and heavy cavalry boots."[26]

Van Dorn lost no time in making his move against Curtis' advancing federal force. Only one day following his arrival in the northeast Arkansas encampment, Van Dorn marched his troops northward out of the Boston Mountains and advanced up the valley of Little Sugar Creek near Bentonville, Arkansas. The tired command reached the Confederate Camp Stephens on the evening of March 6th.[27]

That very same night, Major General Earl Van Dorn set out to outflank the Union position near Pea Ridge, Arkansas, dividing his army into two columns. Learning of Van Dorn's approach, the federals marched north to meet his advance on March 7. This movement—compounded by the killing of two generals, Brigadier General Ben McCulloch and Brigadier General James McQueen McIntosh, and the capture of their ranking colonel—halted the Confederate attack. Van Dorn led a second column to meet the federals in the Elkhorn Tavern and Tanyard area. By nightfall, the Confederates controlled Elkhorn Tavern and Telegraph Road. The next day, Major General Samuel R. Curtis, having regrouped and consolidated his army, counterattacked near the tavern and, by successfully employing his artillery, slowly forced the Confederates to retreat. Running short of ammunition,

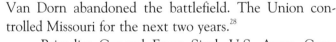

Van Dorn abandoned the battlefield. The Union controlled Missouri for the next two years.[28]

Brigadier General Franz Sigel, U.S. Army, Commanding First and Second Divisions, dispatched his lengthy report to Brigadier-General Samuel R. Curtis on the Battle of Pea Ridge (Elkhorn Tavern) on March 15, 1862:

Samuel R. Curtis. (Author's collections)

On the evening of the 5th the main body of the two divisions was encamped near McKisick's farm, [three] miles southward of Bentonville and [one] mile from the

127

fork of the roads leading west to Maysville and northeast to Pineville. The Second Missouri, under Colonel Schaefer, and one company of cavalry were stationed at Osage Mills, otherwise called Smith's Mill, [five] miles southeast of McKisick's farm, whilst our pickets guarded all the other avenues to the camp. For the purpose of reconnoitering the country towards the Indian Territory and to detain the rebels of Southwest Missouri from following Price's army by the State line road, Major Conrad, with five select companies of infantry, [sixty] men of cavalry, and two pieces of Welfley's battery, was ordered to proceed on the first day to Lindsey's Prairie, where he arrived in the evening, [sixteen] miles southwest of McKisick's farm, on the 2d (the 5th) to Maysville, and to return on the third day to our own camp.

Such was our position on the evening of the 5th, when I received orders from you to send a detachment of cavalry to Pineville, where there were said to be some 200 or 300 rebels, who disturbed and endangered the Union people of McDonald County. I directed Major Meszaros, with [eighty] men, to march at [ten] o'clock P.M. on the northwestern road to Pineville, whilst Capt. Von Kielmansegge was sent to Major Conrad at Maysville, to lead his [sixty] men of cavalry, with one piece of artillery and [twenty] infantry, at [ten] o'clock in the night, from Maysville to Rutledge and Pineville, and to act in concert with Major Meszaros. A Home Guard company, stationed between Pineville and Keetsville, was ordered to occupy at night the roads leading to Neosho and Kent, and thereby prevent the secesh to escape in that direction. Major Meszaros and Capt. von Kielmansegge should approach the town from the east, southeast, and southwest. It was understood that these detachments should attack the town simultaneously at [five] o'clock in the morning.

Just a few minutes before [ten] o'clock in the evening, when Meszaros was prepared to leave the camp, I received news from Colonel Schaefer, at Osage Mills, that his pickets posted in the direction of Elm Springs were fired upon by the enemy. This, in addition to your own dispatches reporting the enemy's force at Fayetteville and a strong party of cavalry advancing towards Middletown, and, besides this, your order to march to Sugar Creek, made me at once aware of the dangerous position of my command. I therefore ordered Colonel Schaefer to break up his camp immediately, to send the cavalry company to Osage Springs to cover his right flank, and to march with his regiment to Bentonville, leaving Osage Springs to the right and McKisick's farm to the left. All other troops I ordered to be prepared to march at [two] o'clock in the morning. In regard to the expedition to Pineville, it was too late to countermand the movement under Captain von Kielmansegge, and I therefore ordered Major Meszaros to begin his march and to accomplish his task with his own detachment and that of Captain von Kielman-segge, but to return to Sugar Creek as quickly as possible, without ruining his horses, so that they could be of some use in the ensuing battle. Major Conrad was made aware of our situation, and instructed to join us at Sugar Creek by some circuitous road leading northeast. The result of the expedition was not very great, but satisfactory.

The attack was made according to the instructions given and at the precise time, but only one captain, one lieutenant, and [fifteen] men of Price's army were found in the town and made prisoners; the others had left some days previous. The commands of Major Meszaros and Captain von Kielmansegge arrived safely on the 6th in our camp at Sugar Creek, bringing with them their prisoners. Unfortunately they had to leave behind and to destroy a printing press and types taken at Pineville, as the roads they took were too bad to bring this important material along.

Major Conrad, with his detachment, found his way to Keetsville and Cassville, which place he left on the 9th, and arrived at the former place, with Colonel Wright, some time after I had opened the road to Cassville on the pursuit of Price's force, which retired from Keetsville to Berryville.

At [two] o'clock in the morning of the 6th the troops encamped at McKisick's farm moved forward towards Bentonville in the following order: Advance guard, under Asboth: One company of Fourth Missouri Cavalry (Fremont Hussars); Second Ohio Battery, under command of Lieutenant Chapman; Fifteenth Missouri Volunteers, under command of Colonel Joliat Train of First and Second Divisions, escorted and guarded by detachments of the respective regiments: The First Division, under Colonel Osterhaus. The flying battery, the Fifth Missouri Cavalry (Benton Hussars), and the squadron of the Thirty-sixth Illinois Cavalry, Captain Jenks.

Before leaving camp I detached Lieutenant Schipper, of Company A, Benton Hussars, with [twenty] men, to Osage Springs, to communicate with Colonel Schaefer, and to bring news to Bentonville as soon as the enemy would approach that place. The advance guard of General Asboth arrived at Bentonville at [four] o'clock, when I directed him to halt until the train had come up more close. He then proceeded to Sugar Creek, followed by the train. Meanwhile the Second Missouri, Colonel Schaefer, and one part of the First Division arrived in town. I ordered this regiment, as well as the Twelfth Missouri, under command of Major Wangelin, the flying battery, under Captain Elbert, and the whole disposable cavalry force, under Colonel Nemett, comprising the Benton Hussars, the Thirty-sixth Illinois Cavalry, under Captain Jenks, and a squad of [thirteen] men of Fremont Hussars, under Lieut. Fred. W.

Cooper, to occupy and guard the town, to let the whole train pass, and remain at my disposition as a rear guard.

At [eight] o'clock the train had passed the town and was moving on the road to Sugar Creek. With the intention not to be too close to the train and awaiting report from Lieutenant Schipper's picket at Osage Springs two hours elapsed, when ten minutes after [ten] it was reported to me that large masses of troops, consisting of infantry and cavalry, were moving from all sides towards our front and both flanks.

After some observation I had no doubt that the enemy's advance guard was before us. I immediately called the troops to arms and made them ready for battle. As Bentonville is situated on the edge of Osage Prairie, easily accessible in front and covered on the right and left and rear by thick woods and underbrush, I ordered the troops to evacuate the town and to form on a little hill north of it. Looking for the Second Missouri, I learned to my astonishment that it had already left the town by a misunderstanding of my order. I am glad to say that this matter is satisfactorily explained by Colonel Schaefer, but at the same time I regret to report that this regiment was ambuscaded on its march and lost in the conflict [thirty-seven] men in dead, wounded, and prisoners.

The troops now left to me consisted of about eight companies of the Twelfth Missouri, with an average strength of [forty-five] men, five companies of Benton Hussars, and five pieces of the flying battery; in all about 600 men. The troops I directed to march in the following order: Two companies of the Twelfth at the head of the column, deployed on the right and left as skirmishers, followed by the flying battery; one company of the same regiment on the right and one on the left of the pieces, marching by the flank, and prepared to fire by ranks to the right and left, the remainder of the regiment behind the pieces, two companies of cavalry to support the infantry on the right and left, and the rest of the cavalry, under command of Colonel Nemett, with one piece of artillery, following in the rear. In this formation, modified from time to time according to circumstances, the column moved forward to break through the lines of the enemy, who had already taken position in our front and in both flanks, whilst he appeared behind us in the town in line of battle, re-enforced by some pieces of artillery. The troops advanced slowly, fighting and repelling the enemy in front, flankward, and rear, wherever he stood or attacked.

From the moment we left the town, at 10:30 in the morning, until 3:30 o'clock in the afternoon, when we met the first re-enforcements-- the Second Missouri, the Twenty-fifth Illinois, and a few companies of the Forty-fourth Illinois—we sustained three regular attacks, and were uninterruptedly in sight and under the fire of the enemy. When the first re-enforcement had arrived I knew that we were safe, and left it to the Twenty-fifth and Second Missouri, and afterwards to Colonel Oster-haus, to take care of the rest, which he did to my satisfaction. It would take too much time to go into the detail of this most extraordinary and critical affair, but as a matter of justice I feel it my duty to declare that according to my humble opinion, never troops have shown themselves worthier to defend a great cause than on this day of the 6th of March.

In the night of the 6th the two divisions were encamped on the plateau of the hills near Sugar Creek and in the adjoining valley sepa-rating the two ridges extending along the creek. The Second Division held the right, the First the left of the position, flouting towards the west and southwest, in order to receive the enemy should he advance from the Bentonville and Fayetteville road. Colonel Davis' division, forming the center, was on our left, and Colonel Carr covered the ground on the extreme left of our whole line.

Early in the morning report came in that troops and trains of the enemy were moving the whole night on the Bentonville road around our rear towards Cross Timber, thereby endangering our line of retreat and communication to Keetsville, and separating us from our re-enforce-ments and provision trains. This report was corroborated by two of my guides, Mr. Pope and Mr. Brown, who had gone out to reconnoiter the country. I immediately ordered Lieutenant Schramm, of my staff, to ascertain the facts, and to see in what direction the troops were moving. On his return he reported that there was no doubt in regard to the movement of a large force of the enemy in the aforesaid direction. You then ordered me to detach three pieces of the flying battery to join Colonel Bussey's cavalry in an attack against the enemy in the direction of Leesville. Colonel Osterhaus was directed to follow him with three regiments of infantry and two batteries.

At about [eleven] o'clock the firing began near Elkhorn Tavern and Leesville. To see how matters stood, I went out to Colonel Carr's divi-sion, and found him a short distance beyond the tavern, engaged in a brisk cannonade. Several pieces, partly disabled and partly without ammunition, were returning, whilst another advanced from the camp. As the enemy's fire was directed to the place where I halted, I ordered two pieces of the battery which came up to take position on an elevat-ed ground to the left and to shell the enemy. After a few shots the fire of the enemy opposite our position became weaker, and I sent the two pieces forward to join their battery. I then returned to look after my own troops, and passing along the road met the Third Iowa Cavalry, which had been sent in advance of Colonel Osterhaus, and which now escort-ed their lieutenant-colonel, who was severely wounded, back into the camp. I immediately sent to you to order the regiment back to Leesville, which order was given, and the regiment returned. I met Lieutenant Gassen, of the flying battery, who reported to me that our cavalry had been driven back by an overwhelming force, and our three pieces taken by the enemy, as there was no infantry to support them. I now ordered Major Meszaros and the two other pieces of the flying battery to re-enforce Colonel Osterhaus, but during their march I learned that Colonel Davis had been directed to advance with his whole division to Leesville, which induced me to send only Major Meszaros to that point, and directed the two pieces of the flying battery to act as reserve, and to join the troops left in their encampment. Proceeding to the camp to see what was going on there and whether we were safe in our rear (towards Bentonville), I found the following troops assembled in their respective positions: The Seventeenth Missouri and a detachment of [sixty] men of the Third Missouri; the Twenty-fifth and the Forty-fourth Illinois ; two pieces of Welfley's battery ([twelve]-pounders); two companies Thirty-sixth Illinois Cavalry, and nearly the whole Second Division, comprising the Second and Fifteenth Missouri, Carlin's battery, and two companies of the Benton Hussars.

It was about [two] o'clock in the afternoon when the cannonading and musket firing became more vehement, and when you ordered me to re-enforce Colonel Carr at Elkhorn Tavern, and Colonel Davis and Colonel Osterhaus near Leesville, as both forces, especially those at Leesville, were, according to your reports, pressed hard and losing ground. I therefore sent General Asboth, with four companies of the Second Missouri, under Colonel Schaefer, and four pieces of the Second Ohio Battery, under Lieutenant Chapman, to assist Colonel Carr. Major Poten, with the Seventeenth Missouri, one company of the Third Missouri, two companies of the Fifteenth Missouri, two pieces of the flying artillery, under Captain Elbert, and two companies of the Benton Hussars, under Major Heinrichs, I ordered to advance on the Sugar Creek road towards Bentonville, to demonstrate against the rear of the enemy. Two pieces of the Second Ohio Battery, with six companies of the Second Missouri, remained in their position to guard the camp and two companies of the Forty-fourth Illinois, with [twenty] men of the Thirty-sixth Illinois Cavalry, under Captain Russell, were sent forward in a northwestern direction, to remain there as a picket between Leesville and the Sugar Creek road. With all other troops—the Fifteenth Missouri, the Twenty-fifth and Forty-fourth Illinois, and the two pieces of Captain Welfley's battery—I marched to Leesville, to re-enforce Colonels Davis and Osterhaus. My intention was to throw back the enemy from Leesville into the mountains and towards Bentonville, and then, by a change of direction to the right to assist General Asboth and Colonel Carr by deploying on their left.

On my march to Leesville, I heard Major Poten's firing on the Bentonville road. Arrived at Leesville, the firing in front had ceased, whilst it commenced with new vehemence on the right, at Elkhorn Tavern. At this moment Captain McKenny, acting assistant adjutant-general, requested me, by order of General Curtis, to send some more re-enforcements to the right, which I did, by detaching five companies of the Twenty-fifth Illinois and four pieces of Captain Hoffmann's battery, stationed in reserve at Leesville, to Elkhorn Tavern. I then proceeded beyond the town to the battle-field, which I found in full possession of Colonels Davis and Osterhaus. As no enemy could be seen except a small detachment on a distant hill, I requested Colonel Davis to protect my left flank, by sending his skirmishers and one regiment of infantry forward through the woods, whilst I proceeded with the Twenty-fifth Illinois and four pieces of Welflcy's and Hoffmann's batteries on the road to the northeast, which was already opened by the Forty-fourth Illinois and Fifteenth Missouri. After making [one] mile and passing two hospitals of the enemy, I ordered Colonel Osterhaus to follow me with the Twelfth Missouri and Thirty-sixth Illinois and a section of artillery, which troops came up promptly, except the two pieces, [twelve]-pounders that remained with Colonel Davis. We advanced slowly, and after making half a mile more we reached an open field, where we took our position, and from which we could easily discern the camp-fires of our friends and those of our enemies near Elkhorn Tavern. I sent immediately to General Curtis to apprise him of my position and that I was ready to co-operate with him. Meanwhile night had fallen in, and although the cannonading was renewed on the right, I did not believe that after a hard day's work the enemy would make a final and decisive attack. In order, therefore, to disguise our position from which I intended to advance in the morning I kept the troops in the strictest silence, and did not allow the building of camp-fires or any movement farther than 200 to 300 paces distance. So we remained until [one] o'clock in the morning, when I found it necessary to remove the troops by a short and convenient road into our common camp, to give them some food, sleep, and a good fire, and to prepare them for battle.

To show the whole position of the First and Second Divisions on the evening of the 7th, allow me, general, to make the following statement: Beginning on the left, Major Poten, with the Seventeenth Missouri, one company of the Third Missouri, two companies of the Fifteenth Missouri, two pieces of the flying artillery, and two companies of the Benton Hussars were stationed on the Sugar Creek and Bentonville road, [three] miles from the camp. The entrance of the road from this side was guarded by two pieces of the Second Ohio Battery and six companies of the Second Missouri. Towards the north (Leesville) two companies of the Forty-fourth Illinois and [twenty] men of the Thirty-sixth Illinois Cavalry remained on picket. On the right, near Elkhorn Tavern, were the following troops: Four companies of the Second Missouri, five companies of the Twenty-fifth Illinois, four pieces of the Second Ohio Battery, and four pieces of Captain Hoffmann's battery. In the field to the left of General Asboth and Colonel Cart, under my immediate command, were the Twelfth Missouri, the Fifteenth Missouri, the Twenty-fifth, Thirty-sixth, and Forty-fourth Illinois, two pieces of Captain Welfley's and two pieces of Captain Hoffmann's batteries. The Fremont and Benton Hussars and one section of Captain Welfley's battery returned to camp with Colonel Davis.

The detachment of Major Conrad, consisting of six companies of infantry detailed from the Third, Fifteenth, and Seventeenth Missouri and Thirty-sixth Illinois, and one piece of Captain Welfley's battery, was encamped a few miles west of Keetsville. One piece of Captain Welfley's battery was spiked and then taken by the enemy, but retaken and unspiked. Three pieces of Captain Elbert's flying battery had been lost near Leesville, the trails burned by the enemy, and the guns left on the battlefield. Another piece of this battery had broken down on the retreat from Bentonville to Sugar Creek, but the gun was recovered and brought into camp.

The different combats of the 7th had fully developed the plans of the enemy. It was evident that his main forces were stationed near and at Elkhorn Tavern, and that he would make all efforts to break through our lines on the Fayetteville road, and thereby complete his apparent victory. I therefore resolved to recall all troops and different detachments of the First and Second Divisions from wherever they were stationed (with the exception of four companies of the Second Missouri and four pieces of artillery from the Second Ohio Battery sent to their original position on Sugar Creek), and to fall upon the right flank of the enemy should he attack or advance from Elkhorn Tavern. At daybreak of the 8th the following troops were assembled near and around my headquarters awaiting orders: First Division, Colonel Osterhaus: Two companies Third Missouri Volunteers; Twelfth and Seventeenth Missouri; Twenty-fifth, Thirty-sixth, and Forty-fourth Illinois; Welfley's battery, five pieces; Hoffmann's battery, six pieces; Captain Jenks' squadron of the Thirty-sixth Illinois. Second Division, General Asboth, Second Missouri, six companies; Fifteenth Missouri; two pieces Second Ohio Battery, Lieutenant Chapman; battalion (four companies) Fourth Missouri Cavalry (Fremont

Hussars); six companies Fifth Missouri Cavalry (Benton Hussars); two pieces of Captain Elbert's flying battery.

It was about [seven] o'clock in the morning when the firing began on the Keetsville road, this side of Elkhorn Tavern. I was waiting for Colonel Osterhans and Lieutenant Asmussen, of my staff, who had gone out to reconnoiter the ground on which I intended to deploy and to find the nearest road to that ground. The Forty-fourth Illinois had already been sent in advance to form our right, when the above-named officers returned and the movement began In less than half an hour the troops were in their respective positions, the First Division forming the first line, the Second Division, with all the cavalry, the reserve, 250 paces behind the first line. To protect and cover the deployment of the left wing I opened the fire on the right with a section of Captain Hoffmann's battery, under Lieutenant Frank, and the five pieces of Captain Welfley's battery. The enemy returned the fire promptly and with effect, but was soon outflanked by our position on the left and exposed to a concentric and most destructive fire of our brave and almost never-failing cannoneers.

After the first discharges on a distance of 800 paces, I ordered Captain Welfley and Lieutenant Frank to advance about 250 yards, to come into close range from the enemy's position, whilst I threw the Twenty-fifth Illinois forward on the right, to cover the space between the battery and the Keetsville road. Colonel Schaefer, with the Second Missouri, was ordered to proceed to the extreme left, and by forming against the cavalry, to protect our left flank. This movement proved of great effect, and I now ordered the center and the left to advance 200 paces and brought the reserve forward on the position which our first line had occupied. I then took a battery commanded by Captain Klauss, and belonging to Colonel Davis' division, nearer to my right, and reported to you that the road towards Elkhorn Tavern was open and we were advancing. About this time, when the battle had lasted about one hour and a half, the enemy tried to extend his line farther to the right, in occupying the first hill of the long ridge commanding the plain and the gradually rising ground where we stood. His infantry was already lodged upon the hill, seeking shelter behind the rocks and stones, whilst some pieces of artillery worked around to gain the plateau. I immediately ordered the two howitzers of the reserve (Second Ohio, under Lieutenant Gansevoort) and the two pieces of Captain Elbert's flying battery to report to Colonel Osterhaus on the left, to shell and batter the enemy on the hill. This was done in concert with Hoffmann's battery and with terrible effect to the enemy, as the rocks and stones worked as hard as the shells and shot. The enemy's plan to enfilade our lines from the hill was frustrated, and he was forced to lead a precipitate retreat with men and cannon. Encouraged by the good and gallant behavior of our troops, I resolved to draw the circle a little closer around the corner into which we had already pressed the enemy's masses, and ordered a second advance of all the batteries and battalions, changing the position of the right wing more to the left, and bringing the troops of the reserve, the Fifteenth Missouri, and the whole cavalry behind our left.

Assisted by Klauss' battery on the right, and co-operating with the troops of the Third and Fourth Divisions, who advanced with new spirit on the Keetsville road, the enemy was overwhelmed by the deadly power of our artillery, and after about an hour's work the firing on his side began to slacken, and nearly totally ceased. To profit this favorable moment I ordered the Twelfth Missouri, the Twenty-fifth and Forty-fourth Illinois to throw forward a strong force of skirmishers and take the woods in front, where the enemy had planted one of his batteries. In the same time I ordered the Seventeenth Missouri Volunteers, which had arrived during the battle from Bentonville road, to climb the hill on our left and to press forward against the enemy's rear. The Thirty-sixth Illinois was also ordered to assist this movement and to hold communication between the Twelfth and Seventeenth Missouri Volunteers, whilst Colonels Schaefer and Joliat, with the Second and Fifteenth Missouri, followed slowly, and Colonel Nemett, with his cavalry, guarded the rear.

The rattling of musketry, the volleys, the hurrahs, did prove very soon that our troops were well at work in the woods, and that they were gaining ground rapidly. It was the Twelfth Missouri Volunteers, under Major Wangelin, which at this occasion took Dallas' artillery and their flag, followed close behind and on the right by part of the Third Missouri, the Forty-fourth Illinois, and Twenty-fifth and on the left by the Thirty-sixth Illinois. The Seventeenth Missouri, under Major Poten, had meanwhile arrived on the top of Pea Ridge, forming the extreme left of our line of battle.

The enemy was routed and fled in terror and confusion in all directions. It was a delightful moment when we all met after [twelve] o'clock on the eminence, where the enemy held positions with his batteries a few minutes before, and when you let pass by the columns of your victorious army. To pursue the enemy I sent Captain von Kielmansegge with one company of Fremont Hussars forward. The Seventeenth and Third Missouri followed in double-quick time, assisted by two pieces of Elbert's flying artillery, other troops of the First Division, all under Colonel Osterhaus, came up and con-tinued their march towards Keetsville.

At the fork of the Benton and Keetsville roads I detached the Forty-fourth Illinois (Colonel Knobelsdorff), two pieces of artillery of the flying battery, and a squad of [thirty] men, Fremont Hussars, to proceed a short distance on the road to Bentonville and to guard that road. Arrived at Keetsville with the greatest portion of my command. I found that one part of the enemy had turned the Roaring River and Berryville, while others had turned to the left. I also received your order to return to Sugar Creek, which I did, and met the army on Sugar Creek at [four] o'clock in the evening of the 9th.

A list of the dead, wounded, and missing of this command has already been transmitted to you, and a special report mentioning those officers and men of my command who deserve consideration for their conduct in action, together with the reports of the different commanders of regiments and corps, will follow to-day, as some of the reports have not come in yet.[29]

Confederate Lieutenant Madison Creasey, who served with the 5,000 men who comprised the First and Second Missouri Brigades at Pea Ridge, wrote: "We have been in an awful battle and our company was cut to pieces. . . . I saw Captain Gibbs fall and started to him when a bullet struck me. . . . I am suffering much. . . . I am afraid many of the boys area hurt. I am very tired and can't write anymore now. Goodbye."[30]

Less than a week following the Confederate defeat at Pea Ridge, forty-mounted bushwhackers under a Colonel Parker attacked Liberty and ripped down the U.S. flag. On March 10th, Quantrill and his band entered Johnson County, Kansas, and killed several persons at Aubrey. Union Colonel Robert H. Graham immediately dispatched Captain John Greelish, Company K Eighth Regiment Kansas Volunteers, to move his command from Olathe, Kansas, to Aubrey and defend its citizens. Two days later, a skirmish took place between thirty men of Greelish's company under First Lieutenant Rose and a portion of Quantrill's band. On his retreat, Quantrill drove a family from their house and set it afire.[31]

One victim of the bushwhackers, Mrs. Permelia A. Hardeman, stated: "We were visited last night about two o'clock by the bushwhackers. I was up with the baby when they came. . . . They got both of the guns and then went up stair, took some of my bed blankets . . . then searched the bureau drawers. They even took as small a thing as a comb and brush."[32]

That same month, Quantrill planned to attack Independence. The bushwhackers met at the home of David George, then rode as far as the Little Blue Church. Expecting to find 300 Jayhawkers in the city, they learned the force was double that figure and rode around to the southwest. On the bridge, they captured a Yankee sergeant. The soldier had dismounted and been disarmed when Quantrill rode up, drew his revolver and shot him. They burned the bridge over the Big Blue River, killing the thirteen guards positioned there and dined that same day at the *Alex Majors*, the freighter, of Russell, Majors, & Waddell.

Eighteen miles southeast of Kansas City, they paused to rest at the Majors' farm. As evening came on, the bushwhackers broke up into four groups and dispersed. Quantrill took twenty-one men with him intending to spend the night at the home of Major David Tate in New Santa Fe, on March 22nd. Unbeknownst to the bushwhackers, Federal Colonel Robert B. Mitchell, Second Kansas Volunteers had learned of the bridge burning and set off in pursuit of the guerrillas. Mitchell dispatched a cavalry squadron under Major James M. Pomeroy to arrest David Tate, who was known to be a confidant of Quantrill's, and Mitchell wanted to question him as to the whereabouts of the guerrilla leader. Quantrill had posted two pickets, but they had fallen asleep as the federals crept up on the house under cover of darkness.[33]

Quantrill, Cole, John Jarrette, Dick and George Maddox, George Shepherd, his cousin Oliver Shepherd, James Little, Stephen Shores, and others were asleep when they were awakened by a heavy knocking on the door. George Shepherd was guarding one of the doors when Pomeroy approached it and demanded they come out with their hands up. Quantrill fired through the wooden door, wounding the officer, who rushed back to his men.[34]

"Quantrill, with a part of his gang, had burned the bridge between Kansas City and Independence, and it was contemplated by Major Banzhaf to march from Kansas City, and in conjunction with Colonel Weer, Fourth Kansas, to surround and entrap Quantrill," wrote Colonel Robert B. Mitchell, Second Kansas Cavalry. "I left camp about 6:30 P.M. of the 22nd instant, reached Little Santa Fe about ten o'clock that night, and Major Pomeroy about three miles from the town, with the instructions to arrest one David Tate, whom I had reason to believe was connected to Quantrill. Major Pomeroy had with him a detachment of Companies D and E, under command of Captain Moore and Lieutenant Stover. When Major Pomeroy reached the house he demanded entrance, and a gun was immediately fired through the door. He then called upon them to surrender, and to send out their women and children if they had any in the house. After waiting some time, after shots were fired from the house, he ordered a volley to be fired into the house. The cries of women were then heard, when he ordered the men to cease firing. The women and children then came out and firing was resumed on both sides. Two of the men then came out of one of the windows and surrendered. They stated to Major Pomeroy that Quantrill was in the house with [twenty-six] men. Major Pomeroy then threatened to fire the house, and upon their continued refusal to surrender, he ordered the house to be fired, and an attempt was made to fire it, but without success. Major Pomeroy and Private Wills, of Company D, were at this time shot. Major Pomeroy becoming disabled, Captain [Amaziah] Moore took command, and sent back to me requesting reinforcements, so as not to let any of the men escape."[35]

Attempting to devise a plan of escape, Quantrill deployed his men throughout the house. Quantrill, Cole Younger, the fierce Dick Maddox, and a few others, defended the upstairs while George Shepherd took charge of the others who occupied the first floor. As Moore shouted warnings that the bushwhackers would be killed unless they surrendered, Cole taunted and cursed him.

When the federals set the house ablaze as they had at the Flannery house, the guerrilla chieftain ordered Cole Younger and the men with shotguns to go out first followed by those with only revolvers. Quantrill led another desperate charge from the weather boarding in the rear of the house, which he had knocked out with a chair, followed by George Shepherd, Cole Younger, the Maddox boys, and the rest of the band. All seventeen bushwhackers made it to safety with the exception of Perry Hoy who was taken to Fort Leavenworth and executed.[36]

Federal reports, however, presented a different scenario: Brigadier General James Totten wrote: "I have the honor to state that I have received official reports from Lieutenant Colonel E.B. Brown, commanding Jackson and Cass counties, to the effect that at daylight on the morning of the 14th instant a detachment of the First Missouri Cavalry, under Lieutenant Nash, attacked Quantrill near the Santa Fe Road, and [twelve] miles from Independence, killing four, wounding four, and taking five prisoners. The report also states that our troops captured all of the horses, arms, accouterments, and most of the clothing of the outlaws."[37]

Lieutenant Colonel E.B. Brown stated in his official report:

Having through my scouts tracked Quantrill for the past five days, I received information last night that gave promise of making a successful attack on his band. After making arrangements with one of our scouts to meet the command at Ray Point with reliable information as to his movements, I ordered Lieutenant G.W. Nash, with [thirty] men of the First Missouri Cavalry, to move to that point at midnight, and be governed in his preparations by the information he there received. The night was dark, and a heavy thunderstorm raged until [four] o'clock in the morning, effectually concealing the movements of the command. At daylight, it reached a small, old log house, two miles from any traveled road and about [twelve] miles from here, in the direction of Santa Fe, where Quantrill was housed. He was completely surprised, and Lieutenant Nash charged on his farm as they were flying to the brush, about [twenty] rods from the brush, killing four, wounding four, and capturing five prisoners, all the horses, accouterments, most of the arms and clothing, most of Quantrill's men running off barefooted and coatless. Lieutenant Nash, for his perseverance in pursuing Quantrill and his bravery in the charge, deserves especial notice of the commanding general.[38]

Mitchell continued his pursuit of the guerrillas and marched at dawn to the Wyatt farm where George Todd and eleven of his men had slept. As the federals approached, the guerrillas fled into the thicket. Because the undergrowth was too dense for pursuit on horseback, several soldiers dismounted and charged into the thicket on foot, capturing three of Todd's men. After an interrogation, the trio was hanged.[39]

An exhausted Quantrill arrived on foot at the David Wilson homestead in lower Jackson County where he dispatched orders to his scattered band to meet at the headwaters of the Little Blue. Quantrill moved from farm to farm, barely eluding his pursuers until he reached the rendezvous site.

On March 31st, Captain Peabody learned that several Quantrill men were at Pink Hill, about nineteen miles south of Independence, and started in pursuit of them. Approaching Pink Hill, Captain Peabody dispatched thirty-five men under Lieutenant White of Company C to scour the area while he and Lieutenant Gurnee of Company D led a force in another direction.

While passing a double log house in an elevated position over the road, Peabody's party was fired upon from the dwelling. Captain Peabody and his men dismounted, and while keeping up a constant firing, converged on the house. At least sixty Quantrill men were in the log house firing from loop holes made by knocking out the plaster from between the logs.

After an hour and a half of fighting, local farmers came to reinforce Quantrill, and before Lieutenant White could come to Peabody's aid, the guerrilla force had increased to 150 men with small arms. When White appeared, Peabody and his men stormed the house, killing six bushwhackers and driving the others from the house. Because Quantrill's party knew the rugged, hilly, and timbered terrain, the federals did not pursue. Captain Peabody's horse had sustained three wounds.[40]

Captain John B. Kaiser, Missouri State Militia, meanwhile led a force from Lexington to Pink Hill where they appropriated ten kegs of powder. Captain Kaiser later reported that upon receipt of a dispatch from Captain Peabody, First Missouri Cavalry, stating he wished reinforcements, as he had found the enemy, he at once ordered Captain Murphy with two lieutenants and fifty men to his assistance. They discovered the enemy, after a march of nine miles, upon a high bluff, on the waters of the Little Sui. Their position was one of great strength and advantage. The rocks of the bluff afforded them a strong breastwork and shelter. Communication with Captain Peabody was impossible, as the bushwhackers were between them. The two forces exchanged volleys before the guerrillas retreated.[41]

Captain Kaiser proclaimed in another report: "The Union people here are suffering greatly from the bands of these ruffians. They are daily driven from their homes and many of them are caught and either hung or shot. No Union man is safe one mile from camp unless a force is with him."[42]

Quantrill and his men rendezvoused again, this time at the home of Reuben Harris, ten miles south of Independence. Deciding to capture Harrisonville, Quantrill moved his men to the home of Job Crabtree, eight miles east of Independence. On the night of April 15th, a torrential downpour forced the bushwhackers to take refuge at the Jordan Lowe house, Quantrill assuming that no federals would be out on such a night.[43]

But Quantrill was wrong. Lieutenant Colonel Egbert B. Brown, Seventh Missouri Infantry, had been tracking him for five days. He and his men surrounded the Lowe house and captured the horses of the irregulars who were tied to a fence. The federals opened fire, causing Quantrill and his men to again run for the thicket.

As Cole Younger dashed from the house, he heard gunfire coming from over his shoulder, and suddenly realized that someone had been left behind. He turned and raced back to the house and found George Todd, Andy

Blunt, and Joe Gilchrist, who had been asleep in the loft, up and firing from the second-story windows. They had not heard Quantrill's order to charge over their own gunfire. Cole managed to save Todd, but in the wild dash to the woods, Gilchrist was killed and Blunt captured.

Captain Peabody, still in Independence learned that Cole Younger had just spent a day at the home of a friend named Blythe. He dispatched a scouting party to the Blythe home, and they quickly surrounded the house. Neither Blythe nor Cole was present, but Blythe's twelve-year-old son was in the house. The federals dragged him out to the barn and began interrogating him, but the boy maintained he knew nothing. Believing he had a chance to break through the guard, young Blythe dashed into the house where he procured a pistol and made for the woods in a shower of bullets.[44]

He was hit before he reached the woods, but as he fell, he rolled over and fired several shots, killing one federal and wounding two others. Before he could get off another shot, the Jayhawkers put seventeen bullets in him. A Negro servant, who witnessed the atrocity, fled into the woods and came across Quantrill and a dozen of his men. After the servant related what he had seen, Quantrill set up an ambush at Blue Cut, a deep pass on the road the soldiers would have to take on their return to Independence.

The road ran between Harrisonville and Independence, and the cut provided the perfect spot for an ambush. Two hills, thirty feet high, loomed on either side of the road and stretched for 150 yards. The bushwhackers tied their horses in the woods and took positions on both sides of the road. The confident federals came in sight, and when the last soldier entered the cut, the guerrillas opened fire. The federals panicked as men and horses fell in mad confusion, dead, wounded, and dying.

With both ends of the pass blocked, the only hope of escape for the Yankees lay in riding directly at their enemies. As one federal soldier and his horse made a mad dash for freedom, Cole Younger grabbed the horse's bridle. The rider lunged at Cole with his sabre but Cole avoided the blow. Drawing his pistol with his left hand while holding the bridle in his right, Cole fired and killed his enemy. Of the thirty-eight federals who went searching for Cole Younger, about half lay dead in the pass that night.

Notes

[1]"War on the Border," Missouri Department of Natural Resources.

[2]*History of Henry and St. Clair Counties, Missouri,* 1883.

[3]A.C. Appler, *The Younger Brothers: The Life, Character and Daring Exploits of the Youngers, the Notorious Bandits Who Rode with Jesse James and William Clarke Quantrill,* New York, Frederick Fell, Inc., Publishers, 1955, p. 31.

[4]Carl W. Breihan, *The Complete and Authentic Life of Jesse James,* New York, Frederick Fell, Inc., Publishers, 1953, p. 222.

[5]Cole Younger, *The Story of Cole Younger by Himself,* pp. 12-13.

[6]A. Huntley, "Cole Younger," *Famous Outlaws of the West,* Fall 1964, pp. 27-28.

[7]E.P. Rogers letter to Charles M. Start dated June 15, 1901. Northfield, Minnesota, Bank Robbery of 1876. Selected Manuscripts Collections and Government Records, Microfilm Edition, Roll 4, Minnesota Historical Society.

[8]A.C. Appler, *The Younger Brothers: The Life, Character and Daring Exploits of the Youngers, the Notorious Bandits Who Rode with Jesse James and William Clarke Quantrill,* pp. 39-40.

[9]Cole Younger, *The Story of Cole Younger by Himself,* pp. 14-15.

[10]William Ward, *The Younger Brothers: The Border Outlaws: The Only Authentic History of the Exploits of These Desperadoes of the West,* pp. 12-13.

[11]Cole Younger, *The Story of Cole Younger by Himself,* pp. 14-15.

[12]William Ward, *The Younger Brothers: The Border Outlaws: The Only Authentic History of the Exploits of These Desperadoes of the West,* p. 14.

[13]Cole Younger, *The Story of Cole Younger by Himself,* p. 15.

[14]William Gregg letter to George M. Bennett dated April 9, 1898. Northfield, Minnesota, Bank Robbery of 1876. Selected Manuscripts Collections and Government Records, Microfilm Edition, Roll 4, Minnesota Historical Society.

[15]James D. Horan, *Desperate Men: Revelations from the Sealed Pinkerton Files,* New York, G.P. Putnam's Sons, 1949, p. 16.

[16]Harry Sinclair Drago, *Outlaws on Horseback,* p. 30.

[17]Shelby Foote, *The Civil War: A Narrative Fredericksburg to Meridian,* Volume II, New York, Random House, 1963, p. 140.

[18]Carl W. Breihan, *Younger Brothers Cole, James, Bob, John,* San Antonio, The Naylor Company, 1961, p. 188.

[19]Dallas Cantrell, *Northfield, Minnesota: Youngers' Fatal Blunder,* p. 143.

[20]William Ward, *The Younger Brothers: The Border Outlaws: The Only Authentic History of the Exploits of These Desperadoes of the West,* pp. 14-19.

[21]J.W. Buel, *The Border Outlaws.*

[22]Report of Captain William S. Oliver, Seventh Missouri Infantry, February 3, 1862. *The War of the Rebellion: A Compilation of the Official Records of the Union and Confederate Armies,* Series I, Volume VIII, Washington, Government Printing Office, 1883, p. 57.

[23]J.W. Buel, *The Border Outlaws*, pp. 29-35.

[24]Carl W. Breihan, *The Complete and Authentic Life of Jesse James*, pp. 233-234.

[25]Richard H. Owens, "Battle of Pea Ridge Deciding the Fate of Missouri," *America's Civil War*, January 2000, p. 44; Colonel William Preston Johnston, *The Life of General Albert Sidney Johnston*, New York, Da Capo Press, 1997 reprint of 1879 original, p. 524; James Willis, *Arkansas Confederates in the Western Theater*, Dayton, Morningside Press, 1998, p. 214.

[26]Arthur B. Carter, *The Tarnished Cavalier Major General Earl Van Dorn, C.S.A.*, Knoxville, University of Tennessee Press, 1999, p. 48.

[27]Phillip W. Steele and Steve Cottrell, *Civil War in the Ozarks*, p. 41.

[28]Richard H. Owens, "Battle of Pea Ridge Deciding the Fate of Missouri," *America's Civil War*, January 2000, p. 44.; George T. Wilson, "Battle for Missouri," *America's Civil War*, January 1990, pp. 27-32.

[29]Report of Brigadier General Franz Sigel, U.S. Army, Commanding First and Second Divisions, on the Battle of Pea Ridge (Elkhorn Tavern) to Brigadier General Samuel R. Curtis, March 15, 1862. *The War of the Rebellion: A Compilation of the Official Records of the Union and Confederate Armies*, 14 R.R., Volume VIII.

[30]Confederate Lieutenant Madison Creasey in 1861 letter. "War on the Border," Missouri Department of Natural Resources.

[31]Report of Colonel Robert H. Graham, Eighth Kansas Infantry, March 19, 1862. *The War of the Rebellion: A Compilation of the Official Records of the Union and Confederate Armies*, Series I, Volume VIII, pp. 335-336.

[32]"War on the Border," Missouri Department of Natural Resources.

[33]Edward E. Leslie, *The Devil Knows How to Ride: The True Story of William Clarke Quantrill and His Confederate Raiders*, New York, Random House, 1996, pp. 113-115.

[34]Carl W. Breihan, "Outlaw George Shepherd," *Pioneer West*, March 1978, Number 2, pp. 22-23.

[35]Report of Colonel Robert B. Mitchell, Second Kansas Cavalry, March 24,1862. *The War of the Rebellion: A Compilation of the Official Records of the Union and Confederate Armies*, Series I, Volume VIII, p. 346.

[36]Ibid; Carl W. Breihan, *Quantrill and His Civil War Guerrillas*, New York, Promontory Press, 1959, p. 169.

[37]Report of Brigadier General James Totten, April 14, 1862. *The War of the Rebellion: A Compilation of the Official Records of the Union and Confederate Armies*, Series I, Volume XIII, pp. 57-58.

[38]Report of Lieutenant Colonel E.B. Brown, Seventh Missouri Infantry, April 16, 1862. *The War of the Rebellion: A Compilation of the Official Records of the Union and Confederate Armies*, Series I, Volume XIII, p. 58.

[39]Edward E. Leslie, *The Devil Knows How to Ride: The True Story of William Clarke Quantrill and His Confederate Raiders*, New York, Random House, 1996, pp. 115-117.

[40]Report of Major Charles Banzhaf, First Missouri Cavalry, April 5, 1862. *The War of the Rebellion: A Compilation of the Official Records of the Union and Confederate Armies*, Series I, Volume VIII, pp. 358-359.

[41]Report of Brigadier-General James Totten, Headquarters District of Central Missouri, April 12, 1862. *The War of the Rebellion: A Compilation of the Official Records of the Union and Confederate Armies*, Series I, Volume VIII, pp.359-360.

[42]Report of Captain John B. Kaiser, Booneville Battalion Missouri cavalry Militia, April 1, 1862. *The War of the Rebellion: A Compilation of the Official Records of the Union and Confederate Armies*, Series I, Volume VIII, p. 361.

[43]Edward E. Leslie, *The Devil Knows How to Ride: The True Story of William Clarke Quantrill and His Confederate Raiders*, New York, Random House, 1996, pp. 117-118.

[44]William Ward, *The Younger Brothers: The Border Outlaws: The Only Authentic History of the Exploits of These Desperadoes of the West*, pp. 21-29; Cole Younger, *The Story of Cole Younger by Himself*, pp. 18- 19; A.C. Appler, *The Younger Brothers: The Life, Character and Daring Exploits of the Youngers, the Notorious Bandits Who Rode with Jesse James and William Clarke Quantrill*, pp. 58-59 .

Chapter Six

Vengeance Is Mine

"Will you follow orders, be true to your fellows, and kill those who serve and support the Union?"
                                                                    —William Clarke Quantrill[1]

I N LATE APRIL, 1862, FRANK JAMES, living at the family home in Kearney, went "wild, shooting his pistol and halloing for Jeff Davis." Learning of the incident, Colonel William R. Penick of the Fifth Missouri State Militia Cavalry, had Frank jailed in Liberty. Zerelda, however, using the influence of Silas Woodson, prominent Missouri politician and future governor, induced the colonel to parole him.[2] Frank took the Oath of Allegiance to support and defend the Constitution of the United States and posted a $1,000 bond for good behavior with Penick.

That same spring, Colonel Henry Younger traveled to New York and purchased seasonal goods to sell in his dry goods store. He immediately commenced advertising his new eastern wares and made an effort to live as if the war and its losses would soon end and his family could return to the lives they had enjoyed before the turmoil.[3]

Early in May, Quantrill's band disbanded for a month to procure horses and ammunition. Captain Quantrill, George Todd, and Cole Younger, attired as Union officers, rode into Hamilton, a small village on the Hannibal

George M. Todd. (Author's collection)

and St. Joseph Railroad. They passed undetected by a company of the United States Seventh Cavalry and checked into a hotel. Moving on to Hannibal, they purchased 50,000 revolver caps and other much-needed ammunition before riding into St. Joseph, which was under the command of Colonel Harrison B. Branch. Near Kansas City, Todd brought the ammunition to the bushwhacker camp in Jackson County. When a federal picket stopped the wagon, Cole and Quantrill slipped off the back and disappeared into the woods unseen.

When Frank Younger learned that Quantrill was in Jackson County, he sought the guerrilla leader hoping to join the irregulars. Having fought under General Price in many battles against the federals, Frank took his oath and, within weeks, was riding with Quantrill, Cole, and the other bushwhackers. One reason Frank joined Quantrill was that the federals would have required him to join the Union militia, placing him at odds with his beliefs and friends.[4]

Frank later remembered: "I met Bill Gregg, Quantrill's First Lieutenant, in Clay County and with him rowed across the Missouri River to this county [Jackson] and joined Quantrill at the Webb place on Blackwater ford of the Sni just a few miles from here [Blue Springs]. This was in May 1863."[5]

Frank saw his first action with Quantrill during a fight at Richfield, Missouri. During one skirmish with Union troops, Frank James and "Hi" (Hiram) George spotted the enemy marching up a country lane, and with the sun ricocheting off their buckles and buttons, they made perfect targets.[6] The two men did not waste the opportunity.

Because of the Union victory at Pea Ridge, Confederate President Jefferson Davis, seeking to re-establish a Confederate presence in the area, created the Department of the Trans-Mississippi on May 26th. The new department included Arkansas, Missouri, Texas, western Louisiana, and Indian Territory under the command of Major General Thomas Hindman.[7]

In June, a federal mail escort, which had left Independence for Harrisonville on the morning of the 11th, with twenty-three men and two non-commissioned officers of Captain Cochran's company of Missouri State Militia, was attacked fifteen miles from Independence. Two men were killed and another two wounded. A scout dispatched by Colonel Buel failed to find the bushwhackers. Colonel Buel reported that he had secured reliable information that Quantrill and sixty men were back in the vicinity of Pink Hill.[8]

Captain J.F. Cochran, Second Battalion Missouri Cavalry, described the attack in his official report: "We had proceeded some [ten] miles when I learned that some of Quantrill's men had been seen in the vicinity. I proceeded very slowly and cautiously, with six men riding by file as an advance. They had proceeded only a short distance when they were fired upon, two of them being killed on the spot and three dangerously wounded. I was about [fifty] yards in the rear with [eighteen] men. We charged in the brush after them and routed them and then dismounted and searched the brush, and fired at them a number of times. I do not know what their loss was, as I had to leave to take care of the mail. The mail is safe. Captain Long, of our battalion, was fired upon from near the same place while escorting the mail a few weeks since."[9]

Major W.C. Ransom wrote Brigadier-General Blunt from Santa Fe, Missouri on June 20th: "Hays, with 100 men, joined Quantrill on the frontier on Tuesday last. Our departure from this station leaves our frontier unprotected from the Missouri River to Cold Water Grove. The people are preparing to leave their homes on our departure. I respectfully suggest to you that the absence of federal troops here will be followed by immediate acts of arson and robbery in Kansas."[10]

That same month, information reached Quantrill that a company of fifty men under Captain Long was foraging along the Harrisonville and Independence Road. Cole Younger was ordered to take twenty-five men and ambush the federals at Blue Cut. Cole learned through spies that a former bushwhacker named Shoat was accompanying the federals. Shoat had enlisted under Quantrill a few months earlier and then deserted, carrying valuable information to the enemy.

Although Cole had suspected Shoat of being a spy, he harbored no ill will towards Captain Long, an old boyhood friend. While Cole posted his men in the gap for an ambush, he begged his men not to kill or injure Long, but to not allow Shoat to escape under any circumstances.

At three o'clock in the afternoon of June 12th, the federals rode into the ambush and fell under heavy fire. Captain Long put up a good fight, but the bushwhackers fought from the summit of the cut, and it was impossible for the federals to reach them. After fifteen minutes of intense fighting, the federal troops began a mad dash out of the cut despite the entreaties of Captain Long.

Cole shot Captain Long's horse from under him and then gave chase after Shoat. The second shot from his pistol hit Shoat in the back, breaking his spinal cord. After making sure the spy was dead, Cole rode back to Major Long, who had been made a prisoner, and conversed with him on friendly terms.[11]

In July, Quantrill's force was increased by twelve men under Jack Rider, who had been attacking the border counties on his own. With his force of seventy-five men, Quantrill decided to leave the Sny Hills and enter Harrisonville, where there was a large stock of provisions guarded by a hundred raw federals. But the federals were everywhere, and with the roads well protected, Quantrill took to the woods with the enemy tracking him.

On Tuesday, July 8th, Major James O. Gower, First Iowa Cavalry received information that Quantrill's band of guerrillas, numbering some 200 men, was encamped on Sugar Creek, near Wadesburg, Cass County, Missouri. Major Gower immediately dispatched Lieutenant R.M. Reynolds, of Company A. First Iowa Cavalry, with Lieutenants Bishop, Foster, and Whisenand, and ninety enlisted men of Companies A, G, and H. First Iowa Cavalry, in search of them.[12]

The detachment set off at 11:00 P.M. with orders to reach and attack Quantrill's camp, if possible, at daylight the following day. Quantrill's camp was discovered about 6:00 A.M. on the 9th, and the advance guard, under Lieutenant Bishop, of Company A., First Iowa Cavalry, led the attack, but, not being supported by the main column as soon as expected, retired without loss, though receiving several volleys. Lieutenant Reynolds charged with his command, but finding the ground unfavorable and the bushwhacker position very strong, he retired with two men wounded and another killed. Quantrill lost one man killed and several wounded.

Upon the return of the detachment, Major Gower sent dispatches to Butler and Warrensburg for reinforcements to meet them at Lotspeich's farm, in Cass County, about one mile west of their camp. Gower marched, with four commissioned officers and seventy enlisted men of Companies A and G, First Iowa Cavalry, at five o'clock on the morning of the 10th, reaching the Lotspeich farm at 11:00 A.M. Awaiting their arrival was a detachment of sixty-five men, First Iowa Cavalry, from Butler, Missouri, under command of Captain William H. Ankeny, with Lieutenants Dinsmore and McIntyre, as well as a detachment of sixty-five enlisted men of the Seventh Missouri Cavalry, from Harrisonville, under command of Captain William A. Martin.

Soon, Gower's command was increased by Lieutenant White and sixty enlisted men of the First Missouri Cavalry, from Warrensburg, under command of Captain M. Kehoe. The federals learned that Quantrill and his men (estimated at 250) had left their camp on Sugar Creek about 4:00 P.M. two days earlier, but Gower received word from Captain Kehoe that he had found their trail and was pursuing them.

Major Gower and his command pressed forward in a northeasterly direction, passing east of Rose Hill, Johnson County, and moving up Big Creek Bottom in a northwesterly direction. They overtook Captain Kehoe at the farm of a Mr. Hornsby, where Quantrill, Cole Younger, and the guerrillas had taken dinner. Having marched fifty miles that day Gower set up camp, distributing his men at farmhouses for subsistence and forage, some of the details having marched without rations.

Meanwhile, according to Major Gower, Captain Kehoe marched without his knowledge in the morning, and in direct disregard of his orders, confronted Quantrill and his band three miles west of Pleasant Hill, at Sears' farm in Cass County, Missouri. Captain Henry J. Stierlin, First Missouri Cavalry, however, claimed that the captain had, in fact, reported to the major that he was sent in pursuit of Quantrill, and knowing that any delay would give the bushwhackers a start, told Major Gower that he would advance at once, and that, if he should meet the marauders, he would dispatch a messenger. Captain M. Kehoe then followed along a creek in pursuit.[13]

He soon struck the bushwhacker's trail at Lincoln Ford, on Big Creek, and immediately dispatched a messenger to Major Gower, requesting him to follow up as soon as possible. Learning from the neighboring farmers, where Quantrill had fed his horses, and that his force consisted of about 250 to 300 men, the captain deemed it prudent to give the First Iowa Cavalry a chance to follow up, keeping up the pursuit in a slow walk.

He arrived at about 7:00 P.M. at a farm-house eight miles west of Pleasant Hill, where Quantrill had again stopped to feed his horses, and at which place he also halted to rest for the night and await reinforcements. Shortly after, Major Gower's command came up and they also encamped for the night. Here it was agreed upon to start again in pursuit of the bush-whackers at daybreak, Friday, July 11th. At the appointed time, Captain Kehoe's command was in the saddle, and Captain Stierlin's report indicates notice was given to Major Gower.

Receiving no answer he started slowly on the trail, giving ample time for the First Iowa Cavalry to follow up. The captain found that Quantrill had passed Pleasant Hill, leaving it to the right, all the time keeping within the brush, when suddenly, about four miles west of Pleasant Hill, the cavalry came upon Quantrill's pickets, and immediately dispatched another messenger to the major, informing him that he was about to engage their advance, and at the same time requesting reinforcements.

In driving in the Confederate pickets, the federals followed them half a mile farther to a house in the brush where Quantrill was encamped. Supposing that this was but a part of the force, it was Captain Kehoe's intention to surprise them, and, immediately ordering a charge, he succeeded in penetrating them. Without warning, he found himself encircled by the whole gang, consisting of men under Quantrill, Upton Hayes, and Houx, who fired from all sides. Captain Kehoe's horse was shot from under him, and he received a ball in his right shoulder. He engaged them for about half an hour. Then deeming it more prudent to dismount the men, he withdrew them from the assault and secured the horses, himself mounting another horse and bringing up the men as skirmishers on foot for the purpose of renewing the attack.

It was at this point he discovered Major Gower's command in the distance. He sent a report of the engagement to the major and also of the bush-whacker position. Kehoe, instead of attacking in a solid body, deployed a part of his command as skirmishers, to cut off, if possible, the retreat of the guerrillas, keeping the remainder with him as an attacking party. Soon the engagement was renewed furiously. Again the captain's horse was shot from under him, and he was compelled to lead his men on foot.

Upon crossing the road from Pleasant Hill to Independence, Major Gower sent Lieutenant McIntyre, of Company L, First Iowa Cavalry, with fifty men, through the timber along the Independence Road, with instructions to march up on the open ground on the west. He and his command continued to follow Quantrill's trail, passing where the bushwhackers had encamped, and reaching the farm of Mr. Sears (where Captain Kehoe was repulsed) at 11:00 o'clock A.M. on the 11th.[14]

Near the Sears farm, Gower found a portion of Quantrill's band, which had fled down a wood road into the Big Creek timber. The federal advance guard, under command of Lieutenant John McDermott, of Company G, First Iowa Cavalry, pursued them, and the head of the column close upon them, came upon Quantrill's main force, lying in the cliffs of the ravines, at Walnut Creek, about half a mile from Sears' house.

The bushwhacker position was very strong, and Cole was sent out with a party of twelve men to forage on July 13th. Upon reaching the home of Joe Larkin, Cole spotted a party of fifteen men approaching in advance of a large force of federals. Cole and his men had left their horses in back of the house to feed, and seeing some quilts washed the day before hanging on a fence, ordered his men to hide in them.[15]

When the fifteen federals reached a spot in the road directly opposite them, Cole and his men opened fire, killing all but one of the men. The main body of federal troops, shocked by the bold attack, formed in line of battle anticipating a charge from a large Confederate force. As 200 men from the Butler County Militia joined them, the federals advanced as Cole and his men mounted their horses and retreated into the bushes.

Just as Cole reached Quantrill, the federals, 400 strong, mounted two charges against the bushwhackers but were driven back both times. The broken federal cavalry retreated to a hill 200 yards away and held a council. About four o'clock in the afternoon, the federals were reinforced by another 200 men and renewed hostilities with a third charge. A hundred Yankees took up positions along the creek, while another 200 was sent to attack the guerrillas from the rear, but the bluffs prevented the latter detachment from reaching a position where they could be effective.

Several charges by the federals, however, took their toll on the weary bushwhackers. Quantrill was hit in the leg, but continued to fight and cheer his men on. Cole Younger's clothing was riddled with bullets and his hat shot off. George Shepherd was hit in the arm. Several of the men lay wounded and dying in pools of blood and half of their horses had been killed.

After repulsing four charges, Cole Younger and two other men were sent out to find a means of escape. Cole crawled into the Union lines in a pouring rain, located every squad and picket, and found a clear passage up a steep bluff. He reported back to Quantrill just before midnight, and the camp moved out. It took over an hour for the men and horses to climb the hill and their movement was detected by the federals, who attempted to follow in the darkness. With Cole leading the way, the guerrillas escaped.

The federal attack, however, had scattered them. According to Major Gower, Quantrill was wounded in the thigh and his guerrillas completely routed and disbanded, fleeing in small squads in all directions. Out of the four commissioned officers in the Gower's command, three were wounded, and the action of the men was highly commendable and entirely satisfactory.[16]

Captain William A. Martin, Seventh Missouri Cavalry, later reported:

> Quantrill, with his forces, fell back half a mile and took position in a ravine, which was surrounded with dense brush, and which had precip‐it[ous] banks on either side from [five] to [seven] feet high, the banks being from [two] to [four] rods apart, giving him a very strong position. The dead of the column advanced and opened fire on him from the prairie, which he returned with great vigor for a few moments, when I came in sight with my command, and, observing the position of the enemy, advanced at once upon their lines. But on riding up within [fif‐teen] paces of the precipice from behind which they were pouring a galling fire upon us I dismounted my men, and, being under so strong a fire, did not wait to form more than [twenty] of my men until I charged upon their lines, not firing a shot until I reached the brink of the precipice, when I opened a volley of fire upon their lines, which were formed not more than [fifteen] feet from my line which produced a most dreadful effect. I at once cried to my brave men to charge the ditch, by which time some more of my men had taken position by my side. We threw ourselves in the narrow defile among them. Then ensued a hand‐to‐hand and bloody struggle for the mastery of the defile; but my gallant men drove them from their strong position with not more than half the

number of men they had on their side. I scaled the opposite bank after them, and drove them back near 100 yards to the edge of the brush, they disputing every inch of the ground. But, as if had been discovered by the major that they were being beaten back toward the open ground, he sent a detachment around to that side, which drove them back, and for a time I and my little band even intermingled with the enemy. They broke entirely past us and formed again in the same defile that they had so stubbornly defended before. I again charged them in their stronghold and again drove them from it, when they took position on another defile, that gave as strong a position as the first; but again I charged their lines and routed them from their position, which partly broke their ranks, and by this time another detachment had been dismounted and sent into the brush, and, by a succession of charges and repulsed we eventually dispersed them in every direction, every man seeking safety and without regard to any one else. Thus ended to bloodiest and most sanguinary guerrilla battle that has been fought in State of Missouri, or probably in the United States, according to numbers engaged. The battle raged one hour and a half, and at no time was my command more than [fifty] feet from their lines, and probably more than half the time within half of that distance, and making seven charges on their lines, and all this with the loss of only [one] man of my command killed, and [one] of the First Iowa, who had fallen in with me, wounded. The number actually engaged was about equal on either side.[17]

After the engagement, the federals rested an hour. Captain Martin's company was first to mount, and they scoured the country until dark and brought in what loose horses could be found. The company ascertained that the greater part of the bushwhackers went northward, but, as Martin's orders were to report to Major Gower, he did not pursue them. Because of the jaded condition of the men and horses, Major Gower deemed it inexpedient to attempt to follow them any farther, At ten o'clock P.M. the different commands left the battlefield of Big Creek for their respective stations.

Quantrill and Shepherd received the best surgical attention but their wounds were slight. Before calling the command together, Cole Younger and George Shepherd were sent into Kansas City to secure ammunition, while Quantrill left for St. Joseph to get arms. Cole and George procured the ammunition, loaded it into a wagon, and started for camp.[18]

While stopping at friend's house five miles from the city for the night, they found themselves surrounded by federal cavalry. Their wagon was secreted in a wheat field behind the house while the horses were tied behind two outbuildings. The federal commander demanded an immediate surrender, but the two bushwhackers drew their revolvers, dashed out the back door, killing four men as they ran, and rode away on their horses. Cole had been hit by three balls, but his wounds were not serious. Shepherd, however, was shot in the shoulder and thigh, which prevented him from riding. Cole rode to his aid, helped him along, and left him with friends where his wounds were mended.

Henry Younger continued on with his life as the difficulties between Kansas and Missouri waged on, trying to remain neutral and run his business. Still, the looting of his business continued. In an effort to reorganize his livery business, he and several of his employees journeyed to Kansas City to sell some horses. There was, of course, a great demand for horses, and Henry planned to buy superior mounts in mid-July. Although he had invested a great deal of capital and had suffered repeated raids on his business, he had netted an impressive profit from his livery business. Everyone was aware of Cole's association with Quantrill, but the colonel simply refused to discuss it by relating his wish to stay neutral on the matter.[19]

Henry Younger decided that while he was in Kansas City, he would speak with someone at the state militia headquarters to see what could be done about the continuous raids occurring in his community. As a small contractor doing business with the federal government, his equipment, horses, wagons, and barns had been guaranteed against loss by the military.[20]

While on this trip, he had conducted some successful business transactions, including the sale of a herd of cattle, and had $1,500 on his person, which he hid in a money belt to begin his trip home. Because of his good fortune, he rewarded his employees by letting them stay in Kansas City a few days. Traveling south along the Westport Road, he talked with two of Bursheba's teenage cousins, who were on their way to Kansas City to purchase provisions for their family. Resuming his journey, he stopped at the home of a friend and allegedly told him he was being followed by a militia gang.[21]

Known to frequently carry large sums of money, he was riding alone in his one-horse buggy on the thirty-mile trip back to Harrisonville. About one mile south of Westport, on July 20, 1862, Henry Younger was shot three times in the back and killed. His horse was tied to a tree, and his body left lying where it had fallen from the wagon.

There are several versions of where Henry was actually shot, but according to the story told by Cole, the above version is correct. Henry's body was found by Mrs. Washington Wells and her son Samuel, "a hairy, crude, semi-illiterate farm boy," on the road from Kansas City to Lee's Summit.[22] Mrs. Wells stayed with the body while her son went to Colonel Peabody of the federal command encamped at Kansas City.[23]

A witness saw Irvin Walley and a group of his soldiers depart shortly after Henry Younger. Although Henry Younger had a substantial amount of cash on him, his body had been undisturbed after his fall from the wagon, so the murder was politically motivated and not a robbery. Charity Kerr and Nannie Harris, cousins of Cole, recognized Walley near the murder scene. Most likely, Walley was seeking vengeance for the earlier incident involving Cole.

Following an investigation, Irvin Walley was charged with the murder of Henry Younger. Missouri State Militia Brigadier-General Benjamin Loan wrote that he had Walley arrested and the motive was robbery. "The evidence of his guilt," wrote Loan, "was so clear and conclusive that he confessed it." Loan ordered the court to try Walley but soldiers of the Fifth Regiment Missouri State Militia, who were expected to testify against Walley, were ambushed and murdered on their way to the trial.

Brigadier General Loan accused Cole Younger of murdering the militiamen. Cole had been unaware that the soldiers intended to testify against Walley and perhaps mistakenly believed Walley was amongst the soldiers in the group. Without the soldiers' testimony, there could be no trial, and Walley was released. Cole later wrote: "During the war I did everything within my power to get hold of him, but failed."[24]

Cole was later asked in an interview as to how much land his father owned at the time of his assassination, to which he replied: "He had 3,500 acres, a greater part of which was under cultivation, with barns, houses, etc. All this property went with the ravages of the war. My part has long since been spent in keeping out of the clutches of mobs."[25]

Todd M. George later described the scene:

> [Colonel Younger] then resorted to the raising of livestock and on one fatal occasion he had sent quite a number of cattle to Westport, the only existing farm market for all kinds of farm produce where on each delivery they were paid in cash. On this same fatal occasion Mr. Younger

had collected about $1,600 from the Westport market and it so happened that some of the Kansas Redlegs saw him make this collection and followed him for about three miles southeast of Westport as he was returning home. They overtook his buggy, stopped him and pulled him out and robbed him of all cash and mangled his body which they dumped by the side of the road. Shortly a Mrs. Wells with her young son was driving to the Westport market when she discovered Mr. Younger's horse and buggy tied by the side of the road and a short distance from it she discovered his mangled body. She stepped out of her buggy and guarded the body as she instructed her young son to turn back and drive to the Younger home and relate what had happened. When this message reached the Younger family someone of the members drove to a country school where Cole Younger, nearing the age of seventeen, and some of his younger brothers and sisters were in attendance. They were driven home to await the arrival of Mr. Younger's body.[26]

Henry Younger's body was returned to the family and buried on the Younger property. They were worried about Walley and his band of soldiers digging up his grave and displaying his body so they left the grave unmarked.

George M. Todd recalled: "In visiting with Cole Younger, he often told me that they buried his father in a very remote place on the farm and left it unmarked, due to the fact that they feared that the Kansas Redlegs might on some occasion molest his grave. The result of all this was the beginning of Cole Younger's career with the Younger brothers to resort to revenge. As much history was made in the days of revenge was the first time that the Younger family had ever swayed from the idea that there should be a separate north or south in this country."[27]

The death of Henry had a devastating effect on the Younger's both financially and emotionally. Cole later stated in an interview: "It was the earliest desire of my parents to prepare me for the ministry, but the horrors of war, the murder of my father, and the outrages perpetrated upon my poor old mother, my sisters and brothers, destroyed our hopes so effectually that none of us could be prepared for any duty in life except revenge."[28]

Union Captain Reuben Smith of Asawatomie, Kansas, later gave an interview which focused upon the early life of the Youngers and the murder of their father. He alleged that during the first week of January 1862, he was at Harrisonville, Missouri, serving under A.G. Nugent's regiment. He was in charge of the quartermaster and commissary stores, and he kept supplies in a long brick storeroom on the north side of the square. He also kept a barrel of whiskey, which had been found in a straw pile a few miles from town. One morning, his superior officer introduced him to a man, who at once struck him as an old Southern planter. He was tall, well built, gentlemanly in manner, language, and deportment. This man, claimed Captain Smith, was Colonel Henry Younger, father of the "notorious" Younger brothers. As long as the whiskey lasted, the two colonels came every morning for the daily drink.[29]

On one of these mornings, insisted Smith, a young, tall man came in a carriage and entered the back of the storeroom, asking if his father was present. When Smith informed him he was with another colonel upstairs, Cole yelled, "Pap, breakfast is ready, and mother wants you to come at once." The young man was Cole Younger.

Smith insisted that the boys' father was not killed for months afterward and the burning of the house, which he himself ordered, did not take place until a year later. Prior to both events, he maintained, Cole Younger and his gang had bushwhacked an escort of Smith's company near Blue Cut, killing one soldier and wounding six others. Mrs. Younger lived nearby, and when Smith talked with her about the bushwhacking, she said Cole had been there and she would continue to feed and harbor him. A few days later, said Smith, she cared for another member of the gang and swore she would help any Southern soldier in the bush or in her home. Smith said Mrs. Younger seemed to think she was running the "whole Confederacy." The home was ordered to be burned by Smith's superior officer.

As to the murder of Cole's father, Smith maintained plunder was not the reason for the act. Three of the men were Missourians and two from Kansas, and they killed for separate reasons. Nothing was taken from the body of Colonel Younger but a gold pin. Smith concluded by saying the Youngers were bandits by choice, since after the war, they could have turned in their weapons and become good citizens.

That same summer, Cole Younger and six companions crept up on a house of ill-repute in Jackson County which was frequented by federal soldiers. Cole rushed forward ordering his men to follow, but four refused to charge. There were six men inside the brothel and three rushed out the back door leaving the other three to fight it out. One of Cole's men was killed in the first round, but Cole fired back and hit two of the enemy. As Cole charged the house, he was hit in the right shoulder by the third man firing from the upper door with a double-barrel shotgun loaded with buckshot. Falling to the ground, Cole rose up and entered the house just as the soldier was attempting to flee out the back door. Cole fired and brought him down as the women fled from the house. Cole then sank to the floor from loss of blood but was carried by his comrades to his horse. The party rode fifty miles before Cole paused to have his wounds dressed.[30]

When Quantrill and Hayes learned that Cockrell's army had entered Missouri, they consolidated their forces with those of Hunter, Coffee, and Tracy. On August 10, 1862, Colonel J.T. Hughes arrived in Jackson County and took command of the combined Confederate force.

On August 11, 1862, Colonel J.T. Hughes's Confederate force, including William Quantrill and 400 irregulars, many of them farm boys, attacked Independence at dawn, in two columns on different roads. The pickets on Spring Street were run over and killed by Quantrill who entered the town from the north. They rode through the town to the Union Army camp, capturing, killing, and scattering the Yankees. Quantrill and his men stormed the prison and released all the Confederate prisoners in it. Most of the federal soldiers had been stationed at a tent camp in a pasture about a half-mile west of the courthouse square while Buel's headquarters were in the Southern Bank Building. Buel's guard company was quartered nearby to the west under the command of Captain W.H. Rodewald.[31]

Lieutenant Colonel James T. Buel, commander of the garrison, attempted to hold out in one of the buildings with some of his men. Buel, wanting to hoist a flag over his headquarters to show his men in the pasture he was still holding out, discovered that there was no flagpole on the building. Two of Rodewald's men climbed on the roof and attempted to tie a flag to the chimney but they were both shot down by the bushwhackers. Two Confederate prisoners were forced to fasten the flag to the chimney, but they were recognized and not fired upon.[32]

Quantrill asked for volunteers to set fire to the building abutting the Southern Bank, and Cole Younger and Jabez McCorkle spoke up. The two men piled wood shavings from a nearby carpentry shop against two doors and lighted them. With the building next to him on fire, Buel, by means of a flag of truce, arranged a meeting with the Confederate commander, Colonel G.W. Thompson, who had replaced Colonel J.T. Hughes, killed earlier. Buel surrendered and about 150 of his men were paroled, the others had escaped,

159

hidden, or been killed. Having taken Independence, the Rebel force headed for Kansas City. Confederate dominance in the Kansas City area continued, but not for long.

Colonel Daniel Huston, Jr., wrote Brigadier-General Totten from Lexington on August 12th: "Two hundred and forty men that I sent yesterday to Independence, under Major Bredett, have just returned, and report that Independence was attacked by 1,500 men, under a Colonel Hughes and Quantrill, and after four hours' hard fighting Lieutenant-Colonel Buel surrendered. It is reported that the rebels are marching on this place. Major McKee has not yet arrived. I shall telegraph Colonel Catherwood to send me two or three companies. I am very anxious in regard to Major Linder, of Harrisonville, with his two companies. He must be on the march to Independence."[33]

Brigadier-General J.M. Schofield wrote General Henry W. Halleck that same day:

> In the southeastern part of the State all is comparatively quiet. I believe there is no immediate danger to be apprehended in that quarter. In the western and southwestern parts of the State the rebels are extremely active and bold. Quantrill succeeded in taking Independence with a few men yesterday. I had ordered a concentration of troops enough in that part of the State to prevent the rebels from gaining any considerable foothold and to break them up in a short time. Coffee, with 500 or 600 men, had succeeded in eluding General Brown's forces and passed up near to the Osage, where he has been joined by a thousand or more recruits. I have two bodies of cavalry after him, and I am sure he cannot gain more than a very temporary success.[34]

Many Independence residents knew of the planned attack and took refuge in Kansas City, but the Union soldiers were, nonetheless, taken by surprise because Buel had refused to believe them. Because Independence was an armed post, Buel felt no Confederate army would dare try to capture it.

Cole later wrote: "It was within a day or two after the surrender of Buell at Independence that I was elected first lieutenant in Captain Jarrette's company in Colonel Upton B. Hays' regiment, which was a part of the brigade of General Joseph O. Shelby. We took the oath, perhaps 300 of us, down on Luther Mason's farm, a few miles from where I now write, where Colonel Hays had encamped after Independence. Millions of boys and men have read with rising hair the terrible 'black oath' which was supposed to have been taken by these brave fighters, but of which they never heard, nor I, until I read it in books published long after the war."[35]

When Colonel Hays camped on the Cowherd, White, Howard and Younger farms, Quantrill and his men had been left to guard the approaches to Kansas City and to prevent the escape from the scattered Confederate commands recruiting in western Missouri. At the same time, he was obtaining from the Chicago and St. Louis newspapers and other sources, information about the northern armies, which was conveyed by couriers to Confederate officers in the South, and he kept concealed along the Missouri River skiffs and ferry boats to enable the Confederate officers, recruiting north of the river, to have free access to the south.

On the night in which Cole enlisted, he was dispatched by Colonel Hays to rendezvous with Colonels Cockrell, Coffee, Tracy, Jackman, and Hunter, who, with the remnants of regiments that had been shattered in various battles through the South, were moving toward Colonel Hays' command. Colonel Hays' planned for them to join him on the 15th, and after a day's rest, the entire command would attack Kansas City, and, among other advantages resulting from victory there, secure possession of Weller's steam ferry. Cole with Boone Muir met Coffee and the rest below Rose Hill, on the Grand River.

On August 16th, 1862, the bloodiest battle fought on Missouri soil took place. But for a twist of fate, it would not have happened at all. As Colonel Jeremiah Vardeman Cockrell marched up from the South with his expedition, his ranks were swelled by the addition of companies, squads, and individuals, giving him an army of 3,200 men. In Butler County, Colonel John T. Coffee, of the State Guards, and Colonel Charles Tracy, of the Confederate Army, joined him with their commands.[36]

The time was opportune for invasions of the state, as Missouri's governor was enforcing his famous order requiring all men of military age to join the State militia or Home Guards. This order sent thousands of men into the woods, all of whom were anxious to reach the Southern Army. Recruitment for the Confederacy was at an all time high, and Cockrell's standard was welcomed everywhere. His brother, General Francis Marion Cockrell, had served for thirty years as a United States Senator from Missouri.[37]

On the night of August 14th the army camped in Johnson County. Captain Jo Shelby, along with his company, went to Lafayette County, which was home. Shelby was acting by orders of the Confederate Government.

Only voluntarily was he subject to Cockrell's orders. Shelby's purpose was to raise a regiment in his home county. In doing so, he was not a participant of the Lone Jack battle.

Being so close to home himself, Colonel Cockrell turned the command over to Colonel D.C. Hunter and headed for Warrensburg. On the morning of the 15th, Hunter moved early and marched all day toward the northeast. At noon of August 15th, Muir and Cole had been in the saddle twenty-four to thirty hours, and lay down in the grass to sleep. Colonel Hays, however, was still anxious to have the other command join him, he having plenty of forage, and being well equipped with ammunition as the result of the capture of Independence a few days before. Accordingly, Cole and Muir shortly awakened to accompany him to Lone Jack, a little village in the southeastern portion of Jackson County, so called from a solitary big black jack tree that rose from an open field nearly a mile from any other timber.

By nightfall, Hunter had arrived in the vicinity of Lone Jack. Colonels' Coffee and Tracy, who were independent of Colonel Cockrell and of each other, camped by themselves. Tracy stopped two miles southeast of Lone Jack on the Dave Arnold farm. Coffee went into camp with his men on the Ambers Graham farm, half a mile southwest of Lone Jack. Colonel Hunter continued through the town another three and a half miles camping on the farm of George Kreeger.

Cockrell was almost home when he learned that a large body of federals, probably Colonel Warren's Iowa troops from the post at Clinton, was moving in the direction his army had gone. He raced back, arriving at Hunter's camp that night. Never had an army been in greater peril than what now threatened the army scattered around Lone Jack. Warren was coming up from the southeast with 800 men; Blunt with 1,500 was heading in from Fort Scott and was near at hand on the southwest; and Major Emory Foster was just a short distance outside of Lone Jack.

Foster had nearly 1,000 cavalrymen, and two pieces of Rabb's Indiana battery that had already made for itself a name for hard fighting. He did not dream of the presence of Cockrell and his command until he stumbled upon them in Lone Jack. The federal troops were converging on the area in retaliation for Buel's capture at Independence on the 11th of August.

Colonel Cockrell had no artillery; he expected no reinforcements except for Hays. Quantrill's troops were in the area, but Quantrill himself was on his way back to Independence to collect the spoils won at Independence, leaving orders that his men were to remain where they were. Cockrell had but slight authority over the men about him—no authority over part of them. He had but one wagon containing only a small amount of ammunition, and he was heavily encumbered with unarmed recruits.

Brigadier-General James Totten of Jefferson City wired Foster at midnight on August 14th that he had been selected to operate against the rebels who were supposed to be near Lone Jack under Hays and Quantrill. Foster had already proceeded from Syracuse to Sedalia, to take command of forces about to march to Lexington. His command was joined by Company H, Seventh Missouri State Militia, Captain Elias Slocum, from Syracuse, two companies of the Eighth Missouri State Militia, Captains Henry D. Moore and Owens, and a section of the Third Indiana Battery, under Lieutenant J.S. Devlin. Foster marched immediately, and reached Lexington, a distance of sixty miles; men and horses very much worn-out, having marched forty-eight hours without food or rest. Foster reported:

> I received an order from you at [one] o'clock A.M. August 15 to march at daylight in the direction of Lone Jack, with 800 men. At daylight I marched with a force consisting of detachments from five companies: Seventh Cavalry, Missouri Volunteers, three companies Sixth Cavalry, Missouri State Militia, two companies Eighth Cavalry, Missouri State Militia, three companies Second Battalion Cavalry, Missouri State Militia, and one company Seventh Cavalry, Missouri State Militia, together with a section of the Third Indiana Battery. In consequence of a jealousy in regard to rank no field officers were sent with me, as you directed should be done. I marched directly for Lone Jack. About noon I reported to Colonel Huston, commanding at Lexington, that the enemy, 1,600 strong, were at Lone Jack, under Coffee, and that I would fight that evening.[38]

Two armies, ignorant of each other's existence, made a long, fatiguing march on the 15th, a dry, blistering hot day. The two approached each other at right angles at Lone Jack, Foster's army from Lexington and Cockrell's army from Johnson County. Upon reaching Lone Jack at eight o'clock in the evening, the federals bivouacked on the streets and in the houses. They placed their cannons in the road, one facing north, the other facing south.

The citizens of Lone Jack had been warned of Foster's approach and remained inside their homes. When Foster learned that Coffee and his men were encamped near town, he decided to attack. Artillerymen of the Third

163

Indiana Light Artillery under Lieutenant James Devlin moved their two six-pounders into position to cover the advance, while skirmishers took positions on both flanks and in front of the enemy.[39]

"We surprised the camp about 9:00 o'clock that evening and completely routed the enemy," recalled Major Foster. "Lieutenant Develin [sic], being drunk, acted very badly, and was arrested, and the artillery placed in charge of Sergeant [James M.] Scott. The men then slept in line in Lone Jack. About daylight the pickets came in and reported that the enemy [sic] were advancing, about 3,000 strong. Several scouts had reported, and no word from Warren, who should have been in supporting distance. Two parties were still out, leaving us about 740 men."

At nightfall, the Indiana battery opened on Lone Jack, and the Confederate commands were cut in two. Captain Milton H. Brawner, Seventh Missouri Cavalry later wrote:

> [We] marched on the 15th instant to Lone Jack, [thirty-two] miles southwest of this place, arriving there about [nine] o'clock same evening. Having ascertained, immediately arriving there, that about 800 rebels, under the command of Colonel Coffee, were encamped about one mile south of the town, we prepared against a surprise. The artillery was brought into position, commanding the lane through which we were passing, while skirmishers were thrown out on each flank and to the front, and the whole column moved forward. After advancing about three-fourths of a mile, between the town and the camp of the enemy, their cavalry charged down the lane upon us, but were received with a volley of musketry, which scattered them in all directions. Their camp was at the same time shelled by the battery with good effect. The enemy having fled, and no further demonstrations on their part being anticipated, the command returned to Lone Jack, arriving at [eleven] o'clock, and encamped for the night.[40]

According to Major Foster: "The attack was made about forty minutes after the pickets came in. The enemy attempted to turn both my right and left, but were unable to do so by reason of a thick hedge, which protected us on each flank and afforded some protection to our front, our rear being protected by a small, deep stream, the crossing of which we held. The enemy's cavalry, being thrown into confusion by the hedge and annoyed by sharpshooters placed behind it, fled in confusion, rejoining the main body, which then attacked us in front."[41]

Coffee retreated to the south, taking his wounded with him, while Cockrell withdrew to the west, and when Colonel Hays and Cole Younger arrived, Cockrell had his men drawn up in line of battle, while the officers were holding a council in his quarters. Foster, meanwhile, had called in his pickets and returned to town. He deployed pickets in the surrounding fields and ordered his men to camp for the night.[42]

With Coffee and his force on the run and Fitz-Henry Warren's First Iowa Cavalry expected to arrive the next day, Foster planned to move westward and attack other Confederate units. Warren's Iowans, however, had gotten lost and went to Harrisonville, some twenty miles out of the way.

The men at Hunter and Tracy's camps had heard the cannon's roar and were apprised of the presence of federals in the neighborhood. Tracy broke camp and making a wide detour, arrived during the night at Hunter's camp. Coffee disappeared in the darkness and did not return until after the battle the next day.

Cockrell, having arrived by this time, thought the cannon belonged to Warren's command from Clinton. During this time, Cockrell was informed by the local citizens that Captain George Webb and Dr. Caleb Winfrey, of Lone Jack, had been organizing a company during the week prior on the George Ingram farm, and they had now joined Colonel Upton Hays on the Frank Harbaugh farm.

He dispatched two swift horsemen to find Hays. Upon the arrival of Colonel Tracy, Cockrell called a council of war with Hunter, Hayes, Jackman, Thompson, and Coffee. The officers debated whether it would be wiser to steal away or fight. Hays and Coffee might come, or might not. The federals in Lone Jack were evidently more than a mere scout, the artillery proclaimed that. They decided to make the attack at daylight the next morning on whatever force might lay before them. It was a bold resolve, although the Confederates were unaware that their force outnumbered the federals 3,200 to 740.

Following the battle of Independence, Colonel Hays had succeeded to the command of all the soldiers who came up from the south with Hughes. Colonel Gideon Thompson, having succeeded when Colonel Hughes was killed, was himself wounded and unfit for battle. Thus the command fell to Colonel Hays. The news that the federals were in Lone Jack was enough. Hays roused his sleeping men and ordered them to mount. The company recruited by Webb and Winfrey had not been organized, but many of the men lived in the neighborhood of Lone Jack and this company was placed in the front. A rapid march was made to Hunter's camp. When Hays arrived with his command at the lane leading up to the Kreeger farm, he found Cockrell and Tracy on their horses waiting in the road.

Cockrell sent orders up to the camp for Hunter to rouse his men quietly and to put his columns in motion for Lone Jack. As the leaders rode forward, they conferred together, and by the time they reached the Noel farm the plan of battle had been agreed upon. They would dismount for the battle and approach the federals stealthily and take them by surprise.

Captain David Shanks, of Hays' command, who was familiar with the region, was to remain mounted and, with forty men, ride around to the north and east to the rear of the federal camp. His instructions were to bring on the battle and cut off retreat. In the confusion among the federals, occasioned by Shanks' feint on the east of their camp, the main attack would be instantly made by those lying ready on the west of their camp. Hunter was to hold the extreme right; Tracy the center; Hays the left. Jackman was at the right of Hays. The battle plan was, indeed, a good one. They expected a repeat of what had happened a few days prior at Independence.

The Confederate forces hurried to the Anderson Long orchard, a mile from Lone Jack. There the men dismounted and the companies were arranged. Six rounds of ammunition were doled out gingerly to those with arms. In the dark before dawn, these reapers of death crept into the weed-grown field west of what was then called the New Town square, where the federals had taken up camp.

As the Confederates moved into position, they waited for Shanks' attack; it never came. Unbeknownst to the waiting army, Shanks was delayed when he encountered a federal picket that was camped in the cemetery just east of town. The plan of battle was disconcerted and then lost when, somewhere down the Confederate line a new recruit, Marion McFarland, accidentally discharged his gun. In an instant the federals were set in motion. Their bugle sounded at arms. The time for attack had come; the time for surprise passed.

On the east side of the street stood a fence, except where a long blacksmith shop was located. On the west side of the street were a few store buildings, residences, a hotel, and some other building. Behind these buildings were garden plots, barns, and plank and rail fences separating the town property from the farmland, overgrown with high weeds and scattered patches of corn. Here is where the battle began. A wild forward rush brought the Confederates to the fences. A perfect shower of lead interchanged across the forty or sixty yards of space between buildings and rear fences.

Captain Brawner later penned:

> On the morning of the 16th, about daylight, we were attacked by an entirely different force, commanded by Cockrell, Thompson, Hays, Quantrill, and others, numbering about 3,200, who, as we afterward learned, had been encamped about nine miles northwest of Lone Jack. They came upon us under cover of cornfields and ridge fences, pouring upon us a most deadly fire, to which we replied with spirit. Our battery of two guns, supported by Company A, Seventh Cavalry, Missouri Volunteers, opened upon them with terrible effect, scattering them in confusion. They rallied, however, supported by overwhelming numbers. The battery was taken, but we retook it. Again it was lost and retaken. The contest at this time was terrible. Two-thirds of the detachment supporting the battery and [twenty-four] of the [thirty-six] men belonging to it are reported among the killed and wounded.[43]

Around the battery the federals were massing in some confusion leading horses forth and keeping up a random firing as Hays' men moved closer. Colonel Hays, cool, calm, observant, noted that the federals were beginning to shield themselves behind their horses and were firing from the saddlebows. He then gave a command, piteous in its execution, the first command and perhaps the last of the day, for this was the privates' battle. He called to his men above the roar of the guns; "Shoot the horses!" For many minutes more horses fell than did men. The poor helpless animals, wounded and dying, groaned piteously.

The two-cannon battery was not idle, by any means. These vicious instruments of death manifested their horrible capabilities by frightful smoke and roar. The cry of, "Take the battery!" ran along Hays' line. Captains Mart Rider and Halloway, and Webb and Winfrey dashed across the street with their companies and captured the battery in a hand-to-hand conflict. It was here that the captors stood and fought without reinforcements. A number of brave men fell in this first contest over the battery.

In the excitement and enthusiasm of this momentary but dearly bought success, a young man leaped on one of the guns and, swinging his hat over his head, shouted, "Hurrah for Jeff Davis!" He was immediately shot and killed. The routed federals returned in a heavy charge and retook the battery, driving Hays' men to the right and left, a part falling back to the line of their comrades across the street and a part taking shelter behind the hedge on the east side of the street. Colonel Hays and Captain Webb were the officers behind the hedge. In a few minutes, Captain Long, with a company of federal cavalry, appeared in the standing corn east of the hedge and a short but terrific fusillade occurred. On the west side of the street a spontaneous impulse was gathering head to capture that deadly battery again. This time Hays' men had support from many parts of the field. The Confederates approached, more sullen and desperate than before. The federals, seeing the storm coming, drew closer about the guns. For a moment there was a lull, not quite a silence, then a wild and frantic charge, Confederates and federals mingling, clubbing, shouting, cursing men falling and men dying. The federals gave back, and the guns were again in Confederate hands. But they were not long retained by their new masters. The Confederates were beaten back with heavy losses and in great confusion.

The battle raged from one end of the town to the other. Captain Caleb Winfrey, whose home was here, led his company in a charge against the federals who were occupying his own house, driving them from it. From the upper windows of the hotel, Foster's riflemen poured out a deadly, ceaseless fire on the Confederates crouching behind the fences, buildings, and whatever shelter they could find. Colonel Hays rode up the line on a black horse (the horse from which he would be shot at Newtonia), and ordered the hotel to be set on fire. Two or three soldiers crept forward. In a few minutes the building was in flames. It was a holocaust. The charred bodies of one or two men and a horse were discovered in the embers after the battle.

Intense fighting lasted for a full five hours across a street only sixty feet in width. There was no skirmishing at long range at Lone Jack. Vicious hand-to-hand fighting ruled, and to compound the horror and agony of the combatants, there was not a cloud in the sky that day, and the heat was terrible.

Riding to the still house where the guerrillas had left the wagon munitions taken a few days before at Independence, Cole obtained a fresh supply and started for the action on the gallop. Of that mad ride into the camp, he later said he remembered little except that his horse ran at full tilt before he came into the line of fire. Although the enemy was within 150 yards, Cole was not wounded. His clothes, however, were creased from bullets in one or two places.

Major Foster, in a letter to Judge George M. Bennett of Minneapolis, later penned: "During the progress of the fight my attention was called to a young Confederate riding in front of the Confederate line, distributing ammunition to the men from what seemed to be a 'splint basket.' He rode along under a most galling fire from our side the entire length of the Confederate line, and when he had at last disappeared, our boys recognized his gallantry in ringing cheers. I was told by some of our men from the western border of the state that they recognized the daring young rider as Cole Younger."

Major Foster later recalled the final struggle over the guns as follows: "We fall upon the Rebels in the middle of the street and struggle with them for guns. The carnage here is frightful. In less time than is required for the telling of it, the sixty federals are forty, and of these all but a dozen are disabled. Captain Long is mortally wounded. Lieutenant Rodgers is sorely hurt. Others lie in heaps-dead and dying . . ."

According to Cole, Foster had overrated the number of Confederates although his account of the fighting was accurate. Foster, however, referred to Confederate regiments that were not at the battle. As to Cole's gallant ride within thirty feet of Union guns, the rousing cheer he was given by the Yankees was not because of his courage but because the enemy thought they had killed him when his horse jumped a fence.[44]

William H. Gregg later called Cole and Jim Younger "two as brave chivalrous soldiers as the Confederate (or any other army) had," during the war. According to Gregg, Cole saved Major Emory S. Foster's life during the Battle of Lone Jack.[45] Although Foster was a Union officer during the war, he later praised Cole Younger for keeping him from being shot. Foster, major of the Seventh Cavalry Missouri State Militia, related that on August 15, 1862, he was in command of 740 Union troops searching for a Confederate force moving from Lexington to Sedalia, Missouri. He found the enemy at Lone Jack. His orders were to attack and hold the Southerners until General Warren, moving from Clinton, could join him. Foster's forces attacked the scattered Confederates, but learned from prisoners, a larger force of Confederates was camped only three miles away.[46]

"After a desperate fight of four hours' duration, the enemy began to fall back," penned Major Foster after the battle. "At this time Lieutenant Devlin came onto the field and, rushing among his men, ordered them to fall back, which they did, leaving the guns. Seeing this, the enemy rallied and made an attempt to capture the artillery but were repulsed with terrible slaughter. Of [sixty] men led by me in this charge, only [eleven] reached the guns, and they were all wounded. In the act of dragging the cannon out of the enemy's reach, I was shot down. Captain Brawner was then in command. After a severe hand-to-hand fight, which lasted about a half hour, the enemy gave way and retreated, leaving us the field and the guns. At this time Coffee came in sight with about 1,500 men, having collected his forces, which were scattered the night before. Captain Brawner fell back, leaving the guns. About an hour after the enemy came up we took possession of the field."[47]

Expecting General Warren to arrive during the night, the Union troops slept in line at Lone Jack. In the morning, they were attacked by, according to Foster, 3,000 Confederate troops. Foster was mesmerized by a brave young Confederate riding in front of his line, distributing ammunition to his men. Foster and his brother, both wounded, were soon captured and locked in a nearby house. A Confederate officer entered their room and said he was going to shoot them with his pistol. Cole Younger rushed in and "seizing the fellow, thrust him out of the room." Cole then placed a guard at the house so no one would disturb the captives.

Wrote Foster:[48]

> About 9:30 A.M. I was shot down. The wounded of both forces were gathered up and were placed in houses. My brother and I, both supposed to be mortally wounded, were in the same bed. About an hour after the Confederates left the field, the ranking officer, who took command when I became unconscious, gathered his men together and returned to Lexington. Soon after, the Confederates returned. The first man who entered my room was a guerrilla, followed by a dozen or more men who seemed to obey him. He was personally known to me and had been my enemy from before the war. He said he and his men had just shot a lieutenant of a Cass County company whom they found wounded and that he would shoot me and my brother. While he was standing over us, threatening us with his drawn piston, the young man I had seen distributing ammunition along in front of the Confederate line rushed into the room from the west door and seizing the fellow, thrust him out of the room. Several Confederates followed the young Confederate into the room, and I heard them call him Cole Younger. He (Younger) sent for Colonel Cockrell (in command of the Confederate forces) and stated

the case to him. He also called the young man Cole Younger and directed him to guard the house, which he did. My brother had with him
about $300, and I had about $700. This money and our revolvers were,
with the knowledge and approval of Cole Younger, placed in safe hands,
and were finally delivered to my mother in Warrensburg, Missouri. Cole
Younger was then certainly a high type of manhood, and every inch a
soldier, who risked his own life to protect that of wounded and disabled
enemies. I believe he still retains those qualities and would prove himself as good a citizen as we have among us if set free, and would fight for
the Stars and Stripes as fearlessly as he did for the Southern flag. I have
never seen him since the battle of Lone Jack. I know much of the conditions and circumstances under which the Youngers were placed after
the war, and knowing this, I have great sympathy for them. Many men,
now prominent and useful citizens of Missouri, were, like the Youngers,
unable to return to their homes until some fortunate accident through
them with men they had known before the war, who had influence
enough to make easy their return to peace and usefulness. If this had
occurred to the Youngers, they would have had good homes in
Missouri.[49]

Both sides expected reinforcements throughout all that terrible morning.
None was forthcoming. About half past nine a force of perhaps 200 men
appeared a mile south of the fighting. They were federals, but they came no
closer. Quantrill's men were in camp about five miles northwest of Lone Jack
on the morning of the battle. Quantrill, having returned the day before to
Independence, left Captain William H. Gregg in command, with orders not to
break camp under any circumstances. For several hours, Captain Gregg obeyed
the order, even after repeated pleas from Colonel Hays to come to their aid.
Finally, when his propensity for fighting could no longer be restrained, he gave
the order for his men to mount, and they galloped into battle.

The dust they raised could be seen from the battlefield, rising away to
the west about two miles. The Confederates shouted, "Hurrah for
Quantrill!" The federals thought they had been fighting Quantrill all morning, and the thought of him now coming into the fray was more than they
could stand. They quit the field in rapid succession. At the close of the battle the cannons were in possession of the federals. From lack of any means
to transport them, they were forced to abandon them, but not before they
put them out of commission by spiking them. There were 110 to 115 dead
horses on the battlefield, all federal horses.

Captain Milton H. Brawner recalled:

> At this juncture the force under Coffee, whom we had repulsed the evening before, again appeared on our left flank, with the evident design of surrounding our worn-out troops and cutting off all retreat. The men being utterly exhausted, and our ammunition almost gone, I deemed it unadvisable to hold the ground longer, and accordingly got the command together and marched off in good order toward this post, unmolested by the enemy. We were forced, much to our regret, to leave the battery behind, the horses attached to it having all been killed and the harness mostly destroyed and other portions of the equipage scattered in all directions. The gallantry of the men was conspicuously displayed after the last recapture of the battery, they being forced to handle the guns entirely without the aid of horses. No horses could be obtained to draw the guns.[50]

As the Confederate victors took over the town site at midday, they began an intense humanitarian outpouring of relief for the broken and mangled bodies clad both in blue and in gray. Captain Caleb Winfrey laid aside his saber and reached for his scalpels, once again becoming Doctor Caleb Winfrey. He was joined by fellow physicians Edward G. Ragsdale of Lone Jack and Minor T. Smith of Raytown. The staggering task of removing the dead began. The local citizens and able-bodied war prisoners buried the fallen men in parallel trenches near the old Black Jack Oak tree from which the town of Lone Jack took its name. One for gray; one for blue!

Every house became a hospital. At the request of the federal surgeon, Dr. W.H. Cundiff, two men, Ambers Graham, and A.L. Snow harnessed a team, gathered up the dead, and removed them to a place of burial, and the wounded to a nearby seminary converted into a hospital. Because of the scarcity of help, none of the federals were buried that day.[51]

Major Wyllis C. Ransom, Sixth Kansas Cavalry, reported on August 17th: "A body of United States troops, some 800 strong, were surprised yesterday morning by the rebel forces of Colonels Coffee, Hindman, and Quantrill, and after a heavy resistance they were obliged to surrender with great loss. Our troops had a battery of two pieces, which is now in possession of the enemy. From all appearances the enemy are moving on to Lexington. Large forces of our troops are moving toward the latter place from north of the river and from Sedalia. In order to keep the enemy from retreating back, though, it will be necessary to throw a heavy force in their rear."[52]

Major Thomas C. Hindman wrote the following in his report of the battle: "The victory won at Lone Jack by Colonels Cockrell and Jackman, aided by Captain Quantrill, was one of the most brilliant affairs of the war, resulting in the complete rout of a superior force and the capture of their artillery—two splendid bronze rifles—with the horses and full equipments, which were safely brought to me, and afterward proved very valuable."[53]

Cole's former teacher, Stephen H. Elkins, a Union sympathizer, witnessed the closing moments of the Battle of Lone Jack, in which Foster was commanding the Union side.[54] Elkins was going to Cass County, Missouri, to visit a young woman, and near Westport, was captured by Quantrill's men.[55]

Because of his allegiance to the federal cause, he was taken prisoner by Quantrill's men and brought into camp by his pickets. The first person he saw in camp that he knew was Cole Younger, whom did not seem to be a member of Quantrill's band.[56]

Elkins knew he was to be shot, and the men composing the picket divided his possessions—his horse, boots, and coat. In their camp, he saw Cole Younger, who had been one of his pupils in school back in Harrisonville. He asked Cole for help

Elkins later recalled: "As soon as I saw Cole Younger, I felt a sense of relief because I had known him and his parents long and favorably, and as soon as I got a chance, I told him frankly what I feared and that I hoped he would manage to take care of me and save me from being killed. He assured me he would do all he could to protect me."

"[Cole] said that he would, but conveyed to Elkins, 'Steve, no living man can tell what this man Qyantrell [sic] will do. He keeps his own counsel and he may conclude to kill you and he may not.' Pretty soon Quantrill came over to where he was sitting, walked around him as if he was inspecting a regiment, and walked away. According to Elkins, Quantrill never looked like a man who could hurt anything.

When Quantrill came into camp, he asked Elkins his name. Cole interjected that Elkins' father and brother were in the Confederate army and were good fighters, and that he had remained at home to care for his mother, that he was a good fellow and noncombatant. When Quantrill left, Cole told Elkins he would stay with him and help him to escape.

173

After being turned over to Cole, Elkins was given his liberty, much to his surprise, for he had feared he would be shot.[57]

According to Cole, he told his friend Elkins, "If any damn hound makes further false charges against you, it's me he's got to settle with, and that at pistol point."[58] Elkins later stated: "I knew Cole Younger when we were boys and also his parents. They were good people and among the pioneers on the western border of Missouri. The Younger brothers maintained a good reputation in the community where they lived and were well esteemed, as were their parents, for their good conduct and character."[59]

Elkins added, "He came of good stock, and it was a matter of surprise that he should have done what he did. I feel especially indebted to him, because during the war I fell into the hands of the enemy, and Cole Younger, I think, saved my life."[60]

When Elkins asked Cole what he should do, he was told: "You see the road there, don't you? I know what I would do." Elkins followed his advice, and was gone in a minute. Elkins believed that but for Cole Younger's intercession in his behalf, he would have been killed. Cole later stated he had pleaded with Quantrill to spare Elkins' life, and the guerrilla leader told him to get Elkins on his way since there were others in camp that planned to kill him. Cole allegedly told Quantrill he would personally defend Elkins against these would-be assassins.

Now of no use, federal "rescuers" began their approach to Lone Jack on Sunday the 17th, in the forms of General Blunt and Colonel Warren. Foster later reported that Warren "had been in sight of the enemy all day," but made no effort to attack.[61] The Confederates, who had fought so hard the day before, were forced to retreat before such superior numbers. Colonel Hays marched out to the west and resumed recruiting and did not go south for about ten days. Colonel Vard Cockrell departed southward with his captured cannons.

Warren Carter Bronaugh, who would later lead the struggle for a Younger pardon, maintained that he met Cole during the battle and was indebted to him for saving his life. He recognized him as the Confederate picket, who in 1862 had stopped him and another soldier from riding into Lone Jack, Missouri, which was held by Union General James C. Blunt and 1,500 Jayhawkers. Bronaugh and his friend had ridden a few miles out of camp to forage for breakfast. When they returned, they found their camp deserted, and galloped away to find their unit. In encountering another

Confederate force, a picket [Cole Younger], informed them that Colonel Cockrell was on the east side of town in full retreat as Union General Blunt was in town with 1,500 Kansas Jayhawkers and Redlegs. For nearly an hour they talked with the picket who had saved them from capture or death.[62]

Bronaugh remembered the young picket, Cole Younger, as an exceedingly handsome young man, "stalwart, alert and intelligent, and every inch a soldier." At his waist, the picket who had saved their lives, carried a brace of fine revolvers, and his face was never forgotten by Warren Carter Bronaugh. He recalled too that during the Battle of Lone Jack, Union Major Emory S. Foster had recounted that during the heaviest fighting, Cole rode up and down in front of the lines distributing ammunition.

Captain Bronaugh was born in Buffalo, West Virginia, in 1841. He was the son of Christopher Columbus Bronaugh and Ann Waters, a descendant of Lieutenant Edward Waters of the English army. Born of French and English stock, he was the grandson of William Bronaugh, a hero of the French and Indian War, Revolutionary War patriot, and member of George Washington's council.[63]

After his family moved, "Wal," as he was nicknamed, grew up in Henry County, Missouri. According to Bronaugh family history, an elderly black woman and former slave, who stayed with C.C. and Ann, remarked about their three sons, Wal, Frank, and Sam. She stated that Wal would talk his way into heaven, Frank would buy his way in, but poor Sam . . . "There just ain't no way."[64]

Wal was the nephew of Confederate Civil War hero, William Yelverton "Buck" Bronaugh, born in 1821, who was killed leading a band of irregulars behind northern lines. Following Buck's death, the band was taken over by John Rafters, and Buck's body was hidden for fear it would be hanged in effigy.[65] Buck's home was destroyed by Union troops. Bronaugh family member, Clara Miller-Dugan, later recalled that when she was a small girl during the Civil War, two men knocked at their door and asked for breakfast. As they sat down to eat, one of the men looked out the window and yelled, "There's Buck Bronaugh. Let's go get him!" They rushed out the door and jumped behind a rail fence at the edge of the yard. As Buck rode into range, they both opened fire on him, inflicting a mortal wound. He rode on for several miles before he died. Clara planted a tree with a spoon in memory of Buck Bronaugh.[66]

While most of Wal Bronaugh's Civil War activities have not been documented, those of his uncle Buck and Buck's son, Yelveton M. Bronaugh, still survive. Fourteen-year-old Yelverton helped the irregulars after his father was killed by bringing them food and supplies. One night he went to meet two fellow irregulars in a grove of trees. Approaching the grove, one of the men ran out waving his arms pointing behind Yelverton. Turning, he saw a band of Union soldiers, and he spurred his horse and rode for his life. The soldiers killed the two irregulars and pursed Yelverton to a neighbor's barn where he was hiding. After the soldiers conducted a vote whether to hang him or let him go, he was released.

In 1861 at the age of twenty, Wal Bronaugh had enlisted in the regular Confederate army at Springfield, Missouri. At the Battle of Lone Jack, in Jackson County, Missouri, August 6th, he fought under Cockrell and thus met Cole Younger.

The federal and Confederate losses were heavy, the losses on both side more or less equal, with a total number of 200 to 250 killed. The number wounded was many times that amount. In the aftermath, thirteen homes and businesses lay in ashes and over 200 men lay dead, dying, or wounded. The citizens of Lone Jack were not without their own sorrow, for some of those who died were boys from their community for the Southern recruiters had been in the area in the days prior to the battle. But perhaps the most sorrowful event of all was the death of a young mother, Lucinda Cave.

Lucinda, along with her husband Bart Cave, ran the Cave Hotel, which Major Emory Foster commandeered as a federal command post the night before the battle. When the hotel was set afire, she and her family were forced to evacuate. She was wounded by a stray bullet as she raised herself from among the weeds where they took refuge, to tend to her infant. She died on September 23, 1862, and was laid to rest in the town cemetery just east of town.

Federal E.F. Rogers related he had in fact been with Major Emory S. Foster at the Battle of Lone Jack when the commander was wounded and taken prisoner. Rogers recalled: "During that time there were several attempts made by a gang of ruffians to enter the house and kill some of the wounded; Major Foster being a special object of their hatred, (some of them having been his personal enemies before the war) and their efforts were persistent and determined."[67]

Rogers said he remembered one incident Foster may have forgotten, since he had been seriously wounded at the time. Some of the "ruffians" did enter the house and began abusing the wounded. Cole Younger, on guard, drew his sabre and rushed the men, ordering them to get out quick while he called them cowardly fiends. Cole told the men he would slaughter every one of them if they did not leave; and added he would protect them over his own dead body if need be. The room was cleared quickly. Had it not been for Cole, rationalized Rogers, the prisoners would have all been slaughtered.

Rogers added he had seen and heard Cole stand up and raise his voice to insults by his men at the Battle of Lone Jack, Missouri. He protected the Union prisoners at the risk of his own life.

Notes

[1] Donald R. Hale, *We Rode with Quantrill*, p. 29.

[2] Ted P. Yeatman, *Frank and Jesse James: The Story Behind the Legend*, pp. 32-33; Carl W. Breihan, *The Day Jesse James Was Killed*, New York, Bonanza Books, 1962, p. 32.

[3] Marley Brant, *Outlaws: The Illustrated History of the James-Younger Gang*, p. 27.

[4] Jack "Miles" Ventimiglia, *Jesse James in the County of Clay*, Kearney, Friends of the James Farm, 2001, p.30.

[5] *Louisville Courier Journal*, September 29, 1901.

[6] Homer Croy, *Jesse James Was My Neighbor*, New York, Duell, Sloane & Pearce, 1949, pp. 216-217.

[7] Peter Cozzens, "Hindman's Grand Delusion," *Civil War Times Illustrated*, October 2000, pp. 29-31.

[8] Reports of Colonel Daniel Huston, Jr., Seventh Missouri Cavalry, June 15, 1862 and Lieutenant Colonel James T. Buel, June 12, 1862. *The War of the Rebellion: A Compilation of the Official Records of the Union and Confederate Armies*, Series I, Volume XIII, pp. 120-121.

[9] Report of Captain J.F. Cochran, Second Battalion Missouri Cavalry, June 11, 1862. *The War of the Rebellion: A Compilation of the Official Records of the Union and Confederate Armies*, Series I, Volume XIII, p. 122.

[10] Major W.C. Ransom letter to Brigadier-General James G. Blunt dated June 20, 1862. *The War of the Rebellion: A Compilation of the Official Records of the Union and Confederate Armies*, Series I, Volume VIII.

[11] J.W. Buel, *The Border Outlaws*, pp. 45-47.

[12]Report of Major James O. Gower, First Iowa Cavalry, July 13, 1862. *The War of the Rebellion: A Compilation of the Official Records of the Union and Confederate Armies*, Series I, Volume XIII, pp. 154-156.

[13]Report of Captain Henry J. Stierlin, First Missouri Cavalry, July 12, 1862. *The War of the Rebellion: A Compilation of the Official Records of the Union and Confederate Armies*, Series I, Volume XIII, pp. 156-158.

[14]Report of Major James O. Gower, First Iowa Cavalry, July 13, 1862. *The War of the Rebellion: A Compilation of the Official Records of the Union and Confederate Armies*, Series I, Volume XIII, pp. 154-156.

[15]J.W. Buel, *The Border Outlaws*, pp. 47-54.

[16]Report of Major James O. Gower, First Iowa Cavalry, July 13, 1862. *The War of the Rebellion: A Compilation of the Official Records of the Union and Confederate Armies*, Series I, Volume XIII, pp. 154-156.

[17]Report of Captain William A. Martin, Seventh Missouri Cavalry. *The War of the Rebellion: A Compilation of the Official Records of the Union and Confederate Armies*, Series I, Volume XIII, pp. 158-160.

[18]J.W. Buel, *The Border Outlaws*, pp. 54-56.

[19]Marley Brant, *Outlaws: The Illustrated History of the James-Younger Gang*, pp. 28-29.

[20]Harry Sinclair Drago, *Outlaws on Horseback*, pp. 25-26.

[21]Ibid; Marley Brant, *Outlaws: The Illustrated History of the James-Younger Gang*, p. 28.

[22]According to several sources, this young man, Sam Wells, later became a James-Younger Gang member known as Charlie Pitts.

[23]Cole Younger, *The Story of Cole Younger by Himself*, pp. 6-7; Harry Sinclair Drago, *Outlaws on Horseback*, p. 28.

[24]Marley Brant, *Outlaws: The Illustrated History of the James-Younger Gang*, p. 30.

[25]J.W. Buel, *The Border Outlaws*.

[26]Todd M. George letter to Owen Dickie dated February 27, 1968, Le Sueur County Historical Society, Elysian, Minnesota.

[27]Ibid.

[28]J.W. Buel, *The Border Outlaws*.

[29]*Minneapolis Journal*, July 10, 1901.

[30]A.C. Appler, *The Younger Brothers*, pp. 81-82.

[31]Donald R. Hale, *We Rode with Quantrill*, pp. 34-35.

[32]Edward E. Leslie, *The Devil Knows How to Ride: The True Story of William Clarke Quantrill and His Confederate Raiders*, p. 136.

[33]Report of Daniel Huston, Jr., August 12, 1862. *The War of the Rebellion: A Compilation of the Official Records of the Union and Confederate Armies*, Series I, Chapter XXV, p. 226.

[34]Brigadier-General J.M. Schofield letter to General Henry W. Halleck dated August 12, 1862. *The War of the Rebellion: A Compilation of the Official Records of the Union and Confederate Armies*, Series I, XXV, p. 562.

[35]Cole Younger, *The Story of Cole Younger by Himself*.

[36]W.L. Webb, *Battles and Biographies of Missourians Or the Civil War Period of Our States*, Kansas City, Missouri, Hudson-Kimberly Pub. Co, 1900.

[37]Lyndon Irwin, "Bronaugh, Missouri History." Unpublished manuscript.

[38]Report of Major Emory S. Foster, Seventh Missouri Cavalry (Militia), March I, 1863. *The War of the Rebellion: A Compilation of the Official Records of the Union and Confederate Armies*, Series I, Volume XXV, pp. 236-239.

[39]William B. Allmon, "Sneak Attack at Lone Jack," *Civil War Times Illustrated*, April 1996, p. 66.

[40]Report of Captain Milton H. Brawner, Seventh Missouri Cavalry, August 20, 1862. *The War of the Rebellion: A Compilation of the Official Records of the Union and Confederate Armies*, Series I, Volume XXV, p. 236.

[41]Report of Major Emory S. Foster, Seventh Missouri Cavalry (Militia), March 1, 1863. .*The War of the Rebellion: A Compilation of the Official Records of the Union and Confederate Armies*, Series I, Volume XXV, pp. 236-239.

[42]William B. Allmon, "Sneak Attack at Lone Jack," *Civil War Times Illustrated*, April 1996, p. 66.

[43]Report of Captain Milton H. Brawner, Seventh Missouri Cavalry, August 20,1862. *The War of the Rebellion: A Compilation of the Official Records of the Union and Confederate Armies*, Series I, Volume XXV, p. 237.

[44]W.C. Bronaugh, *The Youngers' Fight for Freedom*, Columbia, Missouri, E.W. Stephens Publishing Company, 1906, pp. 35-37.

[45]William N. Gregg letter to George M. Bennett dated April 9, 1898. Northfield, Minnesota, Bank Robbery of 1876. Selected Manuscripts Collections and Government Records, Microfilm Edition, Roll 4, Minnesota Historical Society.

[46]Emory S. Foster letter to George M. Bennett dated May 7, 1898. Northfield, Minnesota, Bank Robbery of 1876. Selected Manuscripts Collections and Government Records, Microfilm Edition, Roll 4, Minnesota Historical Society.

[47]Report of Major Emory S. Foster, Seventh Missouri Cavalry (Militia), March 1, 1863. *The War of the Rebellion: A Compilation of the Official Records of the Union and Confederate Armies*, Series I, Volume XXV, pp. 236-239.

[48]Emory S. Foster letter to George M. Bennett dated May 7,1898. Northfield, Minnesota, Bank Robbery of 1876. Selected Manuscripts Collections and Government Records, Microfilm Edition, Roll 4, Minnesota Historical Society.

[49]Cole Younger, *The Story of Cole Younger by Himself.*

[50]Report of Captain Milton H. Brawner, Seventh Missouri Cavalry, August 20, 1862. *The War of the Rebellion: A Compilation of the Official Records of the Union and Confederate Armies*, Series I, Volume XXV, pp. 236-237.

[51]Todd M. George, *The Conversion of Cole Younger: The Early Day Bandit Becomes a Christian Citizen*, Kansas City, The Lowell Press, 1963, p. 36.

[52]Report of Major Wyllis C. Ransom, Sixth Kansas Cavalry, August 17,1862. *The War of the Rebellion: A Compilation of the Official Records of the Union and Confederate Armies*, Series I, Volume XXV, p. 226.

[53]Major General T.C. Hindman Official Report. *The War of the Rebellion: A Compilation of the Official Records of the Union and Confederate Armies*, Series I, Volume XIII, p. 33.

[54]Emory S. Foster letter to George M. Bennett dated May 7, 1898. Northfield, Minnesota, Bank Robbery of 1876. Selected Manuscripts Collections and Government Records, Microfilm Edition, Roll 4, Minnesota Historical Society.

[55]*Clinton Democrat*, September 8, 1903.

[56]S.B. Elkins letter to Charles M. Start dated July 4, 1898. Northfield, Minnesota, Bank Robbery of 1876. Selected Manuscripts Collections and Government Records, Microfilm Edition, Roll 4, Minnesota Historical Society.

[57]Terrell Transcript, April 26, 1907.

[58]Cole Younger, *The Story of Cole Younger by Himself*; St. Paul, Minnesota Historical Society Press, 2000, p. 30.

[59]*Madelia Times-Messenger*, March 14, 1979.

[60]S.B. Elkins letter to David M. Clough dated June 6, 1898. Northfield, Minnesota, Bank Robbery of 1876. Selected Manuscripts Collections and Government Record, Microfilm Edition, Roll 3, Minnesota Historical Society.

[61]William B. Allmon, "Sneak Attack at Lone Jack," *Civil War Times Illustrated*, April 1996, pp. 70-71.

[62]Robertus Love, *The Rise and Fall of Jesse James*, p. 141.

[63]*Kansas City Times*, February 27,1923; Warren Carter Bronaugh obituary, February 1923, Louis Woodford Bronaugh/Pamela Luster Phillips Collection; *The History of Henry and St. Clair Counties, Missouri*, St. Joseph, Missouri, National Historical Company, 1883, pp. 296-298.

[64]Pam Phillips, "The Bronaugh Family," unpublished manuscript from the papers of Louis Woodford Bronaugh.

[65]His grave has never been found.

[66]Pam Phillips, "The Bronaugh Family," unpublished manuscript from the papers of Louis Woodford Bronaugh.

[67]E.F. Rogers letter to George M. Bennett dated January 24, 1901. Northfield, Minnesota, Bank Robbery of 1876. Selected Manuscripts Collections and Government Records, Microfilm Edition, Roll 4, Minnesota Historical Society.

Chapter Seven

Bloody Lawrence

"During the years 1860 and 1861, I was county attorney of Douglas County. During the year 1860, Quantrill was living and operating in the vicinity of Lawrence under the name of Charley Hart. By that time, I prosecuted him in this county, during the summer and fall of 1860, for burglary and larceny, in breaking open and stealing from a powder-house of Ridenour & Baker, for arson, for setting fire to a barn in Kanwaka Township, this county, and for kidnapping. These charges were all pending against him when he disappeared from this county, to turn up here again on the fateful day of August 21, 1863."　　　　　—Samuel A. Riggs[1]

FOLLOWING THE BATTLE OF LONE JACK, Brigadier-General James G. Blunt pursued the Confederate forces. During the chase after Coffee's, Cockrell's, Hunter's, Tracy's, and Jackman's forces, his advance followed them as far south as Carthage, the main column halting at Montevallo. But the Confederates were determined to make good their retreat, and because the federals' stock was being used up, Blunt could pursue them no farther. The bushwhackers and gray-clad soldiers kept the two pieces of artillery (taken from Major Foster) in their advance, and during the chase, Blunt and his command passed many of their horses lying dead along the road, the men taking to the brush when they could not obtain other horses to mount. The road was strewn with hats and caps, which the guer-rillas had dropped from their heads while sleeping in the saddle.[2]

About 300 of the federal cavalrymen, while returning from Carthage, sud-denly, encountered, the forces of Quantrill, Hays, and one Colonel Shelby, from Lexington, with a force estimated at from 800 to 1,200, only eight miles from Lexington. After a short skirmish, the federals retreated, with five men killed and fifteen wounded. Upon learning of the fight, Blunt immediately dispatched reinforcements, but the guerrillas had moved rapidly south.

"It now appears that all of the organized rebel forces south of the Missouri River have gone to Arkansas," wrote Blunt, following the fight. "I would, therefore, suggest that all of the troops in Missouri, except a few to garrison important points, be moved south in mass, the line of march extend-ing across the State east and west, and that they leave no rebels in their rear, but, instead, peace and security to loyal citizens, thus driving them all in front of you to the Arkansas line. You will then be ready to co-operate with my forces on the west and General Curtis' on the east, and we can make a campaign through Arkansas and Texas that will force them either to make a stand and fight or jump into the Gulf of Mexico. Both of those States are rich in supplies to subsist an army, and should be appropriated for the sub-sistence of our forces as well as those of rebels. I trust you will consider the suggestion I have made, and write me your opinion in the matter."[3]

Because of Cole's involvement with the guerillas, his capture became a high priority of the federals. The Younger home was watched constantly as Cole became more involved with the guerillas, and Bursheba and the re-maining family members were constantly harassed. Bursheba was constantly hounded by those seeking her late husband's money, and life for the Youngers would never be the same again. Even her Negro servant, "Aunt" Susie, was beaten.[4]

Upon returning home to check on his family, Cole found one of his sis-ters, Sally, distraught and crying. After consoling her, he discovered that when Sally had been taken to the Kansas City Jail with her sisters, a federal captain had asked her to take a walk outside with him during a party. After the incident between Cole and Captain Walley, she was afraid to decline. She walked outside with the officer and was raped.

Cole vowed that this officer would never touch Sally again. After locat-ing the captain, Cole gathered a dozen of his bushwhacker friends, and they ambushed the captain's company, killing fourteen of the soldiers including the captain. Cole later penned: "I walked out and stood beside the [body] of the captain. I said out loud, 'Sister, I have kept my word.'"

Another night he went home to procure medicine for his men wounded at Lone Jack, whom he was nursing in the woods a few miles away. Captain Davidson, the federal commander at Harrisonville, had gone to see Cole's mother a few days earlier and promised her that he would guarantee safe passage to her and her sons if the family would move out of Missouri. Mrs. Younger accepted the offer in good faith and got word to Cole who slipped home to discuss the offer.

As he was talking with his mother, two of his brothers watching at the window cried out that the militia was surrounding the house. Unbeknownst to the the Youngers, Captain Davidson and a hundred men had been waiting out in the yard. Davidson knocked boldly on the door. Suse opened the door and went outside, only to find several bayonets pushed into her face. Pushing the guns aside with her arms, she commenced screaming when the soldiers ordered her to deliver up Cole to them. During the confusion she created, Cole escaped in a hail of bullets, but he was not hit.[5]

Another account states that "Aunt" Suse quickly removed a quilt from Bursheba's bed, tossed it over her head, and concealed Cole under it, before blowing out the lamp and opening the door. Captain Davidson and his men pushed the door aside and rushed into the house while Suse (and Cole) moved out into a dark corner of the yard. Cole fled into the darkness, and while the federals heard his footsteps, they could not catch him. The angry federals ordered the family out of the house, forcing Mrs. Younger, who was suffering from tuberculosis, from her sickbed.[6]

During each of these visits from the federals, Jim would hide in the woods while his mother and younger brothers were questioned as to Cole's whereabouts. Jim was the oldest son living at home, and Bursheba was convinced the Yankees suspected him of being involved with Quantrill. These same federal militiamen returned and interrogated Bursheba in February 1863. She asked that her family be left alone but the militia captain told her they would be back.[7]

Two months later, the same troops returned to the Younger home in the middle of night, and at pistol point, ordered Bursheba to burn down her own house. She begged to be allowed to wait until morning, as the snow was two to three feet deep, and a trek in the darkness to the nearest neighbor miles away would be difficult with her small children. They agreed on the condition that she put the torch to the house herself. They returned at daybreak, and as the house was consumed in flames, she, Suse, and the four young children began their eight mile trek through the snow to Harrisonville.[8]

"I have always felt that the exposure to which she was subjected on this cruel journey, too hard even for a man to take, was the direct cause of her death," concluded Cole some time later.

From Harrisonville, Bursheba went to Waverly. One of the conditions her life was spared was that she must report to authorities in Lexington weekly. During one of her trips to Lexington, her enemies went to the house where she had left her children and demanded they turn over $2,200 that had belonged to her husband.

Bursheba had concealed the money on the faithful Suse. In order to force Suse to talk, she was hanged by a tree in the yard, but she still refused to divulge any information regarding the money's whereabouts. She was left for dead but was cut down by a friend.

Considering the turmoil of war and how it had affected the Youngers as young men, many esteemed citizens overlooked their dastardly crimes, blaming their acts instead on the environment:

"They [the Younger brothers] were of a good family; their father a prosperous and respected man, their grandfather a judge of the courts," wrote Governor William R. Marshall. "The breaking out of the rebellion was the signal for the renewal of those border troubles between Kansas and Missouri that disgraced the age. Their father was murdered and robbed, their property plundered, and their home burned over their heads. These men were then boys— Cole [seventeen], Jim [thirteen], and Bob [seven]. Four years of war ensued. War in that region was little better on both sides than murder and rapine."[9]

Lizzie [Brown] Daniel, a friend of Cole's, later recalled: "I have known the true character of Cole Younger for many years. At a critical time, while he wore the gray, he did brave and unselfish things for those who were dear to me, now dead and gone. . . . I have learned from the lips of the just dead the true nobility of his inward character."[10]

Todd Menzies George later wrote: "In all my association with Cole Younger, I have never heard an oath or a vulgar word pass his lips. It was a positive fact that at no time did he ever indulge in intoxicating liquor."[11]

Boys such as the Youngers had joined the ranks of such men as William Clarke Quantrill and "Bloody Bill" Anderson to combat what they considered a federal "invasion." Union General John B. Sanborn, who commanded a Union brigade that fought Frank James, the Youngers and other guerrillas who had "infested" southwestern Missouri, later said:

"Those bands of Quantrell [sic], West and Anderson conducted their operations in the most barbarous and ferocious style, and entirely at variance with the principles of civilized warfare. They granted no quarter to their prisoners, and their malice did not even end with the death of their prisoners, whom they mutilated in the most frightful manner. . . . I don't know how many [the Youngers] killed themselves, but their gang killed, I know, scores if not hundreds in their raids."[12]

In August of 1862 Jim Lane, senator and general in the State Militia had undergone the task of recruiting Blacks for the Union Army with fanatical zeal. Many of his first recruits were from the Leavenworth area, but recruiting spread in earnest to cities like Wyandotte, Lawrence, Paola, Fort Scott, and Sac and Fox Agency. In early October 1862 some of the new Black recruits were crossing the Missouri border to liberate slaves to add to their ranks from their base at Camp Jim Lane near Wyandotte. However, their first true taste of combat came on October 29, 1862, at Island Mound near Butler, Missouri, against Confederate Guerillas. This battle was the first in which Black soldiers were engaged during the Civil War.[13]

Also in August, Cole Younger went on a lone spy mission into the midst of federal troops encamped just outside Independence. Hoping to procure information that would assist Quantrill in planning his attack, Cole dressed up as an old woman selling apples and entered the Union camp. His disguise fooled the federal soldiers until the "old woman" on her way out ignored a picket's command to halt. Cole shot the picket and fled, successfully reaching Quantrill's camp with the much-needed information.[14]

Not until September did the federal high command begin monitoring the activities of Major General Thomas Hindman who, in declaring martial law from his headquarters in Little Rock, was drafting nearly every able-bodied man in the state and sending recruiting officers behind Union lines in Missouri. On September 19th, the United States' War Department placed Major General Samuel R. Curtis, the victor at Pea Ridge, in command of the Department of the Missouri, which encompassed Arkansas, Missouri, Kansas, and the Indian Territory. Curtis dispatched Brigadier-General John M. Schofield to pursue Hindman. Schofield immediately created three divisions, which he dubbed the Army of the Frontier, near Springfield, Missouri, and drove the Confederates out of Missouri and south of the Arkansas River.[15]

On October 5th, meanwhile, Captain Daniel H. David, Fifth Missouri Cavalry (Militia) marched with his command, consisting of detachments from Company A, commanded by Lieutenant Bennett; Company B, Lieutenant Bixby; Company D, Lieutenant Fairbrother, and Company K, Lieutenant Dorey, amounting in all to eighty-eight men, in search of the bushwhackers. On the first day, they arrested two men, alleged to be bushwhackers. At the same place, they captured two horses that were concealed in a cornfield, and moved on to the home of an old man named Pruett, a noted Confederate sympathizer. Unable to learn about the movements of Quantrill and his band, the federals scoured the country for about fifteen miles in the neighborhood surrounding Blue Springs. They encamped for the night at the Walker place, having yet learned nothing of the guerrillas.[16]
The following morning, they continued to scour the countryside between Fire Prairie Creek and Snibar in the direction of Sibley, constantly making inquiries in regard to Quantrill, Childs, and their bands. Only two miles from Sibley, they skirmished with bushwhacker pickets, who were posted in a lane near William Hughes' house, on the State road leading from Independence to Lexington. They soon espied pickets posted on Big Hill, near Sibley, on the same road, which was one of the highest hills in the area. The number and position of their pickets indicated that there was a camp not far distant.

In order to ascertain its locality, the federals advanced on Sibley in two columns, one from the north and the other from the northeast. In passing the residence of Mrs. Garrison, one mile from Sibley, they captured two horses bearing government equipments but belonging to the bushwhackers, who fled into a cornfield for refuge. Captain David's cavalry concentrated at Sibley, having ascertained that Quantrill and his men were encamped at a mill about a half a mile from town (reports varying from 150 to 300 strong). Considering the guerrilla force too strong to attack, Captain David sent for reinforcements and secured a position on Big Hill to await their arrival. While on the march to the hill, they encountered the guerrillas, commanded by Colonel Childs and Captain Quantrill, their force numbering about 130 men. They bushwhackers fired upon them from the brush. The federals dismounted and hand-to-hand fight ensued, which lasted about forty minutes, and not any of the time more than forty yards apart. Colonel Childs was captured by the Yankees.

Captain David ordered his men to mount, which they did, on a double-quick, and started in pursuit, though cautiously in moving through the brush. Upon approaching the prairie, the pursuit ended, and the federals returned to the battleground to ascertain their casualties.

After seeing to their wounded, the federals proceeded about five miles to where they encountered their reinforcements, under command of Captain Vanzant. The dead and wounded were taken to camp, and the main command searched the area during the night near Big Hill and Pink Hill, not finding the enemy. But early the following morning, they were confronted by Confederate pickets, and after a brief skirmish, the guerrillas disappeared. Captain David stated in his official report that, "we do not believe that guerrillas can ever be taken by pursuit; we must take them by strategy."

On October 18th, ten prisoners in Palmyra, Missouri, were shot in retaliation for the presumed murder of a local Union man, in what would come to be called "The Palmyra Massacre." The *Missouri Courier* later that week printed this:

> Saturday last, the 18th instant, witnessed the performance of a tragedy in this once quiet and beautiful city of Palmyra, which, in ordinary and peaceful times, would have created a profound sensation throughout the entire country, but which now scarcely produces a distinct ripple upon the surface of our turbulent social tide.
>
> It will be remembered by our readers that on the occasion of [Joseph C.] Porter's descent upon Palmyra, he captured, among other persons, an old and highly respected resident of this city, by name Andrew Allsman. This person formerly belonged to the Third Missouri Cavalry, though too old to endure all the hardships of very active duty. He was, therefore, detailed as a kind of special or extra provost-marshal's guard or cicerone, making himself generally useful in a variety of ways to the military of the place. Being an old resident, and widely acquainted with the people of the place and vicinity, he was frequently called upon for information touching the loyalty of men, which he always gave to the extent of his ability, though acting, we believe, in all such cases with great candor, and actuated solely by a conscientious desire to discharge his whole duty to his government. His knowledge of the surrounding country was the reason of his being frequently called upon to act as a guide to scouting parties sent out to arrest disloyal persons. So efficient-

ly and successfully did he act in these various capacities that he won the bitter hatred of all the rebels in this city and vicinity, and they only waited the coming of a favorable opportunity to gratify their desire for revenge. The opportunity came at last, when Porter took Palmyra. That the villains, with Porter's assent, satiated their thirst for his blood by the deliberate and predetermined murder of their helpless victim no truly loyal man doubts. When they killed him, or how, or where, are items of the act not yet revealed to the public. Whether he was stabbed at midnight by the dagger of the assassin, or shot at midday by the rifle of the guerrilla; whether he was hung and his body hidden beneath the scanty soil of some oaken thicket, or left as food for hogs to fatten upon, or whether, like the ill-fated Wheat, his throat was severed from ear to ear, and his body sunk beneath the wave, we know not. But that he was foully, causelessly murdered it is useless to attempt to deny.

When General [John] McNeil returned to Palmyra, after that event, and ascertained the circumstances under which Allsman had been abducted, he caused to be issued, after due deliberation, the following notice: "PALMYRA, MO., October 8, 1862. JOSEPH C. PORTER: SIR: Andrew Allsman, an aged citizen of Palmyra, and a non-combatant, having been carried from his home by a band of persons unlawfully arrayed against the peace and good order of the State of Missouri, and which band was under your control, this is to notify you that unless said Andrew Allsman is returned, unharmed, to his family within ten days from date, ten men, who have belonged to your band, and unlawfully sworn by you to carry arms against the Government of the United States, and who are now in custody, will be shot as a meet reward for their crimes, among which is the illegal restraining of said Allsman of his liberty, and, if not returned, presumptively aiding in his murder. . . ."

Many rebels believed the whole thing was simply intended as a scare, declaring that McNeil did not dare to carry out the threat. The ten days elapsed, and no tidings came of the murdered Allsman. It is not our intention to dwell at length upon the details of this transaction. The tenth day expired with last Friday. On that day ten rebel prisoners, already in custody, were selected to pay with their lives the penalty demanded. The names of the men so selected were as follows: Willis Baker, Lewis County; Thomas Humston, Lewis County; Morgan Bixler, Lewis County; Herbert Hudson, Rails County; John M. Wade, Rails County; Marion Lair, Rails County; Capt. Thomas A. Sidner, Monroe County; Eleazer Lake, Scotland County, and Hiram Smith, Knox County. These parties were informed on Friday evening that unless Mr. Allsman was returned to his family by [one] o'clock on the following day, they would all be shot at that hour. Most of them received the announcement with composure or indifference. The Reverend James S. Green, of this city, remained with them during that night, as their spiritual adviser, endeavoring to prepare them for their sudden entrance into the presence of their Maker. A little after 11:00 A.M. the next day, three Government wagons drove to the jail; one contained four and each of the others three rough board coffins. The condemned men were conducted from the prison and seated in the wagons, one upon each coffin. A sufficient guard of soldiers accompanied them, and the cavalcade started for the fatal grounds. Proceeding east to Main street, the cortege turned and moved slowly southward as far as Malone's livery stable; thence turning east, it entered the Hannibal road, pursuing it nearly to the residence of Colonel James Culbertson; there, throwing down the fences, they turned northward, entering the fair grounds (half a mile east of the town), on the west side, and, driving within the circular amphitheatrical ring, paused for the final consummation of the scene.

The ten coffins were removed from the wagons and placed in a row [six] or [eight] feet apart, forming a line north and south, about [fifteen] paces east of the central pagoda or music stand, in the center of the ring. Each coffin was placed upon the ground, with its foot west and head east. Thirty soldiers of the Second Missouri State Militia were drawn up in a single line, extending north and south, facing the row of coffins. This line of executioners ran immediately at the east base of the pagoda, leaving a space between them and the coffins of [twelve] or [thirteen] paces. Reserves were drawn up in line upon either bank [flank] of these executioners.

The arrangements completed, the doomed men knelt upon the grass between their coffins and the soldiers, while the Reverend R.M. Rhodes offered up a prayer. At the conclusion of this, each prisoner took his seat upon the foot of his coffin, facing the muskets which in a few moments were to launch them into eternity. They were nearly all firm and undaunted, two or three only showing signs of trepidation.

The most noted of the ten was Captain Thomas A. Sidner, of Monroe County, whose capture at Shelbyville, in the disguise of a woman, we related several weeks since. He was now elegantly attired in a suit of black broadcloth, with a white vest. A luxurious growth of beautiful hair rolled down upon his shoulders, which, with his fine personal appearance, could not but bring to mind the handsome but vicious Absalom. There was nothing especially worthy of note in the appearance of the others. One of them, Willis Baker, of Lewis County, was proven to be the man who last year shot and killed Mr. Ezekiel Pratt, his Union neighbor, near Williamstown, in that county. All the others were rebels of lesser note, the particulars of whose crimes we are not familiar with.

A few minutes after [one] o'clock, Colonel Strachan, provost-mar-shal-general, and Reverend Rhodes shook hands with the prisoners, two of them accepting bandages for their eyes. All the rest refused. A hundred spectators had gathered around the amphitheater to witness the impressive scene. The stillness of death pervaded the place. The officer in command now stepped forward, and gave the word of command, "Ready, aim, fire." The discharges, however, were not made simultaneously, probably through want of a perfect previous understanding of the orders and of the time at which to fire. Two of the rebels fell backward upon their coffins and died instantly. Captain Sidner sprang forward and fell with his head toward the soldiers, his face upward, his hands clasped upon his breast and the left leg drawn half way up. He did not move again, but died immediately. He had requested the soldiers to aim at his heart, and they obeyed but too implicitly. The other seven were not killed outright, so the reserves were called in, who dispatched them with their revolvers.

It seems hard that ten men should die for one. Under ordinary circumstances it would hardly be justified, but severe diseases demand severe remedies. The safety of the people is the supreme law. It overrides all other considerations. The madness of rebellion has become so deep seated that ordinary methods of cure are inadequate. To take life for life would be little intimidation to men seeking the heart's blood of an obnoxious enemy. They could well afford to make even exchanges under many circumstances. It is only by striking the deepest terror in them, causing them to thoroughly respect the lives of loyal men that they can be taught to observe the obligation of humanity and of law.

Because of these executions, General McNeil became known as the "Butcher of Palmyra."[17]

Early on the morning of October 25th, Captain Joseph H. Little and the First Missouri Cavalry (Militia) were ordered to the scene of a mail robbery near the residence of Mr. Luther Green. Mr. Green stated that on the morning of the 22nd, Quantrill, with about twenty-five men, came to his residence and demanded breakfast for himself and men, and while at breakfast the mail-coach passed and was hailed by Quantrill and the mail-bags opened and ransacked. Quantrill, having breakfasted, left in the direction of Chapel Hill. Captain Little ordered immediate pursuit by way of an indirect route, in order to enter Chapel Hill under cover of the woods and surprise the band. Citizens were not permitted to leave until a search was made, which proved fruitless, the band having left the evening before. The federals marched for Hopewell and encountered a bushwhacker, who fled toward Blackwater Grove. Although several shots were fired at him, he gained the bushes and escaped.

The next day, the command marched toward Lexington, having learned that Quantrill's men had been in Wellington one day earlier. At Chapel Hill, several persons were arrested on suspicion; one of whom related information of Confederate recruits lurking around Napoleon. Little ordered his command to Napoleon and captured five men, who reported to have been conscripted, although Little believed they were rebel volunteers.[18]

Philip A. Thompson of the War Department penned a letter to Colonel Penick in Independence on November 6th stating that

> Colonel Catherwood has returned without accomplishing anything. . . . He came on Quantrill encamped for the night in a little grove of about five acres of timber, with prairie in all directions for [ten] miles around, but he so managed as to let them all get away without killing a single man. Twelve of the men murdered by Quantrill when the train was captured were buried to-day with the honor of way. The most of them were teamsters, who were unarmed at the time they were killed; all of them but one were shot through the head, showing conclusively that they were murdered after they were taken prisoners. It was a shocking affair, sending so large a train with an escort of but [twenty] men. Fifteen wagons were piled up and burned; the cattle unyoked and turned loose, but have not yet been found.
>
> They pursued Quantrill and his forces within [ten] miles of Pleasant Gap, near which place Cockrell is represented to be with about 700 men. As it is so difficult to get south, and so many federal forces are in Arkansas, I think it highly probable that the whole force under Cockrell and Quantrill will return and attempt to take Harrisonville and such other points as are most exposed. Quantrill was re-enforced last Sunday with [thirty-three] Enrolled Militia, with new guns and fixtures complete. A negro captured from Quantrill says they are from the north side of the river. Lieutenant Newby verifies the same statement; says he saw the men and guns with his own eyes. All the small bands that have infested Jackson and La Fayette Counties have joined Quantrill, which swells his force to about 300, and leaves the above-named counties clear of any rebel force.[19]

On the morning of November 6th, Major Benjamin S. Henning, Third Wisconsin Cavalry received a dispatch from Captain Breeden stating that he had been attacked about an hour before by 400 men under Quantrill, and that they were still fighting, and asking for assistance. Major Henning immediately sent Captain Conkey with eighty men and Captain Coleman with another thirty, as reinforcements. At nine o'clock Henning learned that Captain Morton's train was at Carthage, and, afraid that Morton would run right into the enemy, he dispatched a messenger to Captain Conkey, direct-ing him to follow on and, if necessary, to fight his way through to the train. Although Captain Conkey killed one of the bushwhackers, he learned that the train had passed west in safety. Major Henning sent Lieutenant Cavert, of the Third Wisconsin, with sixteen men, to Lamar, with a dispatch for Captain Breeden. Upon reaching the town, they discovered that Quantrill had just left, after burning most of the town.[20]

Also on the 6th, Dr. Thomas Hamill wrote Major General Samuel Curtis as a "friend and well-wisher" the following letter:

> I have often thought I would send you a few lines regarding the pro-tecting the State line between Missouri and Kansas. You have heard of Quantrill in Jackson County, Missouri, and his visits over into Kansas. I have been living in Johnson County, Kansas, for four years. I was in Olathe when he came there; he took everything of wearing apparel and all the horses that he could get; he took all of my clothes, a good horse, and a fine gold watch, but we did not care for being robbed, if he had not killed our citizens in cold blood, taking our best citizens from the bosom of their families and shooting them down like so many hogs. It is horrible to relate. Our new State has put into the field thirteen regi-ments; more than any other State in the Union. Now, general, we want to be protected along the line, and we want cavalry, as infantry is of no use but to hold posts, as you are well aware of. There are many families leaving this and other counties along the line. We have two companies of Kansas Twelfth; if they had not been stationed here I do not think there would be scarcely one man left in Olathe. Olathe is some [ten] miles from the line. Nearly all the families have left between us and the line. We would like to have our Kansas troops stationed on the line. I have no motive in saying that we want our Kansas troops stationed along the line, only that all our people would know the country the country and be nearer home. Dear general, you have no idea of the dis-tracted state of this country. I saw our newly-elected Governor this evening, and he said that he was going to see General Lane about hav-ing men stationed along the lines and then see you about it, general. We have elected all the Republican ticket this fall. One thing more: You ought to send a good regiment of Missouri State Militia into Jackson County, and have that notorious bushwhacker Quantrill caught this winter.[21]

In late November, Major General Thomas C. Hindman detached Brigadier General John Marmaduke's cavalry from Van Buren north to occupy the Cane Hill area. Marmaduke's division was comprised of two brigades and an independent regiment of Missourians. Recently, General Hindman had received approval for offensive action but his army was still unorganized. Therefore, the cavalry division was stationed at Cane Hill to protect the still-forming army and prevent federal patrols from gaining intelligence. From here federal movements into Arkansas and the Indian Territory could be monitored.

Hearing of this movement, Brigadier General James Blunt, encamped at Rhea's Mill in Arkansas, advanced with five thousand men and thirty pieces of artillery to meet Marmaduke's command and destroy it, if possible. Outnumbered three to one and possessing only six pieces of artillery, Marmaduke was not prepared for the attack.[22]

Seeing an opportunity to smash the Confederate cavalry, General Blunt moved quickly, putting his division on the direct road to Cane Hill. By 10:00 A.M. on November 28, the Kansas division arrived at the north end of the hill. General Blunt and his escort raced to the front and opened the battle. The Union vanguard encountered Colonel Jo Shelby's brigade, which fought a delaying action to protect their supply trains. Shelby gradually gave ground until establishing a strong defensive perimeter on Cove Creek where he repulsed a determined attack.

Blunt used his superiority in numbers and firepower to drive Marmaduke down Cane Hill, over Reed's Mountain, and through the crucial crossroads at Morrows. After the battle, Marmaduke retreated to Hindman's camps in Van Buren, and the federals withdrew to Cane Hill, while the Confederates returned to Van Buren.

From Cane Hill, Blunt sent a plea to General Herron to take the Second and Third divisions and move to join the Kansas Division in Arkansas. Herron moved immediately, assembling a provisional cavalry brigade under Dudley Wickersham and sending it along to Blunt. The horse soldiers reached Blunt's position during the night of December 6.

On that same day, General Hindman began his counteroffensive. Learning of Herron's approach, Hindman decided to advance and defeat Herron then turn and destroy Blunt. Leaving a cavalry brigade on Reed's Mountain to occupy Blunt's attention, the Confederate army marched up the Cove Creek Road to Prairie Grove Church. Near the church, the advance under Shelby routed the vanguard of Herron's two divisions and drove them across the Illinois River. Rather than build on the momentum gained and continue his advance, Hindman surrendered the initiative to Herron and went over to the defensive, occupying the heights at Prairie Grove.

On December 7, 1862, Major General Thomas C. Hindman's troops collided with the federal army at Prairie Grove, Arkansas. Hindman sought to destroy Brigadier-General Francis Herron's and Brigadier-General's James Blunt's divisions before they joined forces. Hindman placed his large force between the two Union divisions, facing Herron first and routing his cavalry. As Hindman pursued the cavalry, he met Herron's infantry which pushed him back. The Confederates established their line of battle on a wooded high ridge northeast of Prairie Grove Church. Herron brought his artillery across the Illinois River and initiated an artillery duel. The Union troops assaulted twice and were repulsed. The Confederates counterattacked, were halted by Union canister, and then moved forward again. Just when it looked as if their attack would defeat Herron's troops, Blunt's men assailed the Confederate left flank. As night came, neither side had won, but Hindman retreated to Van Buren. Hindman's retreat established federal control of northwest Arkansas.

Julia West Pyeatt, who as a fourteen-year-old girl, witnessed the Battle of Prairie Grove from her family home, the Robert West House, on the northwest side of the battlefield, recalled:

> December the 7th, 1862, will long be remembered especially by those of us who lived here and witnessed the Battle at Prairie Grove. It was a beautiful, cold, frosty Sunday morning. . . . About [ten] o'clock the cannonading began and about noon war began in earnest. When it seemed everyone would be killed. . . . You can never know the horrors of a battle unless you have seen or been in one. The fighting was constant. . . . Families hunted safety in the cellars. Our home being on the north side, we felt we were comparatively safe and our greatest anxiety was for our relatives, neighbors, and friends so we stood out and watched until dark. The fighting continued as long as the soldiers could see.
>
> All the houses were filled with wounded men. Our house was also filled with General [James G.] Blunt's men. The general himself sleeping in mother's baby crib with his feet hanging over. During the night when dispatches came, he would arise up, read it, write answers, or give orders. Men stood and sat around all night with their guns in their hands talking about the fight. . . . All available beds and bedding was used for

the wounded except one bed they left for mother and the children but very few of us slept any. . . .

We were left with hundreds of wounded and dead. For days, people hunted the battleground for some of their missing people. On Monday [December 8, 1862], we saw four houses burn to the ground that was set on fire by the federal troops. The homes belonged to Dr. Rogers, William Rogers, Arch Borden, and the White Taylor home. We lived in the house with the wounded for six weeks.[23]

Caldonia Ann Borden Brandenburg was nine years old when the Battle of Prairie Grove raged around her family's home on the southeast side of the battlefield. She later recalled:

On the sixth of December [1862], the first Yankee was in our home, then two more came and started to tear up things. They turned up the foot of the bed and found Pa's saddle bags which had two handles. Ma got hold of one and the Yankee the other. He dragged her all over the room, and the baby got scared and screamed so loud that Ma had to turn loose.

One early morning [December 7, 1862] Pa told us to move out as there was to be a battle very soon on our hill. We went to a neighbor's a mile away, taking what we could carry and some food. The battle started on the hill where our house was. We could hear the cannons and see their heads rise up to fire. We hadn't had any breakfast; we were too excited to be hungry. About one o'clock in the afternoon the noise got louder and closer. It occurred to Pa that we were in danger, so he rushed us to the cellar just before the shooting started around the [Morton] house where we were. In the cellar there were barrels of kraut, cider and cider vinegar, apples and potatoes, four men, seven women, and eight children.

After dark, it got quiet and we came out of the cellar. There was a dead man across the cellar door, wounded and dying men all around. I can still hear them calling "Help—help—help." The men worked through the night helping the wounded. Yankees and Rebels all got the same care. Four died that night. One soldier's leg was just hanging by the skin, and the doctor cut it off and threw it outside. It sure was scary and pitiful. Some of us got sick.

Pa sneaked back up the hill and found that our beautiful two-story house that was painted light yellow with green trim, the home that we all loved so much, had been burned to the ground after the Yankees plundered the inside. . . . We never got a thing out of our home, not even a change of clothes. They killed and ate our cattle, hogs, sheep, and chickens and used what we had stored in our cellar. . . . They took everything they could use; then set the house on fire. We had [sixty] bushels of wheat stored upstairs and it slowly burned for three weeks in the rubble.

All of the kinfolks and neighbors gave us food, clothing, and bedding and household goods that they could spare, to help us get started again. . . . As soon as it was safe for us kids to go on the battlefields, we went and picked up clothes, canteens, blankets, and anything we found to use. We had to put everything in boiling water to kill the "grey backs" [body lice]. We made bedding out of the cloth we salvaged after cleaning it. The Yankees took our good horses and a beautiful big bay mare, a fine pacer, our work horses, and saddle horses and left us only an old oxen and an old blind mare, but she was still a good plow horse, and we bred her to a good stallion and got a fine colt.

When the Yankees burned our house, they burned Uncle Ed's and Uncle Will's houses the same evening. The officers took Grandma's house for headquarters so it was saved. . . . We had the Yankees in the winter and the Bushwhackers in the summer. . . . We had to hide out everything we could and then sometimes the Yankees found it. We had to live on bran bread sometimes because they took our flour and meat and other foods, so we had poor pickins then. We buried things—some people buried things in the cemetery. They shaped the dirt on top like a grave but the Yankees . . . or Bushwhackers got on to that after a while and began to dig in the fresh graves, and once they found a barrel of whiskey. . . .[24]

Nancy Morton Staples was [thirty-one] years old and living on the southwest side of the Prairie Grove Battlefield at the time of the conflict:

On the 7th day of December, 1862, the advance guard met south of the grove, killing one man. Early in the day the battle commenced on the Borden farm east of the grove, lasting until sunset, winding up on the Morton farm one mile west. The families were ordered west to the first cellar, which was Morton's. Those in the cellar during the battle were N.J. and J.M. Morton, William Morton, William D. Rogers, wife and three children, A. Borden, wife and five children, Eliza Borden, Dr. Rogers, wife and two children. We all remained in the cellar till dark, but I went into the house several times to get victuals [food supplies] and some bedclothes and wraps for the children. They fought through and around the house, the shots flying like hail in every direction, only a few cannon balls striking close. Mrs. Borden's pony stood hitched close to the cook-room, saddled, and was not hurt, and after the firing ceased, she with her . . . children mounted the pony, passed the guards and rode to Mrs. Mock's in safety.

196

. . . The day after the battle we did all we could to relieve the wounded and dying. Such pitiful wails and cries that came from those poor men. We made them tea from herbs and did all we could for their comfort. . . . After the battle Will[iam] Rogers went south, leaving his wife and . . . children with us. The oldest and youngest were taken sick, the oldest dying one day after the battle, the other the next day. . . .

Another shocking affair was my helping to bury Mr. Borden, a brother of A[rchibald] Borden, who was brutally killed in the Pittman lane. He had lain there all night when Eliza and Mary Borden, Martha Butler, and myself got there. Two old men who had previously dug the grave helped us carry him to it and being afraid of scouts they left us to fill the grave. All the implements we had were an old hoe and pieces of boards. We blistered our hands and were worn out when we got home, as we had to walk.

. . . Another trying hour on us was the robbers [who] came and burned my father's feet to make him give up his money. At first they pretended to be friends, and mother and I went to the cellar and got them apples. They talked, enjoyed the apples and were great southern men, of course. My father had gone to bed. After a while one of them went up to the bed and said, "Old man, it's not your politics I care for, it's your money, and we're going to have it."

I cannot express my feelings when they pulled him out and tied him, taking four of them to do it. They heated two shovels, for the night was cold and we had a big fire, and they began burning the bottoms of his feet. I threw water on the shovels with one of them pointing a pistol in my face and striking me over the back and arms until I was black and blue. I then threw water on the fire putting it out. One of them threw a shovel of hot coals on his body, but having on heavy all-wool underwear he was not burned. Then they took him out to hang him, as they had not succeeded in getting him to tell where he had money. They choked my mother for screaming and abused us for looking out of the window. After compelling him to tell them what they wanted to know, they brought him back into the house and ransacked everything in the house, carrying off what paper money he had and destroying some notes. We all then went to bed shivering with cold, afraid to make a fire or light. . . . There was nothing but sorrow, trouble, and worry till peace was declared. . . .[25]

In 1863, Quantrill met Sarah "Katie" King, daughter of Robert King. She later stated in an interview that she had fallen in love at first sight with Quantrill when she was not quite thirteen years old. Because of Kate's age, her parents strongly disapproved of their romance and tried to put an end to it, but Kate persisted in seeing him in secret. When her father found out, they eloped and were secretly married on August 21, 1863, by a country preacher in a church not far from her parents' Blue Springs farm. Sarah took the name of Kate Clarke to hide her true relationship with her husband from his enemies.

An experienced horsewoman, she frequently rode through the Jackson County countryside with her lover. Accounts survive as to how Kate rode along with the guerrillas after her marriage, some even saying she dressed in men's clothing. She may, indeed, have ridden with the men as they changed camps, but she almost certainly did not fight alongside the guerrillas or dress like a man. Kate later insisted she never truly loved any man but Quantrill. She remembered him as handsome, polite and debonair, and inclined to "josh" her.

During the winter of 1862-1863, Cole had remained behind in Jackson County nursing seriously wounded men in the band. Cole had made a lean-to deep in the woods and had piled dirt over the roof to conceal it. As the Yankees continued to search the forest, he found it necessary to continually move his "field hospital" from one hollow to another. When John McCorkle found his camp seven miles south of Independence, he discovered that Cole had restored all his patients back to health and was waiting for spring and the return of Quantrill.[26]

Trouble hit Cole's camp in the person of John McDowell, who had ridden with Cole in one of the Kansas raids. During the raid, they were attacked by a large force of federals, and both sides sustained heavy casualties. Heavily outnumbered, the bushwhackers fled, and when McDowell's horse was shot out from under him, he was wounded. McDowell had called out to Cole for help. Seeing a comrade in trouble, Cole rode back for him, placed him upon his own horse, and carried him to safety.

Following the raid, however, McDowell turned himself in to Colonel Penick in Independence. Suddenly appearing in Cole's camp, he told the bushwhackers that Penick had paroled him, but McCorkle did not believe him. McCorkle insisted that McDowell was working as a spy and urged that he should be immediately put to death. Cole, however, did not believe the accusation.

A few days later, McDowell asked Cole for permission to leave camp and visit his wife. Despite the objections by McCorkle, Cole allowed the man to leave camp. Cole told McCorkle that he was too hard on him, but McCorkle ranted that McDowell was headed straight to Penick.

McDowell returned to camp with sixty militiamen while many of the bushwhackers were out hunting hogs or sitting in the cave hideout. Because the militiamen were disguised as bushwhackers, many of Cole's men mistook them for Todd's men. They were not recognized as the enemy until they had ridden about fifty yards from the cave entrance. Cole drew a pistol as did his men, and they fired away as the federals began shooting at them.

John McCorkle dashed into the entrance of the cave and grabbed his revolver, but in firing the weapon, it merely snapped. Ike Bassham was shot dead in the entrance while Doc Hale sprinted several yards before he, too, was cut down. Cole, Joe Hardin, Otho Hinton, and Tom Talley dashed towards the woods together, but Hardin was shot in the back. Talley attempted to remove his heavy boots as he ran and was assisted by Cole. They made a stand in the woods but Tom Talley's brother, George, was killed.

Cole, on a lone mission in January 1863, stopped at the home of a friend to get something to eat. Cole had mixed feelings over accepting his friend's hospitality because he knew that the old man would suffer dire consequences if the federals learned he had aided a guerrilla. Cole, however, was quite certain that he had escaped detection upon riding up to the house, and his friend fed both him and his horse.[27]

Their after-dinner conversation was interrupted when the two men heard the squeaking of the old iron gate in the yard. While Cole dashed from the house without coat or boots, his friend hid his clothes before the federals were able to search the house. When told that Cole had been spotted in the home, the old man admitted the accusation and said he aided him only because he had been threatened.

A party of federals pursued the fleeing Cole Younger but almost immediately lost his trail. Unable to locate any sign of his footprints, they returned to the house. Cole managed to escape barefooted in the snow by walking for nearly a half mile on top of a rail fence that surrounded the farm.

In June or July, 1863, Cole Younger allegedly decided he must see his sweetheart, Lizzie Brown, and paid her a visit at Wayside Rest. He persuaded fellow irregulars Tom Tally, Will Hulse, George Wigginton, George Jackson, and John McCorkle to act as his bodyguard and protect him while he talked with Lizzie. The irregulars remained in the Harrisonville area for a week with Cole visiting Lizzie every day and every night. They encountered no trouble during the week, despite the presence of 300 federals three miles away in Harrisonville.[28]

Meanwhile, Union authorities, acting out of frustration for losing most all of their encounters with the guerrillas, decided to banish all Southerners in the area who might be assisting these men defend their homes. Federal officials issued orders to execute anyone giving aid to the Partisan Rangers.

In the mid summer of July 1863, federal occupational troops began to arrest and detain many area women (mainly those related to Missouri Partisan

John McCorkle, Cole Younger's bodyguard. (Author's collection)

Rangers) who were said to be spying and gathering food and information for the Partisan Rangers. Among the women detained were close relatives of prominent Partisan Rangers. These included Mary and Josephine Anderson, who were sisters of Bill Anderson, and three sisters of Cole Younger. These women were to be detained until arrangements could be made to transport them to St. Louis, where they would be tried.

All the prisoners were incarcerated in a three-story building named the Longhorn Store and Tavern, located on the site of 1409 Grand Avenue, Kansas City, Missouri. the Longhorn Store and Tavern was a fairly new structure, erected in 1856. Awaiting transport, the Longhorn Store and Tavern had been converted into a make shift jailhouse for women.

On August 13, 1863, after the women had spent six months incarcerated there, the seven-year-old building suddenly collapsed. Four women were killed including fourteen-year-old Josephine Anderson, sister of William T. Anderson. Bill's other sister, Mary Anderson was badly injured (both legs broken). Cole's cousin, Charity Kerr, a sister of John McCorkle, lay helpless in bed with a fever. Her body, frightfully mangled, was later found in the

200

ruins. Mrs. Nannie McCorkle, sister-in-law of John McCorkle, jumped from a window and escaped, but two of Cole's cousins, Susan Vandever and Armenia Whitsett Selvey, were killed.[29]

Word circulated among the guerrillas that Ewing had his men weaken the structure so it would collapse and had thus deliberately murdered his prisoners. The inner structures and supports of the building were allegedly weakened by federal troops so as to make it collapse while appearing to be an accident. Cole believed that the wrecking of the building was planned in cold blood because the downstairs had been used as a grocery store, and just prior to the building's collapse, the grocer had moved his stock from the structure in time to save it from ruin. Many of the guards had been drinking and celebrating after the collapse, and were overheard bragging and boasting as to the sabotage. This event was the reason cited behind the attack on Lawrence and intensified Anderson's hatred of the federals.[30]

Cole's cousin, Mrs. Nannie McCorkle, who had saved herself by jumping from a window of the structure, was the daughter of Reuben N. Harris, who was revenue collector for several years. Because he was an active sympathizer with the Confederacy, Union soldiers ransacked and burned his home in September. A daughter, Kate, was asleep upstairs, but was rescued from the flames by her sister. As the soldiers left, one of them allegedly shouted, "Now, old lady, call on your protectors. Why don't you call on Cole Younger now?"[31]

Cole didn't have to be called by anyone. Believing the federals responsible for the collapse of the building were some of the same men who had killed his father, Cole got permission to track down those responsible. With fellow bushwhackers George Todd, Abe Cunningham, Fletcher Taylor, Zach Traber, and George Clayton, he started for Kansas City, all of them disguised as federal cavalrymen. In one of the barrooms, they found six of the men Cole felt were responsible for bringing down the jail and killed them. Then they returned to Quantrill's headquarters.[32]

Quantrill assembled his captains—Bill Anderson, George Todd, William H. Gregg, Cole Younger—and others and their bands in Johnson County, Missouri. He informed Gregg that "he longed to get even with Kansas," and in a speech to his lieutenants, stated, "We can get more money and more revenge there than anywhere else in the state of Kansas."[33]

Lawrence at the time of the raid had a population of 1,200 people and was referred to by many as the most beautiful town in Kansas. Although it had been in existence for only nine years, it was a prosperous community. Founded by Ann Lawrence in 1854, its wide clean streets were lined with trees, fine stores, and comfortable homes. The people were industrious and, unfortunately, unaware of any impending danger. Lawrence was also a bustling recruiting center for the Union Army, so it was not difficult for the guerrillas to approach the town with the Stars and Stripes flying at the head of their column to avert suspicion.[34]

In the spring of 1863 General George W. Collamoore had been elected mayor of Lawrence, Kansas. He had been quartermaster general of the state under Governor Robinson for two years and was a man of means, well connected in the East. Collamoore was a very active man with a good deal of executive ability, and had an air of self-sufficiency which made him want to do everything his own way and made other people disposed to stand aloof from him. He realized as few others did the danger in which Lawrence stood, and he endeavored earnestly and constantly to arouse the people to a sense of the situation. In this he was partially successful. He organized an effective military company and secured arms for them from the state. He also organized and armed companies in the country about Lawrence. A peculiar notion of his was that the guns should be kept in the armory and not be carried home by the men. The result was that when the attack was made the men were scattered about the city at their homes and their guns were inaccessible.[35]

George W. Collamoore, mayor at the time of the Lawrence, Kansas, raid. (Author's collection)

He appealed to the military authorities to station at Lawrence a body of soldiers sufficient to do picket duty. This would insure a reliable guard, and relieve the citizens of this double service. He insisted that Lawrence could defend herself if she could only be warned in time of the approach of danger. After many efforts he gained his point and some time in May a small squad of soldiers was stationed at Lawrence, and the citizen soldiery was relieved of patrol duty. About August 1st the military authorities withdrew this guard for service elsewhere. They affirmed very positively that the guard was not needed. Lawrence was in no possible danger. The line between Missouri and Kansas was patrolled along its whole length, and no body of guerrillas could pass into Kansas without the fact being reported. General Collamoore protested against the removal of the troops but without avail. The people were disposed to accept the assurance of the military authorities, and nothing was done to revive the old plan of citizen patrol. The result was that Lawrence had never been so thoroughly off her guard, and so thoroughly at her ease, as at this time of her greatest peril

Over the summer of 1863, Union forces appeared to be strong along the Kansas-Missouri border. No large bushwhacker forces had been seen, and the town of Lawrence, Kansas, relaxed until Mayor George W. Collamoore called for a defense of the area. A Lieutenant Hadley, commanding a squad of troops in Lawrence, had received a letter from his brother serving on the staff of General Ewing stating Union spies in Quantrill's camp had learned of an impending raid on Lawrence. Lieutenant Hadley shared the letter with Mayor Collamoore, who immediately summoned the militia to guard the streets of Lawrence. Collamoore, however, failed to convey the message to the town's citizens, who believed the troops were over-reacting.[36]

Disguised as a cattle trader, Quantrill's lieutenant Fletcher Taylor stayed a week in Lawrence's Eldridge House, from where, according to Cole Younger, the Jayhawkers set out and killed 200 men and boys, taken women prisoners, and stolen horses. On August 16, 1863, 310 men met at the home of Captain Purdee on the Blackwater River in Johnson County to hear Taylor's report.[37]

On the night of August 19, 1863, Quantrill assembled 294 men at Columbus, Missouri, where they were organized into four companies, and quietly the plans were made for an attack upon Lawrence. Two of Quantrill's companies were commanded by Bill Todd and Bill Anderson, "two of the most desperate and bloodthirsty of the border chieftains." Others who accompanied him were Dick Yeager and Cole Younger.[38]

Of the men who rode to Lawrence under Quantrill, 100 were raw recruits serving under Confederate Colonel John D. Holt, who on his way south had fallen in with the irregulars by accident. Holt decided to continue on with the bushwhackers so his raw recruits could be initiated into violence.

Fifty others comprised another guerrilla band from the Grand River area south of Jackson County, who joined Quantrill only after the ride to Kansas had commenced.[39]

Quantrill and his men, acting out of retaliation, broke camp in Missouri on August 20, 1863, and headed in a southwesterly direction. Quantrill's scout, John McCorkle, later recalled that the party "went over on the Big Blue to a point south of Little Santa Fe, a town just on the Kansas line." According to McCorkle, Quantrill and his men "halted in the woods, all day, and just about dark he gave the order to mount and crossed into Kansas at a point about ten miles south of Little Santa Fe."[40]

Crossing into Kansas, they rode past a Union cavalry encampment near Aubrey. Quantrill instructed his men not to fire their weapons unless fired upon. Captain Joshua P. Pike, commanding forces at Aubrey, however, was suspicious and sent dispatches north to a camp at Little Santa Fe. Another rider carried messages to General Ewing in Kansas City where a Shawnee Indian named Pelathe (The Eagle) volunteered to ride into Lawrence and warn the residents. But in approaching the town, Pelathe heard the sound of gunfire and knew he had come too late.[41]

Quantrill's border ruffians passed through Gardner, just southeast of Lawrence, about eleven o'clock in the evening. One local citizen recognized Quantrill leading a force of 300 men and recalled: "They passed quietly, riding four abreast with pickets out in all directions. They claimed to be new troops going to Leavenworth to be mustered into service, but their conduct was suspicious and aroused the citizens. Great excitement soon prevailed, and people hid their valuables and ran their horses and cattle to places of safety."[42]

The band moved quietly through Hesper, about ten miles southeast of Lawrence, between two and three o'clock in the morning of the 21st. A local man, Louis J. Rote, later recalled that Quantrill stopped at his house and demanded his brother Jake guide them to Lawrence. Jake initially believed the men were federal troops.

"He was but a boy of sixteen years, and he talked freely with the raiders," penned Louis Rote some years later. "When passing between the banks of the Big Wakarusa on the left and Horseshoe Lake on the right, the man Jake was riding behind turned to him and said, in a very stern voice: 'Young man, do you know who you are riding with?' Jake replied: 'No, and I don't care, so long as you treat me well.' Then the ruffian said: 'This is Marmaduke's command and Quantrill is in the lead.' Jake was quiet after that. But he was forced to go into Lawrence with the guerrillas and hold their horses while they robbed, burned, and murdered. When they were ready to leave Lawrence, they compelled Jake to put on a new set of clothes. They gave him a horse and told him to go home."[43]

The Wakarusa Company, six miles south, assembled the morning of the raid near Blanton's Bridge, but they had no arms. Collamoore saw, as everyone did, that the citizens' guard was very unreliable. While most citizens did their duty when appointed for picket service, others failed, and it was never known whether there was a guard out or not. Besides he insisted that it was unfair to ask men who worked all day to do picket duty all night. It was enough if they held themselves in readiness to rally when danger threatened.[44]

"We reached Lawrence the morning of the 21st," recalled Cole Younger. "Quantrill sent me to quiz an old farmer who was feeding his hogs as to whether there had been any material changes in Lawrence since Lieutenant Taylor had been there. He thought there were [seventy-five] soldiers in Lawrence; there were really 200."[45]

"We had sent a spy into Lawrence, a Negro named John Lobb, to come back and tell how he found things," recalled Quantrill's lieutenant, William Gregg. "Lobb did not get back before we had started. He met us on the way and told us that [Jim] Lane had left town."[46]

The Lawrence raid differed from any other raid in history. The earlier raids of Quantrill and his men were made for plunder largely. They dashed into Olathe at night, ordered all the men to the public square and kept them under guard till they were done. Only one man was killed, and he was killed in a fray. Often raids were made for the purpose of putting out of the way some persons who were obnoxious to them. Houses were burned, horses were taken, and other things stolen such as took their fancy. But in no case was there a general slaughter.[47]

At Lawrence it was butchery from the initial charge to the final shot. The butchering and burning commenced with their approach and hardly ended with their departure. It was not the picking out of a few obnoxious persons as was the case elsewhere. The killing was indiscriminate and mostly in cold blood. There was no provocation, no resistance, and nothing to irritate or provoke. The few who resisted fared better than those who did not resist.

Sophia L. Bissell, a local resident and eye witness to the raid, later recalled: "About [a half] mile away were ever so many men on horseback, coming along very quickly, strung out, oh, I should think there must have been three or four hundred of them. In a few minutes . . . we heard them say, 'Halt!' and then . . . they all separated into bands and went yelling and shooting as fast as they would ride; a band for each street."[48]

There were men in Lawrence whom the bushwhackers hoped to capture and kill. But very few of these were found. Governor Robinson was in town that morning. On account of his position and his prominence in the early difficulties, they would have counted him a valuable prize. But he was permitted quietly to survey the whole transaction from his stone barn on the hillside. They searched for him elsewhere, but did not look in the barn.[49]

Cole had been assigned the task of capturing Jim Lane and taking him back to Missouri for a public beheading. General Lane was in town that morning, and perhaps no man in Kansas would have been dispatched with more relish. As Cole rode towards the Free State Hotel, he was sickened by the slaughter being conducted by his fellow raiders. He yelled to the women and children to run into the cornfields so that they would be spared from witnessing the carnage.[50]

General George Deitzler was in town, having just come from a victorious campaign through the very region from which they hailed. But he was not found. The two Rankins were home on a furlough. They were soldiers and expected no quarters. When they were attacked in the street, therefore, they drew their revolvers and blazed away, and were given a wide berth.[51]

The men the raiders did kill were quiet, peaceable citizens. Few of them had taken any part in the early disturbances or in the border troubles since the war began. There was Judge Carpenter, a very conservative man, never extreme in any line, and having no sympathy with extreme men on either side. There was Edward P. Fitch, one of the quietest of men, a lover of home and of peace, as brave as a lion and gentle as a woman. There was S.M. Thorpe of whom no one could cherish a hard thought. Only a few months before he had been elected to the state senate on the issue of opposition to all irresponsible warfare. He had the utmost abhorrence of all parties on either side who were disposed to take advantage of the condition of war for plunder or prey.

"Almost everyone was abed, and they were all over the city in ten minutes and shot down everyone that showed his head, so that they had no chance to get together to defend the town," related citizen, Hiram Towne.[52] The raid was modeled after the federal attack on Osceola, Missouri, in 1861. During this raid, over 450 men rode to Lawrence with Quantrill, pressing local farmers into service as guides along the way. Some of the guerrillas were members of his gang, but many were Missouri farmers who were greatly angered over the killing of the women. The border ruffians entered Lawrence from the south and continued northeast.

Two horsemen were sent ahead to see that all was quiet in town. Those horsemen rode through the town and back without attracting attention. They were seen going through Massachusetts Street, but their appearance there at that hour was nothing unusual.

At the house of Reverend S.S. Snyder, part of the gang turned away from the main body, entered his yard and shot him. Mr. Snyder was a prominent minister among the United Brethren and held a commission as lieutenant in the Second Colored Regiment. Their progress from here was quite rapid but cautious. Every now and then, they slowed their horses as if fearful to proceed. They were seen approaching by several persons in the outskirts of the town, but in the dimness of the morning and the distance, they were supposed to be Union troops. Upon reaching the homes of Jim Lane and Doc Jennison, Quantrill reminded his men that these men were out looking for them and showing no quarter. He told them to shoot every soldier they saw but spare any woman or child. They passed on in a body until they came to the high ground facing Massachusetts Street, when the command to attack was given and then he dashed down Massachusetts Street firing his pistol.[53]

The attack was perfectly planned. Every man knew his place. Detachments scattered to every section of the town, and it was done with such promptness and speed that before people could gather the meaning of their first yell, every part of the town was full of them. They flowed into every street.

Erastus Ladd was standing on the porch of his home and later recalled: "The shots were accompanied by cheers, or rather yells. In a few moments, as I stood looking, some three or four Negroes . . . came rushing by hallooing, 'The secesh have come!' As I looked, the head of the column of fiends rushed down the street. . . . I saw that, too truly, 'the secesh had come!'"[54]

The bushwhackers scattered to every section of Lawrence and began shooting every male in sight. When several of the riders came upon the raw recruits of the Kansas Fourteenth, a new regiment that had not yet been organized, they fired at the helpless recruits as they tried to run for cover. Seventeen of the twenty-one white recruits were killed while black recruits, camped nearby, fled to safety.

William Gregg remembered:

> We rode into the town from the south by the main street, Massachusetts. Just before we came to the business portion there was a large open space with about [forty] large tents. I don't know how many soldiers were in them. The five men with me halted there for the main body to come up. As we sat on our horses we saw soldiers sleeping on the porches of the nearest houses, we opened fire on them with our revolvers. As soon as Quantrill reached me—he was riding at the head of the column—I pointed at the [forty] tents arranged in the open spaces. Without a halt being made, the command divided, and charged through the camp. Men and horses were brought up to a pitch of frenzy by the all night riding and by the final gallop. The horses made no effort to go between the tents. They plunged right through them. In three minutes there wasn't a man alive or a tent standing in the camp.[55]

"It being very warm, I was up about [five] o'clock on the morning of August 21, 1863," related O.W. McAlaster later. "A noise attracted my attention, and I looked south and saw between 300 and 400 horsemen . . . in an instant they spread out . . . shooting every person they saw. . . . They reached a camp of thirty-two unarmed recruits. . . . I saw them shooting down these men, who ran in every direction, some crawling under sidewalks and into bushes, only about five escaping with their lives. Then I realized that Quantrill and his guerrillas were upon us."[56]

As Quantrill and several bushwhackers reigned up in front of the four-story Eldridge House, one hotel guest gazing out the window saw "men flying in terror, and pleading for mercy, but in every instance unhesitatingly shot down. One man rushed out upon the sidewalk, on the east side of the street, apparently designing to cross, but a trooper riding past, wheeled his horse, and discharged his revolver full at his breast. The man threw up his arms and apparently implored quarter, made the only response made was curses and shots, repeated again and again; under these he sunk to the ground, and probably died on the spot."[57]

The guerrillas ran through the hotel, looking into each of the rooms for any males that might be concealed inside. Two of the raiders broke down a door and dragged a traveler down to the lobby where there were already about [fifty] captives. The traveler described Quantrill thusly:

> Quantrell [sic] would pass anywhere for a well-looking man, and exhibits in his countenance no traces of native ferocity. He is of medium height, well built, and very quiet and very deliberate in speech and motion. His hair is brown, his complexion fresh, and his cunning and pleasant blue eyes, and aquiline nose, gave to his countenance its chief expression. During the few minutes which he spent with us at this time, he conversed freely about himself and the present expedition, receiving with marked complacency some compliments on the completeness of his present success, and not hesitating to express his consciousness, that it was by far the greatest of his exploits.[58]

The bushwhackers moved the guests from the Eldridge Hotel to the two-story brown City Hotel on the river, just opposite the ferry that crossed the Kansas River. Quantrill tipped his hat to the ladies, bid them farewell, and rode south along Massachusetts Street, followed by his guards from the City Hotel. When all of the guards had left, the guests huddled together, hoping the ruffians would not return.

Two drunken guerrillas, however, did come back. They ordered everyone out of the hotel and told the frightened guests to line up in rows. Those who did come out in the street were shot at. Nathan Stone, who ran the hotel, dashed outside and ordered the guerrillas to stop shooting immediately. Stone was shot down and killed.

Brigetta Dix Flintom later stated: "I saw men jumping from windows and fleeing for their lives. Several were killed as they ran."[59]

The hotel guests rushed out the back door. One of them rushed to the river bank and came upon General Deitzler, who was planning to cross the river for help. Calling out to the ferryman to come across the river and pick them up, the pair was taken to the north bank. Deitzler's companion stumbled upon a squad of soldiers and some Delaware Indians carrying guns, bows, and arrows. Forming a party of twenty-five armed men, they crossed the river and fired upon a few stragglers from Quantrill's army. Larkin M. Skaggs, one of the two drunken ruffians at the hotel, was shot and killed, while his companion was killed by arrows from the Delaware Indians.[60]

Other members of Quantrill's band moved through the residential district, looting, burning, and killing. A.K. Allen, who lived in a large brick house, refused to come out when ordered to do so by one of the guerrillas. Mayor George W. Collamoore and a friend, Pat Keefe, rushed out the back door of the house and jumped into a dry well to hide. Mrs. Collamoore remained in the house until it was set on fire by the intruders. Collamoore and Keefe, as well as J.G. Lowe, who tried to rescue them after the bushwhackers had left, all suffocated in the well.

County Clerk G.W. Bell, who lived on the side hill overlooking the town, seized his musket and cartridge box with the hope of reaching the main street before the bushwhackers. His family endeavored to dissuade him, telling him he would certainly be killed. As he dashed out, he found the street occupied by the guerrillas before he could reach it. He decided to go around by the back way and emerge from the ravine west of the street. Along the way, he met other citizens, who urged him to save himself. He turned back, apparently intending to get home again. A friend urged him to throw his musket away, which he did. Finding escape impossible, he went into an unfinished brick house, and climbed up on the joists above, together with another man. A bushwhacker entered and commenced shooting at them, when Bell discovered that the guerrilla was an old acquaintance who had often eaten at his table. Bell appealed to him in such a way that the guerrillas promised to spare both their lives, for old acquaintance sake, if they would come down. They came down, and the bushwhacker took them out to about twenty of his companions and shot him with four balls. His companion was wounded and lay for dead but afterwards recovered.[61]

Mary Carpenter Rankin described the murder of her husband by the bushwhackers: "We had been married ten months. When two of the raiders called at our house and saw my husband, they fired a shot at him and after his race through the yard they fired a second shot. Of what passed around us I know and remember nothing, until I sat beside the body of my husband and saw him in a rude coffin and laid away in a corner of our yard."[62]

Mrs. J.B. Sutliff was a bit more fortunate: "My husband was not killed, he being away on business, and our home was not burned. I saw Mr. Griffith and told him to run to the ravine. He reached it and saved his life. I had to warn Mrs. Griffith to keep away from him. I can hear the pounding of nails yet, for Ira Brown and Hiram Towne made coffins for two nights in their shop just across the alley from my home."[63]

Priscilla Jones remembered: "They were digging graves all night Friday, begun burying just at daylight Saturday morning and worked till dark . . . there was one hundred and twenty-three bodies found, some burnt so you couldn't tell what it was."[64]

W.H. Simpson later explained his family's escape from the marauders:

> When Quantrell [sic] raided Lawrence I was five and one-half years young. My father, Henry M. Simpson, then lived in West Lawrence. Back of our house was a large field of corn, growing as Kansas corn is in the habit of doing, lustily tall and thick. That field, with its "walls of corn" saved our lives. I well remember being hurriedly dragged into the maze of maize just as the rebels came up the front steps looking for abolitionists. The day was hot. It dawned that way. We had no water, no breakfast, and nothing to satisfy hunger except ears of half-green corn. The necessity for keeping quiet was impressed on my mind, but probably I was too badly scared to make a noise, anyway. The flames from our burning house scarcely had died down when we came out of our hiding place and were taken care of by kind neighbors—glad just to be alive.[65]

The surprise was so complete that no organized resistance was possible. Before people could fully comprehend what was transpiring, every part of the town was full of bushwhackers, and there was no possibility of rallying. Even the recruits in camp were so taken by surprise that they were not in their places. The attack could scarcely have been made at a worse hour. The soldiers had just taken in their camp guard, and people were just waking from sleep. When Quantrill's men gained possession of the main street, the armory was inaccessible to the citizens, and the judicious disposition of squads of guerrillas in other parts of the town, prevented even a partial rally at any point. There was no time or opportunity for consultation or concert of action, and every man had to do the best he could for himself. A large number, however, did actually start with what arms they had towards the street. Most saw at once that the street could not be reached, and turned back. Some went forward and perished. Mr. Levi Gates lived about a mile in the country, in the opposite direction from that by which the rebels had entered. As soon as he heard the firing in the town, he started with his rifle, supposing that a stand would be made by the citizens. When he got to town, he saw at once that the rebels had possession. He was an excellent marksman, and could not leave without trying his rifle. The first shot he fired hit one of the attackers, but soon Gates was killed and his head brutally beat to pieces.[66]

Many of the guerrillas celebrated by getting drunk with liquor taken from the local saloons as the town burned. About nine o'clock, however, it was reported that federal troops were approaching the town and the raiders fled back to Missouri. They suffered only two casualties, men too drunk to ride away with the rest of the raiders.

John Jarrette's horse was shot out from underneath him as he started out of Lawrence. He quickly removed his saddle and attempted to place it on a mustang one of his companions was leading. While trying to saddle the mustang, he was nearly surrounded by the federals. Cole rode back and Jarrette got up behind him.[67]

The flight to Missouri became a running battle although Quantrill lost few of his men. Union forces in both Missouri and Kansas were slow to assemble, but Jim Lane gathered a force of about 150 men from Lawrence, fifty volunteers from the Kansas City area, and another 180 from the Kansas border garrisons. They came upon Quantrill and his party near the tint community of Brooklyn, and following a skirmish, continued to chase the bushwhackers to within two or three miles of Paola, Kansas. The guerrillas turned northeast and crossed back into Missouri in the morning.

Disappearing into the brush around Grand River, the bushwhackers disbanded and rode away in different directions. Five miles west of Pleasant Hill, Colonel Bazel Lazear and part of the First Missouri State Militia Cavalry, caught up with the raiders. In the sharp fight that followed, sixteen bushwhackers were killed and several wounded. The raiders who were captured were quickly executed.[68]

"It is not known, generally," said Cole in an interview years later, "but Charley [Wells] was the boy who saved our necks after the raid at Lawrence. If it had not been for his knowledge of the country . . . we would never have been able to get away. There were 1500 men at our rear and 700 men in front of us. They thought that we were going west, but Charley said to go north. It was our only chance, and we got away, but we had to fight our way out after fighting all day under a hot August sun. We were as black as 'niggers' when we got out."[69]

Wells, who was also interviewed, told the reporter that Cole had opposed the Lawrence raid: "It is not generally known either that Cole was the only officer who voted against making the raid at Lawrence."

Cole replied, "I thought it was too dangerous, that was my only reason."

Wells spoke up again: "Cole was [eighteen] then and a captain. I was only [seventeen]. Yes, I was a private, but I was high private, and I knew the country thoroughly. Not a dozen men . . . knew that we were going to raid Lawrence, the day we started out of Johnson County."

When Cole was asked if he and Charley Wells had known each other long, he replied: "Why we were raised together at Lee's Summit. We went through the war together. We were with Quantrill together. We rode through Mexico on mule back and went over the plains to California together after the war. Charley's father was Captain G.W. Wells of Lee's Summit, who was killed in battle at White Oak inst. Old Captain Wells and my father were two of the earliest settlers of Jackson County. Have we known each other long? My, but that's a good one."[70]

Over 150 citizens were killed during the Lawrence raid. Quantrill lost control over his men during this raid, and there was much murder and mayhem. Many of Quantrill's men were sickened by the slaughter. Although no women were killed, they and their children were forced to witness the carnage. Senator Lane, however, escaped across a cornfield in his nightshirt. Quantrill had planned on taking him back to Missouri for a public hanging.[71]

Major John N. Edwards later stated: "Cole Younger saved at least a dozen lives this day. Indeed, he killed none, save in open and manly battle. At one house he captured five citizens over whom he put a guard and at another three, whom he defended and protected. The notorious General James H. Lane, to get whom Quantrell [sic] would gladly left and sacrificed all the balance of the victims, made his escape through a cornfield, hotly pursued but too splendidly mounted to be captured."[72]

Guerrilla Jim Cummins referred to Cole as "the cool and desperate Cole who headed the advance into Lawrence. He was grand, noble looking, and a handsome man, and was respected and well liked by all who came into contact with him. He was far superior to the others."[73]

A.R. Banks wrote Colonel C.W. Marsh, Assistant Adjutant General of the Missouri, from Lawrence on August 21: "I have, with regret, to report that Quantrill, alias Charley Hart, reached this town at about 4:30 . . . this morning; burned the town; slaughtered in cold blood about [sixty] citizens; then left by Blanton Bridge, and by way of the town of Brooklyn. A near as I can estimate, he had about 200 men, armed principally with revolvers. It is said that Lane, with a few men, held him at bay in Brooklyn, and has sent back for help. Quantrill left about [ten] o'clock."[74]

Frank Leslie's Illustrated Newspaper reported the following on September 12th:

> The war has had its terrors. The deep hypocrisy of the Confederate leaders, who, hanging Union men in Tennessee and Missouri as bridge burners, guerrillas, or simply and nakedly as Union men, insulted Heaven and outraged humanity by their mendacious protests against the reprisals occasionally and too seldom made by our kindly-hearted authorities, reaches a climax in the fearful massacre at Lawrence, Kansas.
>
> In atrocity, in bloodthirsty cruelty, in barbarity, rapine and fiendishness, it has no parallel in our history. A town entered treacherously at night, nearly 200 of its people butchered without mercy, the city pillaged and fired, such is, in the sanctimonious eyes of Davis and [P.G.T.] Beauregard, a part of civilized warfare. When Bishop Lynch chanted his *Te Deum* to thank the Almighty that civil war had begun, was it to ask the benediction of heaven on scenes like this?
>
> The immediate perpetrator of the frightful massacre was Quantrell [sic], who has for the last two years, figured in guerrilla war in Missouri, and though often defeated, never captured. His force consisted of 300 picked men from Lafayette, Saline, Clay, and Johnson and other border counties in Missouri. It started on the 20th from Middle Fork, Grand River, fifteen miles from the Kansas border, and crossed the line near the town of Gardner, reaching Lawrence at four o'clock on the morning of the 21st . . .[75]

The *Leavenworth Daily Conservative* of August 23, 1863, headlined the account of the raid as follows: "Total Loss $2,000,000, Cash Lost $250, 000," and described the scene along Massachusetts Street, as ". . . one mass of smouldering ruins and crumbling walls. . . . Only two business houses were left upon the street—one known as the Armory, and the other the old Miller block. . . . About one hundred and twenty-five houses in all were burned, and only one or two escaped being ransacked and everything of value carried away or destroyed."[76]

Richard Cordley concurred: "The walls of the brick and stone buildings were still standing, black, gloomy and threatening. The smoke was still rising from the ruins and in the deep cellars the fires were still glowing."[77]

In a later interview, Cole said he believed he could not have lived his life any differently. He added he had done what any person in his position would have done. "There was nothing in my life so thrilling as my part in the raid on Lawrence during the Civil War," he said to the interviewer. "There is nothing that ever happened that was so misrepresented in literature and history.

> To understand it one must look back into the early history of the war when federal sympathizers had Southerners in Missouri at their mercy.
>
> My father was opposed to the war and had friends on both sides, but was shot down in cold blood and robbed by a gang of federal freebooters as he was driving home from Kansas City. That day changed my whole life. The knowledge that my father had been killed in cold blood filled my heart with lust for vengeance.
>
> I was [nineteen] the day we started from Blackwater, Missouri, about 300 strong, the men in the Quantrill band, I mean. It was August 26, 1863. I was lieutenant in one company of the command.
>
> When we reached a hill in sight of Lawrence we learned from an old hog-feeder that there were 300 regular federal troops in Lawrence and 300 militiamen. They outnumbered us two to one but we can whip them (Cole said he had been told by Quantrill).
>
> Soon we came upon them, there were no guards and we tore open the flaps of their tents and killed them as fast as our guns could work. We lost only four dead and three wounded. Then we rode away and fought for twenty-four hours with pursuers that had been organized. They followed us until we were among friends in Missouri.[78]

Many other Southerners admired Quantrill and the black flag as well, including Miss Annie Fickle, a charming young lady whose aim was to personally meet with the outlaw. And she did! Miss Fickle praised Quantrill and his men, "the faithful Southerners throughout the State of Missouri" and created a slogan:

> "And ever let your battle cry be
> Quantrill and Southern supremacy!"[79]

Annie unfolded a large piece of quilted alpaca, three by five feet in size, with QUANTRILL in bright letters stitched in the center. "Quantrill's black flag was tacked to an eight-foot pole. Cole Younger and Frank James, however, claimed they had never seen such a flag. Upon later being asked what happened to the black flag, Cole answered: "Jim Lane carried a black flag until the fall of 1863, when we captured it, and sometime afterward we sent it to Sterling Price. I think both flags were subsequently cut up and made into over-shirts which some of the boys wore."

Despite the atrocities committed by Quantrill and his men "under the black flag," they did generate some genuine good service to the Confederate cause. They severed Union communications, captured couriers, cut off small patrols, sabotaged buildings, bridges, telephone wires, and railroad lines. They also compelled "the enemy to keep there a large force that might have been employed elsewhere" and succeeded in turning the local population against the enemy.[80]

Occasionally, Quantrill, Cole Younger, Frank James, and company cooperated with regular Confederate forces, as when they assisted in the capture of Independence in the summer of 1862. But most of the time they operated without orders or control from the Confederate military authorities, ambushing federal patrols, attacking Union posts, raiding Kansas border settlements, and terrorizing Missouri Unionists.[81] Years later, Cole Younger maintained:

> In all that time of service in Missouri, I was either a private or subordinate officer, acting under orders. In 1862-1863, I was a lieutenant in Captain Jarrette's company, Shelby's brigade of Price's army. All soldiers. Whether they wore the blue or the gray, know that they take an oath to obey officers appointed over them, and all good soldiers obey the orders of their superior officers. As for the kind of soldier I made, I leave that to the honorable federal and Confederate soldiers that I fought against and with, who now live in Missouri. I know that no one will ever say that he knew me to be guilty of any individual act of cruelty to the wounded or prisoners of our foe. I do not believe there is a brave federal soldier in Minnesota today who, if he knew every act of mine during the war, but what would give me the right hand of a soldier's recognition. I was engaged in many bloody battles where it was death or victory. I tried to do my part, any true soldier would. All articles, such as referred to, are false when they charge me with shooting unresisting men or wounded prisoners. No man who has respect for the truth will say that I ever ordered the execution of a citizen at any place during the war—at Lawrence or anywhere else. Not one of my brothers ever soldiered with me a day. As to a story going the rounds that during the war I captured fifteen men, tied them together and tried to shoot through them all, it is false from beginning to end. I never heard of anything like it having being committed during the war, in Missouri, Kansas, or anywhere else. I know of no foundation for the falsehood.[82]

It is difficult to ascertain Frank James' role in the slaughter. One biographer later stated that Frank "was as ferocious and merciless as a hyena," that day and that "the Youngers did bloody work," although Cole was the only brother there.[83]

On the other hand, an old friend of Frank's, Colonel J.E. Caven, who had served in the same brigade during the war, later told a reporter that Frank was one of the bravest men he had ever known. Colonel Caven related:

> I cannot speak of Frank James without emotion. He was one of the noblest men who took part in the great struggle of the West. I cannot begin to tell of all the instances of his valor in battle, his kindness in camp, his care for his comrades, his noble self-sacrifice. No one but those who were with him in those dark hours can appreciate his spirit. He was only a boy when he joined the regiment, but he soon became the hero of the brigade. It was a grand sight to see him in battle. He was always where the fight was thickest. He was absolutely devoid of fear. Yet while he was as brave as a lion, his courage was not of the wild impetuous sort that led him into foolhardy undertakings. He inspired hope in the hearts of the men, cheered them and encouraged them, and spurred them on to renewed efforts.
>
> I have seen him dismount and give his horse to a tired trooper. In the hospital once I saw him take off his shirt and tear it up for bandages for the wounded, not knowing when or how he was to get another one. I have seen him take off his coat and give it to a soldier who, he thought, was more in need of it. Smallpox broke out among the men. Frank James feared it as little as he did the bullets of the enemy. He would take a soldier with smallpox in his arms and carry him to the most comfortable place that could be secured, and nurse him with the care of a woman. He would brave anything to secure a delicacy for a sick soldier. His heart was so big that he thought of everybody before himself.[84]

Although Cole Younger and Frank James undoubtedly killed their share of men at Lawrence, three guerrillas—Bill Gaw, Allen Parmer, and Dick Maddox—reportedly killed the most. But there were many people slaughtered, and Cole and Frank were as guilty as any.[85] A local newspaper vowed the town would rebuild and not allow the Missourians wipe them off the map:

"Our town will not be like a ruffian hole destroyed. It will rise from its ashes in a space of time which will astonish even Quantrell [sic] himself."[86]

Notes

[1] Kansas Historical Collections, Volume 7, 1901-1902.

[2] Report of Brigadier General James G. Blunt, U.S. Army. August 26,1862. *The War of the Rebellion: A Compilation of the Official Records of the Union and Confederate Armies*, Series I, Volume XXV, pp. 257-258.

[3] Ibid.

[4] Dallas Cantrell, *Northfield, Minnesota: Youngers' Fatal Blunder*, San Antonio, The Naylor Company, 1973, pp. 6-7.

[5] Cole Younger, *The Story of Cole Younger by Himself*, pp. 9-10.

[6] Carl W. Breihan, *The Complete and Authentic Life of Jesse James*, pp. 245-246.

[7] Marley Brant, *Outlaws: The Illustrated History of the James-Younger Gang*, pp. 31-32.

[8] Carl W. Breihan, *The Complete and Authentic Life of Jesse James*, pp. 245-246.

[9] Letter of Governor William R. Marshall of Minnesota published in the *St. Paul Pioneer Press* of July 26, 1886.

[10] Dr. William A. Settle, *Cole Younger Writes to Lizzie Daniel*, Liberty, Missouri, James-Younger Gang, 1994, p. 20.

[11] *Madelia Times-Messenger*, March 29, 1979.

[12] *St. Paul Pioneer Press*, Friday, July 23, 1886.

[13] Eric Uriel Kirkwood, "The First Kansas Colored Infantry Regiment." Internet.

[14] Marley Brant, *Outlaws: The Illustrated History of the James-Younger Gang*, p. 30.

[15] Peter Cozzens, "Hindman's Grand Delusion," *Civil War Times Illustrated*, October 2000, pp. 30-31.

[16] Report of Captain Daniel H. David, Fifth Missouri Cavalry (Militia), October 8, 1862. *The War of the Rebellion: A Compilation of the Official Records of the Union and Confederate Armies*, Series I, Volume XXV, pp. 312-313.

[17] *Palmyra Missouri Courier*, October 1862.

[18] Report of Captain Joseph H. Little, First Missouri Cavalry (Militia), October 27, 1862. *The War of the Rebellion: A Compilation of the Official Records of the Union and Confederate Armies*, Series I, Volume XXV, p. 339.

[19] Philip A. Thompson, War Department, letter to General Penick dated November 6, 1862. *The War of the Rebellion: A Compilation of the Official Records of the Union and Confederate Armies*, Series I, Volume XXV, p. 792.

[20] Report of Major Benjamin S. Henning, Third Wisconsin Cavalry, November 11,1862. *The War of the Rebellion: A Compilation of the Official Records of the Union and Confederate Armies*, Series I, Volume Chapter XXV, pp. 352-353.

[21] Dr. Thomas Hamill letter to Major General Samuel R. Curtis dated November 6, 1862. *The War of the Rebellion: A Compilation of the Official Records of the Union and Confederate Armies*, Series I, Volume Chapter XXV, p. 803.

[22] Edward E. Leslie, *The Devil Knows How to Ride*, p. 159. I

[23] Prairie Grove Battlefield State Park records.

[24]Ibid.

[25]Ibid.

[26]Edward E. Leslie, *The Devil Knows How to Ride*, pp. 160-163.

[27]Carl W. Breihan, *The Complete and Authentic Life of Jesse James*, pp. 244-245.

[28]John McCorkle, *Three Years with Quantrill: A True Story*, Armstrong, Missouri, no date, p. 73.

[29]Cole Younger, *The Story of Cole Younger by Himself*, p. 7.

[30]William A. Settle, Jr., *Jesse James Was His Name*, Lincoln, University of Nebraska Press, 1966, p. 23.

[31]Cole Younger, *The Story of Cole Younger by Himself*, pp. 7-8.

[32]Carl W. Breihan, *The Complete and Authentic Life of Jesse James*, pp. 243-244.

[33]Robertus Love, *The Rise and Fall of Jesse James*, Lincoln, University of Nebraska Press, 1990, p. 21.

[34]Carl W. Breihan, "The Day Quantrill Burned Lawrence," *The West*, January 1972, p. 14.

[35]Richard Cordley, D.D., *A History of Lawrence, Kansas from the Earliest Settlement to the Close of the Rebellion*. Lawrence, Kansas, E.F. Caldwell, Lawrence Journal Press, 1895.

[36]David Dary, *Lawrence Douglas County, Kansas: An Informal History*, Lawrence, Allen Books, 1982, p. 100-102.

[37]Cole Younger, *The Story of Cole Younger by Himself*, p. 41.

[38]Frank W. Blackmar, editor, *Kansas: a Cyclopedia of State History, Embracing Events, Institutions, Industries, Counties, Cities, Towns, Prominent Persons, etc. . . . With a Supplementary Volume Devoted to Selected Personal History and Reminiscence*, Volume II, Chicago, Standard Publishing Company, 1912, pp. 525-527.

[39]Larry Wood, "They Rode With Quantrill," *America's Civil War*, November 1996, p. 62.

[40]John McCorkle, *Three Years with Quantrell [sic]*, Armstrong, Missouri, Armstrong Herald Printing, 1914, pp. 79-80.

[41]David Dary, *Lawrence Douglas County, Kansas: An Informal History*, Lawrence, Allen Books, 1982, pp. 102-103; Frank Triplett, *The Life, Times & Treacherous Death of Jesse James*, New York, The Swallow Press, Inc., 1970, p. 8.

[42]Virginia Armstrong Johnson Gardner, *Where the Trails Divide*, Gardner, Kansas, Gardner News, 1957, p.9.

[43]William Henry Sears, "The Paul Reveres of Lawrence," Collections of the Kansas State Historical Society, Topeka, State Printer, 1928, Volume XVII, p. 841.

[44]Richard Cordley, D.D., *A History of Lawrence, Kansas, from the Earliest Settlement to the Close of the Rebellion*.

[45]Cole Younger, *The Story of Cole Younger by Himself*, p. 42.

[46]Donald R. Hale, *We Rode with Quantrill*, p. 41.

[47]Richard Cordley, D.D., *A History of Lawrence, Kansas, from the Earliest Settlement to the Close of the Rebellion*.

[48]William E. Connelley Interviews Concerning the Quantrill Raid on Lawrence, Kansas, Aug 21, 1863, Ms Collection C4. The complete account from which the above quotation is excerpted is available in the collections of the Osma Room, Lawrence Public Library, 707 Vermont Street and the Watkins Community Museum of History, 1047 Massachusetts Street, Lawrence, Kansas.

[49]Richard Cordley, D.D., A History of Lawrence, Kansas, from the Earliest Settlement to the Close of the Rebellion.

[50]Marley Brant, The Outlaw Youngers, p. 45.

[51]Richard Cordley, D.D., A History of Lawrence, Kansas, from the Earliest Settlement to the Close of the Rebellion.

[52]William E. Connelley Interviews Concerning the Quantrill Raid on Lawrence, Kansas, Aug 21, 1863, Ms Collection C4. The complete account from which the above quotation is excerpted is available in the collections of the Osma Room, Lawrence Public Library, 707 Vermont Street and the Watkins Community Museum of History, 1047 Massachusetts Street, Lawrence, Kansas.

[53]J.S. Broughton, The Lawrence Massacre by a Band of Missouri Ruffians Under Quantrell, August 21, 1863, Lawrence, J.S. Broughton Publisher, 1865, Introduction; David Dary, Lawrence Douglas County, Kansas: An Informal History, Lawrence, Allen Books, 1982, pp. 103-106.

[54]Thomas Goodrich, Black Flag Guerrilla Warfare on the Western Border, 1861-1865, p. 78.

[55]St. Louis Globe-Democrat, September 20, 1898.

[56]William E. Connelley Interviews Concerning the Quantrill Raid on Lawrence, Kansas, Aug 21, 1863, Ms Collection C4. The complete account from which the above quotation is excerpted is available in the collections of the Osma Room, Lawrence Public Library, 707 Vermont Street and the Watkins Community Museum of History, 1047 Massachusetts Street, Lawrence, Kansas.

[57]David Dary, Lawrence Douglas County, Kansas: An Informal History, Lawrence, Allen Books, 1982, pp. 103-106.

[58]Ibid., pp. 107-114.

[59]William E. Connelley Interviews Concerningthe Quantrill Raid on Lawrence, Kansas, Aug 21, 1863, Ms Collection C4. The complete account from which the above quotation is excerpted is available in the collections of the Osma Room, Lawrence Public Library, 707 Vermont Street and the Watkins Community Museum of History, 1047 Massachusetts Street, Lawrence, Kansas.

[60]David Dary, Lawrence Douglas County, Kansas: An Informal History, Lawrence, Allen Books, 1982, pp. 103-106.

[61]J.S. Broughton, The Lawrence Massacre by a Band of Missouri Ruffians Under Quantrell, August 21, 1863.

[62]William E. Connelley Interviews Concerning the Quantrill Raid on Lawrence, Kansas, August 21, 1863, Ms Collection C4. The complete account from which the above quotation is excerpted is available in the collections of the Osma

Room, Lawrence Public Library, 707 Vermont Street and the Watkins Community Museum of History, 1047 Massachusetts Street, Lawrence, Kansas.

[63]Ibid.

[64]Ibid.

[65]Ibid.

[66]J.S. Broughton, *The Lawrence Massacre by a Band of Missouri Ruffians Under Quantrell, August 21, 1863.*

[67]Cole Younger, *The Story of Cole Younger by Himself,* p. 43.

[68]Ted P. Yeatman, *Frank and Jesse James: The Story Behind the Legend*, Nashville, Cumberland House, 2000, pp. 44-45.

[69]*Nevada Daily Mail*, October 26, 1903.

[70]Ibid.

[71]William A. Settle, Jr., *Jesse James Was His Name*, pp. 23-24.

[72]Cole Younger, *The Story of Cole Younger by Himself*, p. 43.

[73]James D. Horan, *Desperate Men*, p. 16.

[74]A.R. Banks letter to Colonel C.W. Marsh, Assistant Adjutant General of the Missouri, dated August 21, 1863. *The War of the Rebellion: A Compilation of the Official Records of the Union and Confederate Armies*, Series I, Chapter XXXIV, p. 585.

[75]*Frank Leslie's Illustrated Newspaper*, September 12, 1863.

[76]*Leavenworth Daily Conservative*, August 23, 1863.

[77]William E. Connelley Interviews Concerning the Quantrill Raid on Lawrence, Kansas., August 21, 1863, Ms Collection C4. The complete account from which the above quotation is excerpted is available in the collections of the Osma Room, Lawrence Public Library, 707 Vermont Street and the Watkins Community Museum of History, 1047 Massachusetts Street, Lawrence, Kansas.

[78]*Honey Grove Signal*, April 2, 1915.

[79]Carl W. Breihan, *Quantrill and His Civil War Guerrillas*, New York, Promontory Press, 1959, pp. 44-45.

[80]William C. Davis, *The Cause Lost Myths and Realities of the Confederacy,* Lawrence, University Press of Kansas, 1996, pp. 86-87.

[81]Albert Castel, *General Sterling Price and the Civil War in the West*, Baton Rouge & London, Lousiana State University Press, 1968, p. 61.

[82]*St. Paul Pioneer Press*, August 1, 1886.

[83]William Elsey Connelley, *Quantrill and the Border Wars*, 1910. Reprint New York, Pageant Book Company, 1956, pp. 360, 384-385.

[84]*Chillicothe Daily Democrat*, November 11, 1904.

[85]David Dary, *Lawrence Douglas County, Kansas: An Informal History*, Lawrence, Allen Books, 1982, pp. 116-118.

[86]*Topeka Tribune*, August 27, 1863, John Speer, "Improvement Commences."

Chapter Eight

The Last Ride

"Well, in March of 1864 one day the Yankees ran onto two of the Southern boys and
the only thing the boys could do was to run as they weren't armed. We were watching and we saw the boys fall. We went closer to see who they were and they were
dead. We knew them, they were our neighbors and it was a half a mile to their house,
so an old man and a woman helped four of us kids move the bodies. Brother Will and
I each took a hand, Tom and Reynold each took a foot and the old man carried the
head and the woman put a board under the hips and shoulders and we carried them
one by one to their folks. That was some time too. A lot I can't tell . . . it shakes me
up so. . . . All we thought of during the war was to save ourselves. We didn't have
time to pray and when we had time we were too tired, but God took care of us. . . .
Well, we lived over it but I don't have any love for a Yankee."

—Caldonia Ann Borden Brandenburg[1]

MAJOR GENERAL J.M. SCHOFIELD WROTE Kansas Governor Thomas
Carney on August 29th:

I have forwarded a copy of your letter of the 24th to the War Department, and requested the President to appoint a court of inquiry, with full
powers to investigate ball matters touching military affairs in Kansas,
and have urged it strongly. I have no doubt the court will be appointed,

and that the responsibility of the sad calamity which was befallen Lawrence will be placed where it properly belongs.

Be assured that nothing in my power shall be omitted to visit just vengeance upon all who are in way guilty of the horrible crime, and to secure Kansas against anything of the hind in future; meanwhile let me urge upon you the importance of mollifying the just anger of your people, or rather of reconciling them to the necessity and propriety of leaving it to the United States troops to execute the vengeance which they so justly demand. It needs no argument to convince you of the necessity of this course. Without it there would be no end of retaliation on either side, and utter desolation on both sides of the border would be the result.

Anything you may require in the way of arms for your militia, and complete outfit for your new regiments of volunteers, shall be furnished at once. Immediately upon the receipt of your letter, I ordered 3,000 stand of arms to be shipped to you at once, and to-day have ordered some horses for the Fifteenth regiment. The arms are not of the best class, but are the very best I have, and are perfectly serviceable.

Permit me to suggest that your militia should be thoroughly organized throughout the State, and that every town should have arms in store, under a small guard, sufficient to arm the militia of the town. The arms can be easily supplied by the General Government. Without such organization, not town in Missouri or Kansas near the border is safe, unless it be occupied by United States troops, and to occupy them all, you will perceive, is utterly impossible with the force under my command.

To entirely prevent the assemblage of such bands of desperate outlaws as that under Quantrill in the summer season is simply impossible without five times my present force. In a State like Kansas, where everybody is loyal, such a state of things could not exist; but when half of more of the people are disloyal of all shades, as in Western Missouri, and consequently cannot be permitted to carry arms, whether willingly or unwillingly, they are the servants of these brigands, and are entirely at their mercy. If they resist their demands or inform upon them, it is at the peril of their lives. I do not wish to extenuate in any degree the crimes of those who are responsible for these inhuman acts; they shall suffer the fullest penalty; but I simply state what, at a moment's reflection, will convince you are facts, to show the necessity for full preparation on your part to assist me in preventing the recurrence of any calamity like that which befell Lawrence.

I am informed that a meeting was held in Leavenworth a few days ago, in which it was resolved that the people should meet at Paola, on the 8th of September, for the purpose of entering Missouri to recover their stolen property. If this were the only result of such expedition, or if their vengeance could be limited to those who are actually guilty, there would be no objection to it; but it is a simple matter of course that the action of such an irresponsible organization of enraged citizens would be indiscriminate retaliation upon innocent and guilty alike. You cannot expect me to permit anything of this sort. My present duty requires me to prevent it at all hazards, and by all the means in my power. But I hope a few days of reflection will show the popular leaders in Kansas the folly and wickedness of such retaliation, and cause them to be abandoned.

I shall confidently rely upon your powerful influence to prevent any such action on the part of the people of Kansas as will force me into the painful position of having to oppose them in any degree, particularly by force. Be assured, Governor, of my earnest desire to do all in my power to promote the peace and security of Kansas. I shall be glad at all times to know your views and wishes touching your State.[2]

Governor Carney replied on September 3rd: "The brutal outrages committed upon the unoffending and unarmed citizens of Lawrence by Quantrill and his ban have not only aroused every man in the State, but shocked the whole country. The wish of both is that the doers of these bloody deeds— their aiders and abettors—shall be steadily pursued and surely punished, for there can be no safety in the present or the future while these miscreants are permitted to live. The 9th day of this month, by order of your district commander, is the day fixed upon to being this summary punishment. That this punishment may be swift and sure, I offer you any forces at my command. You have promptly sent me a sufficient quantity of arms to meet the wants of the State. With these arms in their hands, and organized, our citizens can repel any raid which brutal marauders like Quantrill and his band may attempt, or punish, instantly and severely, those who shall aid or abet them. I have confidence only in organize action, and, satisfied both of your to lead our forces and your resolve to punish the guilty, I shall be happy to place the military of the State at your disposal."[3]

Major General John M. Schofield penned another letter to Governor Thomas Carney that same day:

I am in receipt of your letter of this morning. I fully sympathize with your feeling of anxiety to give security to the Kansas border, and to avenge on the rebels in Missouri the unparalleled atrocities of the Lawrence massacre. My forces in Missouri and Kansas having been greatly reduced by re-enforcements sent to Generals Grant, Steele, and Blunt, I am glad to avail myself of your offer of a part of the Kansas militia to aid the United States forces in this district.

With the chief towns on the eastern border of Kansas garrison by the militia of the State, and with two regiments of volunteers, which I have lately ordered to re-enforce the troops already in the district, the military authorities will be able not only to execute the orders for the expulsion of disloyal persons, but also to pursue and destroy the guerrilla bands which have so long ravaged the border. For the purpose named, I will accept the services of so many companies of militia as may be deemed necessary by you and the district commander to protect the towns referred to.[4]

On the evening of August 20th, Lieutenant Colonel Charles S. Clark, Ninth Kansas Cavalry received a dispatch from Captain J.A. Pike, commanding at Aubrey, that Quantrill, with a large command, was encamped on Grand River, ten miles from the Kansas line. Clark immediately sent orders to Captain B.F. Goss, commanding Trading Post, and to Rockville for the troops to march to Coldwater Grove. He also instructed Captain Pike to watch the movement of the enemy.[5]

At 3:00 A.M. on the 21st, Clark received a dispatch from Captain C.F. Coleman that Quantrill had crossed into Kansas, and was moving in the direction of Paola. Coleman was in pursuit with 180 men, as Clark, with thirty men from Captain Flesher's company, started in direction of Paola. Quantrill had turned north, and Clark followed his trail to Gardner, where he learned that Quantrill had passed at elven o'clock the night before. Being about twelve hours behind, Clark called out the people of Marysville. Upon reaching Paola, following a fifty-five-mile march, they found the citizens in arms. Scouts were dispatched to Osawatomie and Stanton to raise the citizens, and to communicate any and every movement of the enemy.

The scout sent to Stanton encountered Quantrill on his retreat, five miles out along the road to Paola, and returned to report. Clark decided to attack Quantrill at the ford on Bull Creek but the bushwhackers could not be found. After a thorough search of the countryside, they picked up Quantrill's trail at Grand River, where they had dispersed in small bands. Clark's men and horses were exhausted, and many out of cartridges, and, feeling farther pursuit that day useless, the federals halted.

The 24th, 25th, and 26th were spent in thoroughly scouting the country about Pleasant Hill and the tributaries of Grand River. Quantrill, however, made his escape into Johnson County on the 28th. Clark learned that Cole Younger had been seen on the waters of Big Blue, and, dividing his forces, he sent a portion on to the headwaters of Grand River and the rest in the direction of the Blue. But neither Cole nor Quantrill could be found.

Lieutenant Colonel Bazel F. Lazear, First Missouri State Militia Cavalry, also took part in the futile chase upon learning that Quantrill with 250 men had passed twelve miles north of Warrensburg on the 19th. He immediately dispatched messengers to Lexington and Harrisonville, asking for all force that could be sent from those stations to meet him at Chapel Hill at daylight next morning.[6]

Lazear left Warrensburg at ten o'clock with 100 men of Companies C, I, and K. He and his command formed a junction near Chapel Hill with Major Mullins, and 130 men of Companies B, F, G, and H, all of First Missouri State Militia Cavalry. Delayed until late in the evening waiting on a detachment from Lexington, Colonel Neill, with fifty men of the Fifth Provisional Regiment Enrolled Missouri Militia, arrived and the commands pushed on that night as far as Lone Jack.

They followed Quantrill's trail in the morning as far as Big Creek, five miles northwest of Pleasant Hill, where they stopped to feed, and as soon as the advance came out of the brush west of Big Creek, they discovered a body of men only a half mile in front of them. The whole command was immediately ordered up and parties sent out to discover who they were. The unidentified party replied that they were federal troops, but would not say whose command they belonged to. Lazear rode forward and discovered they were bushwhackers and forming line of battle behind a fence; and as they were on top of a ridge, and were still coming up, he thought it prudent to dismount a company to take the advance. While engaged in this, they commenced retreating from their right. After going some three-quarters of a mile, they changed their course to their left, and formed just over a ridge, where Lazear's federals came up with them and exchanged several rounds, when they broke for the brush. As soon as he found they had scattered, Lazear divided his force. Captain H.F. Perry, in command of one of the detachments, came upon the guerrillas late in the evening, and fought them in the brush a considerable time, when they again scattered in every direction.

Brigadier General Thomas Ewing, Jr., U.S. Army, commanding the District of the Border, dispatched his report on August 31st:

Some commanders of detachments engaged in the pursuit of Quantrill are still out after his scattered forces. In advance of their return, I submit a report of the raid, which, in some respect, may be deficient, for want of official information from them. Three or four times this summer the guerrillas have assembled, to the number of several hundred, within [twenty] or [thirty] miles of the Kansas border. They have threatened, alternately, Lexington, Independence, Warrensburg, and Harrisonville, and frequent reports have reached me from scouts and spies that they meant to sack and destroy Shawnee, Olathe, Paola, Mound City, and other towns in Kansas near the eastern border. I placed garrisons in all these Kansas towns, and issued arms and rations to volunteer militia companies there. From reliable sources I learned, toward the last of July, that they were threatening a raid on Lawrence, and soon after they commenced assembling on the Snibar, in the western part of La Fayette County. I at once ordered a company of infantry, which was then coming down from Fort Riley, to stop at Lawrence, which they did for more than a week, and until after the guerrilla force had been dispersed by a force I sent against them.

From this time, though constantly receiving information as to their movements and plans, I could learn nothing of a purpose to make a raid into Kansas. Their forces were again scattered in small predatory bands, and I had all available forces in like manner scattered throughout the Missouri portion of this district, and especially the border counties, besetting their haunts and paths.

Quantrill's whole force was about 300 men, composed of selected bands from this part of Missouri. About 250 were assembled on Blackwater [Creek], near the eastern border of this district, at least [fifty] miles from the Kansas line, on the 17th and 18th instant, and I am informed by Major [J.T.] Ross, Missouri State Militia, who has been scouting in the southwest part of Saline County, that the rendezvous was there. Lieutenant-Colonel [B.F.] Lazear, commanding two companies of the First Missouri, at Warrensburg, heard, on the morning of the 20th, that this force had passed the day before [twelve] miles north of him, going west, and moved promptly after the, sending orders to Major [A.W.] Mullins, commanding two companies of the same regiment, at Pleasant Hill, to move on them from that point.

On the night of the 19th, however, Quantrill passed through Chapel Hill to the head of the Middle Fork of Grand River, [eight] miles northwest of Harrisonville, and [fifteen] miles southeast of Aubrey, the nearest station in Kansas. There he was joined, on the morning of the 20th, by about [fifty] men from Grand River and the Osage, and at noon set out for Kansas, passing [five] miles south of Aubrey at 6:00 P.M., going

227

west. Aubrey is [thirty-five] miles south of Kansas City, and about [forty-five] miles southeast of Lawrence. Kansas City is somewhat farther from Lawrence.

Captain [J.A.] Pike, commanding two companies at Aubrey, received information of the presence of Quantrill on Grand River at 5.30 P.M. of the 20th. He promptly forwarded the information up and down the line and to my headquarters, and called in his scouting parties to march upon them. One hour and half later he received information that Quantrill had just passed into Kansas. Unhappily, however, instead of setting out at once in pursuit, he remained at the station, and merely sent information of Quantrill's movement to my headquarters, and to Captain Coleman, commanding two companies at Little Santa Fe, [twelve] miles north of the line. Captain [C.F.] Coleman, with near 100 men, marched at once to Aubrey, and the available force of the two stations, numbering about 200 men, set out at midnight in pursuit. But Quantrill's path was over the open prairie, and difficult to follow at night, so that our forces gained but little on him. By Captain Pike's error of judgment in failing to follow promptly and closely, the surest means of arresting the terrible blow was thrown away, for Quantrill would never have gone as far as Lawrence, or attacked it, with 100 men close on his rear.

The first dispatch of Captain Pike reached here at 11.30 P.M.; the second a hour later. Before one o'clock Major [P.B.] Plumb, my chief of staff, at the head of about [fifty] men (which was all that could be got here and at Westport), started southward, and at daylight heard at Olathe, [twenty-five] miles from here, that the enemy had passed at midnight through Gardner, [eighteen] miles from Lawrence, going toward that town. Pushing on, Major Plumb overtook Captains Coleman and Pike, [six] miles southeast of Lawrence, at 10.30 Friday, the 21st instant, and by the light of the blazing farm houses saw that the enemy had got 6 miles south of Lawrence, on their way out of the State. The enemy were overtaken near Palmyra by Major Plumb's command, to which were there added from [fifty] to 100 citizens, who had been hastily assembled and led in pursuit by General Lane. By this time the horses of our detachments were almost exhausted. Nearly all were young horses, just issued to the companies, and had marched more than [sixty-five] miles without rest, and without food from the morning of the 20th. Quantrill had his men mounted on the best horses of the border, and had collected fresh ones going to and at Lawrence, almost enough to remount his command. He skillfully kept over 100 of his best mounted and best trained men in the rear, and often formed line of battle, to delay pursuit and give time and rest to the most wearied of his forces. By the time our scattered soldiers and citizens could get up and form line, the guerrillas' rear guard would, after a volley, break into column, and move off at a speed that defied pursuit. Thus the chase dragged through the afternoon, over the prairie, generally following no roads of paths, until night, when Quantrill's rear guard formed line of battle [three] miles north of Paola and [twenty] miles from where they entered the State. A skirmish ensued, the guerrillas breaking and scattering, so that our forces, in the darkness, lost the trail, and went into Paola for food and rest, while search was being made for it. Lieutenant-Colonel [C.S.] Clark, Ninth Kansas Volunteers, with headquarters at Coldwater Grove, was in command of the troops on the border of Little Santa Fe, including the stations at Aubrey, Coldwater Grove ([thirteen] miles south at Aubrey), Rockville ([thirteen] miles south of Coldwater Grove), Choteau's Trading Post ([fifteen] miles south of Rockville), and Harrisonville. There were two companies at each station, but the force out patrolling rarely left [fifty] men in camp at each post. He received Captain Pike's message as to the gathering of Quantrill's forces on Grand River on the night of the 20th, and at once sent for the spare troops at Rockville and Trading Post to march up to Coldwater Grove. At [three] o'clock on the morning of the 21st, he received a dispatch from Captain Coleman, at Aubrey, saying that Quantrill had crossed into Kansas, and he set out with [thirty] men, following Quantrill's trail nearly to Gardner, and thence going south to Paola, reaching there at 5:00 P.M. With this command, and a force of perhaps [fifty] citizens, and a part of Captain [N.L.] Benter's company of the Twelfth Kansas Infantry, which had been garrisoning Paola, he prepared to attack Quantrill at the ford of Bull Creek, [three] miles south of Paola, toward which he was then retreating. But Quantrill, on coming within [four or five] miles of that crossing, soon after dark, formed line of battle, as I stated above, broke trail, turned sharp to the north, and dodged and bewildered the force in waiting for him as well as that in pursuit.

These troops at the ford returned to Paola about the time the command which had followed Quantrill reached there. One of the parties in search of the trail found it [five] miles north of Paola, and reported the fact to Lieutenant-Colonel Clark, who was the ranking officer there, at between [one and two] o'clock. He was slow in ordering pursuit, which was not renewed until daybreak. He, at that time, sent Captain Coleman forward, with [thirty] men of the Ninth Kansas, which he himself had brought to Paola, and [forty] of the same regiment, which had got there from the Trading Post at about [two] o'clock that morning, and about [seventy] militia, chiefly of Linn County. He marched soon after himself with the troops which had followed Quantrill the day before.

Half an hour before Major Plumb started from Kansas City on the night of the 21st, Captain Palmer, Eleventh Kansas, was sent by him from Westport with [fifty] men of his company down the line to near

Aubrey, where he met a messenger from Captain Coleman, directing re-enforcements to Spring Hill, at which point he struck Quantrill's trail, and followed it to within [seven] miles of Lawrence. Thence, learning that Quantrill had gone south, he turned southeast; and at Lanesfield (Union-town) was joined by a force about [eighty] strong, under Major Phillips, composed of detachments of Captain Smith's company, Enrolled Missouri Militia, Captain [T.P.] Killen's Ninth Kansas, and a squad of the Fifth Kansas. This latter force had been collected by Major [L.K.] Thacher, at Westport, and dispatched from there at noon on Friday, the 21st, via Lexington, Kansas. The command of Major Phillips, thus increased to 130, pushed southeast from Lanesfield, and struck Quantrill's trail about sunrise, [five] miles north of Paola, and but a little behind the commands of Coleman and Clark.

Major Linn K. Thacher, commanding the Ninth Kansas Cavalry at Westport when news arrived that Quantrill was returning by way of the Osage Valley, took the rest of the mounted troops on the upper border (Company A, Ninth, and Company E, Eleventh Kansas, numbering 120 men) and moved down the line. He struck Quantrill's trail below Aubrey, immediately in the rear of Lieutenant-Colonel Clark's command.

Quantrill, when, after dark, he had baffled his pursuers, stopped to rest five miles northeast of Paola, and there, after midnight, a squad of Linn County militia, under Captain Pardee, in search of the trail, alarmed the camp. He at once moved on, and between that point and the Kansas line his column came within gunshot of the advance of about 150 of the Fourth Missouri State militia, under Lieutenant-Colonel [W.] King, which had been ordered from the country of the Little Blue, in Jackson County, down the line, to intercept him. The advance apprised Lieutenant-Colonel King of the approach of another force. Skirmishers were thrown out, but Quantrill, aided by the darkness and broken character of the prairie, eluded the force, and passed on. Lieutenant-Colonel King was unable to find his trail that night.[7]

Major Thacher later reported: "I marched with all the available forces I could collect. I had, in all, with me about 120 men. At Olathe, I learned that Quantrill was, when last heard from, aiming for Paola, Kansas, I pressed on in that direction, and, a little after daylight, struck the trail of the enemy about [five] miles north of Paola, leading eastward. I followed this for [ten] miles, and then halted long enough to feed the horses, after which I pressed on until I reached Grand River. There the enemy separated, a part going into the Grand River bottom, and the other steering for Lone Jack and the Sni Hills. I pursued the latter, Colonel [C.S.] Clark being in pursuit of the former. On Big Creek, a half hour before dark, a small party of guerrillas showed themselves as I approached. I charged them, and they fled to the woods, and thus baffled pursuit. There I awaited until daylight, and then followed. They moved direct to the Sni Hills. I scoured the intermediate country and woods, and scouted for three days the Sni country, dividing my command into small parties, and at night secreting my men in squads along the paths and roads I supposed they would pass. For two days I also searched the guerrilla haunts on the Little Blue, running into a party of two of them near Fristoe's place, capturing a revolver and horse of one of them, to my chagrin, killed neither of them. I returned today, after having been out six days and nights, having traveled over many a long and difficult mile, and having failed to accomplish what I hoped to."[8]

Captain Charles F. Coleman, Ninth Kansas Cavalry, reported his part in the pursuit on August 30th:

> On the night of the 20th, at 8:00 P.M., I received a dispatch from Captain [J.A.] Pike, commanding at Aubrey, stating that he had just received reliable information that Quantrill with 700 men was in camp on the head of Grand River, eight miles east of that place. I immediately sent a messenger to Westport and Kansas City with a dispatch stating the facts as I received them. In about fifteen minutes afterward, I received the second dispatch from Captain Pike, stating that Quantrill had passed into Kansas five miles south of Aubrey, with 800 men. The second messenger was immediately sent to Westport and Kansas City with the above news, also one to Olathe, with the request that the word be carried on west.
>
> At [nine] o'clock I started with all my available force, consisting of a detachment of Company M, Fifth Kansas Volunteer Cavalry, and a part of my own company, in all about [eighty] men. At Aubrey I was joined by Captain Pike, Company K, Ninth Kansas Volunteer Cavalry, and Company D, Eleventh Kansas Volunteers Cavalry. My force then consisted of about 180 men. From Aubrey I sent a dispatch to Lieutenant-Colonel [C.S.] Clark, commanding at Coldwater, that at [eleven] o'clock I would start after them. I struck their trail five miles south of Aubrey, followed it some [three] miles, when we lost it, they having scattered and divided their force to prevent pursuit in the night (in again finding it, I lost near two hours).
>
> At Gardner I learned that they passed through six hours before. From Gardner I sent runners south and west to notify the inhabitants that Quantrill had gone north with a large force. I soon could see the smoke

from the burning of Lawrence, and pressed on as fast as our jaded horses would their. When about six miles south of Lawrence, I was relieved from command by the arrival of Major [P.B.] Plumb, Eleventh Kansas Volunteer Cavalry, with about [thirty] men. From there we turned south for Baldwin City, and, when neat there, saw them burning Brooklyn. We halted there a short time to hear from our scouts which way they were moving, who reported that they were on the Fort Scott road, moving south. From Baldwin City we struck southwest, and intercepted them on the Fort Scott road, and engaged their rear with what men we could bet up, we having made a charge for the last three miles, and the most of our horses being totally given out, having traveled them upward of [thirty] miles without feed, water, or rest. After a few rounds their rear gave way and joined their main command. We then divided our command and attempted to cut them off from the crossing of Ottawa Creek, but failed on account of the jaded condition of our horses. We then got together about [forty] soldiers and the same number of citizens (all the rest of the horses having given out), and again attacked them in the rear, and kept up a running fight for the next [eighteen] miles, and till we drove them into the Bull Creek timber west of Paola. Night coming on, we abandoned the chase, having been in our saddles twenty-four hours without food or water for man or horse, and having traveled over 100 miles. The enemy here took around Paola on the north. From the best information received during the day, we killed and wounded about [thirty] of them. We rested at Paola during the night, and in the morning Lieutenant-Colonel Clark took command and resumed the chase.[9]

The raids on Kansas placed considerable pressure on the new federal commanders along the border. Brigadier-General Thomas Ewing, Jr., formerly private secretary to President Zachary Taylor eleven years earlier, moved to Leavenworth, Kansas, in 1856. Two years later, he served as a member of the state's constitutional convention, and in 1861, attended a peace conference in Washington, D.C., Ewing served two years as chief justice of the state of Kansas. In September 1862 he was commissioned colonel of the Eleventh Kansas Cavalry and was promoted to brigadier-general six months later.[10]

Because of the attack on Lawrence and in an effort to cut the guerillas and the Rangers off from their supporters, Ewing issued his infamous Order #11 on August 25, 1863. This order forced all residents in Cass and Bates counties and parts of Vernon and Jackson counties to vacate their homes within fifteen days. All grain, hay and food supplies were confiscated by Union troops and all homes and outbuildings were burned to the ground. These counties became known as "The Burnt District." Basically, this order was a "license to kill" for the Union army, and they ravished these counties, burning everything in site and killing the men and young boys whom they suspected to be Southern Sympathizers. Woman and children were often left with nothing but the clothing on their backs and had to travel great distances to find a safe haven. Many died of starvation and exposure while in route. This action was unique during the Civil War in that it was specifically directed against a civilian population. It affected more than 20,000 individuals. It would be years before many of these families would be able to return home. When they did return home, they returned to burned-out structures and desolate land.[11]

General Ewing's order read:

> First: All persons living in Cass, Jackson, and Bates counties, and in that part of Vernon county within the District, with the exception of those residing within one mile of Union-held towns and except those in that part of Kaw Township, Jackson County, north of Brush Creek and west of the Big Blue River, embracing Kansas City and Westport, are hereby ordered to move from their present places of residence within [fifteen] days. Those who within that time establish their loyalty to the satisfaction of the commanding officer of the military station nearest their present place of residence, will received from him certificates stating that facts of their loyalty and the names by whom it can be shown. All who receive such certificates will be permitted to remove to any military station in this district or to any part of the state of Kansas, except all the counties on the eastern border of the state. All others shall remain out of the district.
>
> Second: all grain or hay in the fields or under shelter in the District from which the inhabitants are required to move within reach of military stations, after the ninth of September will be taken to such stations and turned over to the proper officers there; and report of the amount so turned over made to the district headquarters specifying the names of all loyal owners and the amount of such produce taken from them. All grain and hay found in such district after the ninth of September next, not removed to such stations will be destroyed.

Order #11, from Union officials, forcibly depopulated several Missouri border counties, putting men, women, and children out of their homes, often in the middle of the night, without any means of support or survival. So serious were the actions taken by both sides that the bitterness and hard-feelings lasted for decades and generations. After Order #11 was issued, many of the male citizens were shot on sight and their women and children were left to flee the area with only the clothes on their backs. While seen as an act of retaliation, the actual intent of the order was to deny the support Quantrill and his gang were receiving from border residents. The way the order was carried out by the Redlegs, however, was retaliatory in nature.

The Redlegs, under the command of Lieutenant Colonel Charles S. Clark, entered Jackson County, Missouri, to enforce the evacuation order and to engage and capture Quantrill. Quantrill, however, predictably kept to his guerrilla tactics and avoided the federals. In frustration, Clark elected to execute Missourians whom his intelligence had identified as having aided Quantrill in any way. Among these executions was a group of six men, aged seventeen to seventy-five in what has come to be called the Lone Jack Massacre. Clark reported his victims as bushwhackers to General Ewing.

HEADQUARTERS TROOPS ON THE BORDER,
Cold Water Grove, [Missouri] September 8, 1863.
Brigadier General EWING.

GENERAL:
On the morning of the 4th of September, 1863, I ordered a scout of [forty] men from Companies E and G, of the Ninth Kansas, to accompany me to Pleasant Hill, where I had previously instructed Captain C.F. Coleman to march and join the scout from this station, with Companies D, of the Ninth Kansas, and M, of the Fifth Kansas, which he did on the 5th instant.

The same night we marched [fifteen] miles east [near Lone Jack], concealed our men in the brush, dismounted, and sent out four parties, of [twelve] men each, under Captains Coleman and H. Flesher [early morning of 6 September 1863]. Killed [six] bushwhackers remounted, marched [four] miles south; divided the command; the scout from this station to scour Big Creek, in the direction of Pleasant Hill; Captain Coleman, with his command, was to take in those run off Big Creek, and scour the brush east.

The scout on Big Creek, under Captain Flesher, and myself included, surprised a party at a house; killed [four], captured [eight] horses, saddles, and bridles, and some Lawrence goods, and wounded, as I think, [four] others. Our loss, [two] men slightly wounded, viz, Corporal John Walters, Company E, and Private S. Pentico, Company G, and returned to this station the 7th instant.

Captain Coleman was to remain in the vicinity of Pleasant Hill two or three days, to watch Quantrill's movements. I found a trail of about 100 men [five] miles east of Harrisonville, who had passed the night of the 3rd, twelve hours in advance of my scout, the trail taking a northeast direction.

I am, general, your obedient servant,

C[harles]. S. Clark,
Lieutenant Colonel,
Ninth Kansas Volunteer Cavalry,
Commanding.[12]

Captain Davidson, the federal commander at Harrisonville, also devised a scheme to rid Missouri of at least one bushwhacker. Davidson went to Cole's mother and promised her that he would guarantee safe passage to her and her sons if the family would move out of Missouri. Mrs. Younger accepted the offer in good faith and got word to Cole who slipped home to discuss the offer.

Unbeknownst to Cole, who sat in the house after dark talking with his mother, Captain Davidson and a hundred men waited out in the yard. Davidson was quite certain that Cole was in the house and knocked boldly on the front door. "Aunt" Suse quickly removed a quilt from Bursheba's bed, tossed it over her head, and concealed Cole under it, before blowing out the lamp and opening the door. Captain Davidson and his men pushed the door aside and rushed into the house while Suse (and Cole) moved out into a dark corner of the yard. Cole fled into the darkness, and while the federals heard his footsteps, they could not catch him.

The angry federals ordered the family out of the house, forcing Mrs. Younger, who was suffering from tuberculosis, from her sickbed.

When Frank James with many of the other bushwhackers hid out in Clay County, he frequently stopped at the James-Samuel farm. Mrs. Samuel had learned that the fords across the Missouri River were well guarded, and young Jesse served as a messenger between his mother and the guerrillas. The federals, however, suspected the family's involvement in such espionage and a patrol of the Fifty-first Enrolled Missouri Militia under Lieutenant H.C. Culver.[13]

Because of Frank's involvement with the guerrillas, violence erupted at the James farm that day in 1863. Union soldiers tortured Jesse and Frank's stepfather, Dr. Reuben Samuel, by marching him a hundred yards from the house, placing a noose around his neck, the other end over the limb of a tree, and hoisting him in the air. Dr. Samuel was asked about the whereabouts of Frank, and when he insisted he did not know, the federals repeatedly raised and lowered his body off the ground. Reuben, however, kept his silence and the soldiers finally gave up and left him hanging. Samuel survived the hanging but suffered severe brain damage and later died in home for the mentally insane.[14]

The soldiers then found Jesse James plowing the field, surrounded him, and demanded information about Frank. When Jesse refused, they beat him severely and rode away, leaving him lying bloody, battered, and half unconscious in the field. Jesse crawled back to the farmhouse, only to find his mother trying to revive her husband, with Jesse's sister Susan, half-sister Sarah, and little half-brother John T. looking on. Zerelda, who was pregnant at the time of the raid, was jailed in St. Joseph with her twelve-year-old daughter, Susan,

Jesse James. (Photo by B.A. Bottain. Courtesy of the National Archives)

by her side. When Jesse learned that his sister Susan had contracted a fever in the filthy jail and almost died, he decided to fight the federals. The following year, fifteen-year-old Jesse would join the Confederate cause and ride beside his brother Frank.[15]

Later, John Samuel recalled the incident: "Jesse was out plowing in a field . . . when some Northern soldiers came to the place to look for Frank. Jesse was only [sixteen] [actually, he was fifteen]. They beat him up. Then they went to the house and asked where Frank was. Mother and father didn't know but the soldiers wouldn't believe them They took father out and hung him by the neck to a tree. After awhile they took him down and gave him another chance to tell. Of course he couldn't. So they hung him up again. They did that three times. Then they took him back to the house and told my mother they were going to shoot him. She begged them not to do it, but they took him off in the woods and fired their guns . . . but they didn't shoot him. They just took him over to another town and put him in jail. My mother didn't know until the next day that he hadn't been shot because the soldiers ordered her to remain in the house if she didn't want to be shot too."[16]

Young Jesse rode off, hoping to join his brother in Quantrill's irregulars. Upon meeting with the guerrillas, he was told he was too young and was sent back home. A few days after his return, federal soldiers came back to the Samuel farm looking for Jesse James and Dr. Samuel, although they were not at home. Jesse's mother was, however, and she was placed under military arrest and taken to St. Joseph. After she was released two weeks later, tension was heightened by the constant presence of federal soldiers looking for an excuse to take further action against the family.[17]

In October, 400 men reported to Quantrill in Johnson County, formed into four companies under William Gregg, George Todd, Bill Anderson, and David Poole, and hastily rode south to Texas. Near Baxter Springs, Kansas, they encountered a train of ten wagons carrying General James C. Blunt, guarded by 100 cavalrymen, to Fort Gibson in Indian Territory. Although General Blunt and most of his men escaped, the guerrillas mistakenly thought they had slain him. The wagons were looted for supplies.[18]

In mid-October 1863 Quantrill and his band crossed the Red River at Colbert's Ferry and established winter camp on Mineral Springs Creek fifteen miles northwest of Sherman. Upon reaching Texas safely, the guerrillas were surprised by their reception. Instead of being treated as heroes and soldiers, they found themselves somewhat avoided and not treated cordially by regular Confederate officers.

Quantrill reported at Bonham on October 26th to General Henry E. McCulloch. One of the officers described Quantrill as standing about five feet ten inches, weighing about 150 pounds, with fair hair, blue eyes, and a florid complexion. Lieutenant General Edmund Kirby Smith, commander of the Trans-Mississippi Confederacy, approved of Quantrill and ordered McCulloch to use Quantrill's men to help round up the increasing number of deserters and conscription-dodgers in North Texas. Quantrill's men captured but few and killed several, whereupon McCulloch pulled them off this duty; McCulloch sent them to track down retreating Comanches from a recent raid on the northwest frontier. They did so for nearly a week with no success. Quantrill is credited with ending a near-riot of county "war widows" who were convinced that the Confederate commissary in Sherman was withholding from them such "luxury goods" as coffee, tea, and sugar.

The Missourians spent the winter of 1863-1864 in the vicinity of Bonham, Denison, and Sherman. During his first winter in Grayson County Quantrill and his men may have acted as a police force against cattle thieves who raided farms and ranches from Indian Territory. This winter camp was necessary, in part, for Quantrill's men to escape retribution for two of their recent affairs.

Bloody Bill Anderson had been content to ride with Quantrill until a quarrel between the two bushwhacker leaders erupted in camp. On March 2, 1864, Bloody Bill, while in Texas, met and married Bush Smith, a young girl from Sherman. Quantrill disapproved of the marriage, and following several altercations, Anderson left his command, and in convincing some of the men to follow him, formed his own band of guerrillas.[19]

This band included sixteen-year-old Jesse James, and they became the most feared band of all guerillas. Jim Cummins, a boy about eight months older than Jesse, lived on a farm a few miles from the Samuel homestead, and had befriended him. Jesse, Jim, and two other boys from the area had left home together and joined guerrillas forces under George Todd and Bill Anderson in the spring of 1864 just as the guerrillas were returning to Missouri from Texas. The squad they joined was commanded by Fletcher "Fletch" Taylor, a veteran bushwhacker who saw action at Baxter Springs, Centralia, Independence, Richfield, and Lawrence. Bill Anderson said of the sixteen-year-old Jesse, "For a beardless boy, he is the best fighter in the command."[20]

Jesse James, Jr., later penned the following about his father: "That same spring after Jesse James had been beaten by the militiamen, Fletcher Taylor, a member of Quantrill's guerrillas, and one of the most desperate fighters the world ever saw, came for him and took him to join Quantrill. The exciting life and the horseback riding with Quantrill agreed with my father. He had been a delicate boy, but in one winter he grew so stout and strong that when he returned home the following spring for a short visit, his mother did not know him at first. Fletcher Taylor came home with him on that visit."[21]

Bloody Bill showed no mercy to Union soldiers and killed them on sight. He showed no sympathy to Pro-northerners and raided their homes and stores, murdering those that offered resistance. There is only one known case of when he spared the life of a union officer, and he did so because he admired his bravery. There are other accounts of his band robbing southern sympathizers and returning the loot with apologies when their loyalties were revealed.

Anderson's marriage did nothing to curtail his taste for blood and his need for revenge. They moved to a small farmhouse in Ray County, Missouri. In a letter sent to a local newspaper, Bloody Bill wrote, "I have chosen guerilla warfare to revenge myself for the wrongs that I could not honorably avenge otherwise. I lived in Kansas when the war commenced. Because I would not fight the people of Missouri, my native state, the Yankees sought my life but failed to get me. Revenged themselves by murdering my father, destroying all my property, murdered one of my sisters and have kept the other two in jail for [twelve] months. But I have fully glutted my vengeance. I have killed many, I am a guerilla. I have never belonged to the Confederate Army, nor do my men."

By mid-summer 1864, Bloody Bill Anderson had gained the reputation as one of the most feared bushwhackers on the border. Even though federal presence throughout Missouri restricted guerilla activity, many young men rushed to join Anderson's bushwhacker cause. One enthusiastic recruit later penned: "I determined to join the worst devil in the bunch . . . while [Quantrill] was fierce, he was nothing to compare with that terrible Bill Anderson. . . . I wanted to see blood flow in revenge for the outrages the [federals] had committed."[22]

Soon after joining the bushwhackers, Jesse James was given the nickname of "Dingus" after he accidentally shot off the tip of his third finger while cleaning his pistol. Jesse did not like to use curse words, and allegedly shook his head and quipped, "That's the dod-dingus pistol I ever saw." His guerrillas found his remark so amusing, the name stuck with him for the rest of his life.[23]

Jesse was with the raiders when surprised a party of thirty militia, killing ten and capturing twenty, with Jesse figuring conspicuously in the killings. The guerrillas rode on to Plattsburg where a lieutenant and twenty men defended the town. Jesse captured the lieutenant while the other federals escaped and barricaded themselves in the courthouse. Jesse proposed to murder the officer on the spot unless they came out and surrendered. The bushwhackers plundered the town, appropriated 250 muskets, several hundred rounds of ammunition, $10,000 in Missouri warrants, as well as clothing and supplies.[24]

Leaving Plattsburg, the guerrillas crossed the Missouri River to Independence. Four miles from Independence there was a brothel operated by several women, and it was a resort for the officers of the federal garrison at Independence. The guerrillas allegedly set a trap to catch these officers. Jesse James, dressed as a young girl, rode on horseback up to the house and called its mistress out. Imitating the voice and manner of a girl, he told her that he lived nearby, that he was a girl fond of adventure, and would like to come to the house that night, bringing two or three neighbor girls, "to have a good time."

The mistress of the house consented, and the supposed girl on horseback said he and the other girls would be there that night. The mistress sent word at once to the federal officers in Independence that four new girls would be at her house that night. It was after dark when Jesse James and the other guerrillas rode up to the house, and dismounting, crept up and peered in at the windows. Twelve federal officers were inside one room with five women, and no guards were posted. A cheery fire blazed and crackled on the hearth of the old-fashioned fireplace. Jesse James, with five men, went to one window. Bill Gregg, with five men, moved to another. Each of the nine bushwhackers in the darkness outside selected his man. At a signal that had been agreed upon, all nine men fired, the glass slivered, and nine of the federal soldiers fell dead. The remaining three were killed moments later. The guerrillas mounted and rode away.[25]

With an angry Quantrill remaining in Texas, residents of Grayson and Fannin counties became targets for raids, and acts of violence proliferated so much that regular Confederate forces had to be assigned to protect residents from the activities of the irregular Confederate forces. But while wintering in Texas, there was a second breakdown in discipline, and many of the men left to form bands of their own. Morals became an issue. Even the Confederate authorities became disgusted with their behavior and asked them to leave.

Finally, General McCulloch decided to rid north Texas of Quantrill's influence. On March 28, 1864, when Quantrill appeared at Bonham as requested, McCulloch had him arrested on the charge of ordering the murder of a Confederate major. Quantrill escaped that day and returned to his camp near Sherman, pursued by over 300 state and Confederate troops. He and his men crossed the Red River into Indian Territory, where they re-supplied from Confederate stores and fled back to Missouri.

That summer, Bloody Bill Anderson and his bushwhackers raided central Missouri, killing and allegedly scalping federal soldiers and civilians. Anderson was so filled with hate, that he supposedly tied the scalps to his belt and wore them into battle. He even raided Huntsville, his childhood home, killing one man and robbing the town of $45,000. Anderson did, however, order his men to return money taken from friends he had gone to school with. On July 7th, he wrote several letters to area newspapers warning citizens not to take up arms against him.

"Do not take up arms if you value your lives and property," penned Anderson. "If you proclaim to be in arms against the guerrillas I will kill you. I will hunt you down like wolves and murder you. You cannot escape. . . . I have killed many. I am a guerrilla."[26]

On July 23rd, Anderson and a hundred men gutted the railroad station in Renick. The following day, the bushwhackers ambushed a pursuing company of the Seventeenth Illinois Cavalry. Two slain federals were found scalped. Attached to one of the collars was a note reading, "You come to hunt bush whackers. Now you are skelpt. Clemyent skept you." Eighteen year old Archie had left his calling card.[27]

In mid-August of 1864, a combined federal military force encircled a bushwhacker camp near Dripping Springs, north of Columbia. Four guerrillas were killed and several more wounded or taken captive during this skirmish.[28]

On August 13, 1864, the editor of the *Kansas City Journal of Commerce* penned: "The very air seems charged with blood and death. East of us, west of us, north of us, south of us, comes the same harrowing story. Pandemonium itself seems to have broken loose, and robbery, murder and rapine, and death run riot over the country."[29]

Also in August, Bill Anderson led his men into Rocheport, Missouri, with the intention of capturing the Yankee-owned steamboat *War Eagle*. Concealed behind a tobacco warehouse near the levee with his men, Anderson watched the boat approaching to load. Just as it drew close, a nervous guerrilla accidentally discharged his pistol, causing the pilot to pull the bell and signal the engineer to reverse the engines.[30]

As the rich cargo drew away, the bushwhackers opened fire, and Anderson ordered four of his men to row after it. As the first guerrilla stepped over the gunwales, the pilot blew his right arm off with a shotgun. When the rowboat returned with the injured man, Anderson became furious, and ordered his men to fire and kill every man, woman, and child. When one of his men refused, Anderson began beating him. A group of ladies intervened and begged him to stop while the man crawled away. Bloody Bill ordered Jesse James to go after him and kill him as an example to others. Jesse started after the man, but he, too, had been shocked by Anderson's brutality and gave up the hunt.

A band of guerrillas, under the command of G.W. "Wash" Bryson, on September 7th, stopped a freight train two miles east of Centralia and took off several federal soldiers and forty horses, just what the bushwhackers needed for their raids. After threatening to shoot the prisoners, they were released after a few days.

On the night of September 19th, three-fourths of a mile west of Cherry Grove School near Fayette, Bill Anderson gathered his men together. The company, which included Jesse James, bivouacked for the night near the east bank of Bonne Femme Creek, and at daylight of the 20th, mounted and moved eastward across a farmyard by twos to the Franklin Road. Anderson rode ahead and met with Captains George Todd, Tom Todd, and Dave Poole, who were seated on their horses, engaged in a heated argument.[31]

Following a spirited controversy between these leaders, Bill Anderson rode back to his waiting company and gave the command, "Forward, Men!" Anderson's company leading, moved south along the New Franklin Road one and one-half miles, turning east through the farm of Colonel William Hocker into the Fayette and Maxwell Mill Road seven and one-half miles south of Fayette.

Advancing slowly, they quietly entered Fayette at 10:30 A.M., by way of Main Street from the Rocheport Road. The head of the column approached to within one hundred yards of the Court House Square without their being recognized as guerrillas, when one of the irregulars began firing at a black man dressed in a blue uniform, standing on the sidewalk. Immediately pandemonium broke loose. The whole column of horsemen broke into a run and dashed through town toward the federal garrison at the north edge of Central College campus; one-half mile north of [the] court house.

Approaching the square, fifty men turned up Church Street, the main body continuing west on Morrison Street to Water Street. The divided column linked back up at a ravine. A federal picket stationed at the south corner by Swinney's Factory, fired at the guerrillas instantly killing Thad Jackman. Only one shot by the enemy had been fired previous to Jackman's killing. While passing the court house on Morrison Street, one of the guerrillas had his horse killed from a shot fired from the building by John Patton, a Union private in Company A.

The bushwhackers conducted their first assault on a log house where federal troops had taken cover. As they dashed from the ravine across the open field, the muzzles of muskets protruded from every port-hole, belching fire and lead at the charging guerrillas. Several horses were killed, but only one guerrilla, Garrett M. Groomer, of George Todd's company, was killed; Bill Akin, of Tom Todd's company, mortally wounded, and Tom Maupin and Silas King, of Anderson's company, slightly wounded.

In the second assault, Younger Grubbs, of Anderson's company, was killed, Oliver Johnson, of Todd's company, mortally wounded, Plunk Murray, Lee McMurtry, and Newman Wade, all of Anderson's company seriously wounded. Seeing the utter futility of further attempts to dislodge the enemy, a mere feint was made for the third assault. Oliver Johnson and Bill Akin, both mortally wounded, were rescued from the field of battle by comrades, amid a shower of the enemy's musket balls. One member of the rescue party later penned:

> We secured an army blanket, going to the top of the hill and there found Johnson just over the rise in plain view of the block-houses. Will say to you that when I saw the situation and knew just what was coming, my heart almost ceased to beat. Could the ground have opened up and engulfed me, believe it would have been a relief. . . . When we suc-

ceeded in getting him on the blanket and started over the hill, it appeared to me that every square inch of space around us was filled with musket-balls. Strange to say, not one of us was touched. This was the most scary, as well as the most dangerous, place I have any recollection of ever being in during those dreadful times.

The bushwhackers retreated north along the Glasgow Road. After the fight, Will Hayes, of Anderson's company, while standing in the road, was shot and mortally wounded by a soldier, from the east tower of the Academy, dying a few hours later. But one federal was killed, a man by the name of Renton, and he was shot, in an open field.

On September 23, 1864, a federal wagon train in route to Rocheport from Sturgeon was ambushed at Goslins's Lane by guerrillas led by George and Thomas Todd. Eleven of the federal troops were killed and over 18,000 rounds of ammunition captured. Lieutenant-Colonel Dan M. Draper penned his official report on September 25th:

> We heard yesterday about noon that this place had been captured by 600 bushwhackers under Quantrill, but our horses had just come in from running these same scoundrels. From the direction they took I had no idea that they contemplated an attack upon this place, so I went back to Rocheport after following the trail until it ran out from the scattering of the rebels. The fight here was a most gallant one on the part of the Ninth. I understood your instructions to me were to take what men of Major Leonard's could be spared and move on to Rocheport. I acted accordingly. I do not know whether or not you have had a detailed report of the fight here. The advance guard of the rebels were all dressed in federal uniform and were consequently not suspected until they began firing. The provost guard immediately took post in the court-house and fought the whole command of villains until they left for camp. This gave the men time to rally on camp, which was near the college building. They then went into that and fought them until they got sick of it and left in a hurry, leaving [five] dead on the ground. They probably carried off some dead and many wounded as they pressed wagons, buggies, and carriages on the road as far as we could hear from them.
>
> I congratulate myself on having command of such men as are in my regiment, and hope that I may soon have them all together. General Douglass is giving you such information as he has, so it is not necessary for me to repeat. I differ with him as to the number of them. He thinks the principal force is below yet; I do not. I think they were all here.[32]

Anderson's line was reformed and the march resumed on the road leading to Huntsville in Randolph County, bivouacking near Washington Church, nine miles from Fayette. After an unsuccessful attempt to capture the federal outpost at Huntsville, the march continued into Monroe County. After several days spent in Monroe County, the march was resumed, the guerrillas moving southeast into the eastern part of Boone County, camping the night of the 26th near Centralia.[33]

A key target of the guerrillas was the North Missouri Railroad which ran from St. Louis to Macon where it joined the cross state Hannibal to St. Joseph Railroad. An almost continual series of guerrilla raids on the bridges and tracks of the North Missouri Railroad were carried out to hamper the movement of federal troops and supplies. It was part of this campaign that brought a large force of guerrilla bands to Centralia during the late summer of 1864.[34]

On the morning of September 27, some thirty to fifty bushwhackers, many disguised in captured Union uniforms, under the leadership of Bill Anderson rode into the village of Centralia whose population was less than a hundred. While waiting for the train, they terrorized local civilians, robbing and burning stores and killing a civilian who had attempted to defend a young woman. The stage from Columbia came into the community, and they robbed the passengers. One of the stage passengers was Congressman James S. Rollins, a prominent Boone County citizen who had been identified as the "Father of the University of Missouri" for his role in locating the University in Columbia. Rollins and the other state passengers, which included Boone County Sheriff James Waugh, gave fictitious names and identities to the bandits. The stage coach robbery was interrupted when they heard a train whistle, coming from the east. This was a passenger train that had left St. Charles earlier that same morning.

The train crew saw the guerrilla band as they approached Centralia and decided to run through Centralia at top speed, but Anderson's men had placed a barricade of railroad ties across the track and forced the train to stop. In searching the train they found twenty-three unarmed Union soldiers who were on furlough and heading to their homes in northwest Missouri and southwest Iowa. The civilian passengers were robbed of all valuables. The soldiers were taken from the train, and ordered to disrobe. After isolating one of the soldiers, Sergeant Tom Goodman, the other twenty-two soldiers were shot and killed on the spot, witnessed by the horrified Centralia residents and train passengers. One German civilian on the train, who was wearing military clothing, was also killed, as he could not speak English and tell the raiders of his civilian status. Sergeant Goodman was spared, taken hostage by the Anderson guerrillas, and lived to write of the whole incident in a book after the conclusion of the Civil War. The guerrillas set fire to the Centralia depot, sacked and set fire to the train and then sent it on its way, west, with no crew aboard, to later crash and be destroyed.

W.F. Bassett of the *United States Military Telegraph*, who arrived in Centralia shortly after the massacre and talked with survivors and eyewitnesses, later stated: "About [eleven] o'clock the rumbling of the railroad train could be heard as it thundered down the grade and slowed at the depot, its occupants being entirely oblivious that they were on the threshold of a monstrous tragedy. Scarcely had the train ground to a halt, however, before the soldiers aboard—[seventy-five] [sic] in number—glanced out of the window and at once comprehended the situation."[35]

Brigadier-General Clinton B. Fisk wrote on September 27th:

> The train on the North Missouri Railroad, bound north from Saint Louis to-day, was captured at Centralia Station by Bill Anderson and his friends. Twenty-one soldiers were taken there-from and shot. The passengers were robbed and the train set on fire, and put in motion had been there, ready, an hour when the train came up. They had the citizens of the town under guard, thereby preventing intelligence of their presence being communicated to the approaching train. Perkins and [John] Thrailkill were reported as co-operating with Anderson, being near by and in sight of the depot. General Douglas, Lieutenant-Colonel Draper, Major Leonard, and Major King are each in that neighborhood with an aggregate of 600 troops, and some of them ought to fall upon the villains. More than half of this murdering party are young men from Boone County, fed, protected and encouraged by many of the citizens of this region. We have troops at all the telegraph stations, but it is impossible to guard all stations with the forces at our command. A few of these barbarians can capture, rob, and burn a train at any of the way-stations.[36]

H.P. Hynes, a Minnesotan, later mistakenly insisted theYoungers were responsible for the murder of the federal soldiers:

> Cole, Bob and Jim Younger were the chief movers in taking out of a train on the old North Missouri R.R. at Centralia and murdering along side of the track in 1864. . . . Look at the records in the War Department con-

cerning that event. Their [sic] you will find it-the most cold blooded uncalled for murders perpetrated in the last Civil War. . . . I think it was in April or May 1864 General Clinton B. Fisk was at that time the commander of the Department of North Missouri with headquarters in the Paty [sic] House in St. Joseph. The hospitals in his department were over crowded. In order to better their condition he order [sic] some of the patients to St. Louis. To some of them this was a leave of absence given to go home in the hope they would get well. The train proceeded on its way until it got to Centralia. Their [sic] it was stopped by Bill Anderson's gang of cut throat Gurillias [sic]. The Youngers were his lieutenants. They emptied the cars of all those who had a soldier's uniform on and drew them up in a line on the south side of the track. [The Youngers] had new Winchester rifles that had never been tested. They said they would test them on the 'yanks.' They did so the result of that test (using [sic] their own language) it sent a ball through seven of them by god. Then the work of slaughter began until [sic] the last man was killed. The government had them buried in a ditch where they were murdered and I think put a fence around it later. The Youngers and James boys were born of viciousness, nursed in crime and wickedness. . . .[37]

Word of the massacre spread quickly throughout the area. A unit of the Thirty-Ninth Missouri Infantry searching for the guerrilla bands was immediately dispatched to Centralia. The 300 troops, under Major A.V.E. Johnston, were largely new recruits, riding farm horses and armed with Enfield muskets, a heavy muzzle-loading gun. As the federal troops entered Centralia, the frightened citizens conveyed to them that Bill Anderson's band numbered less than ten men and had moved to the southeast from Centralia. Ignoring warnings from some Centralians that there were more bushwackers bivouacked south of town, the federal Infantry followed the guerrilla trail, expecting to find a relatively small force as had been described to them.[38]

When Anderson learned of Major Johnston's approach, Arch Clements and ten bushwhackers were dispatched towards Centralia as decoys. Johnston and his army rode three miles southeast of Centralia and skirmished with Clements' men and chased them. Within minutes, they became entangled in a guerrilla ambush. Reaching the top of a hill, Johnston looked down and saw 250 bushwhackers under Anderson, George Todd, and John Thrailkill lined up waiting for them. Johnston's men dismounted as the bushwhackers came out to meet them.[39] Major John Newman Edwards later penned:

Major Johnson halted his men and rode along his front speaking a few calm and collected words. They could not be heard in the guerrilla ranks, but they might have been divined. Most battle speeches are the same. They are generally epigrammatic, and full of sentences like these: "Aim low," "Keep cool," "Fire when you get loaded," "Let the wounded lie till the fight is over." But could it be possible that Johnson meant to receive the charge of the guerrillas at a halt? What cavalry books had he read? Who had taught him such ruinous and suicidal tactics? And yet monstrous as the resolution was in a military sense, it had actually been taken, and Johnson called out loud enough to be heard from opposing force to opposing force: "Come on, we are ready for the fight."

The challenge was accepted. The guerrillas gathered themselves up together as if by a sudden impulse, and took the bridle reins between their teeth. In the hands of each man there was a deadly revolver. There were carbines also, and yet they never had been un-slung. The sun was not high, and there was great need to finish quickly whatever had need to be begun. Riding the best and fastest horses in Missouri, the guerrillas struck the federal ranks as if the rush was a rush of tigers. Jesse James, riding a splendid race mare, led by half a length, then Arch Clements, then Peyton Long, then Oll Shepherd. There was neither trot or gallop; the guerrillas simply dashed from a walk into a full run. The attack was a hurricane. Johnson's command fired one volley and not a gun thereafter. It scarcely stood until the interval of three hundred yards was passed over. Johnson cried out to his men to fight to the death, but they did not wait even to hear him through. Some broke ranks as soon as they had fired and fled. Others were attempting to reload their muskets when the guerrillas, firing right and left, hurled themselves upon them. Johnson fell among the first. Mounted as described, Jesse James singled out the leader of the federals. He did not know him then. No words were spoken between the two. When Jesse James reached to within five feet of Johnson's position, he put out a pistol suddenly and sent a bullet through his brain. Johnson threw out his hands as if trying to reach something above his head and pitched forward heavily, a corpse. There was no quarter. Many begged for mercy on their knees. The guerrillas heeded the prayer as a wolf might the bleating of a lamb. The wild rout broke away toward Sturgeon, the implacable pursuit, vengeful as hate, thundering in the rear. Death did its work in twos, in threes, in squads—singly. Beyond the first volley, in which three were killed and one mortally wounded, not a single guerrilla was hurt.

Probably sixty of Johnson's men gained their horses before the fierce wave of the charge broke over them, and these were pursued by five guerrillas, led by Jesse James, for six miles at the dead run. Of the sixty, fifty-two were killed on the road from Centralia to Sturgeon. Todd drew up his command and watched the chase go on. For three miles nothing obstructed the vision. Side by side over the level prairie the five stretched away like the wind, gaining step by step and bound by bound, upon the rearmost riders. Then little puffs of smoke arose. No sounds could he heard, but dashing ahead from the white spurts terrified steeds ran riderless. Night and Sturgeon ended the killing. Five men had shot fifty-two. Johnson's total loss was two hundred and eighty-two, or out of three hundred only eighteen escaped. History has chosen to call this ferocious killing at Centralia a butchery. In civil war encounters are not called butcheries when the combatants are man to man and where over either rank there waves a black flag. Johnson's overthrow, probably, was a decree of fate. He rushed upon it as if impelled by a power stronger than himself. He did not know how to command, and his men did not know how to fight. He had, by the sheer force of circumstances, been brought face to face with two hundred and sixty-two of the most terrible revolver fighters the American war or any other war over produced, and he deliberately tied his hands by the act of dismounting, and stood in the shambles until he was shot down. Abject and pitiful cowardice matched itself against reckless and profligate desperation, and the end could only be, just what the end was. The guerrillas did unto the militia just exactly what the militia would have done unto them if fate had reversed its decision and given to Johnson what it permitted to the guerrillas.[40]

The inexperienced federal troops, with their single-shot rifles followed the traditional warfare practice of advancing on foot, leaving their horses tended by a few soldiers. They marched into a three-sided formation of several hundred hidden guerrillas, each armed with several Colt revolvers, and within minutes, the Union troops were nearly annihilated. The few soldiers that were not killed on the first guerrilla volleys ran back to their horses, but the guerrillas with their faster horses overtook the fleeing troops and within the hour, over 120 soldiers were killed. Some of the soldiers nearly reached the sanctuary of Sturgeon, some ten miles from the battleground, before the guerrillas completed the rout.

David Poole allegedly jumped from one body to another, proving to Archie Clement that he could be just as barbaric. "If they are dead, I can't hurt them," he insisted. "I cannot count 'em good without stepping on 'em."[41]

Among the guerrillas in action on that date were Frank James and his younger brother, Jesse. Some accounts credit Jesse James as the slayer of Major Johnston, commander of the ill-fated Union troops. Cole Younger was

Left to right: Archie Clement, Dave Poole (standing), and Bill Hendricks. Photo probably taken at Sherman, Texas, on Christmas Day 1863. (Author's collection)

also allegedly involved in the fight although he was most likely in Texas during the massacre. Three of the guerrillas, including Frank Shepherd, were reportedly killed in the battle.

Frank James later stated: "We charged up the hill yelling like wild Indians." The federals "fired their first and only volley. We were laying low on our horses. . . . The blood and brains from [Frank] Shepherd splashed on my pants leg as he fell from his horse. . . . But we couldn't stop that terrible charge for anything."[42]

Many of the bodies were recovered and sent back to their homes by federal troops that came to the area shortly after the battle ceased, but seventy-nine of the bodies were buried in a common grave, alongside the railroad tracks in Centralia. The hostage from the Centralia Massacre, Sergeant Tom Goodman, was taken along by Bloody Bill Anderson's band as they moved west to avoid Union troops. On the tenth day of his capture, Goodman managed to escape from the bushwhackers as they prepared to cross the Missouri River at Rocheport.[43]

Frank James, when asked about Centralia years later in an interview, related: "We did not seek the fight. [Johnston] foolishly came out to hunt us and he found us. Then we killed him and his men. Wouldn't he have killed everyone of us if he had had the chance? What is war for if it isn't to kill people for a principle!"[44]

A few days following the Centralia fight, Jesse James and George Todd led a raid from their camp on the Blackwater River into Lafayette County to break up a German federal military organization. The militia knew Todd and his guerrillas were coming, and they formed an ambuscade of 100 men in some hazel brush near the road and sent fourteen cavalrymen down the road to meet the guerrillas, and to fire upon them and to fall back past the ambush.[45]

Jesse James and ten men rode ahead of the main body of one hundred and sixty-three guerrillas. These ten men met the fourteen cavalrymen and charged them, driving them past the ambuscade. Todd and his 163 bushwhackers heard the firing in front and rushed up, and his command was hit by the fire from the ambush. Todd and his men dismounted and rushed into the brush and killed all but twenty-two of the 100 militiamen hiding there. While this was going on, Jesse James and the ten guerrillas with him had killed ten of the fourteen cavalrymen further down the road and were pursuing them, when they ran at full speed into the advance of a federal column

200 strong. There was nothing for the eleven guerrillas to do but turn and run, pursued by the 200 federals, shooting and yelling. Jesse's race mare was killed beneath him while he was shot in the left arm and side. He fell behind his dead horse and fought back. The balance of the guerrilla company came up at this critical time and drove off the federals.[46]

At the same time Centralia was under attack, the regular Confederate Army fought a serious engagement. On the afternoon of September 27, 1864, the peaceful, picturesque Arcadia Valley of southeast Missouri was witness to one of the bloodiest battles of entire war. In the brief span of twenty minutes, more than 1,000 officers and men lay wounded at the foot of Pilot Knob Mountain.[47]

In July, General Kirby Smith had received orders to send his best infantry east for the relief of Georgia and Alabama. Fearful of losing his infantry, Smith notified President Jefferson Davis that he was making plans for a major western campaign, which would be stymied by the loss of his infantry. By August, Davis deferred to Smith, and not a single rifleman was sent across the Mississippi to the aid of Atlanta. The threatened loss of his infantry forced Smith to hastily arrange raids into Arkansas and Missouri.

Smith chose Major General Sterling Price to lead the western campaign. From the outset, however, it was clear that Smith did not intend to gamble many of his organized troops on an ambitious venture. The expedition was to consist of three mounted divisions, each named after its commanding General. The first division was to be led by James Fagan, an Arkansas politician with a meager military background; the second was to be headed by John Marmaduke, a West Point Graduate; and the third by Jo Shelby, a brilliant and tough cavalry officer. The three divisions were to move through northeast Arkansas to the Missouri border, where they would split into three columns and advance twenty miles apart on a quick dash into St. Louis.

Both Fagan's and Marmaduke's divisions were severely undermanned. On his way north through Arkansas, Shelby was ordered to round up as many deserters as possible from behind the Union Lines. Shelby rejoined Price's army near the Missouri border, bringing with him more than 3,000 deserters at gun point to serve in the great campaign. Deserters eventually were to make up nearly a third of Price's force.

Most of the troops were clothed in tattered rags and several thousand were barefoot. Most had no canteens, cartridge boxes or other military issue;

instead they carried water in jugs and stuffed cartridges in their shirts and pockets. Tents and blankets were absent. Arms consisted of an endless variety and caliber of rifles and muskets, making ammunition supply in the field nearly impossible. By the time Price reached Missouri, nearly a fourth of his army were without arms.

On September 19, 1864, Price was ready. A 12,000-man mounted army of military men and misfits, regulars and ragamuffins, Price crossed the Arkansas border into Missouri. Price's advance into Missouri was made by three columns spaced ten to twenty miles apart. By September 24th, two of the columns had converged on Fredricktown to prepare for a thrust into St. Louis. Marmaduke joined Price two days later traveling a longer route.

Meanwhile, in St. Louis, General William Rosecrans, commander of the Department of Missouri, was getting desperate. Early in September, Rosecrans had received reports that Price was advancing toward Missouri with a major force. Constant appeals for reinforcements brought only a handful of infantry to defend the city. By late September, a small garrison of 6,000 men was all that stood between the greatest city west of the Mississippi and Price's invading horde.

In Fredricktown, Price and his three division commanders debated whether to assault the federal entrenchment at Pilot Knob on the way to St. Louis. Having met only token resistance thus far, Shelby wanted to move directly to St. Louis, which he believed could be taken in a day. The others felt it would be a tactical mistake to leave an armed federal garrison unmolested to the rear as the Confederate column moved north.

On September 26, the die was cast. Shelby was ordered to move northwest to Irondale and destroy the St. Louis and Iron Mountain Railroad. The rest of Price's army was to prepare for battle. Without waiting for Marmaduke's entire division to reach Fredricktown, Price ordered Fagan to march north to assault the federal garrison at Pilot Knob.

It was not until the night of September 24 that the Union's General Rosecrans was informed Price's force had crossed into Missouri. As Pilot Knob was his only fortification in south central Missouri, Rosecrans sent St. Louis district commander General Thomas Ewing and a detachment of the Fourteenth Iowa infantry to the area by train. By noon on September 26, Ewing had reached the hexagonal earth works known as Fort Davidson.

The fort lay on the floor of a valley surrounded on three sides by commanding hills. It was situated so that enemy infantry would have to cross hundreds of yards in the open to reach its formidable walls. The fort, however would be vulnerable to any artillery which could be placed on top of the encircling hills. Ewing had about 1,000 men with which to defend the position.

On the afternoon of September 26, Ewing sent two companies of infantry through Ironton to patrol the roads leading to Fredricktown. No sooner had they reached the "Shut-Ins" gap outside Ironton than they ran head-on into Fagan's advance brigades. Fagan's Arkansas troops quickly drove the Union patrol back into Ironton, with brisk rifle and cannon fire. Ewing immediately reinforced his patrol with a detachment of the Fourteenth Iowa, two pieces of artillery, and all the cavalry he could muster. The accurate punishing volleys of the veteran Fourteenth Iowa sent Fagan's untested troops into a near panic, forcing them to retreat to the Shut-Ins Gap. Repeated attacks by the Confederate advance, however, slowly pushed the Union Skirmishers back into Ironton, where nightfall and a heavy rainstorm brought the engagement to an end.

At dawn of September 27, Fagan's dismounted cavalry, reinforced by Marmaduke's, hurled themselves at the Union line fronting on the courthouse, forcing a withdrawal to the gap between Pilot Knob and Shepherd Mountain. When the small Union force came within sight of the fort, Ewing ordered the Fourteenth Iowa to a spur of Shepherd Mountain and his dismounted cavalry to the side of Pilot Knob, opening the gap to the federal artillery in the fort. Heavy skirmishing in the gap resulted in numerous Confederate losses without appreciable gain. Eventually, the desperate Union patrol was overwhelmed and forced to shoot its way back to the rifle pits which extended from the walls of the fort.

Fagan's and Marmaduke's divisions, which already had suffered more than 200 casualties in the first evening and morning of fighting, swarmed over the encircling hills and into the Ironton gap. Ewing found himself completely bottled in the fort with no avenue of escape. At a meeting in the gap, Price determined that his big guns would be placed on top of Shepherd Mountain. He then sent an emissary, Colonel Lauchlan Maclean, to the fort to ask for a Union surrender.

Hot-headed Maclean, a veteran of the Kansas border war, was a personal enemy of Ewing. When the Union general refused to surrender, Maclean returned to Price and urged a frontal assault on the fort, claiming there was no time to bring up all of the Confederate artillery and place it on the mountain. Price soon became convinced that placing the big guns on the mountain would be no easy task when the first attempt at placement saw a Confederate cannon disabled and its gunner killed by the first few volleys from the expert federal artillerymen.

But Price was determined to attempt a frontal assault. For nearly an hour, a hush fell over the peaceful valley. The Confederate commanders commenced forming their brigades for battle among the heavy brush and timber on the mountains. Inside the fort, Ewing ordered his cannons run down from maximum elevation and trained across the flat. Their load was to be canister rounds, each filled with hundreds of half-inch lead balls. Because all the riflemen could not take their places to file from the walls, details were assembled to tear cartridges, load rounds, and pass up the guns as they were needed. At the foot of the encircling mountains, 9,000 Confederates crouched down and waited.

At two o'clock the silence was broken. Confederate cannons in the gap opened on the earthen fort. Soon waves of dismounted southern cavalry poured into the open. The troops, formed in long columns three ranks deep, slowly moved toward the fort. Inside the walled enclosure, the riflemen were ordered to hold their fire and the Union artillery was opened on the advancing Confederate lines. At short range across the flat, the big guns could not miss. Dense clouds of smoke blanketed the fort and rose in columns hundreds of feet high.

The surrounding Confederate mass continued its ill-fated advance. Aware that the rifle pits could not be held, Union soldiers poured into the fort. The confederate horde was only 500 yards from the walls when Union riflemen were ordered to fire. With spent rifles being passed down and loaded ones handed up, the 300 rifles along the top of the walls spewed forth lead. Smoke from the heavy fire obliterated the Confederate lines.

At 200 yards, the southern brigades unleashed their first volley and broke into a crazed running charge. The Union gunners could see only the charging legs as the smoke blocked everything from view. The walls of Fort Davidson blazed as fire leaped from the muzzles of the gun barrels. At thirty yards, Price's troops finally broke and slowly started to fall back.

Spurred on by their officers, the terrified Southerners re-formed their lines and surged ahead. Again, they hesitated, and their officers turned them about. This third charge saw some men actually charge into a dry moat, which surrounded the fort. The Union gunners, with artillery shells fused as grenades, leaned over the walls and tossed them into the huddled Confederate soldiers.

The blood and confusion became too much to bear. Just a few yards from the fort, Price's soldiers finally turned and ran. As the soldiers streamed away from the fort and the smoke had a chance to clear, the incredible carnage became apparent. For 500 yards on the three sides of the fort that were attacked, the ground was covered with dead and wounded men.

The black rainy night which settled in the Arcadia Valley saw every shelter from Ironton filled with Confederate wounded. Price sent messages north toward the Union lines to beg for medical assistance. His entire command lay in a pitiful state of confusion. Most companies were scattered and only a few posted sentries or maintained any semblance of military discipline.

Inside Fort Davidson, General Ewing was deciding on his next move. He correctly surmised that the new morning would dawn with Price's artillery perched on top of Shepherd Mountain, rendering the fort untenable. Near midnight, Ewing hit upon a daring plan; he would attempt to slip his troops out of the fort and through Confederate lines.

At midnight, Ewing muffled the wheels of the six field guns, with the Fourteenth Iowa at the head, marched the column silently out of the fort. The weary Union defenders moved north along the road to Potosi and miraculously marched unchallenged right through the loose Confederate lines. In a few hours, Ewing was miles away from the fort. At two o'clock in the morning, a squad left behind in the fort blew up the powder magazine in the center of the earthen enclosure. Confederates roused by the blast thought the explosion was an accident.

At dawn, Price's dwindling army awakened to find the fort empty, with a large smoking hole in the center. In a fit of rage, Price sent Marmaduke's division after the escaping federals. Although Ewing ran headlong into Shelby, he was able to successfully fight his way to a strong Union fortification in Rolla. Marmaduke and Shelby wasted three days on the futile pursuit. With his best assault troops lost and two of his divisions in disarray, Price knew that an attack on the now reinforced city of St. Louis was out of the question. To salvage something from the ill-fated campaign, Price decided to turn northwest and capture Missouri's capital for the Confederacy. But the week wasted at Pilot Knob and the initial crushing defeat had cost him dearly. Price found that Jefferson City, too, had been reinforced, and he fought only a brief, half-hearted skirmish.

Major General Sterling Price's Missouri Expedition had changed course from St. Louis and Jefferson City to Kansas City and Fort Leavenworth. As his army neared Kansas City, Major General Samuel R. Curtis's Army of the Border blocked its way west, while Major General Alfred Pleasonton's provisional cavalry division was closing on their rear. Price decided that he needed to deal with the two Union forces and decided to attack them one at a time. With Pleasonton still behind him, Price chose to strike Curtis at Westport first. Curtis had established strong defensive lines and during a four-hour battle, the Confederates hurled themselves at the Union forces but to no avail. The Confederates could not break the Union lines and retreated south. Westport was the decisive battle of Price's Missouri Expedition, and from this point on, the confederates were in retreat.[48]

On October 21st, the bushwhackers pushed Generals Blunt, Jennison, and Moonlight two and one-half miles northeast of Independence. Their leader, George Todd, was hit by a federal sharpshooter just east of the Little Blue River in a fight against Major General Samuel R. Curtis and his federal soldiers. (Curtis' son had been killed only a year earlier by bushwhackers at Baxter Springs.)

One account of Todd's demise stated he was cut down in a volley fired by the Second Colorado while his unit was acting as Shelby's advance. Todd was hit in the neck by a Spencer rifle ball, which entered near the base of his throat and exited out his back, just missing the spinal column. Another account claims Todd was leading a small party on a scouting mission near Independence, and upon reaching a ridge, rode forward alone, sat high in his stirrups for a better glimpse of the area, and was shot by a sniper hiding in the grass below. He pitched forward in the saddle and fell to the ground.[49]

Todd was carried by his men to the house of a Mrs. Burns, where he died about an hour later. His men buried him that night in Independence's Woodlawn Cemetery. David Poole then took command of his unit. Because Poole was also with Sterling Price, he merged Todd's unit with his own.

Very little is known about Quantrill after his return to Missouri. What is known, however, is that Quantrill again organized his band of guerillas and partisans, this time to fight in the battle of Westport on October 23, 1864. The Confederate Army suffered their biggest defeat in Missouri during this battle. Union troops known as the "Army of the Border," led by Major General Samuel Curtis overran General Sterling Price's men in the Battle of Westport.

Price's Missouri Expedition had changed course from St. Louis and Jefferson City to Kansas City and Fort Leavenworth. As his army neared Kansas City, Major General Samuel R. Curtis's Army of the Border blocked its way west, while Major General Alfred Pleasonton's provisional cavalry division was closing on their rear. Price decided that he needed to deal with the two Union forces and decided to attack them one at a time. With Pleasonton still behind him, Price chose to strike Curtis at Westport first. Curtis had established strong defensive lines and during a four-hour battle, the Confederates hurled themselves at the Union forces but to no avail. The Confederate force could not break the Union lines and retreated south. Westport was the decisive battle of Price's Missouri Expedition, and from this point on, the Confederates were in retreat.

A 100-mile retreat ensued. Weighted down by wagon trains filled with loot collected during his raids, General Price jeopardized his men and position for the plunder. On October 25th, the wagon train became lodged in Mine Creek and the Confederates employed a rear-guard action rather than lose their bounty. About six miles south of Trading Post, where the Marais de Cygnes engagement had occurred, the brigades of Colonel Frederick W. Benteen and Colonel John F. Phillips, of Major General Alfred Pleasonton's Provisional Cavalry Division, overtook the Confederates as they were crossing Mine Creek. The Confederates, stalled by their wagons crossing the ford, had formed a line on the north side of Mine Creek. The federals, although outnumbered, commenced the attack as additional troops from Pleasonton's command arrived during the fight. They soon surrounded the Rebels, resulting in the capture of about 600 men and two generals, Brigadier General John S. Marmaduke and Brigadier General William L. Cabell. Having lost this many men, Price's army was doomed.

In the final tally, 2,500 Union troops defeated 6,500 Confederate soldiers. Approximately 1,000 Confederates died, were wounded or were captured in the battle. Again, Quantrill and his men disbanded and fled for safety. His authority over his followers disintegrated completely when they elected George Todd to lead them.

On October 26, 1864, just south of Richmond in Ray County, Missouri, Bill Anderson and his guerilla band were ambushed by Captain Samuel P. Cox and his federal troops. They were caught completely unaware. A skirmish ensued, and it is said that Bill and another of his men rode right through the federal line. When his comrade was shot from his horse, Bill turned around to assist him, and it was at this time that he was riddled with bullets and killed. Upon examining the personal items found on his body, he had seven pistols, $600 in cash and two watches. Private papers found in his saddlebags from General Price identified him as William T Anderson.

Bill's body was taken to Richmond, Missouri, where it was propped up in a chair and a pistol was placed in the dead mans hand for photographs. A short time later, the Union troopers decapitated him and placed his head on a telegraph pole at the entrance to the town. His torso was roped and tied to a horse where it was dragged through the streets of Richmond before being buried in an unmarked grave outside of town. The silken cord that Anderson had carried to keep track of the men he had killed, revealed fifty-four knots.

Only two days following the ambush upon Bloody Bill Anderson, General Price's force was in full retreat following its expedition into Missouri. On October 28, 1864, it stopped to rest about two miles south of Newtonia, Missouri. Soon afterward, Major General James G. Blunt's Union troops surprised the Confederates and began to drive them. Brigadier General Jo Shelby's division, including his Iron Brigade, rode to the front, dismounted, and engaged the Yankees while the other Rebel troops retreated towards Indian Territory. Brigadier General John B. Sanborn later appeared with Union reinforcements which convinced Shelby to retire. The Union troops forced the Confederates to retreat but failed to destroy or capture them.

Following the death of Anderson and the Confederate retreat at Newtonia, Edwin Terrell, a Union guerrilla with a fearsome reputation for hunting Confederate irregulars, was hired by John M Palmer to hunt down Quantrill. Early in the war, he had served the Confederacy, but then switched sides and commenced plundering, looting, and killing Southern sympathizers. Terrell was no more than a thief and murderer himself but was put on the Secret Service payroll and paid on a monthly basis.

In an attempt to regain his prestige, Quantrill concocted a plan to lead a company of men to Washington and assassinate President Abraham Lincoln. He assembled a group of raiders in Lafayette County, Missouri, in November and December of 1864, but the strength of Union troops east of the Mississippi River convinced him that his plan could not succeed. Quantrill returned, therefore, to his normal pattern of raiding and then headed east to Kentucky where he met up with some Kentucky guerrillas, but he soon found out the Union forces were better organized than those in Missouri.

Quantrill and several of his men had entered Kentucky in mid-January 1865 near Canton and moved east. Passing themselves off as Missouri federals, the bushwhackers talked and joked with their enemies. On one occasion, however, a federal captain, who was organizing a company of black troops, boasted openly what he and his men would do to the bushwhackers. Soon afterwards, he was killed by Quantrill men.[50]

After fighting in several engagements, Quantrill, Frank James, and the small party of bushwhackers took refuge in the home of a farmer named Dawson that spring. Dawson's daughter, Nannie, was mesmerized by the guerrilla chieftain and asked Quantrill to sign her autograph book. Quantrill obliged by penning her a poem:

My horse is at the door,
And the enemy I soon may see
But before I go Miss Nannie
Here's a double health to thee.

Here's a sigh to those who love me
And a smile for those who hate
And, whatever sky's above me
Here's a heart for every fate.

Though the cannons roar around me
Yet it still shall bear me on
Though dark clouds are above me
It hath springs which may be won.

In this verse as with the wine
The libation I would pour
Shall be peace with thine and mine
And a health to thee and all in door.[51]

In May, Quantrill and his party rode toward Spencer County. Upon reaching the Taylorsville-Bloomfield Pike, a heavy rain drove him and his band to shelter. Terrell caught up with Quantrill on the James H. Wakefield farm, located five miles south of Taylorsville, Kentucky, on May 10, 1865. The men were exhausted and it started to rain. Quantrill and about twenty-one of his men were camped inside the Wakefield barn, many of them asleep in the hayloft, when Terrell launched his surprise attack. Guerrilla John Ross was the first to spot the enemy, and although he shouted an alarm, it was too late to save the remnants of the bushwhackers.[52]

The guerrillas ran to their horses and attempted to flee into the woods rather than organize any type of an offensive. As Quantrill mounted his horse, his stirrup leather broke, throwing him across the back of his horse. The horse immediately panicked and followed the other horses out of the barn. As the terrified mount cleared the barn door, Quantrill was shot in the back. The bullet struck him in the left shoulder blade, angled down and lodged against his spine. He was instantly paralyzed.

As he fell face down in the mud, the federals fired again, a pistol ball severing Quantrill's right trigger finger. When questioned by Terrell and his men, Quantrill gave his name as Captain Clarke of the Fourth Missouri Confederate Cavalry and asked to be allowed to stay on the farm and die. His wish was granted and Terrell and his men trotted off in pursuit of Quantrill. Wakefield sent for a doctor who announced that Quantrill's wound was fatal. Frank James and four other irregulars returned to check on their fallen commander and stated they wanted to hide him on the woods. Knowing the end was near, Quantrill declined.

After learning the true identity of the man who was injured at the Wakefield farm, Terrell and his men returned with a wagon on Friday, May 12. They loaded Quantrill and took him to Louisville, arriving there on the 13th of May. Terrell was paid and dismissed from service after turning over Quantrill. Newspapers announced the capture of Quantrill but on the same day recanted, saying that they had the wrong man. This led to stories that claimed Quantrill was not the one who was killed that day. Quantrill died on June 6, 1865, at the age of twenty-seven years. Before his death, he visited with a priest and asked him to contact a woman who was holding money for him. The priest was to purchase a cemetery plot and headstone and then give the rest of the money to Kate Clarke. He also made a full confession, converted to Catholicism, and took the sacrament of extreme unction.

Quantrill was buried under a tree in the cottage yard of St. Mary's Catholic Cemetery, but his grave was not marked. The priest feared that his grave would be vandalized by his enemies and also ordered that no mound be left over the burial site. In 1887, a boyhood friend of Quantrill's, William Walter Scott, accompanied Mrs. Quantrill to Kentucky to inquire about William's remains. They were shown the burial site and asked to have the grave dug up so Mrs. Quantrill could take the remains back to Dover for reburial. Fearing the legality of removing the bones, they were denied this request, however, it was agreed that the grave would be dug up the following afternoon so that the contents could be viewed.

The following afternoon, brought bad weather, so Mrs. Quantrill stayed in her hotel room while Mr. Scott went alone to the cemetery. When the gravedigger finished digging up the grave, Mr. Scott examined the grave. He removed the head and wrapped it in newspaper. The rest of the remains were placed in a box and reburied near the surface. Mr. Scott took the skull to Mrs. Quantrill who examined it and identified as the head of her son. She was able to make the identity based upon a chipped molar in the lower right jaw. Mrs. Quantrill refused to allow the skull to be returned and devised a scheme to get the rest of the bones and take them back to Dover. She sent Mr. Scott back to retrieve the rest of the bones.

Mrs. Quantrill, curious about her son's endeavors, toured Kentucky and Missouri and visited with some of William's former comrades, trying to learn all she could about her son's death and wartime activities. She returned to Dover in the spring of 1889 and requested that her son's remains be buried in the family lot. The town fathers resisted the idea of the infamous Quantrill being buried in their cemetery but agreed so long as the ceremony remained private and the grave was not marked. Mr. Scott brought the box but had removed the skull, two shinbones, three arm bones and some hair. What was actually buried in the box is unknown. It is known that Mr. Scott attempted to sell the skull of Quantrill to the Kansas State Historical Society and eventually all five bones ended up in their possession. The skull, however, was later sold by Mr. Scott's son and used in fraternity initiations. It was then donated to the Dover Museum where it remained on display until 1992. Quantrill's grave in Dover was marked with a military marker in 1882. His five bones and a hair remnant were re-entered in the Old Confederate Veterans Home and Cemetery in Higginsville, Missouri, on October 24, 1992, with full Confederate honors. On October 30, 1992, the skull of William Quantrill was buried in an infant's coffin in the Dover Fourth Street Cemetery.

Notes

[1] Prairie Grove Battlefield State Park Records.

[2] Major General J.M. Schofield letter to Governor Thomas Carney dated August 29, 1863. *The War of the Rebellion: A Compilation of the Official Records of the Union and Confederate Armies*, Series I, Volume XXXIV. Pp. 577-580.

[3] Governor Thomas Carney letter to Major General J.M. Schofield dated September 3, 1863. *The War of the Rebellion: A Compilation of the Official Records of the Union and Confederate Armies*, Series I, Volume XXXIV, p. 580.

[4] Major-General J.M. Schofield letter to Governor Thomas Carney dated September 3, 1862. *The War of the Rebellion: A Compilation of the Official Records of the Union and Confederate Armies*, Series I, Chapter XXXIV, pp. 578-579.

[5] Report of Lieutenant Colonel Charles S. Clark, Ninth Kansas Cavalry. August 30, 1863. *The War of the Rebellion: A Compilation of the Official Records of the Union and Confederate Armies*, Series I, Chapter XXXIX, pp. 585-587.

[6] Report of Lieutenant Colonel Bazel F. Lazear, First Missouri State Militia Cavalry, August 27, 1863. *The War of the Rebellion: A Compilation of the Official Records of the Union and Confederate Armies*, Series I, Chapter XXXIV, p. 584.

[7] Report of Brigadier-General Thomas Ewing, Jr., August 31, 1862. *The War of the Rebellion: A Compilation of the Official Records of the Union and Confederate Armies*, Series I, Chapter XXXIV, pp. 579-583.

[8] Report of Major Linn K. Thacher, Ninth Kansas Cavalry, August 27, 1863. *The War of the Rebellion: A Compilation of the Official Records of the Union and Confederate Armies*, Series I, Chapter XXXIV, p. 589.

[9] Report of Captain Charles F. Coleman, Ninth Kansas Cavalry, August 30, 1863. *The War of the Rebellion: A Compilation of the Official Records of the Union and Confederate Armies*, Series I, Chapter XXXIV, p. 590.

[10] Ted P. Yeatman, *Frank and Jesse James: The Story Behind the Legend*, Nashville, Cumberland House, 2000, p. 43.

[11] Kansas State Historical Society.

[12] Larry Sullivan, Kansas State Historical Society.

[13] Ted P. Yeatman, *Frank and Jesse James: The Story Behind the Legend*, pp. 38-39.

[14]*Good Bye, Jesse James*, Liberty, Jesse James Bank Museum, 1967, p. 30.

[15]Sharon Gates-Hull, "Not Just Cowboys Women—Wives, Daughters—Played Roles in the Saga of Jesse James," *Northfield News*, Souvenir Edition, Friday, September 11, 1998, p. 6; Phillip W. Steele, *Jesse and Frank James: The Family History*, Gretna, Louisiana, Pelican Publishing Company, 1987, pp. 67-68; Thomas Riley Shouse, "My Father Planned the James' Boys Capture," *Frontier Times*, Summer 1959, p. 17; Carl W, Breihan, *Outlaws of the Old West*, New York, Bonanza Books, 1957, p. 22; *History of Clay and Platte Counties, Missouri*, St. Louis, National Historical Company, 1885, p. 237; William A. Settle, Jr., *Jesse James Was His Name*, p. 26.

[16]Julian Street, "The Borderland," *Collier's*, September 14, 1914.

[17]George Turner, *Secrets of Jesse James*, Amarillo, Baxter Lane Company, 1975, p. 10.

[18]William A. Settle, Jr., *Jesse James Was His Name*, pp. 24-25.

[19]Stuart W. Sanders, "Bloody Bill's Centralia Massacre," *America's Civil War*, March 2000, pp. 36-37.

[20]Robertus Love, *The Rise and Fall of Jesse James*, p. 47.

[21]Jesse James, Jr., *Jesse James, My Father*.

[22]Stuart W. Sanders, "Bloody Bill's Centralia Massacre," *America's Civil War*, March 2000, p. 37.

[23]Robert L. Dyer, *Jesse James and the Civil War in Missouri*, p. 42.

[24]*Good Bye, Jesse James*, p. 31.

[25]Jesse James, Jr., *Jesse James, My Father*.

[26]Stuart W. Sanders, "Bloody Bill's Centralia Massacre," *America's Civil War*, March 2000, p. 37.

[27]Bo Kerrihard, "Bitter Bushwhackers and Jayhawkers," *America's Civil War*, January 1993, pp. 31-32.

[28]Mid-Missouri Civil War Roundtable website, Internet.

[29]*Kansas City Journal of Commerce*, August 13, 1864.

[30]Homer Croy, *Jesse James Was My Neighbor*, New York, Duell, Sloan & Pearce, 1949, pp. 30-32.

[31]Hampton Watts, *The Babe of the Company: An Unfolded Leaf from the Forest of Never-to-Be-Forgotten Years*, reprinted by the Democrat-Leader Press of Fayette, Missouri, 1913.

[32]Report of Lieutenant-Colonel Dan M. Draper, September 25, 1864. *The War of the Rebellion: A Compilation of the Official Records of the Union and Confederate Armies*, Series I, Volume 41.

[33]Hampton Watts, *The Babe of the Company: An Unfolded Leaf from the Forest of Never-to-Be-Forgotten Years*, reprinted by the Democrat-Leader Press of Fayette, Missouri, 1913.

[34]Shelby Foote, *The Civil War: A Narrative Red River to Appomattox*, New York, Random House, 1974, p. 579; Mid-Missouri Civil War Roundtable website, Internet.

[35]James D. Horan, *Desperate Men*, p. 28.

[36]Report of Brigadier-General Clinton B. Fisk, September 27, 1864. *The War of the Rebellion: A Compilation of the Official Records of the Union and Confederate Armies*, Series I, Volume 41.

[37]H.P. Hynes letter to Governor Merriam dated June 24, 1889. Northfield, Minnesota, Bank Robbery of 1876. Selected Manuscripts Collections and Government Records, Microfilm Edition, Roll 3, Minnesota Historical Society.

[38]Jesse James, Jr., *Jesse James, My Father,* Cleveland, Arthur Westbrook Company, 1899.

[39]Stuart W. Sanders, "Bloody Bill's Centralia Massacre," *America's Civil War*, March 2000, p. 39.

[40]John Newman Edwards, *Noted Guerrillas, or the Warfare of the Border*, 1877.

[41]Bo Kerrihard, "Bitter Bushwhackers and Jayhawkers," *America's Civil War*, January 1993, p. 32.

[42]Stuart W. Sanders, "Bloody Bill's Centralia Massacre," *America's Civil War*, March 2000, p. 40.

[43]Robertus Love, *The Rise and Fall of Jesse James*, pp. 22-23.

[44]Stuart W. Sanders, "Bloody Bill's Centralia Massacre," *America's Civil War*, March 2000, p. 82.

[45]Robertus Love, *The Rise and Fall of Jesse James*, pp. 22-23.

[46]Jesse James, Jr., *Jesse James, My Father*.

[47]Missouri Department of Natural Resources Bulletin; Robert L. Dyer, *Jesse James and the Civil War in Missouri*, p. 44.

[48]Alvin M. Josephy, *The Civil War in the American West*, New York, Alfred A. Knopf, 1991, pp. 383-334.

[49]Edward E. Leslie, *The Devil Knows How to Ride*, pp. 334-335.

[50]Stuart W. Sanders, "Quantrill's Last Ride," *America's Civil War*, March 1999, pp. 42-48.

[51]Martin Edward McGrane, *The Home of Jesse and Frank James . . . The James Farm, Kearney, Missouri*, p. 28; Robert Barr Smith, *The Last Hurrah of the James-Younger Gang*, Norman, University of Oklahoma Press, 2001, p. 15.

[52]Marley Brant, *Jesse James: The Man and the Myth*, New York, Berkley Books, 1998.

Chapter Nine

An End and a Beginning

"There is a man who has all the goodness of an angel in his heart. If our Savior was to come on earth and say to me, 'Where can I get a brave and fearless man to assist St. Peter to guard the portals of heaven?' I would say, 'Cole Younger.' And I know he would stick to his post all eternity." —Frank James[1]

F RANK JAMES WAS IN TEXAS during the winter encampment of 1863-1864, and saw Quantrill lose control over his men. William H. Gregg entered the regular Confederate Army with Shelby's Brigade in Louisiana, and other long time guerrillas joined other units in the army.[2]

Cole and a party of bushwhackers started for Texas during the fall of 1863 where they were ordered to report to General Henry E. McCulloch, in command of Northern Texas, in Bonham. Cole had grown tired of guerrilla warfare and joined General Price's regular Confederate army and gone South with it on its campaigns. With the absence of Captain Jarrette, who had rejoined Shelby's command, Cole was, at nineteen, commissioned a captain. Joe Lea became first lieutenant of the company and Lon Railey second lieutenant. According to Cole, all his orders on the commissary and quartermaster departments were signed by him as Captain C.S.A. Cole, commanding 285 men, remained in Bonham doing scouting for General McCulloch.

Cole Younger. (Courtesy of the National Archives)

In November 1863, Cole and his company were dispatched to Shreveport, Louisiana, with orders to report to General Edmund Kirby Smith at the headquarters of the Trans-Mississippi Department. With the invasion of Kentucky a success, General Smith had been appointed to the rank of lieutenant general. Early in 1863, he was transferred to the Trans-Mississippi, where he remained for much of the war.

Cole, in reporting to General E. Kirby Smith, was given an assignment on the Mississippi River in Louisiana.[3] He and his men burned cotton fields along the Mississippi River to keep them out of Yankee hands. Cole fought at Oneka, Goodard's Landing, Harrison's Landing, Joe's Bayou, Lake Providence, and Grand Lake. He then reported to General Jo Shelby at Warren, Arkansas. Younger's company burned several million dollars worth of cotton and captured and killed 500 negroes. The Confederate High Command saw him as a real asset to the Southern cause.[4]

E.G. Bower, who served as Cole's mess-mate during Confederate service, was with him when he was with Shelby's Brigade of Missouri Cavalry in winter quarters on the Ouachita River near Camden, Arkansas. Bower was quite impressed by Cole: "[We] were under General Joe Shelby and knew him [Cole] as well as any man could," wrote Bower, "knew his kindly nature, his warm friendships, his entire truthfulness and heroic gallantry; on the battlefield, he is as calm, thoughtful, sober, cool and intrepid as any man that ever lived. There was never a charge of wrong-doing in Texas against him; he was on the side of law and order."[5]

Due to the Union blockade and then the capture of the Mississippi River, Smith was virtually cut off from Richmond and was forced to deal with matters of how to get food and supplies for his troops. Smith had to keep the blockade-running route to Mexico open. He also kept western Louisiana and Texas in Confederate hands through well-planned defensive campaigns—a difficult task with Union campaigns in Arkansas and Louisiana in 1864 involving thousands of Texans.[6]

Confederate Major General John B. Magruder, commander of the District of Texas, New Mexico, and Arizona felt it was critical to protect the coastal area between the Brazos and Sabine rivers.

"However important the wheat region may be to us as a source of supplies," he argued, "he who commands between . . . the Brazos and the Sabine, controls the heart of Texas, and will have beef and corn enough, even if he should not obtain flour enough, to support his army for an indefinite period."[7]

In March, Union General Nathaniel P. Banks had moved an army of 27,000 men and a naval flotilla up the Red River toward Shreveport, headquarters of the Confederacy's Trans-Mississippi Department and at that time, the capital of Louisiana. He hoped to link up with federal troops under General Frederick Steele, who was moving southward from Little Rock, and then extend federal control over northeast Texas.

This bold attempt, which included a plan to capture Shreveport, comprised one of the largest combined Army and Navy operations of the war and an array of technological innovations, such as the first use of the periscope in battle and the construction of several dams on the Red River. In addition to the tens of thousands of men committed by the United States Army, ninety naval warships and transports moved up the narrow Red River.[8]

Shreveport served as a major cotton exporting center and the hub of a vital war industry with a naval yard, factories, foundries, arsenals, and powder mills. Confederate military units in Louisiana, Texas, Arkansas, Indian Territory, New Mexico, and Arizona were all under the command of the officers in Shreveport.

In an effort to prevent this, Texas troops in Indian Territory commanded by Brigadier General Samuel Maxey-Gano's Brigade, Walker's Choctaw Brigade, and Krumbhaar's battery, which was attached to Gano's Brigade— were moved to Arkansas, where they joined Sterling Price in halting the Union advance at Camden.[9]

Banks, meanwhile, continued his advance in northwest Louisiana. On April 8, 1864, part of his army was defeated at Sabine Crossroads, near Mansfield, by Confederates under the command of Richard Taylor. Texans played a major role in the battle, which halted Banks's advance. Confederates resumed the attack the next day at Pleasant Hill, fourteen miles to the south, but superior Union numbers prevented a Southern victory. Once again Texas units, including Walker's Texas Division; Thomas Green's cavalry, which consisted of five brigades in three divisions led by Hamilton P. Bee, James Patrick Major, and William Steele; and Polignac's Brigade, figured prominently in the fighting. Green, one of the most popular of all the Texans, was killed three days later while leading an attack on the retreating federals at Blair's Landing. Banks continued to retreat and in mid-May crossed the Atchafalaya River, thus ending attempts to invade Northeast Texas.

Captains Jarrette and Poole were in Shreveport, and General Smith gave them all orders to capture cotton growers who were selling their products to the Union forces. The expedition planned by General Smith placed Captain Poole in charge of one company and Cole the other, with Captain Jarrette over both forces.[10]

On June 15, 1864 Stand Watie, the only Indian to become a brigadier-general in the Confederate army, captured the Union steamer, *J.R. Williams*. The federals, attempting to ship provisions up the Arkansas River from Fort Smith to Fort Blunt, loaded the steamer with $120,000 worth of supplies. At Pleasant Bluff, Stand Watie and his Cherokees attacked the steamer with artillery and musket fire. The steamer was beached across the river from Watie's force, and the twenty-six federals retreated to Fort Smith, leaving the valuable cargo to the guerrillas. Watie's success in raids such as this brought him praise from the Confederate High Command and boosted the morale of Confederate forces in the West.[11]

Stand Watie had joined the Southern cause at the outbreak of the Civil War. He was commissioned a colonel on July 12, 1861, and raised a regiment of Cherokees for service with the Confederate army. Later, when Chief John Ross signed an alliance with the South, Watie's men were organized as the Cherokee Regiment of Mounted Rifles. After Ross fled Indian Territory, Watie was elected principal chief of the Confederate Cherokees in August 1862.[12]

A portion of Watie's command saw action at Oak Hills (August 10, 1861) in a battle that assured the South's hold on Indian Territory and made Watie a Confederate military hero. Afterward, Watie helped drive the pro-Northern Indians out of Indian Territory, and following the Battle of Chustenahlah (December 26, 1861), he commanded the pursuit of the fleeing federals, led by Opothle-yahola, and drove them into exile in Kansas. Although Watie's men were exempt from service outside Indian Territory, he led his troops into Arkansas in the spring of 1861 to stem a federal invasion of the region. Joining with

Stand Watie, C.S.A. (Courtesy of the National Archives)

Major General Earl Van Dorn's command, Watie took part in the Battle of Pea Ridge. On the first day of fighting, the Southern Cherokees, which were on the left flank of the Confederate line, captured a battery of Union artillery before being forced to abandon it. Following the federal victory, Watie's command screened the southern withdrawal.

Watie, or troops in his command, participated in eighteen battles and major skirmishes with federal troop during the Civil War, including Cowskin Prairie (April 1862), Old Fort Wayne (October 1862), Webber's Falls (April 1863), Fort Gibson (May 1863), Cabin Creek (July 1863), and Gunter's Prairie (August 1864). In addition, his men were engaged in a multitude of smaller skirmishes and meeting engagements in Indian Territory and neighboring states. Because of his wide-ranging raids behind Union lines, Watie tied down thousands of federal troops that were badly needed in the East.

Confederate General Douglas Cooper advanced against the federal stronghold at Fort Smith. On July 27th, a detachment from Cooper's army, consisting of Stand Watie's Cherokees and Confederate Texans led by Colonel Richard Gano, conducted a surprise attack on a federal cavalry outpost just south of Fort Smith at Massard Prairie. Union Major David Mefford of the Sixth Kansas Cavalry, commanding the camp, rallied his men and directed a fighting retreat towards Fort Smith. But Gano's men had stampeded Mefford's horses and the dismounted federals were soon surrounded by an overwhelming Confederate force.[13]

On July 30th, Cooper and his entire force advanced upon Fort Smith. Stand Watie and his men helped drive back federal troops before the fort's defenses. An artillery duel lasted until midnight when Cooper and his soldiers withdrew to the Indian Territory. The failed assault on Fort Smith constituted the last major defense effort by Confederate Indians outside their territory.

On August 26th, 200 guerrillas made a raid upon the plantations leased by H.B. Tibbetts and Company above Goodrich's Landing, Louisiana, commanded by Colonel A. Watson Webber, Fifty-first U.S. Colored Infantry. They cruelly murdered four white men and several colored people. As the Confederate citizens living immediately beyond Bayou Macon had petitioned the regular Confederate military authorities protectors and raid Yankee lessees, a retaliatory expedition was sent to that vicinity. The villages of Floyd Pinhook, guerrilla rendezvous, were destroyed by fire, some property taken by the guerrillas was recaptured and one captain, a lieutenant, and ten soldiers were killed.[14]

Five miles from Tester's Ferry, on Bayou Macon, Cole and his men encountered a wagon train loaded with cotton and being escorted by fifty federal cavalrymen. Unleashing the frightful "Rebel yell," Cole and his irregulars, who outnumbered the soldiers, charged their enemies. After a heated fight, forty of the Union soldiers lay dead. Before the irregulars departed, they discovered four men coming up behind the wagons, and upon interrogating them, found out they were cotton buyers. The four men were searched. When the guerrillas found $180,000 on them, Cole had them hanged on a cotton gin, and he sent the money to Bastrop, Louisiana, to be used by the Confederacy.[15]

271

Cole's band discovered another cotton train on a plantation a few days later at Bayou Monticello. He later penned: "A more exciting experience was mine at Bayou Monticello, a stream that was deeper than it looked. Observing a cotton train on a plantation across the bayou, I called to my men to follow me and plunged in. Seeing me floundering in the deep water, however, they went higher up to a bridge, and when I landed I found myself alone. I was hard pressed for a time, till they came up and relieved me. There were [fifty-two] soldiers killed here. Other charges near Goodrich's Landing and at Omega put an end to the cotton speculation in that locality."[16]

The Confederate army in this area was not well armed but each man in Cole's company boasted a pair of dragoon pistols and a Sharpe's rifle. General Kirby Smith later conveyed to Cole that he had not seen a band so well armed during the war.

Because of his successful mission in Louisiana, he was sent to Warren, Arkansas, by General Shelby to provide special service for General Maramaduke. "Only twenty and a beardless boy, General Marmaduke looked me over rather dubiously, as I thought, but finally told me what he wanted," remembered Cole.[17]

After Marmaduke looked him over, Cole was singled out for a scouting mission by Adjutant General John Newman Edwards, on assignment from General Jo Shelby, and was dispatched to Little Rock to learn if Union Major General Frederick Steele planned to move against General Price at Camden. As early as August 1, 1863, Major General Stephen A. Hurlbut had written Major General U.S. Grant, then Commanding Department of Tennessee:

> Major General Steele has reported to me from Helena. I have directed him to take all the effective force of Kimball's division and 2,000 men from Helena garrison, open communications with Davidson, now at Madison, and establish a junction at Clarendon; thence to move on Little Rock, where Price is reported to be. Marmaduke is at Jacksonport. I have also directed him to establish a temporary depot of supplies at Clarendon, to which access is easy by White River, and, if the Arkansas is navigable at this time, to seize another point on that river below Little Rock for a second depot. The country from Helena to Clarendon is reported to be utterly desolate and exceedingly dry. I have directed General Steele to ascertain if it be practicable by land; and, if so, to march the troops and send supplies . . . round by the river. Upon unit-

ing at Clarendon, the force will be over 10,000 men, 5,000 of whom will be mounted—more than enough to meet the entire force in Arkansas.

I think the occupation of Little Rock will be simply a question of marching and the holding of it merely a question of supplies. It is evidently the intention of the General-in-Chief to hold the line of the Arkansas River, which again depends upon the water.[18]

In addition to checking upon Steele's whereabouts, Cole Younger also scouted the picket posts from Warren to the Mississippi River, up the Arkansas River to Pine Bluff and Little Rock. Midway between Pine Bluff and Little Rock, he and his men attacked a wagon train of federal soldiers, which was accompanied by an ambulance carrying women. The soldiers escaped to Pine Bluff, but the irregulars captured the wagon. Cole returned by way of the western outpost at Hot Springs.[19]

"We made a thorough examination of the interior of Little Rock," recalled Cole, "and satisfied ourselves that no movement on Price was imminent, and were on our way out before we became involved in a little shooting match with the patrol, from which no harm resulted to our side, however, except a shot in my leg."[20]

Following Cole' scouting expedition, General Edmund Kirby Smith diverted two divisions of troops out of Louisiana to repulse Major General Steele's march into southwest Arkansas. Steele's Camden Expedition ended in a bitter defeat, and by April 27th, his army was in full retreat. The Confederates pursued Steele, the Texans itching for a fight. Captain Julius Bose of the Third Texas Infantry penned: "The Yankees . . . had strewn the road with new overcoats, jackets, pants, knapsacks, tents, cooking utensils, all of which they had rendered unusable. Near farm houses, feathers had been strewn from quilts they had taken from the occupants, all furniture in homes demolished, clothing even torn off children."[21]

John and Bob Younger refused to relinquish their home to the Union troops and kept vigil at the windows with weapons too large for their small bodies to handle. Jim Younger was trying to find a place where the family could relocate. Bursheba, unnerved by worry for her sons, the pressure of trying to survive and distraught over the loss of her beloved husband, soon became ill. On the day the federals arrived to execute Order #11, Bursheba was bedfast and weak. She pleaded with the authorities but was unsuccessful in saving her property, however the commanding officer allowed them to

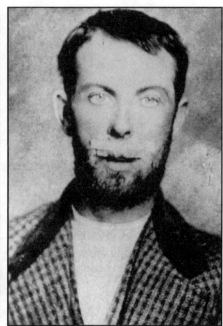

Bob Younger (on left) and brother Jim Younger. (Courtesy of the National Archives)

remain in the home under the condition that they leave in the morning and burn the house and barn themselves. This was agreed to and the following morning, the family loaded Bursheba on a bed in the wagon and commenced with burning their home and dreams. They left to find refuge with relatives.

According to Ex-Minnesota Governor William R. Marshall, Cole Younger was not in Missouri in 1864 and had nothing to do with atrocities committed there. Marshall stated that Cole was at that time a captain in the regular Confederate army in southern Arkansas, Mississippi, and Texas. Marshall was correct in his statements regarding Cole's whereabouts.

Cole later wrote: "For a long time I was accused of the killing of several people at Centralia in September 1864, but I think my worst enemies now concede that it is impossible for me to have been there at the time."[22]

Another accusation that bothered him was that of John McMath, a corporal in an Indiana cavalry company, in Pleasanton's command, who claimed that Cole had mistreated him while he lay wounded on the battlefield near the Big Blue and Cole's home in Jackson County. According to McMath, the incident occurred on October 23, 1863, and while Cole admitted he was still in Missouri on that date, McMath's regiment was not, nor was Pleasanton's command. War records indicate McMath was injured in a fight on the Big Blue on October 23, 1864—a full year later. Cole had, in fact, left Missouri eleven months earlier and was 1,500 miles away when the battle occurred.

Early in 1864, at Bonham, Texas, Cole was ordered by General McCulloch to report to Colonel George S. Jackson in Colorado, and with a detachment of men, cut the international telegraph line extending from Leavenworth, Kansas to San Francisco. After successfully cutting the line, Cole learned that a federal wagon train was moving slowly across Colorado. Cole attacked the wagons but found them empty and the few men escorting the train had fled.[23]

Reaching the Rio Grande, Cole was given special orders to conduct a secret mission for the Confederacy. Letters of marque for two battleships, modeled after the C.S.S. *Alabama*, and built by the British, were to be delivered to Victoria, British Columbia, by a secret service officer named Kennedy. The officer was provided with an escort of twenty men, including Captain John Jarrette and Captain Cole Younger.

Along the way, Cole and his party were attacked by Comanche Indians but the irregulars put up a fight and the Indians retreated back into the desert. The real battle followed soon after when they were engaged in a non-stop, two-day fight with Apache Mojaves. The Confederates killed several Indians with their superior weapons, but, according to Cole, the Apaches unleashed a fierce attack. Not a single irregular was killed, although several of their horses were wounded and they were forced to abandon a wagon.

Cole later penned: "We had a considerable advantage in weapons, but the reds were pestiferous in spite of that, and they kept us busy for fully [thirty-six] hours plugging them at every opportunity. How many Indians we killed I do not know, as we had no time or curiosity to stop and count them. They wounded some of our horses and we had to abandon one wagon, but we did not lose a man."[24]

Starting from El Paso, his next assignment took him into New Mexico where he was to recruit a regiment for the Confederate service. Such a journey was a risky venture with Union troops controlling much of southern Texas. In November 1863, 7,000 soldiers commanded by General Nathaniel Prentiss Banks had landed at the mouth of the Rio Grande and captured

Brownsville, cutting the important trade between Texas and Mexico. Banks then sent one wing of his army upriver to capture Rio Grande City and another column along the coast to capture Corpus Christi, Aransas Pass, and the Matagorda Peninsula. General Jeb Magruder called upon state and Confederate authorities for additional forces to halt the advance. Fortunately for the Confederacy, many of Banks's troops were transferred to Louisiana, where a major Union offensive was planned for the spring of 1864. This allowed Confederate and state troops commanded by John S. Ford to retake most of the area occupied by Union forces. In the summer of 1864 Ford recaptured Brownsville and reopened the vital trade link with Mexico.

When the New Mexico recruiting plan failed, Cole went on to Arizona and was sent into Chihuahua and Sonora, Mexico. This area, including Puerto Peñasco, on Sonora's northwestern Gulf of California coast, was situated in the middle of some of Mexico's most inhospitable territory—hot, arid and desolate. But the devastating heat in the area through which Cole traveled comprised only part of the dangerous challenge. According to an 1857 memoir authored by Sylvester Mowry: "The missions and settlements were repeatedly destroyed by the Apaches, and the priests and settlers massacred or driven off. As often were they re-established. The Indians at length, thoroughly aroused by the cruelties of the Spaniards, by whom they were deprived of their liberty, forced to labor in the silver mines with inadequate food, and barbarously treated, finally rose, joined with tribes who had never been subdued, and gradually drove out or massacred their oppressors."[25]

Lawlessness thrived in this area, luring bandits and persons of low morals, who could rob and pillage without fear of retribution. Wrote Mowry: "We have no remedy but to follow the example so wide spread in the Union, and form a 'Vigilance Committee'—contrary to all good morals, law, order, and society. Can you do nothing to induce the government to establish authority and law in this country, and avert this unhappy alternative?"[26]

Author J. Ross Browne described the area in 1868, only four years after Cole's visit: "A more desolate-looking place than Cocospera [Mission] does not perhaps exist in Sonora. A few Mexican and Indian huts huddled around a ruinous old church, with a ghostly population of Greasers, Yaqui Indians, skeleton dogs, and seedy sheep, is all that attracts the eye of a stranger under the best circumstances. Yet here lives the father-in-law of Pesquiera, Governor of Sonora—a poor old man, with a half-Indian family of children, of whom Pesquiera's wife is one. At the date of our visit the Apaches had just cleaned out the community of nearly all the cattle and sheep it possessed, killed one man, and filled the souls of the remainder with fear and tribulation, so that the place presented a very depressed appearance."[27]

At Guaymas, the party split up, with Captain Jarrette moving up the mainland, while Kennedy, Cole, and three other men took a boat to San Francisco disguised as Mexican miners. Although the voyage took several weeks, the disguised bushwhackers were not detected. From San Francisco, they traveled by stage to Puget Sound where they sailed once more for San Francisco.

When Cole finally reached Victoria, British Columbia, in 1865, he found out that Lee had surrendered his army at Appomattox. And the war was over.[28] Cole remained adamant that while he served in the regular army under General Jo Shelby's Brigade of Sterling Price's army and in the division of General John Sappington Marmaduke, he was never guilty of a cruel or un-soldierly act.

Cole later described the journey: "One of my most interesting wartime experiences was when I went with letters of marque to Victoria, British Columbia, to ship two vessels, the same as the *Alabama*, for the Confederate service. I started from Dallas, Texas, at the head of seventy-five men. We got pack mules and supplies at Fort Worth, issued by Gen. McCullough, then commanding the Northwestern Division of Texas. We crossed into Mexico to dodge the garrison at El Paso. We made our way through Chihauhau into Guaymas, there being only four of us then, and shipped from there to California. When we got there they were planning an outbreak on the federals. We went on to Victoria, delivered our letters of marque, saw the vessels shipped all right, and then hurried back to Sacramento to take a hand in the outbreak. We were just on the eve of the outbreak when we heard of the surrender."[29]

From Victoria, Cole journeyed to San Jose, California, where he visited his father's brother, Coleman Younger. During this visit he heard about to so called Drake Constitution which had just been passed in Missouri. The Drake Constitution stated that all Union soldiers were granted amnesty for any of their acts committed after January 1, 1861. Confederates, however, were to be held responsible for acts done either as soldiers or as citizens. The result of this act was that many Missourians were barred from holding office, voting, attending college, becoming ministers of the gospel or even deacons of the church, or actively participating in business or public life.[30]

Cole had no intention of taking the oath of loyalty and knew that, should he return to Missouri, he would face arrest and possibly a hanging. His mother wrote to him from Jackson County suggesting he stay in northern Missouri with her uncle, Thomas Fristoe, in Howard County. By doing this, Cole's enemies would not be aware of his whereabouts, and he would still be close to home when the family needed him.[31]

"Well, when I went back to my home in Missouri after the war had ended, it was to find that my father had been murdered by a mob out there in Jackson County who wanted his property," recalled Cole many years later. "They tried the same game on me because I had fought for the South. They made several attacks on me to try to kill me, and as a result some of them died. This started me on the downward career. They forced me into fighting and I kept on fighting. . . . After my unfortunate experience with the mobs, I found that I had made for myself a bad name, and it stuck to me. The Drake Constitution which passed during the war was responsible for a lot of this I had to suffer. It disfranchised every man, woman and child who had aided, abetted, or sympathized with the Confederacy."[32]

Cole's adversary, Jim Lane, fared little better. Despite his overwhelming re-election to the Senate in 1865, Lane's political ambitions eventually led to his demise. He supported the Reconstruction policies of Lincoln's successor, Andrew Johnson, in order to maintain his high standing in the eyes of the Executive Office. His constituents sided with the Radical Republican philosophy, and his reputation quickly soured. Physically and mentally exhausted, he committed suicide on a farm near Leavenworth.

Irvin Walley, the man suspected of killing Colonel Henry Younger, returned home to Butler, in Bates County, at the end of the war. He opened the Walley Inn, the first public house in Butler, which also served as a post office and tavern. According to a pension application by his wife in 1894, Walley's death was eventually caused by injuries sustained while serving with the Missouri Home Guards. E.F. Rogers, who had enlisted with Walley, claimed that Walley was injured before January 1862 when he fell from his horse during a battle against bushwhackers. Rogers stated that Walley "was struck in the belly" by the pommel of his saddle, badly "rupturing" him and later died from complications of the prostate and urethra.[33]

"In relation to Walley I will say: if I were what the world paints me, there could be no excuse except cowardice for my neglect to kill him," wrote Cole Younger years later. "During the war I did everything in my power to get hold of him, but failed. . . . When I returned home from the war I could have killed Walley nearly any time but only by assassination. . . . I could not pollute my soul with such a crime."[34]

During the summer of 1864, Jim Younger had joined the bushwhackers, and with Ike Flannery and Warren Welch traveled to Grenton Valley, Missouri, on a mission for George Todd. Linking back up with Todd's band at Pink Hill, they went into camp before moving on to Six Mile Camp where they stayed several days.[35]

After Todd divided his forces, Jim Younger, Ike Flannery, Dick Kinney, and Warren Welch moved on to Waverly where they fought a heated scrimmage with federal infantry. Although Welch's horse was killed, the bushwhackers escaped. After procuring another mount for Welch, Jim Younger's party started in the direction of Miami, Missouri, where they encountered another company of federals. Waiting until nightfall, they started southwest, leaving Marshall to their left, before turning west and reaching Tabo near the Dave Poole farm.

There they found Dave Poole and a company of irregulars encamped and spent a couple days with them. Moving out on their own again, they came upon Davis Creek near the Muir farm. "Old Man Muir," as they referred to him, told them that a company of federals were encamped on the Hutchings farm only two miles away. The Muirs provided them with food, and they returned to camp and reported what they had learned.

Setting out with his company, Jim Younger learned that a squad of federals was moving toward Chapel Hill. The bushwhackers followed their trail, and near the Shore farm, they discovered that the federals had divided into three parties. Jim and his men followed the squad headed toward the old Texas Church and attacked them from a hill above the church.

The federals retreated two miles with the bushwhackers in hot pursuit. Near the Johnson farm on the road leading to the Walton farm, they lost them and went back into camp. At High Grove, they were joined by more of Todd's men, and it was decided to cross the border into Kansas. Near Laynesfield, with several federals in the area, they dressed in blue uniforms and pretended to be Union soldiers hunting for man who had stolen an officer's horse. The federals fell for the ruse as Jim and company moved on to Ottawa and Tauy Creek, before doubling back to Ogletree and the Big Blue where they reported to Pool and Todd.

After Jim's capture and incarceration in an Alton, Illinois, prison, he agreed to take the loyalty oath so he could go home. Jim began searching for his family in Missouri, not knowing for sure of their whereabouts. He felt certain they were still in the state and probably staying with relatives. John and Bob Younger were thirteen and twelve years old at the time of his release from prison and were most likely staying in Independence with their mother's sister, Frances Twyman. The boys wanted to return to the family home in Harrisonville, but Bursheba knew such a move would only bring trouble.[36]

But trouble stalked the Youngers that same year when Caroline Younger Clayton fell ill and died at the age of twenty-three. Caroline left two small children and her husband, former bushwhacker, George Clayton. Bursheba was beside herself with grief but decided she wanted Cole and Bob to return to the family home in Strother, which was then unoccupied. She and the children moved in and prepared the home for the return of her two oldest sons.

Following the death of Quantrill, Frank James and several other bushwhackers assembled under the leadership of Captain Henry Porter, and surrendered to Captain Young of the U.S. Army at Samuel's Depot, Nelson County, Kentucky, on July 25, 1865. With Captain Porter from Quantrill's band were Bill Hulse, John Harris, John Ross, Randall Venable, Dave Hilton, Bud Pence, Allen Parmer, Lee McMurty, Ike Hall, Bob Hall, Payne Jones, Andy McGuire, Jim Lilly, and Frank James. This comprised Frank James' second surrender, the first having been at the Battle of Wilson's Creek. Thus, Frank was in violation of his parole, and had Captain Young been aware of this, Frank would have been shot.[37]

Frank, however, did not return to family and friends back in Missouri because a year earlier he had killed an old man named Alvas Dailey near his home in Clay County. Several persons in the county hated Frank for the murder of their friend, Daily.

Frank remained in Brandensburg, Meade County, Kentucky, an area heavily populated by horse thieves. While Frank was sitting in the hotel office one night, four men entered and demanded his arrest on charges of horse thievery. Frank immediately pulled two revolvers and killed two of the men and wounded a third. The fourth, however, fled after sending a bullet into Frank's hip. Friends came to Frank's aid and carried him off in a carriage.[38]

After the death of George Todd, near Independence, and the retreat of General Price from Missouri, the bushwhackers dispersed; Lieutenant George Shepherd leading a party of twenty-six, which included Jesse James, Matt Wayman, John Maupin, Theodore Castle, Jack Roupe, Silas King, James and Alfred Corum, Bud Story, Perry Smith, Jack Williams, James and Arthur Devers, Press Webb, John Norfolk, James Cummins, William Gregg and his wife, Dick Maddox and his wife, and James Hendrick and his wife. The band started south from Jackson County for Texas, on November 13, 1864.

On November 22, 1864, Shepherd and his veterans were riding southward on Cabin Creek, in the Cherokee Nation where they encountered Captain Emmett Goss of Doc Jennison's old command, riding northward with thirty-two Kansas Jayhawkers. Jesse harbored a special grievance against Goss, who was six feet tall with red hair, and was known as a desperate fighter. When the two commanders lined up and charged each other, Jesse rode directly at Captain Goss. Goss fired at him point blank four times while Jesse struggled to control his horse, which had become unmanageable. Closing in on his enemy, Jesse shot him, and although Goss reeled in his saddle, he held on and refused to surrender. Jesse fired again and killed him. Reverend U.P. Gardner, traveling with the Thirteenth Kansas, attempted to escape, but despite his pleadings that he was a noncombatant, Jesse killed him as well. Of the thirty-two Kansans, twenty-nine were killed and only three escaped.

At Sherman, Texas, Shepherd disbanded his men on December 2nd, and took a part of them into western Texas. Jesse James and seven others remained to take service with Arch Clements and the remainder of Bill Anderson's guerrillas. Clements and his command did not remain in the area long and started on a march back to Missouri.

In the spring of 1865, Jesse and the band of guerrillas returned to Missouri. In Benton County, Jesse and two other bushwhackers captured a militiaman named Harkness and held him while Arch Clements slit his throat. Proceeding to Johnson County, Jesse murdered an old man named Duncan.

With the war over, most of the bushwhackers had surrendered. On March 14, 1865, the guerrillas in Missouri held a conference to talk over a plan of surrender. The Confederate armies everywhere had surrendered

281

with the exception of Shelby's Brigade, which was going into Mexico to espouse the cause of Maximilian. The guerrillas at this conference decided to surrender, with the exception of Clements, Jesse James and a handful of others.

Because all the other guerrillas had turned themselves in, they finally consented and marched into Lexington to surrender to federal authorities at the official surrender station, the Burns School, on April 23, 1865. Jesse rode at the head of the column and bore the white flag of truce. Jesse Hamlett, his longtime friend rode beside him

Following a conference with Major Rodgers, they marched out, Jesse yet in front carrying aloft the white flag, when eight federal soldiers, coming upon them from the rear, fired point blank at them. The guerrillas fought back, killing four of the federals and wounding two. The eight who had charged the guerrillas, were the advance of a body of sixty federals, thirty Johnson County Militia, and thirty from the Second Wisconsin Cavalry.

Jesse Hamlett's horse was shot out from under him. A Wisconsin soldier charged Jesse James, who fired his dragoon pistol; the bullet passed through the soldier's heart. Another Wisconsin trooper charged Jesse, firing as he came. Jesse killed his horse and the soldier sent a pistol ball through Jesse's right lung, his horse falling dead on top of him. Jesse managed to get away, but he was so badly wounded that he hid in the brush.

For three days Jesse lay alone on the banks of Taho Creek, bathing his wound and drinking the water. He had a burning fever from the bullet hole in his lung. At sunset of March 17th, he crawled to a field where a man plowing the field carried him on horseback fifteen miles to the home of a Mr. Bowman. There he was nursed by his inseparable companion Arch Clements, until Poole's surrender on March 21st with 129 guerrillas.

Other accounts state that Jesse reached the Barnett Lankford farm, where he was kept hidden for two days. From there, he rode to another farm near Mt. Hope where he was given medical attention from Dr. A.B. Hereford, a Confederate sympathizer and went on to the Virginia Hotel for additional medical aid. Jesse remained in hiding until he was able to return to the Samuel farm. Although Dr. Samuel administered the best care of which he was capable, Jesse's condition grew worse, and it seemed certain he would die. His lung was badly lacerated and his other wounds did not heal properly.[39]

After several weeks of watching Jesse's condition deteriorate, the family decided to get him away from Missouri before the federals returned looking for him. The Samuel-James family took a steamboat north and settled in Rulo, Nebraska. Rulo, in Richardson County, had served for years as a James-Samuel family retreat. There Zerelda had taught school and her husband attempted to establish a medical practice. Rulo, Nebraska, was close to home and rather safe compared to the Kansas-Missouri border. In addition, Zerelda's Cole cousins, had been among the early settlers crossing into Nemaha County, Nebraska, from Missouri, and Jesse had been named for her brother, Jesse Cole.[40]

Jesse, however, remained seriously ill, and the family decided to take him home to Missouri after eight weeks of rest. Jesse's mother, Zerelda, later recalled the situation: "Jesse was so often near death in the eight weeks he was with me in Nebraska that I would bend over his bed and put my ear to his breast to see if he was breathing or his heart was beating. One day at the end of eight weeks, he drew my face down to him and whispered: 'Ma, I don't want to be buried here in a northern state.' 'My son, you shall not be buried here,' I told him. 'But, ma, I don't want to die here.' 'If you don't wish to you shall not,' I told him and we started the next day. Jesse was so weak and sick that we had him on a sofa and four men carried him to the steamboat landing and put him aboard the boat. He fainted while they were carrying him to the boat, and the people in Rulo tried to dissuade me from moving him. After the steamboat had been going down stream awhile Jesse recovered enough to ask me where he was. I told him that he was on the boat going home. 'Thank the Lord,' he said."[41]

They stopped in Harlem [North Kansas City] and visited Dr. Samuel's sister and Jesse's aunt, Mrs. Mimms, sister of Jesse's father. According to Zerelda, "He was wounded so badly he could not sit up in bed." Jesse remained at Mrs. Mimms' boarding house from late August until late October, nursed by his future wife and cousin, Zerelda "Zee" Mimms. During this period of recuperation, Jesse and Zee became secretly engaged to be married. Jesse was taken back to the family farm and, within a few weeks, was able to walk again.[42]

Unaware of his brother's condition, Frank had remained in Kentucky. He reportedly stayed in the Nelson County area and spent some time with his uncle and aunt George and Nancy James Hite, and his first cousins at Adairville in Logan County, near the Tennessee-Kentucky border.[43]

When he learned that Jesse had been shot and had gone home "to die in the arms of his family," Frank returned to Missouri. Identified as criminals by the federal government, Frank and Jesse, and others like them, felt if they were going to be branded as outlaws, they might as well live the life of the desperado.[44]

Cole Younger never surrendered. His guerrilla friends who did surrender only felt compromised. The promise stated in the terms of the surrender meant little to the men, who believed they were taking the oath of allegiance only because it afforded them the opportunity to remain alive. For most, the war would rage in their hearts for the rest of their lives.[45]

In the fall of 1865, Cole returned to his home in Jackson County to try and pick up the pieces of the ruined family fortune. He was but twenty-one years old. He found that his mother had been driven to take refuge in cabin on one of the family farms. Jim Younger had joined the guerillas after being accused of spying in 1864. His involvement with the guerillas was brief, and he was captured during Quantrill's last battle at Wakefield's house, near Smiley, Kentucky. He remained a prisoner of war in the Alton, Illinois, prison until the end of the war but returned home the same week as Cole. At the time, Cole was twenty-one, Jim seventeen, Bob fourteen, and John twelve.

Less than a year after he had returned to Jackson County, Cole and several others who had ridden with Quantrill at Lawrence, found themselves in trouble with the law. The governor of Kansas was attempting to persuade the governor of Missouri to turn over 300 men listed as participants in the raid.

Several attorneys in Independence offered to defend any Jackson County boys free of charge for any offense except murder if they turned themselves in. Cole later claimed that it was during a trip to assemble some of these men that he met his good friend Frank James' younger brother, Jesse. "Cole didn't like Jesse James and always said he was rough and brutal," recalled Todd M. George.[46]

Mrs. Don Pence, whose husband was a good friend of the James boys was later asked to compare them and concurred with Cole: "Well, my opinion is that Frank is the most shrewd, cunning and capable; in fact, Jess can't compare with him. Frank is a man of education, and can act the refined gentleman on all occasions. Jesse is reckless, and a regular dare-devil in courage, but it's Frank [who] makes all the plans and perfects the methods of escape. Jesse is a fighter and that's all."[47]

Also at this time, a man named Reason K. Judy came looking for Cole whom he claimed had murdered his son in Paola, Kansas. Reason, well known in Cass County, had enlisted in Captain Briggs' Company C, Second Battalion of the Home Guards in February 1862 and participated in the Battle of Lone Jack. Two of Judy's sons, John and James, were also serving in the militia at that time. In October, Reason K. Judy sustained an injury and was released from the army.[48]

During one of Quantrill's raids, one of Judy's sons was killed, for which he blamed Cole. Younger, however, insisted he had been in Austin, Missouri, at the time, relocating wounded gurerrillas, and that all his men knew that the young man was killed by Dick Maddox and Joe Hall. Judy's other son was also killed by Quantrill's men later that year and without Cole's participation. The elder Judy was appointed sheriff of Cass County in March 1863, and he quickly swore out a warrant for Cole's arrest. Cole later related that this action by Judy affected him "so that from 1863 to 1903 I was never in Cass County except as a hunted man."

Cole Younger remained in hiding, oftentimes seeking refuge with the families of his comrades since he was unable to safely return home. Because of the Drake Constitution, men like Cole and Jim Younger and Frank and Jesse James, found it extremely difficult to make money in the state. In discussing their precarious situation, they felt it would be easy to stop travelers passing through the area and relieve them of their money. The more they talked however they realized that much more money could be made by robbing banks and trains.[49]

These men such as the Youngers and Jameses had been caught just budding into manhood at the outbreak of the Civil War and swept into the ranks of bushwhackers and guerrillas. With unformed habits and all of the novelty of enthusiasm and youth, they fell into the hands of older men who educated them in murder and robbery.

In an 1897 interview with a Columbia, Missouri, newspaper, Frank James reminisced about life as a young Confederate guerrilla:

> We usually met hospitable treatment through Missouri, Kentucky, and states farther south. There were enough Southern sympathizers to give us a kind reception, and we had little trouble up to the last days of the war in getting enough food. We lived in the woods, of course; that was our only home. We captured from the federals clothes, horses and

ammunition. We generally carried our coats and overcoats fastened on our saddles. Most of our clothing was the blue uniforms of the Yankees. We wore vests cut low in the front and trimmed with gold lace. Each guerrilla carried two to four pistols. I nearly always carried two. I was small and slender and more than that number would have been too many for me.

At night and when we were in camp we played like school boys. Some of our play was as rough as football. The truth was we were nothing but great big boys, anyhow. . . . If you ever want to pick a company to do desperate work or to lead a forlorn hope, select men from seventeen to twenty-one years old. They will go anywhere you will lead them. When men grow older they grow more cautious, but at that age they area regular daredevils. Take our company, and there has never been a more reckless lot of men, only one or two of them were over twenty-five. Most of them were under twenty-one. Scarcely a dozen boasted a moustache.[50]

The mortality rate of these bands of bushwhackers was frightful, for they neither gave nor received quarter. By the end of the war, most of them had fallen. The others, with very few exceptions, met either violent deaths or went into exile.[51]

"I fought for the south and offered my life on many occasions for my country," explained Frank James years later. "But the North seems to be forgetting the war faster than the South. The war is over, and I thank God for it. I have no bitterness against anyone who wore the blue. The fierce spirit of the rebellion has all died out of my nature, and I am willing to forgive and forget. My son wore the blue in the Spanish-American War, and when he put it on, it looked beautiful and brave. I hated it no longer. For years, I wanted to feel for my pistol when I saw it but I love everybody. Even my old mother eighty years old, has forgiven those who caused her to suffer so deeply in the cruel war."[52]

Quantrill comrade Morgan Mattox once said of Frank. "Ah, he was the fighter for you—never afraid, true always to his comrades, a fine soldier."53

One old rebel, lame from Yankee bullets, later told a reporter that Frank James and Cole Younger were not bad men as they were regarded in the North: "I have a great deal of sympathy for those fellows. They were driven to desperation by bloody war. I was a rebel soldier and can easily see how they drifted into outlawry on the frontier after their loved ones were killed by the federal soldiers."[54]

A Richmond newspaper described Cole and Frank as "two men whose names are two links in the history of the late war." According to the writer, the careers of the two men were marked by a greater number of thrilling adventures than the histories of any other two living men. Deprived of freedom by the fortune of wars, they were hunted for several years by "avengers, detectives, and feudists, who had felt their enmity while the war raged."[55]

In a conversation with another reporter, Frank James said he had no apologies to offer for his past life. "We fought," he said, "simply because we had to fight, in order to live. Our enemies refused to forgive us, and as we asked for no quarter, we gave none."[56]

Of the fury and bitterness of this border warfare between the bushwhackers for the South and the militia for the North, Missourians, and Kansans—neighbors all of them—there can be no conception except with those who were there. The bank and train robbers became the last of the guerrillas. To them, the war had never ended at Appomattox. They came home when peace was declared, and for two years the settlement of old feuds kept the Missouri and Kansas border in constant turmoil and steadily thinned the ranks of the survivors.[57]

Archie J. Clement. (Author's collection)

The hanging of Tom Little at Warrensburg, of Maguire and Devon at Richmond, the shooting of Arch Clements at Lexington on December 13, 1866, of Al Shepherd and Payne Jones in Jackson County, and the murder of Dick Burnes, brought the old Quantrill and Anderson bands nearly down to the number of those robbing the banks and trains. Read was killed in Texas, the McDaniel boys, who were prepared to go wherever others would lead, died full of bullet holes, but never confessing. Jack Kean was sent to a penitentiary in West Virginia. John Younger was killed by Captain Lull near Osceola. Clell Miller and Bill Chadwell died in the streets of Northfield. Charlie Pitts, known as Sam Wells all along the border, was killed in a shootout near LaSalle, Minnesota, and Bob, Jim, and Cole Younger went to Stillwater Prison.

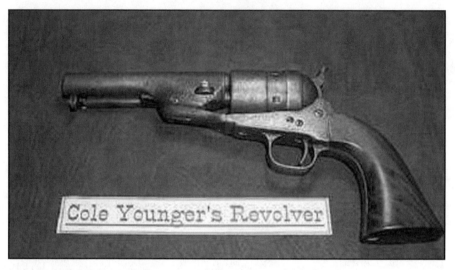

Colt revolver Model 1860 Army, Richards conversion, .44 caliber centerfire.

Although Cole would struggle through twenty-five years in the penitentiary, to John Newman Edwards, his image was never tarnished:

> The character of this man to many has been a curious study, but to those who knew him well there is nothing about it of mystery or many sideness. An awful provocation drove him into Quantrill's band. He was never a bloodthirsty or a merciless man. He was brave to recklessness, desperate to rashness, remarkable for terrible prowess in battle; but he was never known to kill a prisoner. On the contrary there are alive today fully two hundred federal soldiers who owe their lives to Cole Younger, a man whose father had been brutally murdered, whose mother had been hounded to her death, whose family had been made to endure the torment of a ferocious persecution, and whose kith and kin, oven to most -emote degrees were plundered and imprisoned. At Lawrence he was known to have saved a score of lives; in twenty other desperate combats he took prisoners and released them; when the steamer *Sam Gaty* was captured, he stood there a protecting presence between the would-be slayers and their victims; at Independence he saved more lives; and in Louisiana probably fifty federals escaped certain death through Younger's firmness and generosity. His brother James did not go into the war until 1864, and was grave, dauntless, high-spirited boy who never killed a soldier in his life save in fair and open battle.

Cole was a fair-haired, amiable, generous man, devoted in his friendships, and true to his word and comradeship. In intrepidity he was never surpassed. In battle he never had those to go where he would not follow, aye, where he would not gladly lead. On his body to-day there are scars of thirty wounds. He was a guerrilla, and a giant among a band of guerrilla, but he was one among three hundred who only killed in open and honorable battle. As great as had been his provocation, he never murdered; as brutal as had been the treatment of every one near and dear to him, he refused always to take vengeance on those who were innocent of the wrongs, and who had taken no part in the deeds which drove him, a boy, into the ranks of the guerrillas, but he fought as a soldier who fights for a cause, a creed, an idea, or for glory. He was a hero and he was merciful.[58]

Lee's Summit Cemetery. (Photo by Frank Younger)

Notes

[1]*Chillicothe Daily Democrat*, November 19, 21, 22, 1904.

[2]William A. Settle, Jr., *Jesse James Was His Name*, p. 26.

[3]William N. Gregg letter to George M. Bennett dated April 9, 1898. Northfield, Minnesota, Bank Robbery of 1876. Selected Manuscripts Collections and Government Records, Microfilm Edition, Roll 4, Minnesota Historical Society.

[4]Terrell Transcript, April 26, 1907; Carl W. Breihan, *Younger Brothers Cole, James, Bob, John*, pp. 54- 55.

[5]E.G. Bower letter to George M. Bennett dated April 25, 1898. Northfield, Minnesota, Bank Robbery of 1876. Selected Manuscripts Collections and Government Records, Microfilm Edition, Roll 4, Minnesota Historical Society.

[6]Allen Coleman Ashcraft, Texas, 1860-1866: The Lone Star State in the Civil War (Ph.D. dissertation, Columbia University, 1960); Alwyn Barr, "Texas Coastal Defense, 1861-1865," *Southwestern Historical Quarterly* 65, July 1961; Walter L. Buenger, *Secession and the Union in Texas*, Austin: University of Texas Press, 1984; Vera Lea Dugas, A *Social and Economic History of Texas in the Civil War and Reconstruction Periods* (Ph.D. dissertation, University of Texas, 1963); Robert Pattison Felgar, *Texas in the War for Southern Independence, 1861-1865* (Ph.D. dissertation, University of Texas, 1935); Fredericka Meiners, *The Texas Governorship, 1861-1865: Biography of an Office* (Ph.D. dissertation, Rice University, 1974); Stephen B. Oates, "Texas under the Secessionists," *Southwestern Historical Quarterly* 67, October 1963; David Paul Smith, *Frontier Defense in the Civil War: Texas' Rangers and Rebels*, College Station, Texas A&M University Press, 1992; Ralph A. and Robert Wooster, "'Rarin' for a Fight: Texans in the Confederate Army," *Southwestern Historical Quarterly* 84, April 1981.

[7]Margaret Donsbach, "The Third Texas Itch," *Civil War Times*, February 2003, p. 51.

[8]Gary D. Joiner, "Up the Red River and Down to Defeat," *America's Civil War*, March 2004, p. 22.

[9]Allen Coleman Ashcraft, *Texas, 1860-1866: The Lone Star State in the Civil War* (Ph.D. dissertation, Columbia University, 1960); Alwyn Barr, "Texas Coastal Defense, 1861-1865," *Southwestern Historical Quarterly* 65, July 1961; Walter L. Buenger, *Secession and the Union in Texas*, Austin: University of Texas Press, 1984; Vera Lea Dugas, A *Social and Economic History of Texas in the Civil War and Reconstruction Periods* (Ph.D. dissertation, University of Texas, 1963); Robert Pattison Felgar, *Texas in the War for Southern Independence, 1861-1865* (Ph.D. dissertation, University of Texas, 1935); Fredericka Meiners, *The Texas Governorship, 1861-1865: Biography of an Office* (Ph.D. dissertation, Rice University, 1974); Stephen B. Oates, "Texas under the Secessionists," *Southwestern Historical Quarterly* 67, October 1963; David Paul Smith, *Frontier Defense in the Civil War: Texas' Rangers and Rebels*, College Station, Texas A&M University Press, 1992;

Ralph A. and Robert Wooster, "'Rarin' for a Fight: Texans in the Confederate Army," *Southwestern Historical Quarterly* 84, April 1981.

[10]Cole Younger, *The Story of Cole Younger by Himself*, p. 45.

[11]Patricia L. Faust, editor, *Historical Times Illustrated Encyclopedia of the Civil War*, New York, Harper & Row Publishers, 1986, p. 808.

[12]Macmillan Information Now Encyclopedia, "The Confederacy," article by Kenny A. Franks.

[13]Phillip W. Steele and Steve Cottrell, *Civil War in the Ozarks*, pp. 87-88.

[14]Report of Colonel A. Watson Webber, *Fifty-first U.S. Colored Infantry*, August 26, 1864. *The War of the Rebellion. A Compilation of the Official Records of the Union and Confederate Armies*, Series I, Volume 41, P. 295.

[15]Homer Croy, *Cole Younger Last of the Great Gunfighters*, Lincoln, University of Nebraska Press, 1956, pp.38-40.

[16]Cole Younger, *The Story of Cole Younger by Himself*, pp. 45-46.

[17]Ibid.

[18]Major General Stephen A. Hurlbut letter to Major General U.S. Grant dated August I, 1863. *The War of the Rebellion: A Compilation of the Official Records of the Union and Confederate Armies*, Series I, Volume XXXIV, page 424.

[19]Cole Younger, *The Story of Cole Younger by Himself*, pp. 30-31.

[20]Ibid., p. 47.

[21]Margaret Donsbach, "The Third Texas Itch," *Civil War Times*, February 2003, pp. 52-53.

[22]Cole Younger, *The Story of Cole Younger by Himself*, pp. 47-48.

[23]Homer Croy, Cole Younger Last of the Great Gunfighters, pp. 38-40.

[24]Cole Younger, *The Story of Cole Younger by Himself*, p. 48.

[25]Sylvester Mowry, U.S.A. Delegate Elect, *Memoir of the Proposed Territory of Arizona*, Washington, Henry Polkinhom, Printer, 1857.

[26]Ibid.

[27]J. Ross Browne, *Adventures in the Apache Country: A Tour Through Arizona and Sonora, with Notes on the Silver Region of Nevada*, New York: Harper & Brothers, 1868.

[28]*St. Paul & Minneapolis Pioneer Press*, Monday, July 26, 1886.

[29]Ibid.

[30]*Lee's Summit Journal*, July I, 1981; Ronald H. Beights, *Jesse James and the First Missouri Train Robbery*, Gretna, Louisiana, Pelican Publishing Company, 2002, pp. 17-18.

[31]Marley Brant, *Outlaws: The Illustrated History of the James-Younger Gang*, p. 43.

[32]*St. Paul & Minneapolis Pioneer Press*, Monday, July 26, 1886.

33 Marley Brant, *The Outlaw Youngers: A Confederate Brotherhood*, pp. 32-33.

[34]Ibid., p. 31.

[35]Joanne Chiles Eakin, *Warren Welch Remembers, A Guerrilla Fighter from Jacks-on County, Missouri*, Independence, privately printed, 1997, pp. 20-22.

[36]Marley Brant, *Outlaws: The Illustrated History of the James-Younger Gang*, pp. 43-44.
[37]Carl W. Breihan, *The Complete and Authentic Life of Jesse James*, New York, Frederick Fell, Inc., Publishers, 1953, pp. 87-88.
[38]*Good Bye, Jesse James*, pp. 37-38.
[39]George Turner, *Secrets of Jesse James*, pp. 11-12; Marley Brant, *Jesse James: The Man and the Myth*, p. 40.
[40]Emmett C. Hoctor, "Rusticating in Nebraska: 1862-1882," speech presentation to the Friends of the James Farm annual meeting, April 11, 1992, Kansas City, Missouri; "Factoryville, A Nebraska Ghost Town," *Journal of Nebraska History*, Vol. XIV, No. 4, p. 259.
[41]*Boonville Weekly Advertiser*, November 16, 1900.
[42]*Kansas City Daily Journal*, April 4, 1882.
[43]Ted P. Yeatman, *Frank and Jesse James: The Story Behind the Legend*; p. 84.
[44]L.R. Kirchner, *Robbing Banks: An American History 1831-1999*, Rockville Centre, New York, Sarpedon, 2000, p. 14.
[45]Marley Brant, *Jesse James: The Man and the Myth*, p. 41.
[46]Todd M. George letter to Owen Dickie dated September 17, 1969. Le Sueur county Historical Society, Elysian, Minnesota.
[47]*Good Bye, Jesse James*, p. 24.
[48]Marley Brant, *The Outlaw Youngers" A Confederate Brotherhood*, pp. 40-41.
[49]*Lee's Summit Journal*, July 1,1981; Shane Edwards, *Heroes and Outlaws of the Old West*, Santa Monica, Santa Monica Press, 1993, pp. 1127-128.
[50]Martin Edward McGrane, *The Home of Jesse and Frank James*, The James Farm, Kearney, Missouri, pp. 25-26.
[51]*Lee's Summit Journal*, July 1,1981.
[52]*Knoxville Journal*, June 15, 1903.
[53]*Kansas City Star*, Sunday, February 22, 1915.
[54]Ibid.
[55]*Richmond The Times-Dispatch*, June 30, 1903.
[56]Ibid.
[57]*Lee's Summit Journal*, July I, 1981.
[58]John Newman Edwards, *Noted Guerrillas, or the Warfare of the Border*.

Bibliography

BOOKS

Appler, Augustus C., *The Guerrillas of the West, or the Life, Character and Daring Exploits of the Younger Brothers*, St. Louis, Eureka Publishing Company, 1876.

Appler, A.C., *The Younger Brothers: The Life, Character and Daring Exploits of the Youngers, the Notorious Bandits Who Rode with Jesse James and William Clarke Quantrill*, New York, Frederick Fell, Inc., Publishers, 1955.

Arnold, Anna E., *A History of Kansas*, Topeka, The State of Kansas, 1915.

Beights, Ronald H., *Jesse James and the First Missouri Train Robbery*, Gretna, Louisiana, Pelican Publishing Company, 2002.

Blackmar. Frank W., editor, *Kansas: A Cyclopedia of State History, Embracing Events, Institutions, Industries ,Counties, Cities, Towns, Prominent Persons, etc. . . . with a Supplementary Volume Devoted to Selected Personal History and Reminiscence*, Volume II, Chicago, Standard Publishing Company, 1912.

Boyer, Richard O., *The Legend of John Brown*, New York, Alfred A. Knopf, 1973.

Brant, Marley, *Jesse James: The Man and the Myth*, New York, Berkley Books, 1998.

Brant, Marley, *Outlaws: The Illustrated History of the James-Younger Gang*, Montgomery, Alabama, Elliott & Clark Publishing, 1997.

Brant, Marley, *The Outlaw Youngers: A Confederate Brotherhood*, Lanham, New York, London, Madison Books, 1995.

Breihan. Carl W., *The Complete and Authentic Life of Jesse James*, New York, Frederick Fell, Inc., Publishers, 1953.

Breihan, Carl W., *The Day Jesse James Was Killed*, New York, Bonanza Books, 1962.

Breihan, Carl W., *Outlaws of the Old West*, New York, Bonanza Books, 1957.

Breihan, Carl W., *Quantrill and his Civil War Guerrillas*, New York, Promontory Press, 1959.

Breihan, Carl W., *Younger Brothers, Cole, James, Bob, John*, San Antonio, The Naylor Company, 1972.

Bronaugh, W.C., *Youngers' Fight for Freedom*, Columbia, Missouri, E.W. Stephens Publishing Company, 1906.

Broughton, J.S., *The Lawrence Massacre by a Band of Missouri Ruffians Under Quantrell, August 21, 1863*, Lawrence, J.S. Broughton Publisher, 1865.

Browne, J. Ross, *Adventures in the Apache Country: A Tour Through Arizona and Sonora, with Notes on the Silver Region of Nevada*, York: Harper & Brothers, 1868.

Buel, J.W., *The Border Outlaws: An Authentic and Thrilling History of the Most Noted Bandits of Ancient or Modern Times, The Younger Brothers, Jesse and Frank James, and Their Comrades in Crime*, Syracuse, Alvord & Sleight, 1883.

Buenger, Walter L., *Secession and the Union in Texas*, Austin: University of Texas Press, 1984.

Cantrell, Dallas, *Northfield, Minnesota: Youngers' Fatal Blunder*, San Antonio, Naylor Company, 1973.

Carter, Arthur B., *The Tarnished Cavalier Major General Earl Van Dorn, C.S.A.*, Knoxville, University of Tennessee Press, 1999.

Castel, Albert, *A Frontier State at War: Kansas, 1861-1865*, Cornell UP, 1958.

Castel, Albert, *General Sterling Price and the Civil War in the West*, Baton Rouge & London, Louisiana State University Press, 1968.

Connelley, William Elsey, *Quantrill and the Border Wars*, 1910. Reprint New York, Pageant Book Company, 1956.

Cordley, D.D., Richard, *A History of Lawrence, Kansas from the Earliest Settlement to the Close of the Rebellion*. Lawrence, Kansas, E.F. Caldwell, Lawrence Journal Press, 1895.

Croy, Homer, *Cole Younger Last of the Great Outlaws*, Lincoln, University of Nebraska Press, 1999 (reprint edition).

Croy, Homer, *Jesse James Was My Neighbor*, New York, Duell, Sloane & Pearce, 1949.

Cutler, William G., *History of the State of Kansas*, Chicago, 1883, by A.T. Andreas, 1883.

Dary, David, *Lawrence, Douglas County, Kansas: An Informal History*, Lawrence, Allen Books, 1982.

Davis, William C., *The Cause Lost Myths and Realities of the Confederacy*, Lawrence, University Press of Kansas, 1996.

Donald, David, *Lincoln*. New York: Simon and Schuster, 1995.

Drago, Harry Sinclair, *Outlaws on Horseback*, Lincoln & London, University of Nebraska Press, 1998.

Dyer, Robert L., *Jesse James and the Civil War in Missouri*, Columbia & London, University of Missouri Press, 1994.

Eakin, Joanne Chiles, *Warren Welch Remembers: A Guerrilla Fighter from Jackson County, Missouri*, Independence, privately printed, 1997.

Edel, Philippe Charles, *History of Strassburg*, Alsace, France, North Dakota State University, The Libraries, Germans from Russia Heritage Collection, September 1975.

Edwards, John Newman, *Noted Guerrillas, or the Warfare of the Border*, 1877.

Edwards, Shane, *Heroes and Outlaws of the Old West*, Santa Monica, Santa Monica Press, 1993.

Faust, Patricia L., editor, *Historical Times Illustrated Encyclopedia of the Civil War*, New York, Harper & Row Publishers, 1986.

Foner, Eric, *Free Soil, Free Labor, Free Men: The Ideology of the Republican Party Before the Civil War*, New York: Oxford University Press, 1970.

Foote, Shelby, *The Civil War: A Narrative, Fredericksburg to Meridian, Volume II*, New York, Random House, 1963.

Foote, Shelby, *The Civil War: A Narrative Red River to Appomattox*, New York, Random House, 1974.

Fried, Albert, *John Brown's Journey Notes & Reflections of His America & Mine*, Garden City, Anchor Press/Doubleday, 1978.

Gardner, Virginia Armstrong Johnson, *Where the Trails Divide*, Gardner, Kansas, Gardner News, 1957.

George, Todd M., *The Conversion of Cole Younger: The Early Day Bandit Becomes a Christian Citizen*, Kansas City, The Lowell Press, 1963.

Gienapp, William E., *The Origins of the Republican Party, 1852-1856*, New York, 1987.

Good Bye, Jesse James, Liberty, Jesse James Bank Museum, 1967.

Goodrich, Thomas, *Black Flag Guerrilla Warfare on the Western Border, 1861-1865*, Bloomington and Indianapolis, University of Indiana Press, 1995.

Hale, Donald R., *We Rode with Quantrill*, Independence, Blue & Grey Book Shoppe, 1998.

History of Clay and Platte Counties, Missouri, St. Louis, National Historical Company, 1885.

The History of Henry and St. Clair Counties, Missouri, St. Joseph, Missouri, National Historical Company, 1883.

History of Missouri, 1884, Internet.

Horan, James D., *Desperate Men Revelations from the Sealed Pinkerton Files*, New York, G.P. Putnam's Sons, 1949.

James, Jr., Jesse, *Jesse James, My Father*, Cleveland, Arthur Westbrook Company, 1899.

Johannsen, Robert W., *Stephen A. Douglas*, New York: Oxford University Press, 1973.

Johnston, Colonel William Preston, *The Life of General Albert Sidney Johnston*, New York, Da Capo Press, 1997 reprint of 1879 original.

Josephy, Alvin M., *The Civil War in the American West*, New York, Alfred A. Knopf, 1991.

Kirchner, L.R., *Robbing Banks: An American History 1831-1999*, Rockville Centre, New York, Sarpedon, 2000.

Leslie, Edward E., *The Devil Knows How to Ride: The True Story of William Clarke Quantrill and His Confederate Raiders*, New York, Random House, 1996.

Lincoln, Abraham, *Abraham Lincoln: Speeches and Writings, 1832-1858*. Edited by Don E. Fehrenbacher, New York: Literary Classics of the United States, Inc., 1989.

Litwack, Leon, *North of Slavery: The Negro in the Free States*. Chicago: 1961.

Love, Robertus, *The Rise and Fall of Jesse James*, Lincoln, University of Nebraska Press, 1990.

Macmillan Information Now Encyclopedia.

McCorkle, John, *Three Years with Quantrell [sic]*, Armstrong, Missouri, Armstrong Herald Printing, 1914.

McGrane, Martin Edward, *The Home of Jesse and Frank James . . . The James Farm, Kearney, Missouri, Madison, South Dakota*, The Caleb Perkins Press, 1982.

Mowry, Sylvester, *U.S.A. Delegate Elect: Memoir of the Proposed Territory of Arizona*, Washington, Henry Polkinhorn, Printer, 1857.

Nagel, Paul C. Nagel, *Missouri: A History*, Lawrence, University of Kansas Press, 1977.

Neely, Mark E., *The Abraham Lincoln Encyclopedia*. New York, McGraw-Hill, 1982.

Oliva, Leo E., *Fort Scott Courage and Conflict on the Border*, Topeka, Kansas State Historical Society, 1996.

Ray, P.O., *The Repeal of the Missouri Compromise* (1909, reprinted 1965).

Robinson, Sara T.L., *Kansas: Its Exterior and Interior Life*, 1856.

Robley, T.F., *Robley's History of Bourbon County*, 1894.

Scott, John Anthony and Scott, Robert Alan, *John Brown of Harper's Ferry*, New York, Facts on File, 1988.

Settle, Dr. William A., *Cole Younger Writes to Lizzie Daniel*, Liberty, James-Younger Gang, 1994.

Settle, Jr., William A., *Jesse James Was His Name*, Lincoln, University of Nebraska Press, 1966.

Smith, David Paul, *Frontier Defense in the Civil War: Texas' Rangers and Rebels*, College Station, Texas A&M University Press, 1992.

Smith, Robert Barr, *The Last Hurrah of the James-Younger Gang*, Norman, University of Oklahoma Press, 2001.

Steele, Phillip W., *Jesse and Frank James: The Family History*, Gretna, Louisiana, Pelican Publishing Company, 1987.

Steele, Phillip W. and Cottrell, Steve, *Civil War in the Ozarks*, Gretna, Louisiana, Pelican Publishing Company, 2000.

Steele, Phillip W., with Warfel, George, *The Many Faces of Jesse James*, Gretna, Louisiana, Pelican Publishing Company, 1995.

Stiles, T.J., *Jesse James: Last Rebel of the Civil War*, New York, Alfred A. Knopf, 2002.

Triplett, Frank, *The Life, Times & Treacherous Death of Jesse James*, New York, The Swallow Press, Inc., 1970.

Turner, George, *Secrets of Jesse James*, Amarillo, Baxter Lane Company, 1975.

Ventimiglia, Jack "Miles," *Jesse James in the County of Clay*, Kearney, Friends of the James Farm, 2001.

Ward, William, *The Younger Brothers: The Border Outlaws: The Only Authentic History of the Exploits of These Desperadoes of the West*, Cleveland, Arthur Westbrook Company, 1908.

Watts, Hampton, *The Babe of the Company: An Unfolded Leaf from the Forest of Never-To-Be-Forgotten Years*, reprinted by the Democrat-Leader Press of Fayette, Missouri, 1913.

Webb, W.L., *Battles and Biographies of Missourians or the Civil War Period of Our States*, Kansas City, Missouri, Hudson-Kimberly Publishing Company, 1900.

Willis, James, *Arkansas Confederates in the Western Theater*, Dayton, Morningside Press, 1998.

Yeatman, Ted P., *Frank and Jesse James: The Story Behind the Legend*, Nashville, Cumberland House, 2000.

Younger, Cole (edited by Marley Brant), *The Story of Cole Younger by Himself*, St. Paul, Minnesota Historical Society Press, 2000.

MAGAZINES, PAMPHLETS

Allmon, William B., "Sneak Attack at Lone Jack," *Civil War Times Illustrated*, April 1996.

Avery, C.E. Avery and Stolper, Darryl, "Confederate Images," *Confederate Veteran*, Volume I, 1999.

Barr, Alwyn, "Texas Coastal Defense, 1861-1865," *Southwestern Historical Quarterly* 65, July 1961.

Breihan, Carl W., "The Day Quantrill Burned Lawrence," *The West*, January 1972.

Breihan, Carl W., "Outlaw George Shepherd," *Pioneer West*, March 1978, Number 2.

Cozzens, Peter, "Hindman's Grand Delusion," *Civil War Times Illustrated*, October 2000.

Donsbach, Margaret, "The Third Texas Itch," *Civil War Times*, February 2003.

"Factoryville, A Nebraska Ghost Town," *Journal of Nebraska History*, Vol. XIV.

Franks, Kenny A., "The Confederacy", *Macmillan Information Now Encyclopedia*.

Gates-Hull, Sharon, "Not Just Cowboys Women—Wives, Daughters—Played Roles in the Saga of Jesse James," *Northfield News*, Souvenir Edition, Friday, September 11, 1998.

Gilles, Albert S., "Jesse, Frank and Cole," *Frontier Times*, September 1969.

Hinze, David and Farnham, Karen, "Dry Fork Creek," *Confederate Veteran*, Volume I, 1999.

Hosier, Scott, "'Jo' Shelby Goes Home to Missouri," *America's Civil War*, January 2003.

Huntley, A., "Cole Younger," *Famous Outlaws of the West*, Fall 1964.

Joiner, Gary D., "Up the Red River and Down to Defeat," *America's Civil War*, March 2004.

Kerrihard, Bo, "Bitter Bushwhackers and Jayhawkers," *America's Civil War*, January 1993.

Kirkwood, Eric Uriel, "The First Kansas Colored Infantry Regiment." Internet.

McInnes, Elmer D., "The Terrible McWaters," *True West Magazine*.

Monroe, Ph.D., R.D., "The Kansas-Nebraska Act and the Rise of the Republican Party, 1854-1856," Internet.

Oates, Stephen B., "Texas under the Secessionists," *Southwestern Historical Quarterly* 67, October 1963.

Owens, Richard H., "Battle of Pea Ridge Deciding the Fate of Missouri," *America's Civil War*, January 2000.

Page, Dave, "A Fight for Missouri," *Civil War Times Illustrated*, August 1995.

Patrick, Jeffrey L., "The Travels of a Fallen General Brig. Gen. Nathaniel Lyon, USA," *Blue and Gray*, Volume XVII, Issue 2, January 2000.

Rutherford, Phillip, "The Carthaginian Wars," *Civil War Times Illustrated*, February 1987.

Sallee, Scott E., "Porter's Campaign in Northeast Missouri, 1862, Including the Palmyra Massacre," *Blue and Gray*, Winter 2000.

Sanders, Stuart W., "Bloody Bill's Centralia Massacre," *America's Civil War*, March 2000.

Sanders, Stuart W., "Quantrill's Last Ride," *America's Civil War*, March 1999.

Sears, William Henry, "The Paul Reveres of Lawrence," *Collections of the Kansas State Historical Society*, Topeka, State Printer, 1928, Volume XVII.

Shouse, Thomas Riley, "My Father Planned the James' Boys Capture," *Frontier Times*, Summer 1959.

Stottelmire, Marvin, "John Brown: Madman or Martyr?" *Brown Quarterly*, Volume 3, No. 3, Winter 2000, Black History Month Issue.

Street, Julian, "The Borderland," *Collier's*, September 14, 1914.

"War on the Border," Missouri Department of Natural Resources brochure.

Wilson, George T., "Battle for Missouri," *America's Civil War*, January 1990.

Wood, Larry, "They Rode With Quantrill," *America's Civil War*, November 1996.

Wooster, Ralph A. and Robert, "'Rarin' for a Fight: Texans in the Confederate Army," *Southwestern Historical Quarterly*, 84, April 1981.

Manuscripts, Letters, Reports

A.R. Banks letter to Colonel C.W. Marsh, Assistant Adjutant General of the Missouri, dated August 21, 1863. *The War of the Rebellion: A Compilation of the Official Records of the Union and Confederate Armies*, Series I, Chapter XXXIV.

Report of Major Charles Banzhaf, First Missouri Cavalry, April 5, 1862. The War of the Rebellion: A Compilation of the Official Records of the Union and Confederate Armies, Series I, Volume VIII.

Report of Brigadier General James G. Blunt, U.S. Army. August 26, 1862. The War of the Rebellion: A Compilation of the Official Records of the Union and Confederate Armies, Series I, Volume XXV.

E.G. Bower letter to George M. Bennett dated April 25, 1898. Northfield, Minnesota Bank Robbery of 1876. Selected Manuscripts Collections and Government Records, Microfilm Edition, Roll 4, Minnesota Historical Society.

Report of Captain Milton H. Brawner, Seventh Missouri Cavalry, August 20, 1862. *The War of the Rebellion: A Compilation of the Official Records of the Union and Confederate Armies*, Series I, Volume XXV.

Report of Lieutenant Colonel E.B. Brown, Seventh Missouri Infantry, April 16, 1862. *The War of the Rebellion: A Compilation of the Official Records of the Union and Confederate Armies*, Series I, Volume XIII.

Lieutenant Colonel James T. Buel, June 12, 1862. *The War of the Rebellion: A Compilation of the Official Records of the Union and Confederate Armies*, Series I, Volume XIII.

Governor Thomas Carney letter to Major General J.M. Schofield dated September 3, 1863. *The War of the Rebellion: A Compilation of the Official Records of the Union and Confederate Armies*, Series I, Volume XXXIV.

Report of Lieutenant Colonel Charles S. Clark, Ninth Kansas Cavalry. August 30, 1863. *The War of the Rebellion: A Compilation of the Official Records of the Union and Confederate Armies*, Series I, Chapter XXXIX.

Report of Captain J.F. Cochran, Second Battalion Missouri Cavalry, June 11, 1862. *The War of the Rebellion: A Compilation of the Official Records of the Union and Confederate Armies*, Series I, Volume XIII.

Report of Captain Charles F. Coleman, Ninth Kansas Cavalry, August 30, 1863. *The War of the Rebellion: A Compilation of the Official Records of the Union and Confederate Armies*, Series I, Chapter XXXIV.

Confederate Lieutenant Madison Creasey 1861 letter.

Report of Captain Daniel H. David, Fifth Missouri Cavalry (Militia), October 8, 1862. *The War of the Rebellion: A Compilation of the Official Records of the Union and Confederate Armies*, Series I, Volume XXV.

Report of Lieutenant-Colonel Dan M. Draper, September 25, 1864. *The War of the Rebellion: A Compilation of the Official Records of the Union and Confederate Armies*, Series I, Volume 41.

S.B. Elkins letter to David M. Clough dated June 6, 1898. Northfield, Minnesota Bank Robbery of 1876. Selected Manuscripts Collections and Government Record, Microfilm Edition, Roll 3, Minnesota Historical Society.

S.B. Elkins letter to Charles M. Start dated July 4, 1898. Northfield, Minnesota Bank Robbery of 1876. Selected Manuscripts Collections and Government Records, Microfilm Edition, Roll 4, Minnesota Historical Society.

Report of Brigadier-General Thomas Ewing, Jr., August 31, 1862. *The War of the Rebellion: A Compilation of the Official Records of the Union and Confederate Armies*, Series I, Chapter XXXIV.

Report of Brigadier-General Clinton B. Fisk, September 27, 1864. *The War of the Rebellion: A Compilation of the Official Records of the Union and Confederate Armies*, Series I, Volume 41.

Emory S. Foster letter to George M. Bennett dated May 7, 1898. Northfield, Minnesota Bank Robbery of 1876. Selected Manuscripts Collections and Government Records, Microfilm Edition, Roll 4, Minnesota Historical Society.

Report of Major Emory S. Foster, Seventh Missouri Cavalry (Militia), March 1, 1863. *The War of the Rebellion: A Compilation of the Official Records of the Union and Confederate Armies*, Series I, Volume XXV.

Todd M. George letter to Owen Dickie dated February 27, 1968, Le Sueur County Historical Society, Elysian, Minnesota.

Report of Major James O. Gower, First Iowa Cavalry, July 13, 1862. *The War of the Rebellion: A Compilation of the Official Records of the Union and Confederate Armies*, Series I, Volume XIII.

Report of Colonel Robert H. Graham, Eighth Kansas Infantry, March 19, 1862. *The War of the Rebellion: A Compilation of the Official Records of the Union and Confederate Armies*, Series I, Volume VIII.

William Gregg letter to George M. Bennett dated April 9, 1898. Northfield, Minnesota Bank Robbery of 1876. Selected Manuscripts Collections and Government Records, Microfilm Edition, Roll 4, Minnesota Historical Society.

Dr. Thomas Hamill letter to Major General Samuel R. Curtis dated November 6, 1862. *The War of the Rebellion: A Compilation of the Official Records of the Union and Confederate Armies,* Series I, Volume Chapter XXV.

Report of Major Benjamin S. Henning, Third Wisconsin Cavalry, November 11, 1862. *The War of the Rebellion: A Compilation of the Official Records of the Union and Confederate Armies*, Series I, Volume I, Chapter XXV.

Major General T.C. Hindman Official Report. *The War of the Rebellion: A Compilation of the Official Records of the Union and Confederate Armies*, Series I, Volume XIII.

Major General Stephen A. Hurlbut letter to Major General U.S. Grant dated August 1, 1863. *The War of the Rebellion: A Compilation of the Official Records of the Union and Confederate Armies*, Series I, Volume XXXIV.

Reports of Colonel Daniel Huston, Jr., Seventh Missouri Cavalry, June 15, 1862. *The War of the Rebellion: A Compilation of the Official Records of the Union and Confederate Armies*, Series I, Volume XIII.

Report of Daniel Huston, Jr., August 12, 1862. *The War of the Rebellion: A Compilation of the Official Records of the Union and Confederate Armies*, Series I, Chapter XXV.

H.P. Hynes letter to Governor Merriam dated June 24, 1889. Northfield, Minnesota Bank Robbery of 1876. Selected Manuscripts Collections and Government Records, Microfilm Edition, Roll 3, Minnesota Historical Society.

Report of Captain John B. Kaiser, Booneville Battalion Missouri cavalry Militia, April 1, 1862. *The War of the Rebellion: A Compilation of the Official Records of the Union and Confederate Armies*, Series I, Volume VIII.

Report of Lieutenant Colonel Bazel F. Lazear, First Missouri State Militia Cavalry, August 27, 1863. *The War of the Rebellion: A Compilation of the Official Records of the Union and Confederate Armies*, Series I, Chapter XXXIV.

Report of Captain Joseph H. Little, First Missouri Cavalry (Militia), October 27, 1862. *The War of the Rebellion: A Compilation of the Official Records of the Union and Confederate Armies*, Series I, Volume XXV.

Report of Brig. Gen. Nathaniel Lyon, U.S. Army, commanding Army of the West, of operations August 5-9, AUGUST 10, 1861.—Battle of Oak Hills, Springfield, or Wilson's Creek, Missouri. *Official Records of the Rebellion*. Series 1, Volume 3.

Letter of Governor William R. Marshall of Minnesota published in the *St. Paul Pioneer Press* of July 26, 1886.

Report of Captain William A. Martin, Seventh Missouri Cavalry. *The War of the Rebellion: A Compilation of the Official Records of the Union and Confederate Armies*, Series I, Volume XII.

Reports of Brig. Gen. Ben. McCulloch, C.S. Army, with orders and proclamation, AUGUST 4, 1861.—Battle of Oak Hills, Springfield, or Wilson's Creek, Missouri, *Official Records of the Rebellion*, Series 1, Volume 3 [S#3].

Report of Brig. Gen. Ben. McCulloch, C.S. Army to L.P. Walker, AUGUST 10, 1861.—Battle of Oak Hills, Springfield, or Wilson's Creek, Missouri, *Official Records of the Rebellion*, Series 1, Volume 3 [S#3].

Report of Brig. Gen. Ben. McCulloch, C.S. Army to Adjutant General S. Cooper, AUGUST 12, 1861.—Battle of Oak Hills, Springfield, *Official Records of the Rebellion*, Series 1, Volume 3 [S#3].

Brig. Gen. Ben McCulloch, General Order, Number 27, August 12, 1861. *Official Records of the Rebellion*, Series 1, Volume 3 [S#3].

Report of Brig. Gen. Ben. McCulloch, C.S. Army to L.P. Walker, AUGUST 13, 1861.—Battle of Oak Hills, Springfield, *Official Records of the Rebellion*, Series 1, Volume 3 [S#3].

Brig. Gen. Ben McCulloch "Proclamation to the People of Missouri," August 15, 1861. *Official Records of the Rebellion*, Series 1, Volume 3 [S#3].

Report of Colonel Robert B. Mitchell, Second Kansas Cavalry, March 24, 1862. *The War of the Rebellion: A Compilation of the Official Records of the Union and Confederate Armies*, Series I, Volume VIII.

Report of Captain William S. Oliver, Seventh Missouri Infantry, February 3, 1862. *The War of the Rebellion: A Compilation of the Official Records of the Union and Confederate Armies*, Series I, Volume VIII, Washington, Government Printing Office, 1883.

Report of Maj. Gen. Sterling Price, Commanding Missouri State Guard, of Operations from July 25 to August 11., AUGUST 10, 1861.—Battle of Oak Hills, Springfield, or Wilson's Creek, Missouri. *Official Records of the Rebellion*, Series 1, Volume 3 [S#3].

Major W.C. Ransom letter to Brigadier-General James G. Blunt dated June 20, 1862. *The War of the Rebellion: A Compilation of the Official Records of the Union and Confederate Armies*, Series I, Volume VIII.

Report of Major Wyllis C. Ransom, Sixth Kansas Cavalry, August 17, 1862. *The War of the Rebellion: A Compilation of the Official Records of the Union and Confederate Armies*, Series I, Volume XXV.

E.F. Rogers letter to George M. Bennett dated January 24, 1901. Northfield, Minnesota Bank Robbery of 1876. Selected Manuscripts Collections and Government Records, Microfilm Edition, Roll 4, Minnesota Historical Society.

E.P. Rogers letter to Charles M. Start dated June 15, 1901. Northfield, Minnesota Bank Robbery of 1876. Selected Manuscripts Collections and Government Records, Microfilm Edition, Roll 4, Minnesota Historical Society.

Brigadier-General John M. Schofield letter to General Henry W. Halleck dated August 12, 1862. *The War of the Rebellion: A Compilation of the Official Records of the Union and Confederate Armies*, Series I, XXV.

Major General John M. Schofield letter to Governor Thomas Carney dated August 29, 1863. *The War of the Rebellion: A Compilation of the Official Records of the Union and Confederate Armies*, Series I, Volume XXXIV.

Reports of Col. Franz Sigel, Third Missouri Infantry, commanding Army of the West. August 10, 1861.—Battle of Oak Hills, Springfield, or Wilson's Creek, Missouri, *Official Records of the Rebellion*, Series 1, Volume 3 [S#3].

Reports of Col. Franz Sigel, Third Missouri Infantry, commanding Army of the West. August 18, 1861.—Battle of Oak Hills, Springfield, or Wilson's Creek, Missouri, *Official Records of the Rebellion*, Series 1, Volume 3 [S#3].

Report of Brigadier General Franz Sigel, U.S. Army, Commanding First and Second Divisions, on the Battle of Pea Ridge (Elkhorn Tavern) to Brigadier General Samuel R. Curtis, March 15, 1862. *The War of the Rebellion: A Compilation of the Official Records of the Union and Confederate Armies*, 14 R.R.--Volume VIII.

Report of Captain Henry J. Stierlin, First Missouri Cavalry, July 12, 1862. *The War of the Rebellion: A Compilation of the Official Records of the Union and Confederate Armies*, Series I, Volume XIII.

Report of Major Linn K. Thacher, Ninth Kansas Cavalry, August 27, 1863. *The War of the Rebellion: A Compilation of the Official Records of the Union and Confederate Armies*, Series I, Chapter XXXIV.

Philip A. Thompson, War Department, letter to General Penick dated November 6, 1862. *The War of the Rebellion: A Compilation of the Official Records of the Union and Confederate Armies*, Series I, Volume XXV.

Report of Brigadier-General James Totten, Headquarters District of Central Missouri, April 12, 1862. *The War of the Rebellion: A Compilation of the Official Records of the Union and Confederate Armies*, Series I, Volume VIII.

Report of Brigadier General James Totten, April 14, 1862. *The War of the Rebellion: A Compilation of the Official Records of the Union and Confederate Armies*, Series I, Volume XIII.

Report of Colonel A. Watson Webber, Fifty-first U. S. Colored Infantry, August 26, 1864. *The War of the Rebellion: A Compilation of the Official Records of the Union and Confederate Armies*, Series I, Volume 41.

PRESENTATIONS, THESES

Allen Coleman Ashcraft, Texas, 1860-1866: The Lone Star State in the Civil War (Ph.D. dissertation, Columbia University, 1960).

Vera Lea Dugas, A Social and Economic History of Texas in the Civil War and Reconstruction Periods (Ph.D. dissertation, University of Texas, 1963).

Robert Pattison Felgar, Texas in the War for Southern Independence, 1861-1865 (Ph.D. dissertation, University of Texas, 1935).

Emmett C. Hoctor, "Rusticating in Nebraska: 1862-1882," speech presentation to the Friends of the James Farm annual meeting, April 11, 1992, Kansas City, Missouri.

"The Battle of Carthage, Missouri, Friday, July 5, 1861," by Otto C. Lademann, Captain Third Missouri Infantry, U.S. Vols. Companion of the 1st Class, WI Commandery of MOLLUS Read March 7, 1907. "War Papers Read Before the Commandery of the State of Wisconsin, Military Order of the Loyal Legion of the United States," Published by the Commandery. Vol.4, Milwaukee: Burdick and Allen c1914.

"The Battle of Athens" by Hon. George W. McCrary, late Secretary of War, Companion of the 3rd Class, MO Commandery of MOLLUS. "War Papers and Personal Reminiscences, 1861-1865, Read Before the Commandery of the State of Missouri, Military Order of the Loyal Legion of the United States," published by the Commandery, Becktold & Co., St. Louis, MO c1892, reprinted by Broadfoot Publishing Co., Wilmington, NC., 1992.

Fredericka Meiners, The Texas Governorship, 1861-1865: Biography of an Office (Ph.D. dissertation, Rice University, 1974).

NEWSPAPERS

Boonville Weekly Advertiser, November 16, 1900.
Boston News, August 9, 1854.
Chillicothe Daily Democrat, November 11, 1904; November 19, 1904; November 21, 1904; November 22, 1904.
Clinton Democrat, September 8, 1903.
Frank Leslie's Illustrated Newspaper, September 12, 1863.
The Herald of Freedom, May 16, 1856.
Honey Grove Signal, April 2, 1915.
Kansas City Daily Journal, April 4, 1882.
Kansas City Journal of Commerce, August 13, 1864.
Kansas City Star, Sunday, February 22, 1915.
Kansas City Times, February 27, 1923; June 21, 1929.
Knoxville Journal, June 15, 1903.
Leavenworth Daily Conservative, August 23, 1863.
Lee's Summit Journal, July 1, 1981.
Louisville Courier Journal, September 29, 1901.
Madelia Times-Messenger, March 14, 1979; March 29, 1979.
Minneapolis Journal, July 10, 1901.
Missouri Daily Republican (St. Louis), February 1844; June 1844; September 28, 1844.
Nevada Daily Mail, October 26, 1903.
Northfield News, September 11, 1998.
Palmyra Missouri Courier, October 1862.
Richmond the Times-Dispatch, June 30, 1903.
St. Louis Globe-Democrat, September 20, 1898.
St. Paul Pioneer Press, Friday, July 23, 1886; July 26, 1886; August 1, 1886.
Terrell Transcript, April 26, 1907.
Topeka Tribune, August 27, 1863, John Speer, "Improvement Commences."
The True Democrat, Little Rock, Arkansas, July 25, 1861.
Weekly Advertiser, Boonville, Missouri, June 13, 1924.
Newspaper clipping, Northfield Public Library, Newspaper unknown, dated March 22, 1916.

INTERVIEWS

William E. Connelley Interviews Concerning the Quantrill Raid on Lawrence, Kansas, Aug 21, 1863, Ms Collection C4. Collections of the Osma Room, Lawrence Public Library, 707 Vermont Street and the Watkins Community Museum of History, 1047 Massachusetts Street, Lawrence, Kansas.

PUBLIC DOCUMENTS AND RECORDS

Warren Carter Bronaugh obituary, February 1923, Louis Woodford Bronaugh/ Pamela Luster Phillips Collection.
Founder's Library, The 19th Century Letters, Writings and Speeches of Abraham Lincoln.
Kansas Historical Collections, Volume 7, 1901-1902.
Kansas State Historical Society Archives.
Mid-Missouri Civil War Roundtable website, Internet.
Missouri State Archives.
Prairie Grove Battlefield State Park records.

UNPUBLISHED MANUSCRIPTS

Lyndon Irwin, "Bronaugh, Missouri History."
Pam Phillips, "The Bronaugh Family," unpublished manuscript from the papers of Louis Woodford Bronaugh.

Index

Van Buren, Arkansas, 194.
Van Buren County, Missouri, 52.
Van Buren, Martin, 52.
Van Dorn, Earl, 127, 128, 271.
Vandever, Susan, 202.
Venable, Randall, 281.
Vernon County, Missouri, 86, 233, 234.
Victoria, British Columbia, 276, 278.

Wade, John M., 189.
Wade, Newman, 244.
Wadesburg, Missouri, 150.
Wakefield, James H., 262, 285.
Walden, J.C., 76.
Walker, L.P., 100, 103, 104, 269, 270.
Walker, Morgan, 73.
Walker, Samuel, 16.
Walker's Choctaw Brigade, 269.
Walley, Irvin, x, xiii, 118, 119, 157, 158, 183, 279, 280.
Walters, John, 236.
War Eagle, 243.
Ward, H., 103.
Warren, Arkansas, 268, 273, 274.
Warren, Fitz-Henry, 163, 165, 166, 170, 171, 175.
Warrensburg, Missouri, 151, 163, 171, 227, 228, 288.
Warsaw, Missouri, 9, 10, 116.
Washington, D.C., 5, 25, 43, 55, 63, 66, 68, 75, 233, 261.
Washington, George, 176.
Waters, Ann, 176.
Waters, Edward, 176.
Watie, Stand, 270-272.
Waugh, James, 246.
Waverly, Missouri, 44, 185, 280.
Wayman, Matt, 282.
Webb, George, 166-169.
Webb, Press, 282.
Webber, A. Watson, 272, 292, 304.
Webber's Falls, 271.

Weidemeyer, John M., 116.
Weightman, Richard Hanson, 91, 102, 108.
Weiner, Theodore, 47, 49.
Welch, Warren, 280.
Wellington, Missouri, 192.
Wells, Charley, 213, 214.
Wells, G.W., 214.
Wells, Mrs. Washington, 157, 158.
Wells, Samuel, 157, 179, 288.
West Point, Missouri, 112.
Westport, Battle of, 259.
Westport, Missouri, 5, 16, 17, 43, 156-158, 174, 229-232, 234, 258, 259.
Westport Road, 156.
West, Robert, 195.
West Virginia, 52, 176, 288.
Wickersham, Dudley, 194.
Wigginton, George, 200.
Wilkinson, Allen, 47-49.
Williams, Jack, 282.
Williamstown, Missouri, 190.
Willis, S.J., 19.
Wilson, David, 141.
Wilson's Creek, 87, 92-94, 96, 97, 100, 106, 111, 124.
Wilson's Creek, Battle of, 62, 92-112, 124.
Winfrey, Caleb, 166-169, 173.
Woodson, Daniel, 50.
Woodson, Silas, 147.
Worcester, Massachusetts, 14, 17.
Wyandotte, Kansas, 186.

Yeager, Dick, 204.
Young, Brigham, 8.
Young, Samuel, 38, 39.
Younger, Alphae, 3, 51.
Younger, Anne, 3.
Younger, Bursheba, Fristoe, ix, 3, 4, 51, 58, 119, 156, 183-185, 236, 274, 275, 281.

Younger, Carolline, 3, 57, 118.

Younger, C. Frank, 53, 148.

Younger, Charles Richard "Dick," 53, 57, 58, 127.

Younger, Emma, 3.

Younger, Henrietta "Retta," 3.

Younger, Henry Washington, ix, 3-5, 10, 35, 51, 53-55, 58, 117, 118, 122, 147, 156, 158-160, 279.

Younger, Isabella Frances, 3, 57.

Younger, James Hardin "Jim," x, 3, 10, 51, 58, 118, 170, 184, 185, 247, 274, 275, 280, 281, 285, 286, 288.

Younger, John Harrison "John," x, 3, 10, 274, 281, 285, 288.

Younger, Laura, 3.

Younger, Martha Anne, 58.

Younger, Mary Josephine, "Josie," 3, 58.

Younger, Richard, 3.

Younger, Robert Ewing "Bob," ix, x, 3, 10, 185, 247, 274, 275, 281, 285, 288.

Younger, Sally, 3, 118.

Younger, Suse, 183-185, 236.

Younger, Thomas Coleman "Cole," birth and background, 3-10; growing up, 52-58; Captain Walley incident, 117-119; joins Quantrill, 119-127; at Independence, 139-143; at Hamilton, Hannibal, and St. Joseph, 147, 148; at Blue Cut, 149, 150; at Harrisonville, 153-156; father's death, 157-160; attack on Independence, 160-162; at Lone Jack, 152-178; at Lawrence and events leading to, 183-218; hunted by federals, 236; in the South and Southwest, 267-278; to Canada and California, 278, 279; back to Missouri, 285-290; death of, 1, 2.